DOING GOOD BUSINESS IN CHINA

Case Studies in International Business Ethics

DOING GOOD BUSINESS IN CHINA

Case Studies in International Business Ethics

Editors

Stephan Rothlin
Rothlin Ltd, Beijing, China & Rothlin Ltd, Hong Kong

Dennis McCann
Rothlin Ltd, Beijing, China & Rothlin Ltd, Hong Kong

Parissa Haghirian
Sophia University, Japan

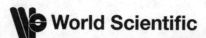

World Scientific

NEW JERSEY · LONDON · SINGAPORE · BEIJING · SHANGHAI · HONG KONG · TAIPEI · CHENNAI · TOKYO

Published by

World Scientific Publishing Co. Pte. Ltd.

5 Toh Tuck Link, Singapore 596224

USA office: 27 Warren Street, Suite 401-402, Hackensack, NJ 07601

UK office: 57 Shelton Street, Covent Garden, London WC2H 9HE

Library of Congress Cataloging-in-Publication Data
Names: Rothlin, Stephan, 1959–   editor. | McCann, Dennis, editor. |
    Haghirian, Parissa, 1970–   editor.
Title: Doing good business in China : case studies in international business ethics / editors,
    Stephan Rothlin, Rothlin Ltd, Beijing, China & Rothlin Ltd, Hong Kong;
    Dennis McCann, Rothlin Ltd, Beijing, China & Rothlin Ltd, Hong Kong;
    Parissa Haghirian, Sophia University, Japan.
Description: USA : World Scientific, 2021. | Includes bibliographical references and index.
Identifiers: LCCN 2021005218 | ISBN 9789811231698 (hardcover) |
    ISBN 9789811233654 (ebook) | ISBN 9789811233661 (ebook other)
Subjects: LCSH: Business ethics--China. | Social responsibility of business--China. |
    Corporate governance--China.
Classification: LCC HF5387.5.C6 D65 2021 | DDC 174/.40951--dc23
LC record available at https://lccn.loc.gov/2021005218

British Library Cataloguing-in-Publication Data
A catalogue record for this book is available from the British Library.

For any available supplementary material, please visit
https://www.worldscientific.com/worldscibooks/10.1142/12145#t=suppl

Desk Editors: Balasubramanian Shanmugam/Pui Yee Lum

Typeset by Stallion Press
Email: enquiries@stallionpress.com

Printed in Singapore

This book could not be more timely. It brings together a careful selection of well-written short cases that illustrate a number of situations and dilemmas faced by leaders and managers operating today in China. The immense value of this book stems also from the power of the case method: a proven teaching vehicle appreciated by managers because of its great relevance for learning from the chunk of reality it brings and from the teacher's skills to use research results, frameworks, and concepts to help understand complex dilemmas. The case discussion indeed enhances awareness, sharpens judgment, and broadens the choice among alternative actions before the necessary decision. Rothlin, McCann, and Haghirian have produced an invaluable book also because the cases are presented in a way that guides the analysis for the reader, for the student. In fact, the book will be a precious resource for anyone trying to understand better the changing business ecosystem in China, with its many ethical challenges seen through different lenses.

Henri-Claude de Bettignies, Emeritus Professor, INSEAD, and Distinguished Emeritus Professor of Globally Responsible Leadership, CEIBS

This wonderful book is a collection of 46 business ethics cases, which is the result of the hard work and great efforts made by Dr. Stephan Rothlin, Dr. Dennis McCann, and their team of Rothlin Company, Beijing & Hong Kong. These cases, strictly based on first-hand information from China and guided by international business ethics and essential Confucian ethical ideas, involve various issues of business ethics arising from the business in China. The analysis of the cases is full of insight. Anyone who

reads this book can have a clear idea of how to do good business in China and how to deal with all kind of challenges and to create a win–win situation in the business.

Hengda Yang, Professor of Renmin University of China

This volume of 46 case studies is much more than a collection of particular challenges of enterprises in China. Not only does it explain the broader Chinese context and thus help to overcome widespread ignorance and prejudices but it also provides ethical and legal guidance by drawing on Confucian values and national and international standards of corporate responsibility. While courageously critical in its analysis, it shows many innovative ways for GOOD business in China.

Georges Enderle, John T. Ryan Jr., Professor Emeritus of International Business Ethics, University of Notre Dame, USA

This innovative and inspiring work book on a wide range of controversial business cases from mainland China makes a strong point for ethics in business. By its persuasive three-step method of Seeing–Judging–Acting, it encourages business students to adopt the moral point of view and to bring the values from their own cultural tradition in perspective with global moral standards. It is highly recommended.

Gerhold K. Becker, Founding Director of the Centre for Applied Ethics of Hong Kong Baptist University

About Rothlin LTD.

Rothlin International Management Consulting, Ltd. (Rothlin Ltd.) is a socially responsible management consulting firm located in Beijing and in Hong Kong. We represent a diverse international team that has come together to work toward the development of new paradigms in the application of corporate social responsibility (CSR) in China. Our pledge is to sustainably inspire, empower, evolve, and advance the dialogue between corporate interests and stakeholder rights about CSR toward the common good.

More information can be found at www.rothlin.org.

About the Editors

Stephan Rothlin is the Director of the Macau Ricci Institute (www.riccimac.org). He serves also as the Founder and CEO of Rothlin International Management Consulting Ltd., located in Beijing and in Hong Kong (www.rothlin.org). His teaching and research interests are focused on international business ethics and responsible entrepreneurship with a focus on China. He provides educational consulting services to encourage the practice of corporate social responsibility, and advocates among business communities and society at large the values of honesty, integrity, respect, transparency, and responsibility as indispensable elements for excellence in business.

Dr. Rothlin completed his academic studies in 1991 with a Ph.D. in moral theology at the State University of Innsbruck, Austria, and is fluent in six languages, including Mandarin Chinese, English, Spanish, Italian, French, and German. From 1992 to 1998, he was the executive director of the Academic Centre, AKI, in Zürich and a research fellow at the Institute of Empirical Research in Economics of the University of Zürich in Switzerland. From 1998 to 2012, he served as a guest professor of international business ethics at The Beijing Center for Chinese Studies in Beijing. Since his relocation to Beijing in 1998, he has become a sought-after speaker on international business ethics, having taught at various business schools throughout Asia, including Renmin University, Peking University, Tsinghua University, the Central Party

School in Beijing, Hong Kong University, and INSEAD Business School, Singapore. From 2005 to 2013, he was secretary general for the Centre for International Business Ethics, Beijing, and chairman of the Association of International Business Ethics in Hong Kong.

His personal hobbies include playing classical piano and tennis.

Dennis P. McCann is the Research Director for the Rothlin International Management Consulting (Beijing). He was Professor Emeritus of Agnes Scott College, Atlanta/Decatur, Georgia, USA, from which he retired in 2011. McCann taught business ethics in the USA for over 30 years, and has been involved in research, lecturing, and teaching on business ethics in China and SE Asia for the past 20 years. He has been particularly concerned to identify culturally appropriate teaching materials for China and Asia, based on his ongoing research in the fields of philosophy and religious studies. McCann received his Ph.D. from the University of Chicago Divinity School in 1976, and his Licentiate in Sacred Theology (S.T.L.) from the Gregorian University in Rome, Italy, in 1972. In addition to his current focus on Asian business ethics, his fields of academic expertise include comparative religious ethics, philosophy of religion, Christian social ethics, and Catholic Social Teaching. The author of several books and dozens of scholarly articles, most recently he co-authored, with Stephan Rothlin, *International Business Ethics: Focus on China*, published by Springer-Verlag in 2015. Along with Prof. Lee Kam-hon and Ms. Mary Ann Ching Yuen, he published a book, *Christ and the Business Culture*, in 2012 (Chinese University Press in Hong Kong). Over the past 20 years, McCann has taught courses, given workshops, and lectured in universities in Hong Kong, China, Philippines, Malaysia, Japan, Thailand, Indonesia, East Timor, and India. Currently, as a Faculty Fellow at Silliman University, Dumaguete, Philippines, McCann teaches courses in the graduate school of the College of Liberal Arts and Sciences: "Ethics and Organizational Behavior", "Ethics and the Professions", and "Religion and Psychology".

Parissa Haghirian is Professor of International Management at Sophia University, Tokyo. She has lived and worked in Japan since 2004 and is an internationally renowned expert in international management with a focus on Japanese management.

Ms. Haghirian studied Japanese Studies at the University of Vienna (MA 1999) and holds a Master's Degree (2000) and Ph.D. in Business Administration (2003) from the Vienna University of Economics and Business Administration. She is also a visiting professor at Aalto University, HEC Paris, Keio University, Waseda University, and the University of Vienna. From 2011 to 2012 she held a professorship in Japanese Management at Ludwig-Maximilians-Universität München (LMU).

She has published several books and articles on the topic of International and Japanese management, and is the author of *Understanding Japanese Management Practices* (Business Expert Press, 2010), *Multinationals and Cross-Cultural Management: The Transfer of Knowledge Within Multinational Corporations* (Routledge, 2010), and *Successful Cross-Cultural Management: A Guide for International Managers* (Business Expert Press, 2011). She is also the editor of *Japanese Consumer Dynamics* (Palgrave Macmillan, 2011), *Case Studies in Japanese Management* (World Scientific Publishing Company, 2011), *Routledge Handbook of Japanese Business and Management* (Routledge, 2016), and *Business Development, Merger and Crisis Management of International Firms in Japan: Featuring Case Studies from Fortune 500 Companies* (World Scientific Publishing Company, 2018). In 2019, she edited the free e-book *Japanese Business Concepts You Should Know*.

Professor Haghirian advises companies on intercultural cooperation and coaches top-level managers searching for new perspectives and the potential for success. She regularly gives keynote lectures at conferences and corporate events across Europe and Asia. She currently lives between Tokyo and Vienna. More information on her can be found at www.haghirian.com.

Contents

Part 1
Introduction

Chapter 1

Becoming a Confucian Entrepreneur: The Search for Truth in Case Studies in the Chinese Context

Stephan Rothlin

The term "Confucian Entrepreneur" can easily be abused by both entrepreneurs and self-styled scholars in order, masked, to continue doing business or conduct business in a ruthless way that completely lacks any ethical and legal norms. But, not all who claim to be "Confucian Entrepreneurs" are fraudulent. The challenge is learning to know the difference between what is real and what is fake. This article limits itself to pointing out the prime importance of case studies as a reality check in an ongoing search for the necessary benchmarks to distinguish fake from genuine Confucian entrepreneurs who can and do contribute to sustainable economic development.

The Copyright Law in China adopted on September 7, 1990, which has been amended for the first time on October 27, 2001 and for the second time on February 26, 2010 (http://en.ncac.gov.cn/copyright/contents/10365/329083.shtml) making reference to current news including statements in official state sanctioned media, is an impediment for obtaining a Copyright in China. This seems to indicate a general trend, which is by no means restricted to one country, that prevents people from getting access to vital background information. A common excuse for restricting such access to reliable news is the claim that media would be overwhelmed with "Fake News".

3

The present collection of case studies was not yet subject to these restrictions. Moreover, we have to bear in mind that there have always been enormous obstacles for scholars intending to better understand business and economic matters in Chinese contexts. Already 10 years ago when I conducted a research project on the implementation of the UN Global Compact in China in the period from 1999 through 2009, only a small fraction of the firms which had signed the Global Compact were willing to answer questions related to the implementation of these codes (Rothlin, 2010, pp. 3–13). Already a first look on the related websites of the firms which signed the Global Compact indicated that the duty of regular reporting on progress and setbacks was consistently disregarded.

Only a genuine awareness of complex and socially significant facts will make the teaching of economics and ethics truly meaningful for all concerned stakeholders. However, to engage in a thorough and nuanced social analysis is far more demanding than it appears at first sight. A host of preconceived ideas and prejudices tend usually to seriously affect the process of acknowledging facts. Often, the students who have to analyze case studies come from a privileged social background that makes it difficult or even impossible for them to properly understand the often harsh and brutal conditions in which folks from lower social backgrounds find themselves trapped. Moreover, in the case of China, a worsening trade conflict between the US and the European Union (EU), and China, may easily result in a biased and negative view of China and its business practices, perceiving them as ruthlessly profit and money driven and lacking in any ethical considerations.

The term "Confucian Entrepreneur" is by no means restricted to an Asian context. It refers to a business person who is typically not shaped and influenced by a specific religious creed, but is committed to sticking to a certain set of basic human values of honesty, integrity, truthfulness and reliability. What makes these basic human values distinctively Confucian, is the way they have been defined in Chinese moral education over the centuries (Yang and McCann, 2018). Let us start with the so-called Golden Rule, so readily used to summarize Confucius' teaching.

> Zi Gong asked, saying, 'Is there one word which may serve as a rule of practice for all one's life?' The Master said, 'Is not RECIPROCITY (shu 恕) such a word? What you do not want done to yourself, do not do to others.'" (Analects 15:24).

Reciprocity is best understood by considering the parent–child relationship, and the ideal of filial piety (*xiào*孝). The parent nurtures the child for three years, and the child eventually mourns the parent for three years. Over time the child will learn what is expected by way of filial piety, and those expectations will change as he or she eventually becomes responsible for its parents. Fulfilling the meaning of the reciprocity will evolve as relationships change. What may not change is the common desire to be treated as a human being, and the common aversion to all things that detract from our humanity: "What you do not want done to yourself, do not do to others".

Even today, though the contexts in which filial piety and reciprocity may have changed, the ideal of *Junzi* leadership is still informed by these constants. A leader following the *Junzi* ideal will start with a core assumption about his rivals, his employees, and all the stakeholders based on what he knows about himself. For example, since he does not expect hate from others, so he should be inclined toward benevolence (*jen*, 仁) and righteousness (*yi*, 義) in his relations with others. A *Junzi* leader must love all people and be just and fair to them. The attitude to oneself and to others should be equally the same.

How one learns to live by the Golden Rule is not a spontaneous result of experience. The education of anyone becoming fully human must proceed through the study and practice of ritual propriety (*Li*, 禮). The proper rituals communicate who we are — that is, the objective nature of the relationships in which we find ourselves — and what we must do to achieve harmony with Heaven, Earth, and Humanity as a whole. What is accomplished through such practices Confucian tradition remembers as "the rectifications of names" (*Zhèngmíng*, 正名). This is a hallmark of *Junzi* leadership, insofar as good governance depends on calling things by their proper names and acting accordingly.

Junzi leadership, nowadays, forms the core of "Confucian Entrepreneurship." Where to begin, then, in achieving the harmonious relationships that Confucius thinks are possible? The answer lies at the core of in ritual propriety, namely, the practice of self-cultivation. How can a leader reach the point of always keeping *ren*, *yi* and *shu* in mind, and responding to others through *li*? The ever-expanding virtuous circle depends upon universalizing the practice of self-cultivation "from the Son of Heaven down to the mass of the people."

The *Analects* provide a number of insights into the practice of self-cultivation.

Achieving such a state of personal equilibrium or tranquility requires more than study in the conventional sense. Apparently, maintaining ritual propriety requires some form of meditation or personal reflection, beyond what is normally associated with acquiring knowledge through mastering facts and theories:

> Zi Lu asked what constituted the superior man. The Master said, 'The cultivation of himself in reverential carefulness.' 'And is this all?' said Zi Lu. 'He cultivates himself so as to give rest to others,' was the reply. (Analects 14:42)."

In order that lofty terms like "Confucian" and basic human values may not easily be abused not only as meaningless empty rhetoric but even as masking unscrupulous business practices, it seems to be necessary to keep alive certain principles that provide benchmarks enabling not only an individual but also firms, institutions, and governmental agencies to stick to their values. Therefore, providing access to a constantly updated set of case studies seems to be crucial to ensure a reliable way to monitor, more effectively, how rules, promises, and ethical standards are concretely implemented.

In each cultural context, it is a challenge to come to grips with the amazing complexities of its social fabric. However, it seems to be especially true in Asia where linguistic barriers may cloud mutual understanding. Even more problematic are the various prejudices which prevent individuals, firms, and institutions from genuinely understanding cultural patterns and engaging in successful business. More specifically, a widespread prejudice can be recognized in the *idée fixe* that business cultures across Asia are pervasively corrupt and that the only possible response from entrepreneurs eager to forge ahead with successful business deals would simply be to "go with the flow" and engage as much in bribing while at the same time — as in the case of foreign Multinationals as well as with State-Owned Enterprises — merely paying lip service to the rhetoric of Ethics and Corporate Social Responsibility.

Case studies highlighting the long-term effects of such practices may therefore become the main battleground where it becomes evident how ill-advised this notion proved to be on a wide range of issues: obviously first of all in the devastating deterioration of the natural environment with massive pollution of air, soil, and water as well as in the widespread erosion of trust spawned by corrupt and incompetent forms of governance.

The reference to moral principles such as honesty, integrity, and truthfulness remains meaningless without a constant reality check within a given socio-cultural context. The exploring of different components of complex social realities seems to us an important antidote to different forms of ideological indoctrination.

"Confucian Entrepreneurship" therefore is very much a "work in progress" as it aims to not only state the obvious that Asian countries including India and China are becoming more and more the main drivers of economic development but that Asians are becoming key players in practicing the values of integrity, honesty, and truthfulness.

The term "Confucian" needs to be taken in its dynamic sense because values are subject to historical development. Values that have been dominant in a certain socio-political context may evaporate in other circumstances. Thus Asian countries seem more eager to recover wisdom and religious traditions which for centuries have already taken root in their cultures. This is the case of religions in China especially Buddhism and Christianity, which seem to attract growing audiences in both urban and rural areas, while traditionally Christian communities in Europe have either completely vanished or have been significantly reduced in numbers. Therefore, the term "Confucian" delineates an openness to embrace key elements of religious and wisdom traditions without which the reference to Confucius risks becoming meaningless jargon and rhetoric.

The case studies in this book explore different dimensions of the crisis in implementing key Confucian values. "Filial piety" ("孝", *Pinyin: "xiao"*), for example, refers to the respect we owe to parents, teachers, and superiors. However, it is obvious how modern life, mobility, and new patterns of life and work disrupted key values. As the values keep eroding, it is not easy to find a surrogate in rigorous law enforcement, as in the case of parents who feel so abandoned by their offspring who hardly visit them any more on a regular basis. This seems to have provoked the passing of a rather awkward new law in China which makes it a monthly legal requirement to visit one's parents.

1.1 Seeing–Judging–Acting

The case studies follow the classical three steps of *Seeing–Judging–Acting*, which takes its origin in a conceptual framework developed by a Belgian Cardinal Joseph Cardijn in the context of the Catholic social teaching. Along these lines, case study analysis recognizes with *Seeing* the enormous opportunities and challenges for Responsible Entrepreneurship. Within a business world characterized by empty rhetoric and a system that seems to favor entrenched corrupt and dishonest business practices the tendency is to think that following the rules and the law is for inferior people. But, *Seeing* also reveals a business world which has become more and more interconnected, characterized by social innovation with new IT solutions, and products enhanced with social messaging. With *Seeing*, we aim also to better recognize the underlying cultural and religious components of ongoing changes.

A critical process is the second step *Judging*, as the reality we see is tested. In the light of ethical principles and the law, we need to ponder if the products and services meet genuine human needs and serve the common good. Is a business or a government agency truly a community of persons which respect each other or does it just reflect another destructive caste system with cronies at the top who become more and more alienated from the genuine needs of their employees and customers as they are only obsessed with satisfying their own narcissistic needs?

Acting: The previous steps of *Seeing* and *Judging* cry out for action which has constantly in mind the dignity of each person in service to the common good. It is certainly also important to fulfill the financial and legal benchmarks of a business as an institution. However, the genuine Confucian Entrepreneur demonstrates his skills and uses natural resources wisely. Practical wisdom should prevent him from getting into the trap of corruption and cynicism.

Confucian Entrepreneurship is fully committed to serve those most in need. In particular, the pandemic of COVID-19 has revealed the growing gap between the rich and the poor. Earning the trust of shareholders and stakeholders during such a health crisis requires us to go the extra mile with those who struggle to survive. Only on the level of genuine action does it become clear whether moral principles have become confused and obfuscated through incompetence and corruption or if they get a chance to become fruitful in the midst of a fiercely competitive marketplace.

Case studies are a key argument to counter the cynical *idée fixe* that there is ultimately no real way to change a deeply entrenched dishonest and unfair way of doing business. Dominant economic paradigms focused on profit maximization, shareholder value, and overall cost cutting are often tainted with a negative view on Asian cultures, which they consider basically as corrupt and only money driven. The Confucian Entrepreneur needs to have a firm grasp of the influence of social milieus on the values of individuals and institutions in order to be able to stick to them in the midst of adverse challenges and pressures toward corruption.

Another key issue in a thorough analysis of case studies true to the ideals of a Confucian Entrepreneur is the awareness of the interwovenness of micro-, meso-, and macro-levels in a case study. With the micro-perspective, each individual may be put in the shoes of the key actors of a case so that questions arise such as the following: How would I understand such and such dilemma? How would I ponder the odds? How would I make sure that my actions are truly tuned to my conscience?

However, the micro-level perspective needs to take into account how much it is shaped by different institutional bodies within firms, associations, consumer associations, etc., that come into play on the intermediate or "meso"-level as well as through the interconnectedness of markets, countries, and supra-national organizations on the "macro"-level. Within such a conceptual framework, it may become more understandable why someone's original set of values of integrity as fostered through different educators, and not just one's family, may become seriously at risk in an ethically and legally toxic environment which operates as if there were no ethical foundation.

Bibliography

Rothlin, S. (2010). Towards a socially responsible China: A preliminary investigation of the implementation of the global compact. *Journal of International Business Ethics*, 3 (1), 3–14.

Yang, H., and McCann, D. P. (2018). The ideal of Junzi leadership and education for the common good. *Macau Ricci Institute Journal*, 3 (November 2018), 15–25.

https://doi.org/10.1142/9789811233654_0002

Chapter 2

What's to Learn From the Study of Ethics?

Dennis McCann

Ethics may be a new and unfamiliar word for you. It may seem foreign, as it does come from the traditions of Ancient Greece and Rome. You may find it taught as an academic subject in philosophy departments. And, you may find it in various qualified forms as "applied ethics", "professional ethics", "medical ethics", "business ethics", and other specialties. Our concern with it here is whether there is anything important to learn from it, as we examine case studies in business.

Ethics is theory. It is the study of what people do when they are expressing moral attitudes, like approval or disapproval, or evaluating various actions and policies, or determining the best way forward in approaching difficult choices. What makes such choices difficult may itself be complex. Nash (1990) has identified two types of moral difficulties with which we all are familiar:

(1) Type A situations where we simply do not know the right thing to do, usually because we are confronted with a decision involving conflicting moral values or priorities. Ethics, and the ways it is reflected in various codes, catechisms, and manuals of instruction, can be very useful in resolving such conflicts, clarifying what the priorities should be, what the right choice may involve in such situations.

(2) Type B situations where we know the right thing to do, but find ourselves unwilling or unable to do it. Type B situations are best

11

approached, not by studying ethical theory, but by involving ourselves in some kind of spiritual practice or therapy that helps to strengthen our capacity to become a responsible person. This is the kind of strengthening — call it "salvation", or "liberation", or "enlightenment" — that is offered by the wisdom traditions in various cultures. All the great religions of China, as well as elsewhere, provide various ways to become a responsible person, that is, one who is capable of acting humanely, who is not guided exclusively by narrow self-interest.

One relevant example of an effective response to Type B situations is the Way of Confucian moral philosophy, which distinguishes concretely between the *junzi* (or morally enlightened person) and the *xiaoren* (or small-minded person), who can see no further than his or her own immediate self-interest. While these terms may appear in some of the case studies featured here, the point is not to provide a general introduction to Type B situations and proper responses to them. The assumption animating our case studies, on the contrary, is not that our readers are either saints or sinners, neither morally perfect nor hopelessly depraved. Instead, we assume that our readers, like us, are seekers after truth, responding in good faith, genuinely seeking a solution that optimizes both practicality and morality, that is, a solution that tries to maximize benefit for all concerned or at least is fair to all the stakeholders identified within the case study. In other words, the case studies are meant to highlight Type A situations, in which the right thing to do is unclear, for one reason or another, where there may be honest disagreement about what the way forward actually is. We assume that readers who are practical problem solvers will normally be capable of acting in good faith, animated by some basic notions of appropriate or virtuous behavior, but who may not be sure how their personal moral beliefs actually apply in complex situations.

Here is a practical example that may help clarify this distinction: Gifts and Bribes. Gift-giving is a time-honored custom in many cultures, especially in Asia. It is also a standard part of business negotiations, an integral part of the rituals through which business partners come to trust each other and acknowledge their mutual interests. But, these practices have also come under suspicion as forms of corruption. There are laws, as in Hong Kong's *Prevention of Bribery Ordinance* and in the USA's notorious *Foreign Corrupt Practices Act*, that are designed to penalize acts of bribery and extortion, particularly as these may occur in the course of doing business, public or private. The legal statutes and penalties are fairly clear in the abstract that bribery involves accepting a personal benefit in exchange for doing something that is contrary to one's role within the organization, say, a government agency or a business firm. But, how does that differ from accepting a gift from a client or prospective business partner? This situation is clearly not a Type B situation. The one asking such a question is not tempted to violate the law or any relevant code of ethics or corporate policy. Rather, it is Type A, insofar as the question involves trying to understand the distinction and how it applies to his or her particular circumstances. We believe that business ethics case studies are most effective in helping readers learn to identify Type A situations and discover resources for dealing with them responsibly.

Assuming that Type A situations are typically featured in business case studies, are there general points from the study of Ethics that may be useful when working with these studies? Modern analytic moral philosophy, shaped by the cultural traditions of post-Enlightenment Western philosophy, generally starts with observations of what people think, say, and do when they make moral decisions. What is a moral decision? It is one that answers the question, is it right or wrong to do this or that? Analyzing the language we use to express approval or disapproval, ethics helps us to distinguish the meaning of right and wrong, and distinguish it from related terms, good and bad, appropriate and inappropriate. Analysis suggests that in common usage these terms are not convertible to one another. The pair, right and wrong, implies imperatives, a sense of obligation, an urgency that is beyond expediency. By contrast, good and bad, implies ideals, or attitudes expressing intentions and consequences, that reflect preferences that may change according to circumstances. The third set, appropriate and inappropriate, shifts the focus to the importance of context, usually cultural context. Since such judgments are not readily generalizable, or reducible to those expressed in the first and second sets, they are acknowledged in this third set.

Having established the logic of these three sets — right vs. wrong, good vs. bad, and appropriate vs. inappropriate — the study of ethics shows how each of these has given rise to distinctive and irreducible forms of ethical theory. Right vs. wrong, with its emphasis on duties and obligations, has given rise to deontological theories of ethics, the most impressive of which is Immanuel Kant's system derived from the so-called Categorical Imperative, memorably stated in the maxim, "Treat persons as ends and never as means only". Good vs. bad, with its emphasis on intentions and consequences, has given rise to teleological theories of ethics, the most memorable of which is Utilitarianism, so named by John Stuart Mill, and well stated in the maxim, "The Greatest Good for the Greatest Number". Appropriate vs. inappropriate, with its emphasis on cultural contexts, has given rise to a number of theories that may be labeled hermeneutical, insofar as they seek to interpret cultural contexts in which moral attitudes and dispositions are cultivated. Confucian ethics, the tradition emerging from the Confucian Classics, is a useful example of this type that presupposes a worldview, while also providing concrete guidance for becoming truly human. The Way of Confucius is not reducible to either deontological or teleological ethics, but establishes a path toward the practice of virtues indispensable for living well.

Being aware of the diversity of moral attitudes expressed in these three sets is useful in examining business ethics case studies because it provides patterns for understanding the basis for disputes regarding the best solution to a particular problem. One of the deepest challenges in achieving moral wisdom is learning to understand the basis for moral disagreements. If someone disagrees with our opinion, that does not mean the person disagreeing is evil or stupid or captive to some hidden agenda. Disagreement, when examined rationally, may involve diverging sets of facts and how they are interpreted. At a deeper level, disagreement may result from conflicting priorities among values shared in common or from entirely different sets of values. If such disagreements can be understood, the way forward may become clearer for mutually agreeable compromises that create win–win situations for all concerned. Business negotiations can proceed more smoothly if all the parties to a dispute are willing and able to recognize the basis for their disputes.

One important example of such diversity is captured in traditional comparisons between Western individualism and Asian communalism. The contrast suggests that persons formed in Western cultures are taught to be highly individuated, valuing individual liberty, prioritizing individual human rights, and generally promoting solutions that maximize freedom of choice. Persons formed in Asian cultures, on the contrary, traditionally are expected to sacrifice self-interest to the apparent necessities of the community. The centrality of filial piety (*xiao*) in Confucian tradition is an example of this pattern, since it may shape the corporate culture in Asian businesses in ways that Westerners may find troubling, insofar as it favors respect for hierarchy, solidarity within one's group, even to the extent of tolerating apparent violations of abstract legal norms, like the rule of law, or anti-discrimination policies that reflect universal standards of human rights. If such patterns can be identified in any dispute over the proper application of business ethics and corporate policy, recognizing them may be an important first step to resolving them. This may be especially useful in addressing the tensions that typically arise in joint ventures involving Asian firms and Western partners, or in integrating Asian offices into a multinational corporation that formally adheres to Western standards of ethics.

Type A situations generally arise because of organizational complexity, especially in international business, where problems occur that involve multiple and conflicting moral values. The conflict is not a simple choice between right and wrong, or good and bad, but among a number of rights claims or multiple good outcomes to be realized. Can ethics help managers to sort out such conflicts? We believe that it can, and here are a few rules of thumb that may put things on the right track.

The first of these is to recognize the priority of deontological claims. If such claims are valid, that is, that they can be verified by a reasonable observer, the first step is to identify and address these fairly and expeditiously. Deontological covers duties and obligations. If there are any clear duties or obligations, for example, promises made, these must be resolved before any other issues are addressed. We might call this a "Deontological Override", in that fulfilling promises already made, such as duties and obligations, must be the first element in any solution, and not simply regarded as a point for negotiations and compromise, unless, of course, those to whom the promises have been made have agreed to accept such an outcome.

A second rule of thumb is to respect the ethical assumptions governing teleological perspectives like Utilitarianism. If a situation yields a number of competing good outcomes, among which a manager must decide, the rule is to seek "the Greatest Good for the Greatest Number". Maximizing the greatest good requires acknowledging the interests of all stakeholders in a given situation, including stakeholders beyond the firm's own agents and owners. This is what distinguishes utilitarian or consequentialist ethics from "Cost Benefit Analysis", a managerial tool that all too often places exclusive focus on the costs and benefits to the firm and ignore externalities imposed on other stakeholders. Of course, a "Cost Benefit Analysis" so narrowly focused, arguably, is a perverse misuse of this tool, and one that is likely to create as many problems as it solves. The more "Cost

Benefit Analysis" includes the interests of all stakeholders in a given situation, the closer it is in spirit to utilitarianism.

Our first rule of thumb, the "Deontological Override", not surprisingly, is not so simple in application. What if — as is often the case — there are multiple duties, obligations, or promises to be fulfilled? How is a manager to prioritize among them, especially when each of them raises a valid deontological claim? Deontological theories, like the Universal Declaration of Human Rights, may provide some guidance. If there are multiple deontological claims, can they be prioritized in terms of seriousness or urgency? For example, if the conflict is between one group's right to life and another group's right to private property, normally the right to life would override the right to private property. A manager would choose not to ignore the clear risks to life and limb, either for employees or members of the community, simply in order to maximize profits to investors. The promises made to investors, which are real and deontologically valid, can only be fulfilled ethically in policies and practices that insure the health and safety of employees and other stakeholders. The manager's challenge is to balance the interests of all stakeholders, honestly and fairly. Ethical theory applied to business case studies cannot and will not support theories of the firm that urge managers to maximize returns to shareholders while ignoring all other stakeholders. When there is a conflict among equally valid deontological claims, the manager will seek to achieve an equitable balance among them. Arguably, this is but another example of the utilitarian principle of seeking "the Greatest Good for the Greatest Number".

What, finally, are the lessons that can be learned from hermeneutical theories of ethics that focus on distinguishing appropriate from inappropriate responses within a given cultural context? The most important of these is to respect the cultures of others as well as one's own. Everyone, every moral agent, participates in a culture, however unaware they may be of it. Westerners sometimes give the impression that respect for cultures is somehow esoteric, a luxury for other people, but not relevant to their own work. This is a remarkably short-sighted view, for it is blind to the history of ethics in Western civilization, and its ongoing impact even on post-Enlightenment ethical theories. The ethical assumptions built into the systems of both Kant and Mill are unintelligible apart from the long-term influence of Christian traditions in the West. This often is more obvious to Asians viewing Western culture from afar than it is to Westerners who take their culture for granted. If we can all recognize that each of us participates in a culture, and that no one possesses a point of view that completely transcends culture, then we all may be ready to participate in dialogue, working together to solve the world's problems.

The other big lesson from hermeneutical theories of ethics is what elsewhere we have described as "the natural priority of virtue" (Rothlin and McCann, 2015). Ethical theories may provide a framework for understanding moral choices and their logic, but they are no substitute for a personal commitment to the practice of moral virtue. A good manager must first learn to become a good person, however that is defined, as in the world's various wisdom traditions. As we have seen in the previous chapter, Confucian Entrepreneurship defines an ideal of business leadership whose authenticity depends upon the steady pursuit of Confucian virtue. The pre-Enlightenment traditions of Western philosophy, starting with Socrates, Plato, and Aristotle, as well as the teachings of Jesus and the Hebrew Scriptures, and the achievements of Hellenistic moralists like the Stoics, all emphasize the necessity of cultivating virtue for success in any walk of life. These traditions offer paths of personal enlightenment and development that are still essential for achieving happiness or the good life. As you will see in the case studies offered here, the practice of virtue in business management and leadership remains the key to any authentic learning from the study of ethics.

Bibliography

Nash, L. (1990). *Good Intentions Aside: A Manager's Guide to Solving Ethical Problems*. Cambridge, MA: Harvard University Press.

Rothlin, S. and McCann, D. (2015). The natural priority of moral virtue [Chapter 2], in *International Business Ethics: Focus on China*. Springer. Chapter Two.

© 2021 World Scientific Publishing Company
https://doi.org/10.1142/9789811233654_0003

Chapter 3

Teaching Asian Business Ethics with Case Studies

Parissa Haghirian

3.1 The Use of Case Studies in College Classrooms

Cases are not simply stories for entertainment. They are stories with a message. They are stories to educate (Herreid, 1997, p. 92), and it is no surprise that the use of case studies in colleges has established itself as the most popular practice in the teaching and learning process. Case studies provide a link between theory and practice and allow the learner to apply theoretical knowledge already learnt in the classroom (McFarlane, 2015).

Business schools in particular have preferred the use of case studies over other teaching methods (McFarlane, 2015). Also, other disciplines have successfully used case studies to prepare learners for future challenges (e.g., Bonney, 2015; Robinson, 1997).

3.1.1 Why are Case Studies Good Teaching Tools?

Luo (2004) describes the case study method as "not only a method to teach students how to pick up 'knowledge,' but also how to acquire a 'learning' technique. Consequently, students will be more creative and more able to 'put ideas' into practice" (Luo, 2004, p. 75). Case studies support critical thinking (Herreid, 2004) and motivate learners to look at a problem from very different perspectives.

19

Now, what makes a good case study? (Herreid, 1998)

- A good case tells a story and focuses on a topic of interest.
- A good case creates empathy with the main actors.
- A good case is relevant to the reader.
- A good case is conflict provoking.
- A good case is decision forcing and has pedagogical influence.

Case study teaching differs from conventional teaching, which emphasizes systematic and structural learning. Learners learn in a systematic way. Case studies on the contrary stress exploratory and creative learning (Luo, 2004).

"Humans are story-telling animals" (Herreid, 1997, p. 92). Case studies tell stories and allow the listener to get involved. Case studies are often emotional stories; they feed our need for information and allow us to feel compassion for others and increase interest in a certain topic. The case study method is a method centered on students (Luo, 2004). Complex and controversial topics can be discussed very well with the use of cases. Many case studies deal with real social problems such as global warming, pollution, environmental degradation, and medical problems (Herreid, 2004).

Moreover, case studies help develop learners' interpersonal skills as they engage in role play; they can understand different perspectives and problems from case characters' points of view. Learners can further engage in role play and simulated discussions. They can further take the role of a consultant and investigate, analyze, and identify processes to solve organizational issues and problems, or to capture opportunities.

Chakrabarti and Balaji (2007) divide cases into two groups. On the one hand, a case is a chronological description of facts or situations designed in an order which would facilitate a scope for extensive discussion and analysis (McDade, 1995 in Chakrabarti, and Balaji (2007)). On the other hand, a case study represents a model of real life which supports the practice of decision-making. A case study thus helps develop the managerial skills of students (Richardson, 1994).

3.2 Challenges When Teaching Business Ethics

A major issue when teaching business ethics is to show students that not every "unethical behavior" is illegal. There are laws in all countries that regulate what companies can and cannot do. The state has the task of guaranteeing the general welfare of the citizens and must therefore prevent activities endangering it.

Companies, on the contrary, usually have profit goals. They try to use their resources and abilities in the best possible way to increase sales and decrease cost. All these management activities are regulated by local laws, but governments often find it very difficult to keep up with economic and social changes and to enact laws in a timely manner. Often, laws restricting corporate actions more severely take years to be discussed and established. In many cases, this only happens after big scandals or strong demands by the public.

Multinational companies face different laws in every country. Management decisions and consequences can be illegal in one country, but are not yet forbidden in another. For companies operating in many different markets, the question arises of which standard to establish when making management decisions. Is it enough to abide by local laws or should other factors and viewpoints also be considered? For most companies, the legal aspect is the most important; but, are management practices only based on local laws ethical as well? And, what happens in countries, such as the People's Republic of China, where many laws protecting consumers and society are still weak or not even enacted.

One of the cases described in the book describes this dilemma quite well. IKEA (Chapter 21) recalled a specific product in North America. In the USA and Canada, this is required by law. A product recall is expensive and always has a negative impact on the company's reputation. As a result, many states have very strong consumer protection laws to protect buyers from defective and dangerous products. In China, these laws are not quite as strong; IKEA did not have to and did not launch a recall. Legally, this approach was not a problem, but it was also an ethical issue. Should one simply resell a product that is sure to endanger the health and life of the buyer?

In this case, some questions arise that should be asked in many companies:

(1) What is ethical management?
(2) What is more important to us, the law or consumers, the environment, and the society in which we do business?
(3) How can we ensure that our company and our employees make good, people-oriented decisions in every market?

Another important point of discussion when it comes to business ethics is the general public. Many companies do not address critical or ethical issues until there is a scandal that may damage corporate reputation and sales. In recent years, the Internet and online communities have established themselves as the most controlling factor in international business ethics. Until a few years ago, only mass media played an important role in uncovering scandals, but today every individual can question corporate practices and their consequences for society with the help of social media channels.

This new power of consumers and the Internet increases pressure on companies to address ethical issues and develop strong and reliable corporate codes to avoid unethical decision-making in their firms.

The People's Republic of China is a very interesting place when discussing these questions. Many laws in China are not yet specified in such a way that a company must adhere to the laws and still not always have to comply with ethical principles. Ethical principles are not always clearly defined and, in many Chinese companies, economic interests dominate over traditional Confucian values. China is a large country and the world's second largest economy. Developing and establishing new laws can therefore be very difficult. In addition, the state has its own interests and wants to control companies strategically and efficiently. Ethical aspects are not always the main concern here.

On the contrary, in China, there is a very active and interested online community that puts pressure on companies and discusses ethical issues very critically. All these factors make the People's Republic of China a very interesting place to learn about different aspects and attitudes when discussing business ethics.

3.3   Teaching Business Ethics with Case Studies

The case studies in this book address the complexity of this topic and show how difficult it is to develop and enforce ethical standards and processes in a world where everything is constantly changing. They differ from the "classic" case studies that are published in different organizations for the business classroom. They are shorter and describe a situation from several perspectives. The focus is — as the title suggests — on business cases that are problematic from an ethical and legal point of view. The cases show several sides, those of the actors and those of the victims of unethical behavior. The case method has the real potential to develop the skepticism that students should learn to develop when in college (Herreid, 2004).

3.4 Using this Book

Anyone teaching business ethics and management in Chinese and East Asian settings knows how important it is to have culturally and socially relevant materials to explore with students. This is the need that we are seeking to address.

Rothlin Ltd has developed an approach that varies significantly from the standard paradigm usually described as "Applied Ethics" or "Applied Moral Philosophy" (AE). This approach is developed progressively but not systematically in Rothlin and McCann, *International Business Ethics: Focus on China* (Springer, 2016). AE applies post-analytic (primarily Anglo-American) moral philosophy to the resolution of moral dilemmas, by the application of ethical principles distilled from the traditions of deontological ethics (Kant) and utilitarian ethics (Mill). Once the dilemma is resolved philosophically, the manager (or student) is left to figure out how to apply that resolution to the issue at hand. AE, then, provides a rationalist perspective that tends to dismiss the problem of how to follow through on our professed moral principles.

By contrast, our approach — which could be identified as a perspective in "virtue ethics" — tries to go deeper to confront the question of embracing or cultivating a level of moral seriousness that will enable practitioners to work creatively with the principles they claim to follow. The virtue ethics paradigm consists in a creative synthesis of Confucian and Aristotelian thinking about human nature and moral excellence, and how precisely to respond to the exigencies of both consistently. Both traditions acknowledge the spiritual dimension of moral excellence, and demonstrate the importance of spiritual practice of self-cultivation, either through the traditional Confucian ideal of *Junzi* moral leadership or the religious practices of Christian saints and theologians, adapted to contemporary lifestyles and sensibilities. These converge in the contemplation techniques embraced by both traditions that support the development of moral character or virtues, deemed indispensable for moral leadership in business. The cases in this book introduce this paradigm to students, encouraging them to explore it as a possible way to approach the challenges managers face in addressing stakeholder concerns.

The case studies we propose to include have all been completed, and most have been copyrighted in China. They represent a selection from the 60+ original case studies researched, written, and archived by the Rothlin Ltd. Case Studies Archive. All the case studies in this book come from actual social activities and describe real-life situations, and each case describes a business or social scenario with a series of questions. The questions do not have a single, correct answer. The cases are open-ended with multiple possible answers which should lead to discussion in the classroom and help learners to understand the complexity of the issue discussed, the different viewpoints that all stakeholders have, and that it is often very difficult to find a "correct" answer for the ethical dilemma presented in the case study.

The cases in this book discuss various topics, such as pollution, labor issues, or the rapid changes in Chinese society. All cases and stories were featured in Chinese and international media and allow further research by students and learners. We hope to strengthen their interest in these current topics of business ethics and modern Chinese society.

The cases in the book can be used in various ways. In some of them, it is not entirely clear whether the behavior and management practices described are unethical and/or violate the law. Different viewpoints are presented, and critical questions asked. We want to initiate a discussion in classrooms in which learners can fill the different roles and empathize with them. This makes the different points of view clearer and also the reasons why unethical business decisions are made. It also allows learners to wonder whether they understand the person's approach and how they would have acted in that situation. The cases so support classroom discussions by showing different opinions and inviting further information searches and research.

The overall aim of this book is to encourage managers, students, and entrepreneurs by showing concretely how this quest for optimal solutions can be made sustainable, a routine, a habit promoted by a healthy corporate culture in which moral leadership is valued as an important contributor to business success.

Bibliography

Bonney, K. M. (2015). Case study teaching method improves student performance and perceptions of learning gains. *Journal of Microbiology & Biology Education*, 16 (1): 21–28.

Chakrabarti, D. and Balaji, M. S. (2007). Perception of faculty on case study method of teaching in management education: An empirical study. *The ICFAIAN Journal of Management Research*, 6 (10): 7–22.

Herreid, C. F. (1997). What is a case? Bringing to science education the established teaching tool of law and medicine. *Journal of College Science Teaching*, 27 (2): 92–94.

Herreid, C. F. (1998). What makes a good case? Some basic rules of good storytelling help teachers generate student excitement in the classroom. *Journal of College Science Teaching*, 27 (3): 163–165.

Herreid, C. F. (2004). Can case studies be used to teach critical thinking? *Journal of College Science Teaching*, 33 (6): 12–14.

Luo, D. (2004). Practicing and researching the environmental case study teaching method in middle schools. *Chinese Education and Society*, 37 (4): 75–80.

McDade, S. A. (1995). Case study pedagogy to advance critical thinking. *Teaching of Psychology*, 22, 9–10.

McFarlane, D. A. (Win, 2015). Guidelines for using case studies in the teaching-learning process. *College Quarterly*, 18 (1).

Richardson B. (1994). Towards a comprehensive view of the case method in management development. *Industrial and Commercial Training*, 26 (9): 3–10.

Richardson, C. P. (1997). Using case studies in the methods classroom. *Music Educators Journal*, 84 (2): 17–21.

Part 2

Internet and Social Media Issues

Chapter 4

Baidu Tieba: A Case of Unhealthy Health Forums

Mark Pufpaff, Helen Xu, and Dennis P. McCann

Abstract

In 2016, Baidu Inc., China's most successful online search engine faced consumer protest when internet users accused the company of selling administration rights of online health forums to unqualified doctors, private hospitals, and pharmaceutical companies. Users expressed that Baidu Inc. was commercializing these forums and ignoring the social impact that health forums have on consumers. The company was accused of putting profit over its social responsibility.

Keywords: Internet, safety, information, consumer protection, consumer rights

4.1 Seeing

On January 10, 2016, Baidu Inc., the primary search engine for over one billion Chinese Internet users, found itself confronted with severe criticism from thousands of these users from across China almost simultaneously. The protest came in response to a post on the information sharing website Zhihu, the Chinese equivalent of Quora in the United States, explaining how Baidu had sold the administration rights to its disease-related forums on Tieba to unlicensed private hospitals, unqualified doctors, and pharmaceutical companies. The author of the post, who acted under the alias "Ma Yi Cai", claimed to be a former administrator of the Tieba forum on hemophilia, a disease that weakens the regular blood-clotting ability of a patient, who had been removed and replaced without notice by Liu Shanxi. Liu, a purported doctor and supposed expert on hemophilia, had been publicly discredited in 2014 as unreliable, according to a news report published by the Chinese media source *Xinhua*. Baidu's decision to approve him as the new administrator of this specific forum thus provoked widespread controversy.

Regular users of the hemophilia forum reported that with the appointment of Liu there was a significant increase in disingenuous and sometimes completely counterfeit advertisements promoting inauthentic cures, remedies, and prescriptions for treating hemophilia. It was also alleged that Liu was censoring discussion posts that challenged the effectiveness of the products and services he was promoting. Similar experiences were reported from users of other health-related forums on Tieba as well. Another Zhihu user, "ytytytyt", researched forum ownership and estimated that up to 40% of Tieba's health-related forums had been sold to untrustworthy administrators like Liu.

Baidu began commercializing its Tieba forums in 2014 through its "Partnership of Forum" campaign, which allowed companies and individuals to buy the administrative rights to a given forum, one that was presumably related to their particular business interests. Baidu was supposed to administer a verification process, to determine whether the purchaser was seeking to self-operate the forum or operate by way of an agent. The annual fee for each of these options started at RMB 30,000 and RMB 60,000, respectively; however, a report by the *Beijing Youth Daily* stated that health-related forums in particular were priced much higher, reaching over RMB 2,00,000 in some cases. With over 19 million forums on Tieba potentially for sale, Baidu stood to make windfall profits.

The Tieba forums, and in particular the health forums, were intended to create online communities of support, encouragement, and experience sharing whereby members learn about the diseases they may have and how to manage them. Many members expressed discontent because they felt that by commercializing these forums Baidu was neglecting its social responsibility and contradicting its values as a company. With pressure both from the State Internet Information Office and the Chinese public, Baidu pledged to investigate and restructure its forum administrator approval procedures, repeal the current administrators and discontinue the commercialization of the health forums.

4.2 Judging

When we consider this episode within the context of consumer rights, we run into some immediate questions. What can a health forum user reasonably expect from Baidu regarding the accuracy of its content and the authenticity of its advertisements? What measures does Baidu have to take to uphold the dignity of persons participating in its health forum communities? Baidu is a publicly listed company on the Nasdaq stock exchange. Does the need to generate profits for its shareholders give Baidu the right to place profit maximization above the rights of even one of its users? What, then, are the rights of its users?

All of these questions point to one, general, and perennial concern: when money is on the line, ethics is typically off the table. Sadly, it *ought* to be the exact opposite. When money is on the line, ethics is the surest way to safeguard it against mismanagement and ill investment.

There is also a difference between what is legal and what is ethical. It is not uncommon for businesses to make decisions based only on what is legal in their respective markets or the countries in which they operate. However, whether that decision is ethical, that is, whether it respects human dignity and is directed toward the common good, is a different consideration altogether. It requires an exercise of freedom that looks beyond the minimum required by law in order to discern best business practice. In the case of Baidu, its freedom to both profit from advertising and to change its forum administrators at will may have been legal, but it was exercised poorly. There are two points where this can be argued.

4.2.1 One is Advertising

Advertisements are meant to inform, not coerce. They are also meant to attract, not intrude. One of the most obvious violations Baidu committed was enabling unscrupulous health forum administrators, many of whom were driven purely by the desire to maximize profits, to take advantage of vulnerable and unsuspecting users through the use of deceptive advertisements. This not only undermined the solidarity that such online communities were supposed to create, but actually damaged their capacity to work together to help each other by promoting misleading information and counterfeit products and services. Their rights were violated because their dignity, which demands honesty, was neglected.

4.2.2 *The Other is Verification Processes*

Verification processes are not arbitrary formalities. They serve a crucial purpose, which is simultaneously to secure the interests of the company and protect the rights of the customers. Baidu, on both fronts, though in differing ways, failed to fulfill this purpose. It failed to secure its own interests because it allowed a short-term profit motive to obscure the due diligence required in verifying and approving its forum administrators. Not only is it now under legal scrutiny, but it has incurred financial losses and long-term damage to its reputation. Baidu failed to respect its users by putting profits over consumer rights and exposing them to harm, especially those who used Tieba's health forums as a trusted source of advice on products and services.

4.3 Acting

Put yourself in the position of both Baidu and one of its health forum users. What would you do? How would you respond? What course of action is directed toward justice, toward the common good?

If I were Baidu...
The primary question for Baidu is how to rebuild consumer trust. It was reported that Baidu has, at present, taken the following actions:

- Limited the administrator rights to its health forums to public service organizations only.
- Improved the existing complaint channel to encourage the reporting of suspicious behavior.
- Implemented a user-based supervision mechanism to monitor for illegal behavior.
- Adopted the Internet Users Rights Protection Plan to protect and reimburse cheated Tieba users.

Are these actions enough? Are they sincere and aimed at resolving the trust issues at hand? Or are they simply telling the public what they want to hear? Does it show real commitment by Baidu to change its current practices?

For contrast, Alibaba took drastic measures to rebuild trust after a high-profile fraud scandal in 2011, involving around 100 salesmen who were shown to have aided criminal organizations in setting up "Gold Supplier" storefronts on Alibaba.com to imitate legitimate businesses with the intention of defrauding consumers. Even after investigative reports absolved Alibaba's top management of any involvement in the scandal, their CEO, David Wei, and COO, Elvis Lee, resigned. What message does this send to the public? Is it comforting to know that, even while innocent, top executives are willing to take responsibility for the actions of the staff under their oversight? Does this inspire consumer trust? Does it recover hope in Alibaba's commitment to integrity?

In responding to crises, there are three fundamental principles that are aimed at rebuilding trust, honesty, ownership, and sincerity: honesty in communicating the problem, ownership of responsibility for the problem, and a sincere commitment to solving the problem. With this in mind, how would you advise Baidu in its efforts to restore the trust of its users and repair the damage to its reputation?

If I were a health forum user...
Consumers have more power than they may realize to change business behavior. Companies, no matter how autonomous they may sometimes seem in their operations, are completely dependent upon the consumer marketplace. They know this, but it is often that we, the consumers, do not. What responsibility do you, as a consumer, have in response to distasteful business practices? What kind of message are you sending by your consumption behavior?

If you were dissatisfied with the business practices of Baidu, what could you do? What action could you, personally, take? Do you feel the response from the Tieba health forum communities was justified? Would you have reacted similarly? Would you continue using Baidu as a search engine or begin using a competitor like So 360 or *Sogou*?

The responsibility of consumers is to avoid complacency in the marketplace. Companies can and do become comfortable with a certain standard of operations, losing sight of their innovative capacity and the ever-evolving needs of society. They may also see consumer complacency or indifference as an opportunity for profit maximization or even exploitation, as perhaps we saw here with Baidu Tieba.

4.4 Conclusion

Baidu is currently relied upon by over one billion people. It provides services, such as its search engine, Tieba forums, and micro-segmenting platforms that have been a source of community and empowerment for people across China. Going forward, and in light of this crisis, its growth model would profit by innovating away from a dependence, for example, on medical advertisement, as a commitment to its users in its health-related forums. Trust between businesses and consumers is achieved through business practices that are ethically consistent. To accord with the wisdom of an editorial from the *People's Daily*, Baidu must reduce short-sighted behavior if it is to rebuild consumer trust and see ahead to a sustainable future.

4.5 Discussion Questions

1. What are the moral issues in this case? List and explain them.
2. Was it inevitable that Baidu's decision to monetize its Tieba forums would end in scandal? Is there a way to implement such monetization ethically? If so, how? If not, why not?
3. Do you think Baidu's actions after the scandal broke were enough? What would you have done differently, if anything?

Bibliography

Kan, M. (2011). Alibaba.com CEO and COO resign after fraud investigation. *Yahoo News*. Retrieved February 16, 2016, from https://www.computerworld.com/article/2747592/alibaba-com-ceo-and-coo-resign-after-fraud-investigation.html.

Lee, C. (2016). Baidu slammed for monetizing health forums. *ZDNet*. Retrieved February 16, 2016, from http://www.zdnet.com/article/baidu-slammed-for-monetizing-health-forums/#!.

Meng, L. (2016). Baidu to halt commercialization of Tieba health forums. *China Daily*. Retrieved on February 16, 2016, from http://www.chinadaily.com.cn/business/2016-01/12/content_23052646.htm.

Securities Daily (2016). 百度贴吧被曝"野蛮"商业化 运营权3万元起售 (Baidu Tieba exposed to "Barbaric" commercialization, selling commercial operation rights from 30,000 yuan). *People.com.cn*. Retrieved on February 16, 2016, from http://finance.people.com.cn/gb/n1/2016/0113/c1004-28046062.html.

Xinhua (2016a). Search giant Baidu under fire for profiting from medical forums. *China.org.cn.* Retrieved on February 16, 2016, from http://www.china.org.cn/business/2016-01/14/content_37572013.htm.

Xinhua (2016b). Baidu's unlearned lesson. *China Daily.* Retrieved on February 16, 2016, from http://www.chinadaily.com.cn/business/tech/2016-01/14/content_23088458.htm.

Xinhua (2016c). Baidu faces punishment over porn, libel. *Chinadaily.com.cn.* Retrieved February 16, 2016, from https://www.chinadaily.com.cn/china/2016-01/16/content_23117379.htm.

Chapter 5

Charity Fraud or Unethical Personal Behavior?

The Essential Differences between Public Fundraising and Individual Appealing

Helen Xu and Dennis P. McCann

Abstract

In 2011, Tencent, one of the most influential Chinese Internet companies introduced a new service called "WeChat", which has become the most relevant chat service in China. Another year later, official accounts were also introduced, which allowed users to monetize their account and also receive donations. The service was confronted with severe criticism when a user published information on his young daughter's illness and received donations from other users. Publicizing details about the illness and receiving these donations was seen as "bloody marketing", which led to a discussion about charity fraud and Internet services supporting it.

Keywords: Fraud, Internet, social responsibility, charity

5.1 Introduction

Following the popularization of the Internet all around the world, the concept of "We Media" was first recognized by Dan Gillmor in 2002, one of its defenders in the blogosphere. One year later, Chris Willis and Shayne Bowman defined the underlying concept as "Participatory Journalism": "the act of a citizen or group of citizens that played an active role in the process of collecting, reporting, analyzing and disseminating news and information," with "the intention of providing independent, reliable, accurate, wide-ranging and relevant information sharing in a democratic way." In other words, "We Media" consists of information exchange platforms, such as Blogs, Microblogs, WeChat, and BBS, in which each account could be seen as a news source and used to exchange messages generated by the general public.

In 2011, when Tencent, a Chinese Internet giant, first introduced "WeChat" as a free messaging App for Chinese Internet users, only few people had expected it to be a great success. Compared with SNS, WeChat could not only offer video and voice calls but also share instant messages and make quick connections with others all around the world. By the third quarter of 2016, WeChat had become one of the most outstanding technical innovations with 846 million active users.

In August 2012, WeChat launched a public platform with official accounts, in order to create a better user experience and to open a new era of "interactive marketing." The official account, differing from the common user account, consisted of three types:

- Subscription Accounts: These are available to individuals and enterprises and are used to convey information to all subscribers.
- Service Accounts: These are not applied to individuals, but can offer interactive services and powerful user management tools to public organizations, such as banks and governments.
- Enterprise-Specific Accounts: These are used for internal communications which will enhance good connections within the business.

Any individual, enterprise, government, media, or organization is allowed to apply for a public account by completing the registration form, and verifying it by using an individual's identity card, or by arranging prior qualifications for the organization. A properly registered public account provides a significant benefit in the form of a "Reward" functionality. Thus, owners of such accounts — like WeChat — are able to make profits from their subscribers and viewers who choose to express how they like the service or posting by assigning a certain amount of "Reward" to them. It is this "Reward" functionality and its use in soliciting charitable donations that sets the stage for discussing the issue in this case.

5.2 Seeing

Mr. Luo Er, a former chief editor of *New Story Magazine* in Shenzhen City, Guangdong Province, is one of the beneficiaries who operates a subscription account with a "Reward" functionality for a living. However, a tragic disaster occurred in Luo's family on September 8, when his 5-year-old daughter, Luo Yixiao, was diagnosed with leukemia, a type of cancer characterized by the abnormal proliferation of leukocytes. It is not hard to imagine how sad this family was when it suddenly learned the bad news, but Luo refused to seek assistance from the NGOs or charitable foundations, which was like "begging" in his view. Instead, he decided to start writing and to sell his stories on WeChat. At that time, nobody could have predicted that Luo would be regarded as a swindler one day.

The turning point came with an article posted by Luo on November 25, which he named *Luo Yixiao, Stay Where You Are*. In the story, Luo provided an update on his daughter's situation with a commentary at the top and bottom announcing that "the Xiao Tong Ren Company will give RMB 1 to Luo for every single repost of this journal entry." Once the story was verified and confirmed by well-known web portals, for instance, *Sina News*, the posting quickly went viral, thus amassing numerous "Rewards" from generous netizens. More than RMB 2.62 million yuan was raised within five days, "of which RMB 0.5 million yuan were the promised 'aid' pledged by Xiao Tong Ren Company."

Unexpectedly, however, the heart-wrenching story was soon denounced as a "bloody marketing promotion." The first challenge came out in the "Moments" of WeChat user, Doctor Hu, where he revealed the following:

> "One of my senior fellow apprentices works in the department of the Children's Hospital in Shenzhen, and he mentioned that, (1) Daily expense of Luo Yixiao is approximately RMB 5,000 yuan; (2) 80% of her expenses are covered by the reimbursement of social security, which means that Luo's family affords about RMB 20,000 yuan so far... The hype of the [Xiao Tong Ren] Company is so disgusting that [it] not only takes advantage of people's sympathy, but also exaggerates the treatment and cost..."

On the afternoon of November 30, the Children's Hospital in Shenzhen also publicly disclosed the treatment fee for Luo Yixiao, stating the following:

"The total of hospitalization expenses of Luo Yixiao by November 29, 2016 reaches RMB 204,244.31 yuan, of which RMB 36,193.33 yuan (17.7%) was paid by Luo's family, while the rest was covered by the social security."

What's more, the "good Samaritan", Xiao Tong Ren Company, turned out to be a new media operation and digital marketing company, and its Legal Representative, Mr. Liu Xiafeng, years ago worked for the same publisher alongside Luo. In light of these revelations, some members of the public dismissed the whole event as "charity fraud", since both parties were suspected of gaining sympathy and attention by making use of a sick child. The financial status of Luo was also exposed by Mr. Liu, who admitted the following:

"He [Mr. Luo] has three apartments indeed, one in Shenzhen and the other two in Dongguan with a loan of RMB 420,000 yuan. However, he cannot sell them off because he didn't have the property ownership certificates so far."

This entirely different picture of Mr. Luo's affairs drew a heated response on the Internet, prompting the Civil Affairs Bureau of Shenzhen to begin an investigation on December 1. Negotiations based on the Civil Affairs investigation led to an agreement that Mr. Liu Xiafeng, Mr. Luo Er, and Tencent would return the income — every cent of it, a total of RMB 2.62 million yuan — back to the users of WeChat. Although the final decision was issued promptly, it was too late for them to take further action in light of the increasing public outcry. Sadly, as reported by the media, Luo Yixiao died at Shenzhen University Health Science Center on December 24, and her parents then donated her body to Shenzhen University for future clinical research.

5.3 Judging

Beyond everyone's expectations, the whole story had become very clear after the Bureau of Civil Affairs' intervention. The feelings of anger and outrage of netizens who accused Luo of betrayal and deceit were understandable, especially when they realized that Luo's family could already afford his daughter's medical expenses. Meanwhile, a number of people also questioned the authenticity of the information published via WeChat, the online platform, as well as the unspoken intentions of Luo and Xiao Tong Ren Company. However, no party — at least in this case — was punished by the local government.

Why did the government not take further action? According to Mr. Kan Ke, "The penalty depends on how Luo's behavior been identified in this case." Mr. Kan, a former Deputy Director of the Criminal Law Office of the National People's Congress, and also the lawmaker who participated in the legislation of the new charity law, raised the best question: What are we to think of what Luo and Xiao Tong Ren Company were doing? Under China's new Charity Law, should we regard it as a case of "'charity fraud' and 'individual appealing'?"

5.3.1 *Charity Fraud in the New Charity Law*

It is widely acknowledged that the new Charity Law that came into effect on September 1, 2016, was designed to find the solutions to the increasingly urgent problems in the field of charity. At the same time, it promotes proper supervision of the organizations, donations, services, and information disclosure on the basis of the actual condition of China's economic and social development. It also is meant to meet the needs for innovation in social governance mechanisms. In this context, Luo's case was regarded as a primary challenge to the enforcement of the new law.

According to the interpretation by the Chinese Charity Federation, the initiation of fundraising activities is limited to charitable organizations that aim to benefit an unspecified group of people, while individuals are prohibited from public fundraising because of the problems involved in holding them accountable. Moreover, "the charitable organization who wants to carry out the public fundraising shall obtain the credential in advance" (Provision 22). In other words, a charitable organization is allowed to launch such activity on the condition that it has been legally registered and already has obtained approval from the Civil Affairs Department. For the individuals who do not possess the credentials, they may ask for the assistance of qualified organizations that can initiate "the public fundraising based on a charitable purpose" (Provision 26). For the violators, whether organizations or individuals, "the Civil Affairs Department will send the warning or order the suspension on the certain activities, or fine between RMB 20,000 and 200,000 yuan if it's difficult for them to return the illegal income" (Provision 101).

5.3.2 *Definition and Management on Individual Appealing*

Individual appealing, according to the literal meaning, refers to an individual, or a family, who turns to others for help. Nowadays, everyone has the right to post messages online and ask the public for help on the basis of truthful information disclosure in order to solve problems for themselves or their family. In this context, the relationship between donors and recipients "is not covered by the Charity law, nor supervised by any juridical entity." In Luo's case, the "aid" pledged by Xiao Tong Ren Company, dependent on the journal repost, was defined as the advertising income since its commercial purpose was prominently labeled in the article, at least as interpreted by Mr. Kan.

Since neither concrete standards nor punitive measures were ever issued by the Chinese government in this matter, what kind of standards shall those in need follow in order to comply with the law? The answer seems to point to self-discipline, in other words, individual morality. The big change in Mr. Luo's attitude before and after may be instructive here. At the very beginning, Luo was adhering to moral principles which led him to take the path of self-reliance. However, faced with a long and difficult treatment cycle, he changed his mind because Liu's proposal — a so-called win-win strategy — looked very appealing. It would not only bring great benefits to the marketing promotion of Xiao Tong Ren Company but also address Mr. Luo's urgent family problem. Therefore, what is important is the morality of both the help seeker and the online operator, which ought to be highly correlated with the Confucian virtues, such as integrity, truthfulness, and uprightness. This is reminiscent of a similar case involving Baidu. Due to unethical online advertising and an irresponsible approval process for advertisers, a 22-year-old student named Wei Zexi died after using an unapproved experimental treatment being advertised on Baidu's search results page.

The amazing income raised in a short period of time shows how benevolent and generous people are nowadays. Nevertheless, due to the moral deficiencies and fierce competition in the business world, especially in China, corporations, like Xiao Tong Ren Company, apparently intend to take advantage of legal loopholes and people's kindness to achieve their marketing goals. If their actions go unchallenged, the result would be just the opposite to what benevolent and generous people would hope for. Not surprisingly, Luo and Xiao Tong Ren Company saw their reputation and credibility diminished in the whole society, which suffered further erosion of the trust that people ought to have in each other.

Undoubtedly, WeChat, as the Internet platform used for conveying and passing information between the givers and the recipient in this case, is partly to blame for failing to verify the information disclosure in Luo's case. *The People's Daily* commentary pointed out that the proper "public spirit" was shown by the users who responded to people in need. However, "We Media" made huge cost reductions by failing to verify the claims made by those seeking help. As a result, their expenditure on information filtering is expected to increase in the future. Advanced technology and its adoption in "We Media" should raise higher demands on the platform operator's sense of responsibility, authority, and managerial effectiveness.

5.4 Acting

How do you judge Luo and Xiao Tong Ren Company's behavior? Can you excuse Luo's concealing some facts in order to gain the sympathy of the netizens? And, what do you think of the responsibility of a "We Media" platform like WeChat?

If you were the parent of a child who was diagnosed with leukemia...
Putting yourself in Luo's position, would you like to seek help from the foundation, or raise money by other means, like using a "We Media" platform? You must feel tortured by your child's serious disease; at the same time, you also realize that quite a long process will be involved in applying for the treatment fee from a foundation, not to mention the difficulties involved in getting a mortgage loan from the bank to pay for your child's treatment. On the one hand, online platforms, such as WeChat, seem to be the fastest and easiest way for your family to earn money; on the other hand, you know for sure that disclosing your financial status will delay or even generate more challenges to your fundraising. What would you do?

Under no circumstances should we do anything to violate the moral principles or fundamental ethical codes — intending to safeguard the basic quality of our humanity. In China, there are 12 core socialist values encouraged and advocated by the central government, which are classified into three dimensions:

- National Dimension: Prosperity, Democracy, Civility, and Harmony.
- Social Dimension: Freedom, Equality, Justice, and Rule of Law.
- Citizen's Dimension: Patriotism, Dedication, Integrity, and Friendship.

"All citizens shall be mobilized to foster and practice these core socialist values," said Xin Ming, Professor of the Party School of the CPC Central Committee, and "only by doing so can we transfer the values into social group consciousness and conscious action." Moreover, Confucius also indicated the following: "I do not know how a man without truthfulness is to get on. How can a large carriage be made to go without the crossbar for yoking the oxen to, or a small carriage without the arrangement for yoking the horses?" (Chapter 22, Book II of *The Analects*). Therefore, the core values are not only the extensions of Confucian virtues but also relevant for guiding the development of the codes of ethics that we live by.

If you were the manager of the WeChat, Tencent...
For sure, the "Online Pay" and "Reward" functionalities opened up new possibilities to promote the development of charitable activities in China. They can expand the scope of both donors and recipients in comparison with traditional methods. Beyond what is already being done by entrepreneurs and generous groups, everyone can now take part in and extend a hand to those in need. As an intermediate structure, the online platform plays a key role that could not only ensure the truthfulness and transparency of the information but also the effectiveness of management in order to be fully responsible for all users and stakeholders.

It is widely acknowledged that the legislation and supervision of charitable activities are still in a stage of continuous exploration and development in China. Luo's case was a wake-up call for both the government and the whole society. Someone should work out the best solutions to standardize online fundraising and verify the authenticity of information to eliminate the "grey area" as soon as possible. The lapse in WeChat's management may result in damage to the reputation of the whole company; at the same time, users would also feel hurt when misled and exploited by fake news. As one of the Internet giants in China,

Tencent was supposed to be better; while being the role model in corporate social responsibility implementation, Tencent should concentrate on cultivating best practices. If the company would like to cooperate with local government proactively, and work out positive ways to promote self-discipline and ensure the accuracy of information disclosure, all businesses may benefit from it. Such incidents can be avoided in the future.

No matter whether Luo concealed the facts deliberately or not, it is undeniable that his inconsistent behavior before and after appears to be immoral at least. Even if there is no rule or regulation used to define what is legal in this case, both Luo and Xiao Tong Ren Company did wrong and should be blamed. In the cyber world, it is more and more difficult for people to tell truth from falsehood in all the massive information and news they have access to. However, this should not excuse the irresponsibility of "We Media" such as WeChat. As the old saying goes that "Do not do any evil no matter how insignificant it is, do not miss doing any good no matter how insignificant it is." Moreover, guaranteeing the rights and interests of all stakeholders is fundamental to any business, especially an Internet-based business.

As you can imagine, the worst outcome from this case is not that it challenges the enforcement of the new Charity law, nor that we should worry so much about the final destination of the millions of "rewards" generated from the public at large. The worst outcome would be that vulnerable groups really in need may feel helpless because they are unable to gain public trust and support, after being exploited and cheated by society so often before. "The Wolf is Coming" story indicated that the shepherd who used to tell lies may not be rescued when a really dangerous situation emerges. How about others who were never telling lies? Are they not still reliable and do they not still deserve to be helped?

5.5 Discussion Questions

1. Do you think Luo's case is a moral issue? Why or why not?
2. What do you think is the responsibility of Luo and Xiao Tong Ren Company in this case?
3. What do you think is the responsibility of Tencent in addressing the problems of people seeking help through "We Media"?
4. If you were in trouble and could not afford the treatment fee for your family members who were diagnosed with cancer or any other malignant disease, what would you do? Why?

5. If you were asked to advise "We Media" moving forward after Luo's case, on how to promote charitable activity in China, what would be your strategic recommendations?

Bibliography

Beijing Times (2016). 罗尔获捐约 270 万策划者:好事做到底, 不怕风凉话 (Luo Er received about 2.7 million donations). *news.163.com*. Retrieved from https://news.163.com/16/1130/17/C74V5DM50001875P.html.

Bowman, S. and Willis, C. (2003). We Media — How audiences are shaping the future of news and information. *Hypergene*. Retrieved on January 4, 2017 from http://www.hypergene.net/wemedia/download/we_media.pdf.

People's Daily Online (2016). Dad flooded with criticism after journals about daughter's leukemia go viral. *China Daily*. Retrieved from http://usa. chinadaily.com.cn/china/2016-12/01/content_27534898.htm.

Tencent News (2016). 罗一笑事件时间线梳理 (Timeline of Luo Yixiao Incident). *Tencent News*. Retrieved from http://news.qq.com/cross/20161202/ 15DS6Ux1.html#0.

Chapter 6

Social Media Contents:
The Tencent Case

Mark Pufpaff and Dennis P. McCann

Abstract

In 2017, Tencent Holdings Limited, China's Online giant faced the rage of its users after publishing an emoji featuring World War II sex slaves called "comfort women" on the International Memorial Day for Comfort Women. The company officially apologized, and the third-party provider that had designed the emoji was forced to stop its operations for two months by the government. The case discusses the freedom of speech, corporate communication, and moral issues of the events.

Keywords: Social media, history, privacy rights

6.1 Seeing

On August 20, 2017, Tencent Holdings Limited came under attack from the public in China for allowing emojis — which are small, digital images intended to convey feelings or sentiments in instant messaging or group chats — of World War II sex slaves, called "comfort women",[1] on its

---

[1] "Comfort women" were women and girls in Japanese occupied territory that the Japanese Imperial Army forced into sexual servitude before and during World War II. The victims were organized into "comfort stations" where Japanese military personnel would rape

social media platform Qzone.[2] The emojis were created by a third-party provider, named Siyanhui Co., and featured picture content from a recent documentary called *Twenty Two*, launched on August 14th in accordance with International Memorial Day for Comfort Women. The pictures were overlaid with Chinese text, translated into English as "I am lost", "I was really wronged", and "speechless and choked up." An example of what they looked like is provided below:

Enraged Chinese citizens took to the Internet to denounce Tencent for allowing such offensive content on its platform. A sampling of the responses is given as follows:

> "You [Tencent] cannot use something very serious ["comfort women"] to make emojis which are used for teasing people…it's immoral and disrespectful to those poor war victims." — Chinese netizen
>
> "You [Tencent] take everything for the purpose of entertainment and don't realize the pain of the old women at all, let alone the pain of the entire people at that time." — Weibo blogger
>
> "The people who made these stickers [Siyanhui Co.] are heartless, using other people's pain for their own entertainment." — Weibo blogger

---

them at will. The fact of these horrific crimes against innocent women, from China, South Korea, the Philippines, and many more countries, has been a historical and ongoing source of tension between these countries and Japan. Moderate estimates put the number of "comfort women" at around 200,000.

[2]Qzone is used primarily for blogging, diary keeping, music and photo sharing, and watching videos. It is linked to QQ, one of Tencent's instant messaging and file-sharing platforms.

"I hope they [Tencent] issue a serious apology. This kind of thing is not 'entertainment'. Absolutely not." — Chinese netizen

"What brutes produced these stickers [emojis]? How would you feel if this was a member of your family? If it was your mother?" — Weibo blogger

These reflect the attitudes of thousands, if not millions, of Chinese netizens nationwide. Their outrage prompted an apology from Tencent. Part of their public statement is as follows:

"The incident has exposed flaws in our content supervision and reviewing system. We will conduct self-investigation and improve the related systems. We will take this as a lesson to firmly prevent a repeat of this incident."

While Tencent seemingly issued their apology independent of political pressure, Siyanhui Co. has been fined RMB 15,000 (USD 2,258) by the government and had their operations suspended for two months. They, too, issued an apology after appearing in court. Authorities justified the fine and suspension of operations on the grounds that it was illegal to create and spread offensive content — such as emojis — that made light of the sufferings of China's "comfort women."

6.2 Judging

Why might the proliferation of the "comfort women" emojis be prohibited, and the company responsible for creating them fined? A relevant starting point for interpreting this response on behalf of the government is the Chinese constitution. In it, there is not only an enumeration of rights, freedoms, and protections but also a social vision that is to form the basis for interpreting how such rights, freedoms, and protections shall and shall not be enjoyed by the public. Let us begin with Article 35, which states that the "citizens of the People's Republic of China enjoy freedom of speech, of the press, of assembly, of association, of procession and of demonstration." It is important to note that while these are legitimate freedoms, the freedom of speech being perhaps the most relevant to this case, they must be interpreted within the political, legal, social, and philosophical environment in which they are being exercised. In other words, it is not unreasonable to ask what freedom of speech *means* in the context of China. There is a rather significant difference between, say, the freedom to do as one wishes and the freedom to be and do good. Is not the government's suppression of Siyanhui's "comfort women" emojis a lesson in how freedom is to be exercised in China, namely, with a view toward the common welfare?

Next, let us look at Article 38, which states that "the personal dignity of citizens of the People's Republic of China is inviolable. Insult, libel, false accusation or false incrimination directed against citizens by any means is prohibited." This lends further weight to the notion that freedom has limits, and must be bound by a set of values amicable to societal flourishing. That the violation of a person's dignity is likely to incur some degree of punishment by the government sheds light on why the "comfort women" emojis generated the reaction they did. Not only did the government act against Siyanhui (and possibly Tencent — we do not know) but their action was in alignment with and responsive to the reactions of the public. In other words, the government brought closure to the desires of some of its people through the exercise of its power to punish, a closure that the concerned citizens themselves, even collectively, may not have been able to bring about on their own. It also reflects the kind of values that the people of China will and will not tolerate (e.g., making light of the experiences of World War II Chinese sex slaves). While emojis of all kinds — including many morally questionable ones[3] — permeate the Chinese blogosphere and social media community, there are some, like these "comfort women" emojis, that seemingly go too far, and threaten the very core of the Chinese character. Is not the protection of such values a legitimate justification for curtailing the freedom of companies like Siyanhui to produce content that arguably goes against them?

Finally, and perhaps most importantly, in Article 51, we read that the "citizens of the People's Republic of China, in exercising their freedoms and rights, may not infringe upon the interests of the State, of society or of the collective, or upon the lawful freedoms and rights of other citizens." That the exercise of "freedoms and rights... may not infringe upon the

---

[3] There are whole hosts of emojis, stickers, and GIF (Graphics Interchange Format) images that raise moral questions. Some of the genres include race, gender, homosexuality, violence, pornography, and ethnicity. While this case is attempting to deal specifically with the morality surrounding the creation of the "comfort women" emojis and the response by the public and the government, there is much to say about why some of these other kinds of emojis are permitted at the expense of those mocked. Is the government applying fair standards? This could be the subject of further case studies.

interests of the State" is central. We might use this as the interpretive key for understanding not only the Chinese constitution but also the way in which the government sets up its regulatory framework for society. In short, freedom is not to be viewed as absolute in China, and thus is not absolutely protected by the government. It can and, given the case at hand, seemingly does come into conflict with the interests of the State. When such conflicts arise, it is vested in the power and discretion of the government to suppress that which it deems destructive to the common good and vision of Chinese society.

The "comfort women" emojis, it may be said, not only make light of the experiences that these women went through — and thus affect the capacity for the State and its people to stand in solidarity with them — but also may have implications in international relations — for example, the desire of the Chinese government on behalf of these "comfort women" to reconcile historical tensions with Japan. The issue of China's "comfort women" is certainly a sensitive one, and one that the government itself has been heavily involved in over the years. Using a documentary aimed at dignifying such women to create emojis for use in social media exchanges is "playing with fire", and Tencent and Siyanhui, as they say, are "feeling the burn."

6.3 Acting

Another aspect of this case study is the responsibility of corporations in self-censorship and regulation. What principles should guide how corporations like Tencent monitor their platforms for abuses?

An important principle of business ethics is "do no harm." This principle is relevant for a number of reasons. It presupposes not only a desire to avoid whatever commonly might be considered harmful in any given business context but also includes a recognition of the need for compliance with applicable laws. In other words, corporate activity is not to be considered independent of government regulation or preexisting societal values. Obliging by them (regulations and laws) and conforming to them (societal values and ethical norms) are thus ways for a business to act responsibly in the communities in which it operates. Beyond the question of harm is a strategic consideration. How can corporations structure their operations so as to incentivize good behavior and provide disincentives to bad behavior? Let us make a brief comparison between the response of Tencent to the negative feedback from the public about the existence of the "comfort women" emojis in their Qzone and the self-governance policy of a US-based company called Quora.

As noted previously, Tencent apologized and removed the "comfort women" emojis from circulation because of negative public feedback. This indicates that Tencent was willing to make censorship decisions based on the prevailing moral sentiment of its users. Quora, a US-based question-and-answer sharing platform, has what they call a "Be Nice Be Respectful" (BNBR) policy, whereby answers to questions that include certain types of character attacks, identity attacks, and unnecessarily offensive content are removed by Quora's forum moderators. Such content is regularly reported by the Quora community itself, but is also identified by moderators using algorithms that flag potentially inappropriate answers or questions for review. While answers suppressed because of a perceived violation of the BNBR policy can be appealed, it is an example of a company imposing a norm aimed at deterring *destructive* and encouraging *constructive* interactions, even among those who disagree with each other. Tencent's apology and censorship of the "comfort women" emojis is similar in kind to Quora's censorship of offensive answers in its forums. Both have an aim in mind, namely, the creation of an environment that is respectful and directed toward humane ends — connection and communication in Tencent's case, information sharing and learning in Quora's case.

While the emergence and suppression of the "comfort women" emojis seems to be an isolated incident, it still raises an important question for corporate governance. Tencent is a pioneer in social media technology in China. They have revolutionized the social landscape of the country and have penetrated many international markets. What kind of message should they be sending to their users and stakeholders? How can they regulate the usage of their platforms and applications in view of the common good?

6.4 Discussion Questions

1. What are the moral issues in this case? List and explain them.
2. Do you think the government was right to fine Siyanhui and suspend their operations for two months? Why or why not?
3. Do you think Tencent was right to remove from circulation the "comfort women" emojis being used in Qzone? Why or why not?
4. What do you think of Quora's BNBR policy? Do you think more social media companies — such as Tencent — should adopt such policies? Why or why not?

Bibliography

Beijing Youth Daily (2017). 慰安妇纪录片《二十二》遭截图制作表情包 腾 讯致歉: 第三方提供 (Comfort Women Documentary "22". Emoji package was produced by screenshots, provided by a third party). *www.guancha.cn*. Retrieved on October 16, 2017 from https://www.guancha.cn/culture/2017_08_22_423868.shtml.

People Daily Online (2017). 把"慰安妇"做成表情包,你的良心不会痛吗?腾讯 QQ空间道歉 (If you Make "comfort women" an emoticon, doesn't your conscience hurt? Tencent QQ space apologizes). *hxnews.com*. Retrieved on October 16, 2017 from http://m.hxnews.com/news/yl/ylxw/201708/23/1289984.shtml.

Sixth Tone (2017). Tencent under fire for emojis of WWII sex slaves. *Sixthtone. com*. Retrieved on October 16, 2017 from http://www.sixthtone.com/news/1000723/tencent-under-fire-for-emojis-of-wwii-sex-slaves.

The Paper (2017). 因制作慰安妇表情包,上海似颜绘科技有限公司被处罚 (Shanghai Siyanhui Technology Co., Ltd. was punished for making a comfort woman emoji package). *www.thepaper.cn*. https://www.thepaper.cn/newsDetail_forward_1776417.

Chapter 7

Baidu: Is Online Advertising Reliable for the Treatment of Severe Diseases?

Helen Xu, Dennis P. McCann, and Mark Pufpaff

Abstract

On April 12, 2016, a 22-year-old student named Wei Zexi died of synovial sarcoma, a rare soft tissue cancer. He was diagnosed with the disease two years earlier and documented his experiences seeking treatment on Zhihu, a popular question-and-answer website in China. The title of his testimony was called "What do you think is the greatest evil of human nature?" His answer? Baidu, China's largest and most prominent search engine. This case will detail the controversy that has surrounded his death and the moral dilemmas it presents.

Keywords: Corporate social responsibility, social media, online information, medical treatment

7.1 Seeing

On April 12, 2016, a 22-year-old student named Wei Zexi died of synovial sarcoma, a rare soft tissue cancer. He was diagnosed with the disease two years earlier. After Wei's diagnosis, he underwent chemotherapy treatments at a hospital in Shaanxi Province which, unfortunately, did not cure him of his disease. He then turned to Baidu to search for more options. He discovered, as the top result on the first page of one of his searches on Baidu, an experimental cellular immunotherapy treatment named Dendritic Cells and Cytokine-Induced Killer (DC-CIK), originally discovered by the Stanford School of Medicine, being offered by the Second Hospital of the Armed Police Beijing Corps (Second Hospital). This brought hope to Wei and his family. However, what was not indicated in this search result was the fact that DC-CIK was still in its testing phase and had a low rate of success.

After following the link, Wei contacted the hospital. He met with a doctor who claimed that DC-CIK had an 80–90% success rate and that Wei was "guaranteed" to live more than 20 years after the treatment was complete. This could not have been further from the truth. Not only did the treatment fail but it also cost Wei and his family precious time and over RMB 200,000 (USD 31,000), most of which had to be borrowed from family and friends. By the end of the treatment, they were out of time and out of money. Even though Wei and his family found a subsequent, more reliable treatment, it was too late.

After Wei's death, there was outrage from the Chinese public and investigations were launched into Baidu and Second Hospital. The points of controversy are as follows:

1. Baidu did not differentiate its "paid search" results from its ordinary search results. This meant that Wei did not know that the advertisement promoting DC-CIK and Second Hospital was, in fact, an advertisement.
2. Baidu did not display any additional information regarding the status of the DC-CIK, which, as mentioned above, was still in its testing phase and had a low effective rate. Wei only learned of this when an overseas student helped him search the treatment on Google.
3. Baidu did not do its due diligence in screening the integrity of the products and services, and the organizations offering them, being advertised on its website.
4. Second Hospital allegedly outsourced the department where Wei sought treatment to an unqualified, undisclosed private medical group.

Stanford University responded by saying the following: "Stanford Health Care and Stanford School of Medicine have no connection to this hospital, or to this case. Stanford has never had any cooperation with any Chinese hospitals in the cellular treatment sector, including the hospital involved in the case."

7.2 Judging

A lot of people die of cancer in China each year. According to *Cancer Statistics in China 2015*, there were 4,292,000 people diagnosed with cancer in China in 2015 (almost 12,000 diagnoses/day) and 2,814,000 cancer-related deaths (average of 7,500 deaths/day). What exactly makes Wei's stand out?

It is not that Wei died, but it is that his chances of survival were diminished through questionable corporate behavior. The National Health and Family Planning Commission in China released a statement saying that DC-CIK was "never approved as a formal therapeutic tool for [cancer] treatment in China." The fact that Second Hospital offered it and Baidu allowed them to promote it in its search engine should raise instant suspicions as to their intentions. Were Second Hospital and Baidu seriously looking out for the interests of those who might rely on them for lifesaving treatments and information? Or was money-making, regardless of consequence, their prime objective?

7.2.1 *Second Hospital of the Armed Police Beijing Corps*

Second Hospital was explicitly blamed by Baidu for the death of Wei after the controversy broke and investigations began. This was due to Second Hospital's relationship to the Putian Health Industry Association (Putian), a mysterious and historically controversial group run by a group of medically unqualified businessmen in Southern China's Fujian Province.

Their history began in the 1980s when they were ineffectively treating prostitutes and their customers for sexually transmitted diseases. During the market-oriented medical industry reforms in the 1990s, led by Chinese Premier Zhu Rongji, state-run hospitals became responsible for running themselves. That and military reforms around the same time resulted in the military opening hospitals as a way to increase their diminishing revenues. This provided Putian with an unprecedented opportunity. They began to offer themselves as contractors to medical departments, both military and state-run, and eventually began operating their own hospitals.

Putian-run hospitals and departments became infamous for pushing treatments and medications that were ineffective, unnecessary, and expensive. They generate the majority of their business by buying medical advertisements on Baidu. In fact, they are one of Baidu's biggest customers for the health care advertising sector.

Second Hospital's Biological Treatment Center, where Wei was administered the DC-CIK treatment, was serviced by Shanghai Claison Biotechnology Co. (Claison). The chairman of Claison is a man named Chen Xinxian. His brother, Chen Xinxi, is the founder and legal representative for Kangxin Hospital Investment and Management Co. (Kangxin), the operator of Second Hospital as a whole, and was Claison's controller until December, 2015. Kangxin was responsible for registering Second Hospital's website, which was what Wei referenced after following the Internet link found on Baidu. Both brothers are allegedly heavily involved in the Putian network of departments and hospitals.

Since the controversy broke, Second Hospital suspended all operations, its website went offline, Stanford University's Medical Center was removed from Claison's list of official partners, and Kangxin covered up the registration details of Second Hospital's website. There is good reason.

The State Council of the People's Republic of China banned public hospitals from outsourcing departmental work to private medical groups in 2010, most of them affiliated with the Putian network. The People's Liberation Army's (PLA) General Logistics Department banned military-affiliated hospitals from doing the same in 2011. However, enforcement has been negligible and the Putian network has managed to retain strong links to the Chinese health care system despite the bans.

In light of this, it is not surprising the Baidu attempted to pass the blame to Second Hospital. It is clear they broke the law and violated any and all standards of medical professionalism and moral aptitude. But, is Baidu off the hook?

Baidu, Inc.
Even though under law Baidu has not committed a crime by allowing Second Hospital to take out ad space to promote DC-CIK, the outrage from Chinese citizens is startling in its intensity. What is the source of the anger? Since Wei's death, the discussion among Chinese netizens has concerned two contentions:

1. Unethical online advertising:
    Baidu makes a fortune from online advertising. Even though the firm claims it is merely the provider of information and does not have any specific duty to certify the authenticity of content found in its search results, many feel it is being purposefully indifferent to its social

responsibilities, especially when it comes to paid advertising. First, Baidu does not differentiate between paid ads and generic search results, even though it intentionally places the paid ads at the top of every page of search results they relate to. This is deceptive to browsers, because it is common for the first and second search results to be considered the most trustworthy. It was ultimately fatal for Wei. Second, Baidu is paid by advertisers based on the number of clicks on their ads. The more visible its ads are, the more they will be clicked. They more they are clicked, the more money Baidu makes. So, there is a distinct financial incentive to make paid ads look as if they are the top search results, since those results will receive the most clicks.

2. Irresponsible approval process for advertisers:
   Baidu has been accused in the past of putting profits over the dignity of its users. In a related incident in January, 2016, Baidu was found guilty of selling the administrative rights to a significant number of its Tieba health forums, particularly the one concerning hemophilia, to unqualified private doctors and hospitals merely because they paid the most. The greedy doctors then started promoting inauthentic treatments and counterfeit products on the forums, putting people's health at risk. A similar policy is under scrutiny in this case, where Baidu overlooked the quality of the advertisers and the integrity of their products and services and focused exclusively on maximizing profits. The consequences of this kind of business practice are compounding. No one died as a result of the Tieba scandal. But, someone, Wei, did die this time.

So, is Second Hospital only to blame? It does not seem so. Baidu's apparent negligence amounts to an exceeding degree of indifference to the common good of Chinese society. Ignorance, in light of Wei's death, is not bliss. They cannot remain indifferent when they are profiting off the deaths of their own citizens.

7.3 Acting

It is clear that both Baidu and Second Hospital have made grave errors in judgment and practice. But, they are capable of change. They are in a position to make new commitments. For example, on April 19, 2016,

Chinese President Xi Jinping, at a symposium on cyber security and informatization, identified Baidu in particular as a company that can and should begin shouldering social responsibilities. As they say, a clean hand needs no washing. How would you clean up this mess?

If I were Baidu...
Where would you start? It is clear, in both this case and the Tieba health forum scandal, that health care-related policies are causing major problems. They are negatively affecting the Baidu brand as a whole and causing harm to society. How would you begin damage control? How would you begin to rebuild trust?

A good precedent is Google's response to a similar scandal in 2011, whereby the search engine was found guilty of selling advertising space to illegal online pharmaceutical companies or drug stores from Canada. They were fined USD 500 million as a consequence. In response, they changed their advertising policies. Depending on the country, Google does not allow advertisements that promote medical treatments, prescription drugs, or procedures — period.

It is reported that Baidu is still promoting health care-related treatments, products, and organizations linked to the Putian network of departments and hospitals. If you were Baidu, would you continue to allow that?

If I were Second Hospital of the Armed Police Beijing Corps...
Your situation is delicate. A patient just died at your hospital, on your watch, under your care. And, it was due to your own doctors lying about the effectiveness of the treatment, which was not even approved for use in the first place. You have lost all trust and all credibility. What do you do? How should you, as a manager, respond to such a seemingly hopeless scenario?

Start with what you have control over. For instance, stop advertising on Baidu. Cut all affiliation with the Putian network. Review the profiles of all your medical staff to ensure they are qualified. Remove any and all experimental treatments. Shut down the Biological Treatment Center. Focus on what you have historically done well. Keep a low profile once you are allowed to open back up for business. What else?

In China, doctors are considered a sacred profession. The amount of trust that is put in a doctor by a patient is overwhelming. But, when a doctor, whose vocation it is to save people's lives, is proven untrustworthy, what hope is there for people like Wei? Are they just doomed to die? Is there really not a moral standard that all doctors should actively adhere to, and where possible, surpass in excellence?

7.4 Conclusion

It is common for corporations to equate being good with doing no harm. But, for hospitals, it is not so simple. The outcome of their work is either life-giving or life-taking and must adhere to a higher standard. They cannot be allowed to make certain decisions merely because they will result in higher profits. They are in a position of service, and must live up to the expectations of those patients who put their trust in them. Likewise for Baidu. Though Baidu is not a hospital, it is a platform for providing information on hospitals and treatments. It is, in a sense, an extension of a hospital's outreach to the people. And, there is a responsibility that comes with that capacity. This case dealt with the death of Wei Zexi at the hands of negligent corporations. As China mourns this tragedy, there is no better time to reflect on what it means to be a responsible business leader.

7.5 Discussion Questions

1. What can you learn about management from this case? About leadership?
2. What moral issues are involved in this case? Why do they matter?
3. If you were the CEO of Baidu, how would you respond to public concerns? What would you say if asked about Wei's case?
4. If you were the Director of the Second Hospital of the Armed Police Beijing Corps, how would you respond to this crisis? Would you make an apology? Would that be enough? How would you reestablish trust with the Chinese society you claim to serve?
5. How should the government respond? What would be the appropriate punishment for this kind of activity? What could the government do to avoid such a case from happening again?
6. What do you think is the most efficient way to manage online information as with a search engine? Is a code of conduct necessary? If you had to write one, what would it say? How would you enforce it? How else would you propose to regulate the business practices of search engines like Baidu?

Bibliography

Beijing Youth Daily (2016). 调查组公布"魏则西事件"调查结果 (Investigation team announces the findings of the "Wei Zexi Incident"). *www.chinanews.com*. Retrieved on January 26, 2017 from http://www.chinanews.com/gn/2016/05-10/7864143.shtml.

China Net (2016). 从魏则西事件看互联网平台企业的社会性 (Judging Social Interaction of Internet Platforms looking at the Wei Zexi Incident). *www.china.com.cn*. Retrieved on January 26, 2017 from http://it.people.com.cn/n1/2016/0511/c1009-28342129.html.

Sohu.com (2016). "魏则西事件"的伦理审视 (An Ethical Review of the "Wei Zexi Incident"). *jkb.com.cn*. Retrieved on January 26, 2017 from https://www.sohu.com/a/75211329_269298.

Wanging, C. *et al.* (2016). *A Cancer Journal for Clinicians* 66: 115–132.

Chapter 8

The Ethics of Online Peer-to-Peer Lending Firms — Good or Evil?

Helen Xu, Dennis P. McCann, and Mark Pufpaff

Abstract

Alipay is one of the leading third-party online payment platforms in China. One of the company's services is "I Owe You" (IOU), a lending service in which users can lend money to each other. In 2016, Alipay terminated this service after the suicide of a user who was unable to repay his debt. But, there are other corporations still very active in Chinese P2P (peer-to-peer) lending. The case discusses this phenomenon and its effects on Chinese society.

Keywords: Internet, social media, Alipay, finance

8.1 Seeing

Alipay, a part of Ant Financial Service Group (Ant Financial), is one of the leading third-party online payment platforms in China. It was launched in 2004 and has become widely known due to its integration of a variety of consumer-oriented features, including "payment, lifestyle service, civil services, social networking, wealth management, insurance and public welfare." It also boasts "over 450 million registered users and 200 financial institution partners" as of June, 2016.

Alipay has produced a number of updates since its inception. At the launching of Alipay 9.0, a financing platform titled "I Owe You (IOU)" was introduced. It was well received among younger generations, especially those at university and working far away from their hometowns. To use IOU, the only requirement is that the lender and borrower are mutual "friends" — for example, on WeChat or a related Chinese social media application. Once the friendship status is established, the steps for acquiring a loan are as follows:

1. Choose the friend you would like to ask for a loan.
2. Choose the IOU function.
3. Fill in a form, including information on the amount to be borrowed, period of repayment, suggested interest rate, and purpose of the funds.
4. Send the form to the friend specified in step 1 until the money you have requested is transferred into the account.

However, after nine months of operation, Alipay terminated its IOU function. Why? On March 9, 2016, a sophomore in Henan Province, going by the alias of "Zheng Xu", committed suicide because he was unable to pay back the money he had borrowed (RMB 600,000 in total) from several online lending firms, Alipay's IOU among them. Zheng, having come from a poor, agrarian background, was a model student in secondary school. It came as a shock to find out he had compiled such a massive debt liability, and even involved 28 of his classmates in his borrowing activity. However, it came to an unfortunate conclusion when Zheng, feeling depressed and hopeless under the weight of the debt, left a final message to his family before ending his life:

"As a son of yours, I feel very sorry to you. But I'm not up to [living anymore], especially when I found [that all of my efforts in life were in vain]…I heard that jumping from the building may feel very painful, but I'm really tired! I do appreciate your help and the meticulous care you showed me as always, and I'm so sorry to all of you…"

After Zheng's suicide, Chen Zijun, a lawyer from Shanghai, mentioned that the rise of peer-to-peer (P2P) lending practices on college campuses poses real challenges, both ethical and legal, and such practices currently lack substantial regulation. He stated the following:

"According to the *Interim Measures for the Administration of Personal Loans*, the personal loans shall be in accordance with the legal compliance, principle of prudent operation, equality, voluntary, fairness and sincerity (Article 4). In consideration of the particularity of college students, the legislation shall take into full account their repayment capacity, enhance a healthy consumption concept and protect their lawful rights and interests."

It was in response to Zheng's death that Alipay removed its IOU function from its list of services, but not for long. Several days after it was removed, the Ministry of Education and the Chinese Banking Regulatory Commission issued its *Notification on Strengthening the Risk Prevention and Educational Guidance of Bad Online Lending Practice on Campus*, which requires "colleges and universities to establish a monitoring and precautionary system to protect students from the schemes of irregular online lending firms." Since August, 2016, Alipay's IOU function is back in operation.

Another P2P lending platform, Jiedaibao, was established by Kunwu Jiuding Capital Holdings Co., Ltd. Like Alipay, Jiedaibao has a relatively basic loan approval process, but claims to go further in terms of privacy, especially for the lender. Lenders on Jiedaibao enjoy what the firm calls "unidirectional anonymity", which prohibits the borrowers from knowing who their loans are originating from. This operational model was praised by the industry, and garnered a number of awards, including the Annual Most Influential Brand by the 2015 Global Mobile Internet CEO Summit, New Financial Service Award by the National Business Daily, and The Most Innovative APP in Financial Field by the CNR News.

However, Jiedaibao found itself at the center of controversy at the end of November, 2016, when a substantial number of nude pictures and videos were leaked online. The pictures and videos were collected as a substitute for installments on loans borrowed by (mostly) female college students. The *China Daily* newspaper reported the following:

> "Many Chinese university students were found to have used their nude pictures as IOUs on some online lending platforms, putting themselves at the risks of having everybody — including their parents — see them naked."

It was also reported, which may have contributed to the fact that these women could not pay their installments, that some lenders were charging obnoxiously high interest rates, 1,564% being one of the highest. These revelations created public outcry. A collection of sentiments from Chinese social media are given as follows:

"I will never ever understand such behaviors taken by female students who took nude picture in order to borrow one or two thousand yuan, while some of them lent out one thousand yuan at an excessive rate of interest. [...] Most of college students are adults, who had to learn to take responsibility for their own mistakes. Meanwhile, they must stand out for rights violation." — Dianfeng Juanke

"'Taking nude pictures for loan' revealed a crucial point of social reality that for young ladies of those pictures, the indignity of being poor has now far exceeded the indignity of being naked — this feeling forced them to put their entire privacy and networking at risk for [a few] thousand yuan." — Caiwang

"Their 'buy first, pay later' idea was easy to sell. Credit service users could choose between delayed payments and repayments in installments. Students need to spend just five minutes to fill in the consumer credit application online." — *China Daily*

In response to the resulting outrage, Jiedaibao posted an official statement clarifying the following:

"Jiedaibao is an online P2P lending platform adhering to the principle of lawfulness and compliance. The company has never appeared or stored any nude pictures. These inappropriate photos came from private deals between users and third parties through irregular operations.

Concerning the spreading of nude pictures online, the Department of Legal Affairs has collected the relevant evidence and already reported this to the responsible public security organ. We intend to take legal actions to crack down on the persons responsible for the illegal lending practices and for [disseminating the nude photographs]."

8.2 Judging

P2P lending, which is an offshoot of a more general borrowing trend on college campuses, is becoming more popular among students. Quick access to cash without the barriers that traditional banks impose, on the one hand, gives students more freedom of choice at university. On the other, however, it can be a temptation that smothers one in debt. Such a situation can result in tragedies like those described in the SEEING section. According to a survey distributed by Beijing Zhicheng Credit Service Co., Ltd., in April, 2015, 78% of college students responded that they experienced a shortage of funds either frequently or occasionally. 2.6% of respondents reportedly applied for microcredits and 8.6% indicated that they investigated online P2P firms. 15.5% stated that they addressed their financial shortcoming through traditional bank loans. Another survey, within the *Consumption Report of Online P2P Lending in College Students*, revealed that 29.03% of respondents applied for loans, of which over 60% obtained financing through a P2P platform.

As P2P lending grows in prevalence, questions are emerging as to the responsibilities of platforms such as Alipay and Jiedaibao to their users, both lenders and borrowers. Given their role as intermediaries who simply provide the means for lenders and borrowers to facilitate financing transactions, are they absolved from responsibility if, for example, lenders engage in predatory practices? Are they responsible if lenders begin demanding nude photos from female borrowers? Or if lenders are charging over 1,000% interest? The basic requirement for entering into a financing transaction using Alipay's IOU is that the lender and borrower be "friends." This assumes that, by virtue of their status as "friends", the parties will carry out their exchanges within reason, and without exposing one or the other party to undue risk. The examples in the SEEING section certainly exemplify how lenders can abuse borrowers. But, given the rather sketchy requirements for borrowers to obtain financing, there is certainly the possibility of lenders being taken advantage of, especially because companies like Alipay and Jiedaibao do not guarantee the loans transacted on their platform. There is good reason for this. In August 2015, the Supreme People's Court of China ruled that "online P2P lending platforms who offer guarantee for the loan shall bear the responsibility for bond" (Article 22). In other words, Alipay and Jiedaibao do not have much incentive to guarantee loans, given the risk of having to assume liability for loan defaults.

Another area of concern is whether Alipay and Jiedaibao are enabling predatory lenders to exploit needy borrowers, due to their all-too-easy requirements for borrowers obtaining credit. The four steps for obtaining a loan through Alipay's IOU could not be more basic, and reveal nothing of the borrowers' credit history or current financial standing. This can put borrowers — and potentially their families — in desperate situations if they borrow more than they can repay. Perhaps that is why, in April, 2017, the China Banking Regulatory Commissions declared that "offering online lending service to college students under 18 years old is prohibited." This is likely because young, uninformed borrowers are at a higher risk of entering into financing agreements they are unable to uphold, and thereby at a higher risk of being sued, or worse exploited, by unsympathetic lenders.

A parallel example of how a platform might allow predatory behavior is Baidu. Their Tieba forums were the cause of scandal, when in 2016 the company began bidding out their administrative rights. This decision allowed predatory, for-profit organizations to begin pushing their own products and services to the users of the forums. The result? Many users who decided to buy the products or procure the services soon found out that either the offers were fabricated or not at all what they expected. In other words, Baidu was the platform through which exploitative exchanges were being facilitated. Public outrage eventually forced Baidu's hand, and they altered their policies to curb the abuse, but the damage was done. Such responses are becoming increasingly common in the P2P industry; it would behoove companies like Alipay and Jiedaibao to engage in proactive self-governance instead of waiting for either government regulations to catch up or a public scandal to force a reactionary adjustment.

A related area of concern surrounds the idea of disclosure. In the *Consumption Report of Online P2P Lending for College Students*, 68.26% of college students reported that they received less than RMB 1,500/month for living expenses, mostly from their parents. This has caused students to look for additional sources of income, one of those sources being P2P companies. However, P2P companies seem to have done a poor job ensuring that new borrowers are well informed of their debt obligations. For example, in the study cited above, only 22% of those who borrowed money "understood the terms of loans well". This is a major problem, because had they understood the terms of their loans thoroughly, they may not have gone through with it in the first place. As Confucius said,

"Riches and honors are what men desire. If it cannot be obtained in the proper way, they should not be held. Poverty and meanness are what men dislike. If it cannot be avoided in the proper way, they should not be avoided." — Book IV, *Analects*

Building on this wisdom, a commentary from Netease.com on the P2P phenomenon on college campuses in China stated the following:

> "A normal financial ecology [on college] campuses means that: college students take responsibility for [loan] defaults; financial institutions who issue [illegal] loan bear the losses [of such activity] themselves; financial supervisory departments offer financial education [for students] and punish [those engaged in] abusive mortgage lending."

8.3 Acting

As P2P lending grows and becomes more prevalent, what can pioneer platforms like Alipay and Jiedaibao do to hedge against the kind of tragedies and abuses described above?

1. They can proactively work with the Chinese government to develop consumer-centric industry regulations. Firms like Alipay and Jiedaibao bring valuable industry experience, experience that can help regulatory agencies develop appropriate guidelines for the marketplace. This is advantageous because the firms who contribute to this process will not, except in cases of willful disregard, find themselves in trouble with the law. It also sends a message to their consumers that their best interests are being taken to heart. Lastly, it is simply good business to *want* to be compliant, transparent, and fair. This kind of behavior creates win-win outcomes for all stakeholders involved.
2. They can offer values education to college students. As P2P lending becomes popular on university campuses in China, there is an opportunity for leading companies like Alipay and Jiedaibao to educate prospective borrowers about the risks involved in obtaining financing. Informing borrowers about predatory lending, illegal loan outlets, interest rates, and amortization tables, and living within ones means, will not only create better and more responsible borrowers but also position certain brands as trustworthy authorities within an industry. The more trust a firm demands from the market, the more likely they will be top of mind when prospective borrowers begin searching for credit. Examples of how firms could conduct values education would be by setting up on-campus lectures or workshops or offering a live hotline for borrowers to learn about financing and the specific risks facing them as students.

3. They can partner with universities to provide scholarships or related aid. If Alipay, for example, wanted to penetrate a given university, they could provide incentives — such as scholarships — to students in exchange for promotion as a viable source of credit for those students in need. This would encourage the university to do its due diligence, to ensure they are not promoting an exploitation platform to their students, while incentivizing the platform to hold itself accountable to strict standards of excellence, so as not to tarnish its image among its target market.

4. They can set standards of excellence in the industry. P2P lending firms would be wise to target those borrowers who can demonstrate an ability to pay back their debts. Establishing a more robust qualification process will weed out unfavorable borrowers and assure lenders that their borrowers will make good on their loans. This is win-win. It allows borrowers to acquire needed cash and lenders to make money from interest payments. It protects borrowers from entering into lending situations they do not fully understand, and prevents lenders from exploiting gullible borrowers. It hedges against scandal and promotes sustainability.

8.4 Discussion Questions

1. What is P2P lending? What are the advantages and disadvantages of this kind of lending model?
2. Should Jiedaibao be held responsible for the behavior of the lenders using their platform, such as requiring that female borrowers submit nude photos of themselves in exchange for installment payments? Why or why not?
3. If you were a college student, would you consider taking out a loan from a P2P lender, such as Alipay? Why or why not?
4. If you were a Product Manager at Alipay or Jiedaibao, how would you interpret the China Banking Regulatory Commission's statement that "offering online lending service to college students under 18 years old is prohibited"? How might that influence your product strategy going forward?
5. What role, if any, do you think Alipay and Jiedaibao could play in the promotion of financial literacy on college campuses in China?

Bibliography

China Daily (2016). Nude pics as IOU: A new, risky online loan among Chinese university students. *China Daily*. Retrieved on April 11, 2017 from https://www.chinadaily.com.cn/china/2016-07/14/content_26089898.htm.

Daily Business News (2017). 女大学生借5000元滚成26万元，裸贷何时休? (Female college students borrowed 5,000 yuan, which turned into 260,000-yuan debt. When will naked loans be forbidden?). *Business Daily*. Retrieved on April 11, 2017 from http://www.nbd.com.cn/articles/2017-04-11/1093253.html.

Jiang, X. (2016). Careless on the Chinese campus. *China Daily*. Retrieved on April 11, 2017 from http://africa.chinadaily.com.cn/business/2016-09/26/content_26893195.htm.

Sohu.com (2016). 学生负债自杀案令人惊恐,校园借贷为何失控 (Student debt suicide cases are frightening — Why campus borrowing is out of control). *www.sohu.com*. Retrieved on April 11, 2017 from https://www.sohu.com/a/64506841_381439.

Southcn.com (2016). 图解: 大学生网贷现况调查报告. www.southcn.com. Retrieved on April 11, 2017 http://tech.southcn.com/t/2016-08/15/content_153644135.htm.

Tencent Finance (2017). 校园网贷 诱人馅饼还是吃人陷阱? *www.finance.qq.com*. Retrieved on April 11, 2017 from http://finance.qq.com/a/20170411/034929.htm.

Part 3
Labor Issues

Chapter 9

Should a Venture Capital Company Invest in Female CEOs?

Gender Equality and Women Empowerment

Helen Xu, Dennis P. McCann, and Mark Pufpaff

Abstract

In 2017, Luo Mingxiong, CEO of Jingbei Investment and one of the most popular angel investors in China stated publicly that his company is not investing in companies or start-ups that have a female CEO. Luo's comment provoked outrage from women, human rights groups, and especially female entrepreneurs. This case discusses gender equality, female entrepreneurship, and venture capital investments in China.

Keywords: Gender equality, *guanxi*, diversity

9.1 Seeing

Internet finance, a process by which "deposits, loans, investments and other financial services [are] provided through online channels rather than through traditional financial institutions such as banks," is a recent and fast-growing phenomenon in China. From Alibaba Group to Tencent Holdings to smaller-scale venture capital (VC) firms, Internet-based financial institutions are injecting immense amounts of investment dollars into China's bustling entrepreneurial ecosystem.

Jingbei Investment (Jingbei), one such Internet finance VC firm, was founded in 2014 and, as of the end of 2016, had invested in 36 companies. They target companies from a wide range of industries, including Internet insurance, consumer finance, supply finance, big data accumulation and analysis, and philanthropy. Its CEO, Luo Mingxiong, was hailed for his leadership and received the "2015 Most Popular Angel Investor in Zhongguancun" and "2015 Excellent Angel Investor in Zhongguancun" awards as a result. However, his time in the limelight was short lived.

On January 6, 2017, during a keynote speech at the *2nd New Year Summit of Chinese CEOs*, Luo made the following comment during a discussion about the rules Jingbei operates by when deciding what companies to invest it: "Rule number 10: We usually don't invest in female CEOs." His rationale is as follows:

> "It's not because of any kind of prejudice. Just think about it carefully, besides giving birth to children, what can women do better than men? Nothing. […] If the company CEO is a man, but a lot of the chairmen are women, we typically won't invest either. Why? Because it shows that the entrepreneur can't recruit equally excellent and ambitious male executives."

Luo's comment was immediately condemned as gender discrimination and provoked outrage from women, human rights groups, and especially female entrepreneurs. It also generated opposition from the Chinese blogosphere, corporate CEOs, and even a lawyer, who claimed Luo violated the Law on the Protection of Rights and Interests of Women, which states that "women shall enjoy equal rights with men in all aspects of political, economic, cultural, social and family life," and that "offender[s] who debase or injure a women's personal dignity through public media or other channels shall be subjected to administrative sanctions." However, no charges have been pressed against Luo as of yet.

At the summit itself, where Luo first made his controversial remark, Huang Huan, CEO of Beijing Huanfou Information Technology Company and honored guest at the event, stated as an implicit response to Luo:

> "When women start their own businesses [and are described] as powerful she-devils [or other] derogatory terms, this is prejudice for sure. Considering arguments like 'we never ever invest in women', 'women are unreliable' […] whatever it is, we do not care [for] such investors!"

Outrage also quickly poured in from the Chinese blogosphere. Two of their sentiments are as follows:

"As the Director of the Internet Finance Institute of Shanghai Jiaotong University, Luo describes his prejudice as criterion... Feel bad for his female students, [and his] wife and daughter if [he has] any."

"Women have historically been subjected to educational and working deprivation due to a patriarchal society, [although] they [have been] eligible to enjoy the same rights as men over the past 100 years. Obviously, women are [less] privileged than men, but there are a lot of outstanding women [who have] emerged in a relatively short period. More are expected to emerge in the future."

These comments, from Huang and the netizens from the blogosphere, contrast with Luo's perception of professional women.

9.2 Judging

What is gender equality? The United Nations defined it as follows:

"Equality between women and men (gender equality) refers to the equal rights, responsibilities and opportunities of women and men and girls and boys. Equality does not mean that women and men will become the same but that women's and men's rights, responsibilities and opportunities will not depend on whether they are born male or female. Gender equality implies that the interests, needs and priorities of both women and men are taken into consideration, recognizing the diversity of different groups of women and men. Gender equality is not a women's issue but should concern and fully engage men as well as women. Equality between women and men is seen both as a human rights issue and as a precondition for, and indicator of, sustainable people-centered development."

The global strategy for mainstreaming gender equality throughout all dimensions of political, economic, and social life was established through the Platform for Action at the United Nations Fourth World Conference in Beijing in 1995, and defined in the Economic and Social Council's agreed conclusions in 1997. In China, the Law on the Protection of Rights and Interests of Women was adopted at the Fifth Session of the Seventh National People's Congress (NPC) in 1992 and was amended in 2005, which aimed to guarantee that women enjoy the same rights as men throughout all aspects of life. All levels of governments are thus obliged to respect these rights by creating jobs and educational opportunities, improving women's employment conditions, and empowering female entrepreneurs to innovate new businesses. Gender discrimination, by contrast, is defined as follows:

> "Any distinction, exclusion or restriction made on the basis of sex which has the effect or purpose of impairing or nullifying the recognition, enjoyment or exercise by women, irrespective of their marital status, on the basis of equality of men and women, of human rights and fundamental freedoms in the political, economic, social, cultural, civil or any other field."

Such discrimination has numerous concrete manifestations, including sexual harassment, pregnancy discrimination, and unequal pay. In this case, Luo is accused of gender discrimination on the basis of merit, or capacity. "Just think about it carefully, besides giving birth to children, what can women do better than men? Nothing." These were Luo's words, which indicate an assumption that women, in comparison to their male counterparts, are inferior. He uses this assumption to then conclude that companies with female CEOs should not be invested in by his firm, given their inferiority, presumably in terms of business acumen and decision-making capacity, to companies with male CEOs. Is his position justified?

There are several preliminary problems. First, Luo is assuming women are inferior to men as business professionals. Given the emergence of the female workforce over the past century or more, this assumption needs to be tested. For example, a report from Bain & Co shows that "75 percent of working-age women in China were employed in 2014, compared with 67 percent in the United Kingdom, 66 percent in Australia, and 62 percent in the United States." This shows that women not only have the capacity to work but they are getting and holding jobs in China. Moreover, another survey carried out by Grant Thornton revealed that "24% of senior roles were held by women globally, while the proportion in mainland China was 30% in 2016," indicating that China is above the global average for employing executive-level women. Discussions about any prevailing glass ceiling aside, these numbers stand in stark contrast to the assumption by Luo that women are inferior to men or somehow incapable of succeeding in senior roles. Finally, according to a white paper on gender equality and women's development in China, "the number of (Chinese) female entrepreneurs keeps growing, now accounting for one quarter of the total number of entrepreneurs, and about 55 percent of new Internet businesses [were] founded by women in 2013." Although we are unsure of the failure rate of these new businesses, it is evident that women have entered the entrepreneurial scene in China with fervor.

Second, Luo is also assuming that women, in order to be successful or taken seriously, must be as closely aligned with the male executive or CEO archetype as possible. In other words, women, if they want to make a name for themselves in business, need to think and act like men. Although such sentiments do prevail in some pockets of the feminist movement, which started in the United States in 1848, and have been responsible for such achievements as the women's right to vote, improved working conditions, and greater participation in the public and private sector workforces, it is generally viewed as contrary to the founding feminist principles of nondiscrimination, nonviolence, and justice for all. The perception that a woman must imitate a man to succeed is just another form of stating that a woman, as a woman, is inferior, regardless of how well she imitates the male persona. Is there no such thing as a distinctly feminine approach to leadership, one that is both effective and dignified? Luo seems to think not, but it is unclear why, as existing leaders in China and around the world have done their part to affirm not only the capacity of women to run businesses but the necessity of their contribution in terms of industry innovation and creative thinking.

For example, Sheryl Sandberg, COO of Facebook and the author of *Lean In*, a book about gender equality issues in the workplace, was a guest speaker at Tsinghua University's School of Economics and Management in 2015. There she stated, "The world would be better when men run half the homes and women run half the organizations and companies." Although such a ratio is naturally unrealistic given the ever-changing professional and private interests of men and women and the dynamism of socio-economic development across the world, she is touching upon the risks of sticking too firmly to so-called "traditional" roles, ones that might restrict the capacity for women to participate meaningfully in economic life, and contribute *as women*.

Jack Ma, the Founder and Chairman of Alibaba Group, is optimistic about the opportunities for female entrepreneurs with the emergence of Internet finance, a development his firm is an integral part of. He stated that women obtain microfinance loans with ease due to their perceived credibility and integrity, have five times more active storefronts on Taobao than men, and their default rate for such storefronts is 25% less than their male counterparts. Such qualitative and quantitative data challenge Luo's perception, or rather rule, that only male CEOs are worth investing in.

Liu Nan, the CEO of mia.com, is one of the beneficiaries of Internet finance. In 2011, she opened an online store providing goods for babies and adolescents using Taobao. After surpassing RMB 13 million in sales during her first year of operations, she founded her own business in 2013 — independent of Taobao — using RMB 1 million in venture capital obtained from two VC firms. Three years later, in 2016, mia.com was valued at RMB 1 billion. Liu's success should indicate to Luo that, in business terms, she would have been a good investment, and in moral terms, she is deserving of respect and fair consideration. Although Luo's statement could have been misinterpreted, due to him poorly wording his meaning, a commonsense reading of it leaves much to be desired.

9.3 Acting

How did Luo respond to the outrage from the public to his statement? If in fact he means what he says, namely, that "It's not because of any kind of prejudice" that his firm, as a rule, does not invest in female CEOs, one would expect a concerted and convincing response in defense of such a claim, given the circumstances. However, it seems that no such attempt to assuage concerns about gender discrimination was made. His only response has been to double down on his position in a post on his website, merely reaffirming his original statement that his firm does not invest in female CEOs. If we are to take Luo seriously, should we not expect something more? As Confucius said, "When the great way prevail[s], the world community [is] equally shared by all."

VC firms, to be sure, have a tough job. Analyzing the potential of entrepreneurs and start-up companies is as time-consuming as it is complicated. Enter the role of investment methodologies. For example, Zhou

Hongyi, Chairman of Qihoo 360, has three criteria to be fulfilled before an investment decision is made:

1. Ability of an entrepreneur to self-reflect, self-learn, self-improve, and self-correct.
2. Ability of an entrepreneur to collaborate and maintain an open mind.
3. Ability of an entrepreneur to persevere, especially during the early stages of starting up.

Notice how these criteria are gender neutral. The decisive factor for Qihoo 360, therefore, has less to do with gender as such and more to do with individual capacity, or merit. But, not all methodologies emphasize the same traits, or attribute the embodiment of such traits in such a gender-neutral way. Rui Ma, former investor at 500 Startups, a start-up accelerator and seed fund investor in the USA, made the following observation:

"For entrepreneurs, especially CEOs, a lot of [investors] are [looking] for pure aggressiveness, ruthlessness, [and] speed, especially in China. And that is seen as a very, very male trait."

Why might this be the prevailing perception? Moreover, why are these qualities the paramount ones in determining between CEOs? And, why might women be perceived as lacking them, if they are, in the end, so essential? Anna Fang, female CEO and Partner of ZhenFund, an angel investment fund that focuses on the telecommunication, media, and technology (TMT) sectors, stated the following:

"All investors are looking for a 'unicorn' [The term was coined in 2013 by venture capitalist Aileen Lee, choosing the mythical animal to represent the statistical rarity of such successful venture. Thus this term is used to describe a startup who has achieved a USD 1 billion or more valuation]; their determinations [on who to invest in] depend on entrepreneurial potentials — whether the entrepreneur has the potential to [successfully] guide the company [to a unicorn status] — not gender."

The emphasis on potential and not on gender is an important distinction. What Fang is telling us, however implicitly, is that both women and men have potential, and that within the context of entrepreneurship, such potential should not be determined solely by a set of predetermined, so called gender-exclusive qualities. Pocket Sun, female Founder of SoGal Investors, a VC firm focused on technology start-ups in Asia and USA, stated the following:

> "When I heard of Luo's comment, I actually laughed. I was thinking to myself, 'he's missing out.' We will invest in female CEOs and make returns from them. He clearly doesn't see where the future of [the] economy is going."

Even if men have historically dominated the entrepreneurial scene in China, Luo would do well not to assume that such a trend will continue indefinitely. In fact, the evidence suggests that he is already out of step — according to the All-China Women's Federation, an organization dedicated to the empowerment of women in China, more than RMB 290 billion in small loans were offered to female entrepreneurs nationwide by the end of 2015, and 8,100 entrepreneurship centers were established for female college students, offering training and guidance for those interested in starting businesses.

These numbers should indicate the growing market value of female entrepreneurs. For male investors like Luo, the price of discrimination is high. Should the resulting outcry against his statement, "We usually don't invest in female CEOs", not have been a chance to change his attitude and realign his investment methodology to include the burgeoning marketplace of female-run firms? Did he lose his chance with his response?

9.4 Discussion Questions

1. Do you think Luo's statement about female entrepreneurs is true? Should it be regarded as gender discrimination? Why or why not?
2. If you had to write an investment methodology for Jingbei Investment, what would it say?
3. If you were a female entrepreneur seeking funding for your business, and were rejected from a VC firm primarily because you were a woman, what would you do? Is there any way to turn such a rejection into an opportunity? What do you think of the Chinese organizations cited above that are ready to support female entrepreneurs?
4. If you were asked to advise Jingbei in their response to the public backlash, what would be your strategic recommendations?

Bibliography

Ma, Q. (2017). 直男癌碰上女王范. *Chinaventure.com.cn*. Retrieved on February 10, 2017 from https://www.chinaventure.com.cn/cmsmodel/news/detail/307807.html.

Sina.com (2017a). 蜜芽3年估值过百亿 自有现金超10亿 因一个原则 (Mibud has been valued at more than 10 billion in 3 years, and its own cash exceeds 1 billion). *Sina.com*. Retrieved on February 10, 2017 from http://news.sina.com.cn/o/2017-01-06/doc-ifxzkfuk2521224.shtml.

Sina.com (2017b). 罗明雄说不投女CEO 回应: 性别歧视的钱何必稀罕 (Luo Mingxiong said he would not vote for female CEOs). *sina.com*. Retrieved on March 28, 2021 from http://tech.sina.com.cn/other/cy/2017-01-09/doc-ifxzkfuk2983803.shtml.

Sohu.com (2017). 京北投资罗明雄: 不投女CEO 也不投企业全是女高管的男CEO (CEO Jingbei Investment Luo Mingxiong: No female CEO). *Sohu.com*. Retrieved on February 10, 2017 from https://www.sohu.com/a/123640741_470090.

UN Women (2021). Concepts and definitions. United Nations Entity for Gender Equality and the Empowerment of Women. Retrieved March 28, 2021 from http://www.un.org/womenwatch/osagi/conceptsandefinitions.htm.

Weibo.com (2017). Sentiments from Chinese blogosphere. *Weibo.com*. Retrieved on February 10, 2017 from http://weibo.com/1726276573/Epxy449jq?refer_flag=1001030106_&type=comment#_rnd1486540624610.

Wikipedia (2021). Unicorn (Finance). *www.wikipedia.com*. Retrieved on March 28, 2021 from https://en.wikipedia.org/wiki/Unicorn_(finance).

Xinhua (2015). China issues white paper on gender equality, women's development. *China Daily*. Retrieved on February 10, 2017 from http://www.chinadaily.com.cn/china/2015-09/22/content_21947110.htm.

Chapter 10

Gender Discrimination in the Chinese Workplace: Second-Child Policy vs. Women's Employment

Helen Xu, Dennis P. McCann, and Mark Pufpaff

Abstract

China is well known for its "One-Child Policy" introduced in 1979, which intended to curtail the growing population rate. In 2015, it was replaced by a "Two-Child Policy" and numerous new regulations to support families to have two children. The new policy is not as successful as planned, since many Chinese women decide against a second child. The main reason is their fear of facing discrimination at their workplaces and negative effects on their careers. This case discussed the effect of the new policy and whether the two-child policy has contributed to gender discrimination in China.

Keywords: Gender equality, society, employment, discrimination

10.1 Seeing

Under Mao Zedong, the founder of the Chinese Communist Party, China's population grew from 500 million in 1949 to 900 million in 1974. After Mao's death in 1979, the government officially implemented its "One-Child Policy" (jì huà sheng yù zhèng cè, 计划生育政策) on

September 25, 1980. The policy was aimed at curtailing China's then rapidly growing population rate. Such population growth, the creators of the policy thought, would put a strain on the country's natural resources and exacerbate already existing social, economic, and environmental problems. Although it is perceived to have reduced the population growth rate in China since 1980, and averted between 100 and 400 million births, it has also produced a number of difficulties that are being felt today:

- There is a 3–4% disparity in the ratio of males to females in Chinese society.
- There are a disproportionate number of elderly people (60+ years old) in China, resulting from the decreased birth rate concurrent with an increase in life expectancy.
- There is a shortage of labor, or working-age people, relative to the economic goals of the country.

In 2015, the one-child policy was abolished, and was replaced by the current two-child policy. The two-child policy was conceived primarily in response to the disparity between China's working-age population and its aging, or elderly, population. For example, according to the National Bureau of Statistics, China's working-age population decreased from around 911 million in 2015 to 907.5 million in 2016 — a decrease of 3.49 million people — while its elderly population increased from 222 million people in 2015 to around 231 million people in 2016 — an increase of 9 million people. To achieve China's social and economic goals, the country's top leadership has put a priority on building up its labor force. It has established several incentives to entice families into having a second child. They are as follows:

- Female employees are entitled to a 98-day maternity leave.
- Female employees can be awarded — at the discretion of a given provincial government — a 30-day leave on top of their 98-day entitlement.
- Female employees' salaries or employment cannot be reduced or terminated during lactation.
- Female employees can apply to have their maternity leave extended for up to three months on top of their 98-day entitlement.

The rationale for the two-child policy can be summed up in a public statement issued by an advisor to China's State Council:

"The two child policy realigns China's resource limitations with economic and social development. It will slow down but may not revert the aging population trend. We need to grow the labor force before it drops sharply. China used to rely on the population scale for cheap labor, but now we have to shift the focus to improving the labor quality. This is a new impetus for our economic growth."

Despite the implementation of the two-child policy and the associated government-sponsored incentives for having a second child, women are reluctant to do so. In a report by National Career Women, nearly 60% of females polled stated they would not have a second child. In a survey of 14,290 women carried out by zhaopin.com, a recruiting site in China, 56% of respondents stated they did not want to have a second child because of the financial pressures involved, limited time and energy, employment concerns, and marital risks. Although concerns vary as to why women in China are hesitating to have two children, one issue is gaining notoriety: *employment discrimination*. Based on an online poll of enterprises carried out by *Doctorjob.com.cn*, 75% of respondents expressed concerns about hiring female employees due to the implementation of the second-child policy, and 72% of respondents believed that female employees would invest more time and energy into raising their children than carrying out their job roles.

Given this, a growing number of women in China feel that they are being discriminated against in the recruitment process for job positions. Xiao Chen, a postgraduate student in Wuhu City, Anhui Province, claimed the following:

"I often get asked privacy questions, for instance, whether I have a boyfriend and if I have any plan to get married. However, male candidates would never encounter the similar questions."

Similar sentiments were expressed by Wang Li, a mid-level manager in a Top 500 software company. She stated the following:

"It's widely acknowledged that no matter how capable a female leader is, she will be perceived as less dedicated to her job after giving birth. I [would] lose my position after maternity leave [if I decided to] have a child."

However, not all women in China agree. Feng Lijuan, a human resource professional at *51job.com*, a job-hunting platform, holds a contrary view. She argued,

> "Taking the economic situation into consideration, it is not realistic to require companies, especially fast-growing startups, to provide absolute equality when choosing their employees. Chinese women shoulder more family responsibility. […] If a job requires frequent business trips, extra work and more attention to work instead of to the family, a capable male candidate would be more suitable. In conclusion, it is not about gender choice, but a market choice."

Although companies in China have historically worried about their female employees or potential employees having children,[1] the implementation of the two-child policy brings a unique challenge, as some women feel that having a baby, while encouraged by the government, may not be congruent with their own career ambitions.

10.2 Judging

Do companies have a right to refuse the hiring of a female candidate simply because she intends to start a family in the future? Are women entitled to a position they are qualified for, regardless of whether they have or plan to have children? Are these questions with self-evident answers, or is there any legal or ethical grey area in them?

"Invisible discrimination" is a term that refers to "hidden barriers" for women seeking a job or a promotion. The barriers are caused by "unspoken rules or conventions", which implicitly discriminate based on physical conditions (health, height, disability, etc.), gender, age, and educational background. Although explicit hiring discrimination — for example, stating in job posts that only male candidates will be

---

[1] According to a survey conducted by the All-China Women's Federation in 2014, 59.11% of female undergraduates admitted that they were asked during interviews whether they intended to have two children. Another survey showed that 80.2% of female undergraduates thought "inconsistent employment standard" was present during the recruitment. "Inconsistent employment standard" refers, for example, to a hiring manager's preference for male candidates or imposing a higher education requirement for women applicants.

considered — has by and large been eliminated in China, women still face challenges in being fairly weighed in comparison with male candidates.

In the Labor Law of the People's Republic of China, article three states, "Laborers shall have the right to be employed on an equal basis, choose occupations, obtain remuneration for their labor, take rest, and have holidays and leaves"; article 12 continues, "Laborers shall not be discriminated against in employment, regardless of their ethnic community, race, sex, or religious belief." Moreover, article 5 of the Special Rules on the Labor Protection of Female Employees states that "Employers shall not reduce the wages of female employees, [nor] dismiss or rescind the labor or employment contracts with female employees due to pregnancy, giving birth, or lactation." From a legal perspective, then, it is clear that discriminating against a woman as a woman is prohibited. But, would it also be inappropriate to condition a female candidate's employment on an understanding that she would not have, or have any more, children? Enforcing such a policy is easier said than done, and not only in China but around the world. A 2014 survey from Australian law firm Slater & Gordon questioned 500 managers about their perceptions of hiring women with current or prospective family commitments. The results can be summarized as follows:

- 40% stated they would be wary of hiring a woman of child-bearing age.
- Around 40% stated they would be wary of hiring a mother for a senior role.
- 25% stated they would rather hire a man to avoid issues stemming from maternity leave and child-care once the mother was back to work.
- 44% stated the financial costs to their businesses because of maternity leave were a significant concern.
- 33% stated that women are not as good at their jobs after they return from maternity leave.

Pairing the experiences of Xiao and Wang in the SEEING section with the concerns of managers in the Slater & Gordon survey, one must question how the two-child policy is affecting the perception of female professionals by their current or prospective employers. One result has been the establishment of what are becoming known as "reproductive schedules", aimed at avoiding "simultaneous pregnancies" and thereby multiple women on maternity leave at the same time. A testimony from a woman in Jilin Province stated that, if she was to be hired, she would have to apply for pregnancy approval at least a full year in advance of the time she planned to get pregnant. A firm in Henan Province sent out a notice to its employees after the two-child policy became official, stating the following:

> "An employee birth plan has been established and will be strictly enforced. Employees who do not give birth according to the plan and whose work is impacted will face a one-time fine of 1,000 yuan and will not be considered for promotion."

Many female professionals have found the idea of a "reproductive schedule" distasteful, and have been opposing it throughout the Chinese blogosphere:

> "In the past, women at marriageable age faced discrimination in finding jobs. Now there are further discriminations on whether they will have a second baby."
>
> "How idiotic are these leaders to come up with such a policy? Where is our right to give birth?"
>
> "I suggest men should also have maternity leave after wives give birth. This will help reduce discrimination."

However, some businesses are standing their ground and defending the necessity of such policies. Mr. Zhang, a manager of a private enterprise in China, discussed the situation in his firm on social media:

> "There are six women at my department in total, and three of them are now pregnant. Because of a limited budget, it's almost impossible to recruit new people; thus, some other colleagues may need to take extra work during the leave of pregnant workers."

Zhang's sentiments have found support among some women in China. One female blogger on Sina Weibo stated the following:

> "Some women get pregnant as soon as they start a job. It's those people who don't work hard and use the excuse of taking care of their baby that have caused some organizations to be afraid to recruit women."

There are clearly two sides to this debate. The law explicitly states that women cannot be discriminated against simply because they are women, nor can they be discriminated against because of any pregnancy-related issues, such as taking maternity leave. Given this, "reproductive schedules" are likely to be challenged as ethically questionable, since they focus on the issue of maternity leave and react negatively against it. But, does this mean that the business concerns associated with maternity leave are inherently illegitimate? Could it be that "reproductive schedules" are just an inappropriate reaction to the two-child policy, which after all will require businesses to make significant adjustments? Is there not a response that could properly balance the interests of both female professionals and companies with a concern for efficiency and profitability?

The words of the Weibo blogger who suggested that some women use their pregnancies and child-raising responsibilities as an excuse to work less, or work less hard, bring up an important point. It is reasonable for a company to have basic performance expectations for their employees, regardless of their personal circumstances, and that their employees have a responsibility to fulfill those expectations. Would it therefore be discriminatory for an employer to fire an underperforming female employee, even if such underperformance was due to the demands of her domestic commitments? If pregnancy cannot be used by an employer to reject a female candidate, for hire or promotion, should it not likewise be prohibited for a female employee to use her family responsibilities as an excuse for underperformance? The wisdom of Confucius and Mozi may help us address these questions:

> "The gentleman will employ a man on a distant mission and observe his degree of loyalty, employ him close at hand and observe his degree of respect. He will hand him troublesome affairs and observe how well he manages them, will suddenly ask his advice and observe how wisely he answers. He will exact some difficult promise from him and see how well he keeps it, turn over funds to him and see with what benevolence he dispenses them, inform him of the danger he is in and note how faithful he is to his duties." — Lieh Yu Kou, *Chuang Tzu*

This passage from the *Chuang Tzu* expresses basic performance expectations in the relationship between employer and employee.

> "The virtuous and the excellent who are firm in morality, versed in rhetoric, and experienced in statecraft — since these are the treasures of the nation and props of the state, they should also be enriched, honored, respected, and commended in order that they may abound." — Exaltation of the Virtuous, *Mozi*

Here, Mozi is encouraging employers to establish incentive systems for talented people to enhance employee loyalty.

10.3 Acting

What can businesses do to ensure there is no pregnancy discrimination in their workplaces? The two-child policy has clearly created a difficult situation for some businesses, as female employees of these companies seek to have a second child to which they are entitled. Anne Hathaway, a distinguished American actress, described what she claims to be the effect that polices such as maternity leave are having on women:

> "Maternity leave, or any workplace policy based on gender, can — at this moment in history — only ever be a gilded cage. Though it was created to make life easier for women, we now know it creates a perception of women as being inconvenient to the workplace."

Although this should not be taken as a generalizing view of how all companies feel about their current or prospective female employees, it does highlight the issue of "unintended consequences." What was intended to help women entering the workforce has, at least to a degree, become an obstacle confronting them. However, Hathaway's pessimistic view of maternity leave is not shared by all women. Yang Lan, Chairman of Sun Media Group, stated the following at the "2016 Her Village International Forum — Inclusive Society, True Partnership" forum:

> "It has been proved by international experiences that extending the maternity leave may cause more concerns in the process of enterprise recruitment. Obviously, the cost of hiring a female employee is higher than male on condition that only women take maternity leave. In light of this, we are appealing to public policy to encourage man to take paternity leave as well. [...] The double bias results in the absence of father and anxiety of mother in many Chinese families. In contrary, parental leave may bring more fun to father who would like to share parenting responsibilities with his wife, because the true life partner asks couples to better balance the conflicting demands of work and family".[2]

---

[2]http://cul.qq.com/a/20160330/027753.htm.

Moving forward, there are a number of options businesses can take to navigate the issue of pregnancy discrimination:

1. Providing competitive compensation: Providing all employees, male and female, with a competitive salary and benefits package is important for empowering them to high degrees of productivity and job satisfaction. Employees who enjoy their work, feel supported by their employers, and are provided the means to live a comfortable life outside of work are more likely to achieve performance targets at or above expectations.
2. Offering maternity and paternity leave: Women will feel less discriminated against, or at least less pressured, if they know their husbands also have the option of taking time off to help raise their children, as one blogger suggested in the JUDGING section. This opens up options for splitting the amount of time spent at home and the possibility for women to avoid and overcome the negative connotation some companies put on maternity leave.
3. Becoming an employer of choice: Companies offering an environment that supports women who are free to choose their lifestyle in any way they wish are more likely to attract the best of the female applicant pool. All employees, male and female, want to work for companies that understand their needs and enact policies that anticipate, as opposed to react to, them.
4. Offering flextime and telecommuting: In an age of digitalization that will only deepen in reach as time goes on, companies offering flextime and the option to telecommute when needed can be a mechanism for avoiding the temptations that often lead to discriminatory female hiring decisions. Giving female employees the option to meet company expectations on their own time, or at home, puts the responsibility on them to prove themselves. Flextime and telecommuting can be empowerment tools.

10.4 Discussion Questions

1. What is gender discrimination? Do you think the two-child policy has contributed to gender discrimination in China?
2. If you were a hiring manager and you were told by your boss to hire an under qualified male candidate over a highly qualified female

applicant because the company could not risk the female applicant going on maternity leave, how would you respond?

3. Do you think women who choose to be stay-at-home moms or housewives are compromising their potential? Why or why not?

4. If you were asked to create the hiring policy at a company in China after the two-child policy was implemented, what would it say?

5. What do you think of "reproductive schedules"? Are they distasteful or merely realistic? If they are a form of subtle discrimination, what might be a better alternative?

6. What do you think of "invisible discrimination"? Why might it be necessary to go beyond what is already legislated in prohibitions against various visible forms of discrimination?

Bibliography

CCTV (2015). 河南焦作一单位规定女工按时怀孕 否则罚款千元 (Company unit in Jiaozuo, Henan requires female workers to become pregnant on time, otherwise they are fined 1,000 yuan). *http://china.cnr.cn/*. Retrieved on March 6, 2017 from http://china.cnr.cn/xwwgf/20150702/t20150702_519049750.shtml.

Nan, X. (2017). 职场二胎妈妈"生"还是"升 (Second child or promotion? The question for mothers in the workplace). *Zhejiang News*. Retrieved on March 6, 2017 from https://zj.zjol.com.cn/news/334681.html.

Xinghua News Agency (2015). Two-child policy approved by the Fifth Plenary Session of the 18th Communist Party of China (CPC) Central Committee. *Xinhuanet.com*. Retrieved on March 6, 2017 from http://www.xinhuanet.com//politics/2015-10/29/c_1116983078.htm.

Zhang, Y. (2017). 二孩时代"女性就业遭遇歧视怎样应对 (How to deal with discrimination faced by women in employment having a second child). *Xinhuanet.com*. Retrieved on March 6, 2017 from http://www.ah.xinhuanet.com/20170301/3669609_m.html.

Chapter 11

Ending the Debt Bondage of Foreign Domestic Helpers in Hong Kong

Dennis P. McCann and Mark Pufpaff

Abstract

Foreign Domestic Helpers (FDHs) in Hong Kong are playing an important role in domestic households. Many of them are women, mothers with children of their own at home, who are working overseas in order to pay for school fees, and all the other needs of their families in Indonesia and the Philippines. A newly established NGO, Hong Kong's "Fair Employment Agency" (FEA), states that the crucial problem is "debt bondage", namely, that incoming FDHs typically pay very high fees to the agencies through which they obtain their contracts in Hong Kong and support FDHs to enter Hong Kong under fair conditions. The case discusses social businesses and asks whether introducing cheap labor is actually a social business idea.

Keywords: Employment, abuse, labor rights, society, domestic helper

11.1 Seeing

Foreign Domestic Helpers (FDHs) have become a very visible part of Hong Kong's life since the 1970s. At first, they came primarily from the Philippines, but in the past decade or so, slightly more than half of them hail from Indonesia. Whatever their country of origin, the FDHs are attracted to Hong Kong because of the prospect of relatively high wages — that is, relative to what they were likely to earn at home — and the promise of better protection under the Hong Kong Special Autonomous Region's (HKSAR) vaunted "rule of law." The reality, however, is often far different from what the FDHs were led to expect. Most of them are women, mothers with children of their own at home, who are working overseas in order to pay for school fees, and all the other needs of their families. Though they generally manage to save prodigiously to send remittances home — it is reported that 96% of the FDHs send more than 50–60% of their salaries home — they report that they have been unable to meet the economic goals that led them to work abroad.

A recent study, "Modern Slavery in East Asia" (Farsight, February 2016), contains a survey of over 4,000 FDHs in Hong Kong and Singapore. Of those who participated in the survey, the study reported, "only 6 per cent… return home feeling they have saved enough money. Ten per cent go home with no money at all and 50 per cent return with only material things. Of those who return with nothing, 13 per cent still owe money to recruiters. And of those who have returned home, 65 per cent of Indonesians and 89 per cent of Filipinos say they want to migrate again." These statistics confirm what local NGOs — like the well-established Mission for Migrant Workers (MFMW) — have been arguing for years, namely, that the system is rigged so that most of the FDHs cannot fulfill their economic goals, and must sign on for additional labor contracts, whose costs must be paid before any savings can be realized.

There have been a range of proposals for improving the conditions of the FDHs and their families back home, including several efforts either to increase the "Minimal Allowable Wage" (MAW) specified for them in the HKSAR's regulations or to have them covered by Hong Kong's existing minimum wage laws. While the MAW is currently set at HKD 4210 a month, compliance with this figure typically has negative consequences. Instead of stipulating a minimum, it becomes the maximum that Hong Kong employers are willing to pay the FDHs. Any increase in the MAW, while always welcome, is likely to be used to similar effect. It will still define a ceiling for wages, rather than establish a floor, below which they cannot fall. To be sure, many FDHs complain that what they actually receive from their employers already falls short of the MAW.

On the contrary, some see a solution in revising the HKSAR's minimum wage law to include the FDHs. It is estimated that that if they were paid the statutory minimum wage of HKD 33.50/hour, it would more than double the amount they receive on a monthly basis. Though some organizations such as the Asian Migrants Coordinating Body (AMCB) have advocated this change, others point out that there are advantages as well as disadvantages to the current system regulating compensation and living conditions for FDHs. It is not clear that the FDHs would be significantly better off were they to be covered under the HKSAR's minimum wage law, especially if other provisions related to the MAW, such as the provision of adequate housing and food allowance, were to be dropped along with it.

A newly established NGO, Hong Kong's "Fair Employment Agency" (FEA), has taken the lead in pursuing a very different approach. Based on a painstaking study of the actual challenges faced by FDHs, the founders of this philanthropic "social business", Scott Stiles and David Bishop, concluded that the crucial problem was "debt bondage", namely, that incoming FDHs typically pay very high fees to the agencies through which they obtain their contracts in Hong Kong. Since most of the FDHs normally cannot afford to pay these fees out of pocket, they are forced to take out loans, often at usurious rates of interest, which in many cases means that the bulk of their wages (estimated at 70–80%) are garnisheed for several months until the loans are paid off. Such repayment schemes, indeed, are illegal in Hong Kong; but, as with many other questionable business practices, the employment agencies rarely, if ever, are investigated and penalized for them.

Since the totality of these exactions amounts to a system of "debt bondage", Stiles and Bishop founded the FEA to demonstrate the sustainability of an alternative. The costs involved in matching a prospective FDH with a Hong Kong employer, which the Agency estimates at HKD 7500, are paid by the employer and not the employee. This fee covers the cost of transportation to and from the FDH's country of origin, usually the Philippines or Indonesia, as well as a work visa, medical examination, and any orientation program needed to make the transition as smooth as possible. With the up-front cost of an employment contract shifted from employee to employer, the FDHs can begin their service debt free and start to send home remittances, as well as establish their own savings plans, immediately.

The FEA operates under the slogan, "Fair to Workers, Fair to Employers, Fair to Hong Kong." David Bishop explains, "Currently, all three groups are being taken advantage of. Domestic workers are being loaded with illegal debt, employers are paying money for a service that is not as good as it should be, and they are participating in trafficking unknowingly or against their will. And then you have the Hong Kong people who are being criticised by the global media for the marginal cases like [that of] Erwiana Sulistyaningsih" — an Indonesian domestic worker whose case gained international attention after she had been both brutalized by her employer and victimized by the illegal exactions of the employment agency that brought her to Hong Kong. "Our goal is to right the wrongs on each side. The best way to do that is to solve the debt problem."

Since their opening in September 2014, the FEA has fulfilled that goal for many FDHs and their employers. It is clear why the FDHs might be attracted to the FEA. Who would not want to start their overseas employment debt free? But, why would employers be attracted to it? They must pay 100% of the cost of recruiting, vetting, and transferring their new employee to Hong Kong. Why would they be willing to do that? The FEA is not for profit, and its fees seem reasonable. But, it is the quality of its service that is most appealing. Working through the FEA, employers are more likely to hire an employee that has been properly trained, and one who is free of the understandable anxieties that usually accompany crippling debt. A more secure employee is a happier employee, and a more productive employee. The FEA seems to have found expatriate families in Hong Kong most receptive to its strategy, since such people may be more aware of the problems accompanying globalization, especially with regard to human trafficking. Choosing the FEA when they are in need of domestic assistance is one way to ensure that their own actions become part of the solution, no longer part of the problems facing FDHs.

11.2   Judging

It is clear that the innovation that lies at the core of the FEA's social business strategy responds to the standards proposed by the United Nations' International Labor Organization (ILO) regarding debt bondage and its direct connection with forced labor and human trafficking. The problems of FDHs in Hong Kong are not simply local, but indicative of a systemic weakness that has become more severe in and through the processes of globalization. As labor markets have become increasingly global, so have the challenges of ensuring that these are well regulated, and that those participating in them do so ethically. Coerced labor, however subtle its forms, is still slavery by another name. Coercion through a system of debt bondage — in which one's freedom of movement, choice of employers, opportunities for redress of grievances are severely restricted, as they are for FDHs in Hong Kong — is a violation of universal standards of human rights. Article 23 of the Declaration on Human Rights, passed by the United Nations General Assembly on 10 December 1948, states the following:

(1) Everyone has the right to work, to free choice of employment, to just and favourable conditions of work and to protection against unemployment.
(2) Everyone, without any discrimination, has the right to equal pay for equal work.
(3) Everyone who works has the right to just and favourable remuneration ensuring for himself and his family an existence worthy of human dignity, and supplemented, if necessary, by other means of social protection.
(4) Everyone has the right to form and to join trade unions for the protection of his interests.

The labor laws of all member states, including the People's Republic of China, as well as the HKSAR, are meant to conform with this Declaration. Thus, it is not surprising that the business practices of employment agencies are regulated, with the expectation that Hong Kong's commitment to the "rule of law" should be observed in this area just as effectively as it is in any other.

One major challenge for anyone promoting the "rule of law", however, is the nearly universal discrepancy between theory and practice, between stated ideal norms and actual compliance, between the capabilities of law enforcement agencies and the communities to be served and protected by them. That the HKSAR should be having a problem achieving compliance in its labor laws when the employers are mostly Chinese and the employees are foreigners, in this case FDHs who are particularly vulnerable to exploitation and abuse, should come as no surprise. We need not suppose that the employers of Hong Kong are significantly less moral than their employees, but to be realistic we should recognize that there are limits to what can be achieved through legislation and rigorous law enforcement.

Governments and the citizenry in general have learned through experience the necessity of cultivating the institutions of a civil society. Social businesses — initiated as philanthropies and sustained through innovation — may make a contribution that is beyond the power of governments to achieve. If a social business, like the FEA in this case, develops an exemplary employment agency that is not only ethical but also compliant with the highest international legal standards and consistent in delivering superior service to all its stakeholders, then such a social business may provide a model to be explored if not imitated industry-wide, even by its competitors. One of the surest ways of making social progress on any issue is to show how businesses — for-profit as well as not-for-profit — can turn problems into opportunities. The difficulties faced by FDHs can become an opportunity to demonstrate how their needs can be met within an innovative as well as ethical business plan. Debt bondage, as the FEA's leaders have shown, is a problem for all of Hong Kong society, and not just for the victims but also those who prey upon their vulnerabilities and the law enforcement agencies devoted to providing justice for all. If the FEA's business plan is sustainable, it may be imitated by others, and the costs incurred by tolerating debt bondage and other abuses can be reduced for all stakeholders. The big "if", of course, is whether it is sustainable. Can such a model lead to real change in the Hong Kong labor markets for domestic helpers?

11.3 Acting

A review of the FEA's website indicates that it has survived its first two years of operation. The news media reports available on the website are uniformly positive in their praise of the firm's achievements. These may be cross checked against all stories involving the FEA on the Internet, with similarly favorable results. The impression created is that progress in achieving the FEA's goals is steady and very encouraging. At the same time, it is clear that the FEA may not yet be self-sustaining. It still solicits philanthropic donations, which suggests that this social business is not yet able to cover all its costs simply on the basis of the fees it charges those who avail of its services. While there is ample precedent for a start-up social business to depend initially on philanthropic or charitable donations, the question remains whether and when it will be sustainable apart from such donations. Similarly, if its innovative policies are to be adopted by other employment agencies, how can these be integrated into a for-profit business plan? After all, it is highly unlikely that the labor markets any time soon will be dominated by employment agencies that are managed as social businesses.

If the FEA's core concept — namely, the FDHs' recruitment fees should be paid by employers and not by the employees themselves — is to be widely adopted, how might that happen in a for-profit employment agency?

- First of all, such agencies must understand that the ILO's "Fair Recruitment Initiative" (2014), among other things, specifically recommends measures to "ensure that recruitment fees or costs are not charged directly or indirectly to workers." Since the FEA's business plan is in compliance with ILO standards, it can provide a useful model for other employment agencies.
- Second, the standard Labor Contract for FDHs in Hong Kong, recruited from abroad, stipulates that the employer will be responsible for all fees incurred in recruiting and transporting the employee from and to his or her home or place of origin. Furthermore, if the employee has paid any such fees to an employment agency, the employer shall reimburse him or her promptly, once the receipts for such payments have been produced.
- Third, in light of such stipulations, the FEA's policy must be regarded not as a radical change, but simply as a good faith attempt to comply with existing regulations. The policy, then, should be adopted generally by any recruitment agency that is operating within the law, regardless of its for-profit or not-for-profit status.

The challenge to employment agencies, then, comes down to this: Does their business plan enable them to operate within the law and still make a profit? Understood in this way, one may well ask why they should be different from any other business. Why should they be exempt from compliance? If they cannot make a profit while complying with the law, they ought not to be in business. The FEA's initial success suggests that many, if not most, employment agencies specializing in the recruitment of FDHs are actually criminal enterprises that, from an economic point of view, deliberately extort illegal rents from those whom they are pledged to serve. The labor markets of Hong Kong, as well as other places where the system of forced labor through debt bondage is practiced, would be far better off, let alone more efficient for all participants, were such criminal enterprises abolished.

11.4 Discussion Questions

1. The FEA is a social business initially supported through philanthropic activities or charitable donations. Its purpose is to bring justice or fairness to the labor markets through which FDHs are recruited in and for Hong Kong. Do you think this is a legitimate purpose for philanthropies and charitable individuals to be supporting?
2. Do you think it is possible to make a profit operating an employment agency while in full compliance with relevant laws and regulations? If so, how so? If not, why not?
3. The FEA understands its business plan as an alternative to engaging in usually fruitless political controversies over raising the MAW or expanding minimum wage law coverage for the FDHs. Do you think that attacking debt bondage directly is more likely to improve the finances of FDHs and their families more than further changes in the MAW or minimum wage law in Hong Kong? If so, how so? If not, why not?
4. What is debt bondage? How does it work? Why do the founders of the FEA, as well as the ILO and other international agencies, condemn it for undermining the freedom of efficiency, and fairness of labor markets?
5. Is debt bondage an inevitable byproduct of capitalist economic development, or is it an indication of anti-capitalist corruption in international labor markets?

Bibliography

Fair Employment Agency (2021). Our Story. *www.fairagency.com*. Retrieved March 28, 2021 from https://www.fairagency.org/our-story/#our-story-pane.

Mission for Migrant Workers (2021). Mission for migrant workers. *www.migrants.net*. Retrieved March 28, 2021 from https://www.migrants.net/who-we-are.

SEEFAR (2016). Modern Slavery in East Asia. https://modernslavery.seefar.org/assets/seefar-modern-slavery-in-east-asia.pdf.

United Nations (2021). Universal Declaration of Human Rights. *www.un.org*. Retrieved March 28, 2021 from https://www.un.org/en/universal-declaration-human-rights/index.html.

Chapter 12

Wages for Coal Mine Workers?

Dennis P. McCann and Mark Pufpaff

Abstract

This case discusses the problems coal miners in Heilongjiang Province faced when not being paid. They staged massive protests after not getting their wages for six months. The case discusses the issue from various perspectives, the company claiming to have great debt, the workers asking for their rights, and the Chinese media reporting on labor and health issues.

Keywords: Wages, labor relations, employment, environment

12.1 Seeing

Failing to pay wages owed to coal miners seems like adding insult to injury. Working in a coal mine is among the most hazardous occupations in China, if not also the dirtiest, even if government reports are to be believed concerning the reduction of deaths attributed to coal mine accidents. Yet recently in Heilongjiang Province, coal miners staged a massive protest in Shuangyashan city, claiming that they had not been paid their wages for six months or more. "Give us our wages back! Give us our wages back! We need to eat!" chanted the demonstrators who also carried banners reading "We want to survive!" or "The Communist Party owe us money!"

While hundreds of riot police were called in to break up the demonstrations, the governor of Heilongjiang Province, Lu Hao, tried to assure the press in Beijing that "not a penny was overdue" in wages from the Longmay Mining Holding Group, the largest state-owned coal mine in the province. However, his assurances were dismissed as a "fat lie" by protesters, and as their numbers grew over the weekend, the government was forced to admit that there had been a "mistake", that Governor Lu had been misinformed, and that now inquiries were underway on how to return the Longmay mines to financial solvency.

If the authorities at Longmay are to be believed, their actions were not simply a matter of naked greed. The company was in serious debt and unable to pay its bills, and under those circumstances slowed down payments to their workers while directing whatever money they had on hand to their creditors. Such a stratagem may have worked in the past, when workers may have been more docile and accepting of hardships when there seemed to be no other choice. But, in today's China, with workers becoming increasingly resourceful in pressing their own legal and moral claims, and with the Chinese news media now more than ever likely to report on labor unrest and other protests, Longmay's refusal to pay could only create more problems than it was designed to solve.

12.2 Judging

Defaulting on one's promise to pay wages for work already completed, by all accounts, is morally outrageous. It is also illegal in China. Chapter Five of the Labor Law of the People's Republic of China, promulgated in 1995, establishes the framework in six articles. Article 50 states that wages "shall be paid to laborers themselves in the form of currency (yuan) on a monthly basis", and shall "not be deducted or delayed without reason." Other articles make it clear that while wages may be freely set by mutual agreement of the employer and employees (Art. 47), with "distribution according to the principle of work and equal pay for equal work" (Art. 46), workers are to be paid "no lower than the local standards on minimum wages" as determined by the State (Art. 48–49). Wages shall also be paid for legally recognized holidays, including "leaves for marriage or mourning" and "participation in other social activities in accordance with the law" (Art. 51). Employers may be subject to legal prosecution if they fail to comply with the law in the following instances:

"(1) Deduction or unjustified delay in paying wages to laborers; (2) Refusal to pay laborers wage remunerations for working longer hours; (3) Payment of wages to laborers below local standards on minimum wages; (4) Failure to provide laborers with economic compensations in accordance with this Law after revocation of labor contracts" (Art. 91). While the Chinese Labor Law is clear about wages, its moral basis should be equally clear. The basic transaction between employers and their employees is a form of promise-making and keeping. Workers agree to provide their labor in exchange for the employers' promise to pay them mutually agreed-upon wages. Failure to pay means breaking a promise. If the work has already been done, the failure is especially serious since the promise was relied upon. If the failure was deliberate, that is, if the employer never had any intention of paying what he or she promised, then it amounts to theft, a form of fraud based on deception. There can be no more basic form of corruption than this. If done deliberately, as a matter of policy or choice, wage theft reveals the employer as totally lacking in integrity.

Whatever the legal consequences of failure to pay mutually agreed-upon wages, the moral judgment depends on whether or not the failure was deliberate. The standard is one of "reason." Are there, or can there ever be, good reasons for not paying wages for work already done? Can there be any legitimate excuse for the decision of the Longmay Holding Group to either suspend or delay the payment of wages for over six months? Perhaps we can imagine some possibilities: if the company has not received payment for its products, and therefore has no revenue with which to meet expenses; but, that is highly unlikely. Let us try to be more realistic. What if the price of coal has plummeted, or the tonnage of coal supplied to its customers is down, and thus revenues are much less than expected? If that were true, it might make for a legitimate excuse. But, what if the budgetary shortfall occurred because the firm had to make a large payment on its debt to one of China's major investment banks? Would that make it reasonable to withhold scheduled wage payments? Or what if the firm had to cut a number of budget items — including its employees' wages and benefits — in order to secure the retirement accounts of its senior managers? Would it be reasonable then? Or what if the firm was required to purchase and install new and expensive equipment, designed to prevent accidents in the coal mines, or mitigate the environmental hazards of coal mining?

Surely, each of these "what if" scenarios might have some merit as providing a reasonable basis for delaying payments. At this point, we do not know which, if any, of these apply to what happened at the Longmay Holding Group. But, it is likely that some combination of them may have created the situation, since the State's response to the coal miners' strike was to begin an investigation into the firm's financial problems, and the need for some kind of bailout that would make it possible for the wages to get paid sooner rather than later. Even if the managers at Longmay were caught in some kind of financial crisis, questions still remain on how they handled the situation, and whether they could have acted in ways that addressed the workers' legitimate claims without forcing them to call a strike.

12.3 Acting

If you are commerce student, undergraduate or MBA level, you are likely to be preparing for a career in business management. How would you handle this situation? What would you do differently from what Longmay's managers did? We do not know for sure, but apparently management at Longmay did not bother to inform their workers about the firm's financial crisis and the impact it would have on wage payments. They probably did not want the workers to get upset, or slow down production until they were paid. You may recall the joke about labor in Poland during the days of Communist Party rule: "We pretend to work, and they pretend to pay us." Longmay's managers may have decided that "Silence is Golden." Keep the workers in the dark, and hope for the best. But, obviously, that strategy does not work anymore. So, what might you have done differently? If you were advising top management at Longmay, what would you recommend?

What would you need to know in order to answer this question realistically? Well, for example, is there a workers' union or other labor organization at Longmay? Does it enjoy the support of the workers? If it were to negotiate with management in order to craft some kind of solution, would its efforts have credibility with the workers? Or what about the track record of Longmay's management? Have they tried to show genuine concern for their workers' needs, addressed their legitimate grievances, or promoted coal mine safety procedures? Or have they only been interested in meeting their production quotas and securing their own economic advantages and political favoritism? If labor relations had been relatively healthy in the past, that is, conducive of mutual respect,

Longmay's management might have been able to disclose the firm's financial prospects, and obtained the workers' agreement to forego some portion of their wages, at least temporarily, until some solution to the crisis was achieved. Do you think that is a realistic possibility? If you were advising Longmay's management, what options might you give them other than to flat out lie to their workers, and call in the riot police whenever their outrage boils over into organized protests?

12.4 Conclusion

Though it should be obvious to everyone, we need to take to heart the fact that coal miners are human beings, just like everybody else. They, their lives and families, their hopes and concerns, need to be taken seriously, just as seriously as we do those of our own parents and others close to us. Confucius and the other great sages East and West had it right in formulating the Golden Rule: "Do not do to others, what you do not want them doing to you." Or, in positive terms, "Do unto others, what you would have them do unto you." Each of us knows how we would react if others were to disrespect us, or try to steal from us, especially through acts of fraud or other deceptive practices. We know in our hearts how the anger provoked by such evil acts may provoke further acts of protest and even violence. Why should we expect coal miners to be any different? It is tragic that life in the city of Shuangyashan was disrupted by a coal miners' strike that has embarrassed China internationally. But, who bears responsibility for it? What could be done differently to avoid such embarrassments in the future?

12.5 Discussion Questions

1. Imagine that you are a coal miner who has not received his or her wages for several months. What would you do? Would you join the others in organizing a strike, as workers did in Shuangyashan? Would you participate in the strike, even if you knew it might lead to violence, either your arrest or some kind of riot? What would you do?

2. Imagine you are a manager at the coal mine, and you know that the firm is facing a financial crisis and will not have the money to meet its obligations next month. There is some money that could be allocated for some payments, but how would you prioritize among

them? Would workers' wages be at the top of your priority list? If not, why not?

3. You are a manager at the Shuangyashan coal mine, and the strikes and social unrest have already occurred. Now what? What would you do to reestablish enough harmony to allow the coal mine to reopen? Would you try to reopen communications with the strikers and their representatives? Would you try to persuade them to go back to work with threats or promises? Would you threaten to call in the police to compel them to work, or would you promise them not only to pay what is owed them but also to provide other benefits, for example, medical exams, to improve their lives?

4. Sometimes we hear that business bluffing is ethical. But, what is bluffing, and when is it ethical? Both managers and workers may be tempted to tell lies to try to get what they want in situations like the crisis at Shuangyashan. What do you think about telling lies to workers, making promises that you know you cannot keep, just to keep them from going on strike? What do you think about strikers telling lies to other workers to get them to participate in their protests? If bluffing means lying to people to whom you owe the truth, what is the good of it?

5. We hear a lot about "transparency" and "accountability" in business ethics. How might these values be translated into policies that help managers and workers cooperate to solve their problems at the Shuangyashan coal mine? Both might involve thinking through what can be done both short term and long term? What would you do to create a "win-win" situation here?

Bibliography

Goh, B. *et al.* (2016). China coal firm quells protests, pays out wages. *Yahoo news*. Retrieved on April 11, 2016 from https://news.yahoo.com/china-coal-firm-quells-protests-pays-wages-133712205.html.

Liu, X.T. (2016). 同舟共济, 共守难关 — 双鸭山煤矿工人向政府讨薪 (Together, we will help each other to overcome difficulties — Shuangyashan coal miners demand wages from the government). *www.inews.ifeng.com*. Retrieved on April 11, 2016 from http://inews.ifeng.com/mip/ 47838792/news.shtml.

Shuangyashan Daily (2016). 双鸭山通报龙煤拖欠工资职工上访事件 (Shuangyashan informs Longmei's employees of the petition incident). *www.guancha.cn*. Retrieved on April 11, 2016 from https://www.guancha.cn/economy/2016_03_14_353858_s.shtml.

Part 4
Corporate Social Responsibility

Chapter 13

PepsiCo Philanthropy in China: Too Good to be True?

Dennis P. McCann and Mark Pufpaff

Abstract

PepsiCo GCR, an MNC producing popular brands of soft drink beverages, integrated philanthropic activities into their business activities in China. It donated over RMB 53 million yuan for various projects supporting water safety all over China. Their activities affected more than 600,000 people. One of the most memorable projects is called "Water Cellars for Mothers." The case discusses PepsiCo GCR's involvement in the "Water Cellars for Mothers" project and asks whether these community-oriented activities of the firm are merely a public relations coup, dictated by strategic business considerations, or a genuine act of corporate philanthropy.

Keywords: Corporate social responsibility, water safety, customer relationships, philanthropy

13.1 Seeing

Everyone knows that we need positive role models if philanthropy, not to mention business ethics in general, is to flourish in China. PepsiCo GCR, an MNC producing both popular brands of soft drink beverages and internationally recognized snack foods, has been operating in China for a

111

long time, since 1981, to be exact. Although their path has not always been easy, over the years PepsiCo has made it a lot smoother by integrating its philanthropic activities into a comprehensive sustainability strategy resonant with its ongoing commitment to China's social and economic development.

One significant program that illustrates PepsiCo's success is its partnership with the China Women's Development Foundation (CWDF) of the All-China Women's Federation (ACWF), to support the "Water Cellars for Mothers" project that tries to address the lack of safe drinking water for families and schools in central and western China. Through the CWDF, PepsiCo GCR has supported the building of water cellars, which function as underground containers for collecting and storing rain water. Typically, people in these regions have relied upon water pits that were leaky and inefficient because of inadequate construction materials and poor design. The "Water Cellars for Mothers" project has provided resources allowing local communities to mitigate, if not entirely overcome, such water shortages. With the building of the water cellars, not only has the health of women and children been improved thanks to better access to clean water but also agricultural production in the surrounding areas has increased.

PepsiCo GCR reports that "as of the end of October 2013, PepsiCo Foundation, PepsiCo GCR and PepsiCo employees had contributed a total donation of over RMB 53 million yuan for the building of 1,500+ water cellars, the building or upgrading of more than 170 small-scale safe drinking water projects, the construction of more than 90 school safe drinking water projects, and the training of over 170,000 rural residents." June 2011 saw the announcement of an additional grant of USD 5 million for the project, which is PepsiCo's largest single charity donation in China. "As of October 2013, over 655,000 people in 30 counties of 8 provinces had benefited from the project during the first two years of its implementation."

The "Water Cellars for Mothers" project represents an investment not only of financial resources but also of employee volunteers, who over the past 10 years have worked in remote villages and schools in the communities supported by the project. As PepsiCo GCR's Sustainability Report indicates, as of June 2013, personal donations from its employees in China had exceeded RMB 2.2 million yuan. Apparently, PepsiCo GCR's collaboration with the CWDF has been so successful that the two organizations announced, in 2012, the development of a five-year strategic partnership that will expand their activities into related projects, thereby building upon the impact of "Water Cellars for Mothers."

13.2 Judging

What PepsiCo GCR and the CWDF have achieved together is very impressive. But, what can others — other foreign businesses operating in China as well as local NGOs — learn from their experience? Is PepsiCo GCR's involvement in the "Water Cellars for Mothers" project merely a public relations coup, dictated by strategic business considerations, or is it a genuine act of corporate philanthropy? Is it too good to be true? Should we be skeptical of their claims for it, and be looking for hidden agendas or corporate wrongdoing that the project is meant to cover up?

If we are to judge, it is always useful to search for more information. Only here, we may be dealing with the proverbial "dog that didn't bark", since the blogosphere and other sources seem remarkably free of stories accusing either PepsiCo GCR or the CWDF of malfeasance. Assuming, then, that their good reputations are well deserved — PepsiCo, for example, consistently ranks in the top 50 firms listed in *Fortune Magazines* "World's Most Admired Companies" and in 2013 was named one of the "Top Employers in China" by the CRF Institute, a market research organization based in the Netherlands — our concern is to understand what they are doing and why.

It may be useful to review certain basic assumptions about philanthropy, corporate philanthropy, and corporate social responsibility. Philanthropy, as such, means roughly the same as "charity." Literally "love of humanity", philanthropy overlaps with the Chinese term, "benevolence" (仁, *rén*), which refers to the good feeling a virtuous person experiences when being altruistic. Philanthropy is a personal act of altruism, motivated by a concern for the good of another. In traditional Confucian teaching, such benevolence is innate, but it must be cultivated. It is first learned in one's family, expressed in the love of a parent for his or her child, and then it expands, as the person matures, to include all of humanity. The Chinese practice of philanthropy is readily apparent in the way ordinary people pitch in with donations and other assistance in the aftermath of natural disasters, like earthquakes, monsoon floods, and severe drought.

Corporate philanthropy builds upon this basic instinct to help others in need, but channels it in ways that are — and ought to be — consistent with the overall purpose of a business. Corporate philanthropy may be understood as but one part of a comprehensive strategy for exercising corporate social responsibility. Corporate philanthropy is likely to be shaped by a business's strategy or overall business plan. After all, a successful business is supposed to make a reasonable profit. We may hesitate to embrace the term "profit maximization" because it is too narrow, with a tendency to obscure all the other goals or promises that a business must fulfill to its various stakeholders if it is to stay in business. "Optimizing profit" may be a more useful term, since it assumes that making a profit for its owners or investors is essential to a business. At the same time, optimizing is consistent with budgeting for other legitimate expenditures, including philanthropic grants and contributions. Corporate philanthropy, in short, must be consistent with a firm's overall business plan, conceived and organized so that it contributes, rather than undermines, its capacities for achieving its legitimate business goals.

It is therefore not sheer serendipity that PepsiCo GCR should target its corporate philanthropy toward the problem of safe and adequate water supplies in western China. Given that its two major product lines, beverages and snack foods, both depend on access to safe and adequate water supplies, it is very smart for PepsiCo GCR to build upon its expertise in water management to address the needs of women and children, as well as farmers, in drought-prone areas of China. If the "Water Cellars for Mothers" project is successfully replicated throughout the region, more safe water will be available for human use, thus alleviating some of the pressure on water supplies allocated for commercial uses, such as manufacturing and bottling the range of beverages marketed by PepsiCo GCR. As PepsiCo GCR continues to learn new conservation methods for reducing their water intake for commercial uses, similar improvements can be extended to a range of non-commercial uses, as in the water cellars project. In one area — inner Mongolia — where the project has taken root and achieved success, PepsiCo GCR has opened experimental farms to optimize irrigation methods for cultivating potatoes, which of course are a major ingredient in the snack foods they produce and market. Local families benefit from their enhanced access to safe water supplies, and local farmers are enabled to produce crops that may be sold to PepsiCo GCR, thereby creating not only good will among the local people but also enhanced economic opportunities.

Given that the "Water Cellars for Mothers" project is likely to yield positive outcomes enhancing PepsiCo GCR's bottom line, should we dismiss or denigrate its claim to represent a model of corporate philanthropy? Some may be inclined to skepticism, since evidence that philanthropic activities are based on anything other than purely altruistic motives will prompt them to dismiss such activities as merely a clever example of public relations management. In such cases, however, demanding absolute purity of motive may be counterproductive. Imposing an impossibly high standard on corporate philanthropy may tend to discourage firms from doing what they can to help others. A more realistic approach may be to accept a firm's claims to corporate philanthropy at face value, knowing that mixed motives — for example, doing good while doing well — are inevitable in business.

In such an approach, the focus shifts from analyzing the donor's motives to investigating the results of his or her actions. No one has denied that hundreds of thousands of households in western China have seen the quality of their lives improved thanks to PepsiCo GCR's partnership with the CWDF. In light of their success, the inquiry should focus on basic issues of transparency and accountability, that is, how decisions are made regarding who gets the grants, whether and how due diligence is exercised in determining the needs of applicants, how the funds once transmitted are put to use, whether the NGO partner — in this case, the CWDF — facilitates honest and mutually respectful communication between the donors and recipients, and whether the NGO partner is successful in helping both donors and recipients to develop sustainable relationships that may be mutually beneficial now and in the future. While studies on the "Water Cellar for Mothers" projects have documented its positive economic consequences, they have not analyzed certain developmental issues that inevitably arise in the management of philanthropic partnerships. What is clear is that PepsiCo GCR encourages the participation of employee volunteers, who visit the sites where water cellars and other improvements have been made, and occasionally serve as instructors teaching proper methods of health maintenance and water conservation. Though the evaluation of the PepsiCo GCR–CWDF partnership thus remains incomplete, what is known is very encouraging.

13.3 Acting

Suppose a foreign MNC wants to support philanthropic activities in China. What lessons can be learned from PepsiCo GCR's successful participation in the CWDF's "Water Cellars for Mothers" projects?

First, experience counts. PepsiCo GCR has been operating in China since 1981, and has seen first-hand the development of China's markets in an era of economic and social reform. Through trial and error, they have learned to work with Chinese organizations, not only to develop their overall business plan but also to target for philanthropic response the needs of real people that might be addressed in ways consistent with their business strategy. Water management, and the conservation of scarce water resources, is strategically important to PepsiCo GCR; it is also strategically important to the people helped by them in western China.

Second, find the right Chinese partner with whom to do business. The CWDF is an integral part of the All-China Women's Federation (ACWF), founded on April 3, 1949, to unite Chinese women of all ethnic groups and from all walks of life, strive for their liberation and development by upholding women's rights and interests, and promote equality between women and men. Established in 1988, the CWDF is "a non-profit social welfare organization registered with the Ministry of Civil Affairs and approved by People's Bank of China," actively sponsoring and supporting programs focused on "women's education, training, poverty alleviation and disaster rescue." PepsiCo GCR realized, well before many others, that corporate philanthropy in China will only be sustainable if it builds on partnerships with local institutions that contain the requisite local knowledge and expertise. What better choice than the ACWF-CWDF, an NGO with a well-established reputation in its field, as well as the appropriate legal certifications permitting it to cooperate with foreign donors?

Third, develop the partnership in ways that will ensure a convergence of values, reflected in mutual efforts to achieve appropriate levels of transparency and accountability. Though PepsiCo has been in China for over 30 years, it remains a foreign-based MNC, with its own distinctive corporate culture, including a Vision and Mission statement, and a list of Six Guiding Principles — "(1) Care for our customers, our consumers and the world we live in. (2) Sell only products we can be proud of. (3) Speak with truth and candor. (4) Win with diversity and inclusion. (5) Balance short-term and long-term. (6) Respect others and succeed together" — all of which may resonate better at PepsiCo's headquarters in Purchase, New York, than they do in western China. PepsiCo's Guiding Principles, as well as the original recipes for its beverages, may have been formulated in the USA, but like all such formulas, they can be translated into Chinese and integrated into best business practices specific to PepsiCo GCR. The mutual learning that emerges from its successful philanthropic partnership with the ACWF-CWDF surely has had an impact on how the company has come to understand what mutual respect, honesty, fairness, and integrity mean in and for China. Reciprocity (恕, *shu*) is the core value enshrined in Confucian ethics (Analects XV.24) that is convergent with PepsiCo's stated aspirations. Developing sustainable relationships with Chinese partners, especially in the area of corporate philanthropy, and based on such values, is perhaps the best way to achieve mutual understanding.

13.4 Discussion Questions

1. What is corporate philanthropy, and how does it differ from personal charity, on the one hand, and corporate social responsibility, on the other?
2. How did PepsiCo GCR get involved in the "Water Cellars for Mothers" project? Was the company simply responding instinctively and collectively to the needs of poor women and children, or were there other considerations involved?
3. If PepsiCo's corporate philanthropy is not motivated purely by altruism, does that mean that it is not really philanthropic? Why or why not?
4. A business must earn a profit if it is to be sustainable. Normally, profits are earned in order to fulfill a business's promises to its investors or ownership group. Assuming that business managers have an obligation to their investors, on what basis can they justify allocating any of their profits for philanthropic activities?
5. Is there any moral justification for corporate philanthropy? Or should all philanthropic activities be acts of personal charity, leaving it to the discretion of individuals to dispose of their wealth and income? Why or why not?
6. If you were a manager of an MNC operating in China, and your firm had a tradition of supporting philanthropies in other countries where you do business, how would you advise the firm on doing philanthropy in China? Is there anything for you to learn from the successful partnership that PepsiCo GCR has developed with the CWDF? What would you advise your colleagues on how to proceed in China?

Bibliography

PepsiCo GCR Sustainability Report (2014). https://www.pepsico.com/docs/album/sustainability-report/regional-and-topic-specific-reports/gcr_sustainability_report_en_final.pdf?sfvrsn=8717cb72_4.

Qing, J. (2009). PepsiCo supports safe drinking water project. *China Daily*. Retrieved on August 12, 2016 from http://www.chinadaily.com.cn/bw/2009-11/23/content_9020376.htm.

The All-China Women's Federation (2015). Water Cellars Improve Lives of Mothers in W China. Retrieved on August 12, 2016 from http://www.womenofchina.cn/html/photo/15120917-1.htm.

Chapter 14

The Business of Elderly Care in China
Filial Piety in the 21st Century

Mark Pufpaff, Dennis P. McCann, and Helen Xu

Abstract

China's population is aging. The ratio of retirees to workers is increasing at the same time as the size of the average family is decreasing. This is putting a strain on China's working population, who are responsible for taking care of their retired family members. This tradition of parent/child reciprocity in China is called filial piety. However, with changing dynamics and demographics, how it is or ought to be practiced in the 21st century is in need of fresh reflection. This case study thus presents the challenges and opportunities facing the practice of filial piety and explores mutually beneficial options for both children and parents.

Keywords: Filial piety, cross-generational home, elderly care, loyalty, business models

14.1 Seeing

"If my children ever put me in a nursing home, I would feel like I was being abandoned." — Huang Liangbao, 83

Huang, an aging parent and grandparent in Shanghai, is not alone. Many in China, where elderly housing services like nursing homes and assisted living facilities are still viewed unfavorably and generally as undesirable, still prefer to be cared for by their children as they age. Such a practice of reciprocity, where parents provide for their children when they are young with the expectation that their children will care for them once they are old, is part of the historical traditional of filial piety (孝, *xiào*). However, there are a number of emerging trends posing challenges to the practicality or feasibility of this tradition, at least in its current form.

China has a growing elderly population. According to the *China Daily*, in 2014, there were 212 million people above the age of 60; by 2050, that number is estimated to rise to 480 million, or more than double. Researchers from the United Nations (UN) found that, in 2005, there were 16 retirees for every 100 workers in China; they project that by 2025, this ratio will rise to 64 retirees for every 100 workers. Wang Jianjun, standing deputy director of the National Working Committee on Aging, stated that China's population is on a trajectory of accelerated aging, the effects of which will have a significant impact on public policy (i.e., the provision of State-funded nursing homes and related accommodations).

A driving factor in this trend is China's now reformed one-child policy, originally introduced in 1979, which effectively prohibited a majority of Chinese families from having more than one child for over 35 years. This has led to what has become known as the "4:2:1" problem, that is, where in a given family there are four grandparents, two parents, but only one child. While not the situation for all families, it is a situation facing many, thus making filial piety, and the cross-generational housing model[1] it so often represents, difficult. There are a couple of reasons why. First, there is a trend of rural-to-urban relocation among students and young professionals. In increasing numbers, children of rural families are studying and working in cities (and even abroad), while their parents and grandparents oftentimes remain in their hometowns. Second, even when these children do stay in close geographical proximity to their parents and grandparents, the ability to house and serve them adequately — being for all intents and purposes perpetually "on call" — is becoming increasingly untenable. This is due to the disproportionate number of elderly members compared to working-age members in such families. Third, the costs for one child (or even multiple children, as in some cases) to support the

---

[1]Cross-generational housing is when family members from multiple generations live within a single housing property over the course of their lives.

health care needs of their parents and grandparents can be overwhelming. For example, Fan Yan, the daughter of Huang Liangbao, stated the following in an interview:

"Having professional staff to take care of my mother would really relieve me and my brothers from worrying all the time."

A parallel driver has been an increase in life expectancy among Chinese citizens due to improvements in health care. While in 1970 the average life expectancy was just over 58 years, by 2015 it had risen to almost 76 years. With China's elderly living longer into their retirement years, paired with the lingering effects of its one-child policy, a rethinking of the country's public policy agenda may be in order. Luo Shanzhen, director at CHJ-Care Lezhi, a Beijing-based senior living service provider, indicated as much when she stated the following:

"Over the next 15 years, as the first generation of parents affected by the [one-child] policy enters their 70s and 80s, they will need more professional care and attention…residential compounds for the elderly — especially the upscale ones — will be in greater demand."

It may very well be that the luxury market grows first, or fastest. Luo is seeing a change in attitude from the wealthier and more highly educated in Beijing, many of whom see in upscale retirement compounds a fulfilling life. This is partially due to the services and the quality of life offered there, but also because they will not receive the same treatment staying with their children or grandchildren.[2] To accommodate their higher-end lifestyle demands, Luo outlines the value proposition of luxury residences:

"At some luxury apartments in Beijing, older people are lining up to live there. Lower-tier cities have started to develop the upscale market as well. Such institutions provide daily care, entertainment, exercise, trips, and classes such as English, calligraphy, and knitting — all tailored to the elderly."

---

[2]According to Luo, "A coming demographic shift will quickly grow demand for [luxury homes for the elderly] in the years to come. China's one-child policy was introduced in 1979, which means more and more Chinese who need regular elderly care don't have the traditionally large families to cater to this need."

If the prospects for the luxury nursing and retirement home market in China look good, what about the low to middle range of the market? The government has indicated that providing for such people is an important priority. Li Jianguo, vice chairman and general secretary of the Standing Committee of the National People's Congress, stated as far back as 2011 that there needed to be a serious increase in the number of government-funded nursing home beds available for the elderly going forward. His desire did not go unheeded. In 2012, there were approximately 4 million beds available; by 2015, that number had risen to 6.7 million, and is only set to continue rising. Much of this increase was directed toward those at the lower end of the economic spectrum, where the government perceives the greatest need.

However, it is not just providing quality facilities for the less wealthy but also changing perceptions. Fan, speaking on behalf of her mother Huang, stated the following:

> "[My] mother is reluctant, because she thinks of all nursing homes as the sparsely adorned rooms and run-down facilities of many state-run institutions."

However, with the development of more upscale facilities, paired with the fact that an increasing number of elderly — regardless of financial status — are choosing to reside in nursing homes, such negative perceptions may diminish over time. One reason is social. Living alone is a direr prospect than living in a senior facility. Confirming this, Gao Lanzhi, a 75-year-old woman now living at the Happiness Senior Citizens Care Center in Beijing, stated that living by herself, even with an in-home nurse whom she had hired after knee surgery, was unbearable; after moving to the care center, she found being in the company of the 200 other residents deeply fulfilling. In her own words,

> "The nursing home provides me a quiet and reliable place to do what I like and to meet more peers."

However attractive the social dimension is, by itself it does have its limits for attracting the elderly to nursing homes. According to the *China Daily*, "the aged care service industry in China faces the awkward situation of lacking qualified professionals." China's Ministry of Civil Affairs set the national professional standard for aged care staff; however, of the over one million industry workers, less than 40,000 of them meet the requisite standard. Many prospective residents like Gao are having to do a substantial amount of shopping before committing to a care center or nursing home, with the patience, knowledge, and attentiveness of the staff being a deciding factor. Hu Tongwei, director of the Happiness Senior Citizens Care Center, stated that of the 24 staff working there, "most of them [are] without professional aged care training." But, as the industry grows, and demand for such professional qualifications increases, the disparity between qualified and unqualified workers is projected to decrease. As Gao mentioned, "it's high time for governments to increase the training of nursing home workers."

14.2 Judging

What do these developments within the elderly care industry mean for the tradition of filial piety?

Filial piety represents the first of the Confucian relationships — parent/child — and expresses the Confucian value of reciprocity. The Chinese character for filial piety — *xiào* (孝) — is a combination of two characters; the top character derives from *lǎo* (老), which translates as "old", and the bottom character is *zi* (子), translated as "son". This symbolically presents the parent being supported by the child, which in practice is descriptive of the way children should act toward their parents in China. However, the reason why children should act in this way is due to the upbringing they were given by their parents, and the sacrifices they made for their child's benefit (providing a home, healthy food, an education, emotional support, etc.). Thus, when the children give back to their parents what was originally given to them, they are embodying the value of reciprocity and continuing on the tradition of filial piety.

The details of how children reciprocate and care for their parents as they age can take many forms depending on the resources, lifestyles, and needs of a given family. However, historically, there *was* a common context in which filial piety was carried out, namely, the cross-generational home. As discussed briefly in the SEEING section, it is a home that includes family members from different generations. For example, a given household may include grandparents, parents, and children. It may also be the case that the home is the same residence the parents grew up in and inherited, and then passed on to their children. This inheritance and passing on of real estate reinforces the cross-generational home model so often seen in the practice of filial piety.

Does the present-day rise in nursing home occupancy somehow undermine the practice of filial piety? If a child invites a parent to visit a nursing or retirement home because they feel it will give them a better quality of life, is that showing a lack of reciprocity?

Some, like Huang, may say yes. They may feel their child was abandoning them, and by extension neglecting their filial duties. But, many others are saying no. The caveat is that many who are turning toward and embracing elderly care homes are China's so-called high-net-worth individuals (HNWI). According to the *Jing Daily*,

"Preference [by HNWIs in China] for senior living communities has grown by 87 percent in the past year. A total of 28 percent of HNWIs have listed "medium- to high-end elderly care homes" as their personal post-retirement plan, marking a jump from 15 percent in 2015. Meanwhile, the percentage of those planning on "home retirement" has declined from 77 percent in 2015 to 57 percent in 2016."

For those HNWIs nearing retirement age, the desire not to burden their children and the necessity of having adequate health care services on call are two of the driving reasons for the acceptance of life in a retirement home. But, this does not mean their children are out of the picture. *Jing Daily* continues,

"While more wealthy aging parents may be living away from their children, they're still getting a significant amount of support from them. For now, the cost of post-retirement healthcare and living is being taken care of by a combination of the parents' savings (37 percent), funding from their children (30 percent) and social insurance (30 percent), with commercial insurance only funding around 2 percent."

Not only are children funding a significant portion of their parents' post-retirement costs but they are also remaining in close touch with them through telecommunications technology. According to the *China Daily*,

"Modern technologies, particularly social networking, has made [parents] feel closer to their children."

Gao Lanzhi, referenced in the SEEING section, stated in an interview that she "lives her life in full without the feeling of loneliness and fear, although her daughters live abroad." This feeling of closeness, however incomparable to being in person, is being facilitated through smartphone applications such as WeChat. So effective has the emergence of such technology been in keeping children and parents in daily contact that technology companies such as Tencent (who owns and operates WeChat) and the government itself have supported projects and initiatives embedding such technology into the elderly care industry. The *China Daily* continues,

> "Seniors in China are owning more and more electronic gadgets…many of them have mastered applications on smart phones. Chinese tech companies have taken on the project of connecting the elderly with their relatives, communities, and hospitals, using big data on the Internet. Data from daily life, including health index, [is] collected and uploaded through wearable devices to the cloud platform, [whereby] family members, living afar, receive updates. In 2013, the State Council asked local governments to support enterprises in applying the Internet and other new technologies to the industry."

If the prospects for retirement home life are positive for HNWIs in China, what about the less financially well-off?

14.3 Acting

The Chinese government has indicated that the growth of the elderly care industry must accommodate those who need such housing and services the most. Wu Yushao, director of the China Research Center on Aging, stated the following in an interview:

> "There should be a screening system to ensure that those most in need are admitted to nursing homes. Without the evaluation of physical and economic conditions, healthy and rich old people with lower ages [will] occupy the nursing resources…those without the ability to care for themselves, [and] who are in financial difficulty, are kept outside."

Until the supply of nursing home beds, especially among state-run institutions, rises to a level whereby such discretion is unnecessary, a rationing of beds in favor of those most in need is advisable. Such a policy would accommodate the desire of children — who may not be able to adequately support their parents by themselves — to give parents the care they deserve, and thus carry out their filial responsibilities. How else might the government and the elderly care industry work together to preserve the idea of filial piety?

One way, as discussed in the JUDGING section, is to adopt digital technology. A law requiring that new homes be outfitted with enough digital technology to allow all residents to contact their children on a regular basis would be appropriate, given the rate of digital technology adoption in China.[3] While HNWIs may already be flush with digital technology,[4] such a policy would be all the more relevant and necessary for homes catering to the less wealthy, many of whom may not even own a smartphone, computer, or tablet. The provisions of the law could, for example, require that each room come with a basic smartphone and Internet access. It could also require that a class on how to use applications such as WeChat be made available to those who do not have much experience using such software.

Another way is to encourage the children of residents to participate in structured activities — such as cooking meals, going for walks, or taking a community class — with their parents on a regular basis. This would of course be dependent upon whether the child lives in close geographic proximity to the home where their parents are residing. But, insofar as they do, making it a requirement for admittance into the home would be consistent with the ethic of filial piety, and would give children an opportunity to serve their parents. For children residing far away from their parents, requiring at minimum a weekly WeChat video call — or some such equivalent — would help assuage the fear of parents like Huang that their children are abandoning them.

China is going through a transition, not only sociologically but also in terms of how its historical values and traditions are to be thought of and applied in the modern age. Filial piety is one of many such traditions in transition. How can we be sure that China's elderly receive the care and services they so deserve? As Huang Liangbao said,

"I want to fade away with dignity."

---

[3] 56% of the Chinese population owned smartphones in 2017. That percentage is predicted to rise to 63.3% by 2019, without any signs of stopping.
[4] For example, Gao Lanzhi has two smartphones and an iPad.

14.4 Discussion Questions

1. Is the issue of elderly care a moral issue? Should business take care of elderly care? Why or why not?
2. Do you think traditional notions of filial piety are a barrier to the development of the elderly care industry? Or do you think filial piety, with its reciprocal characteristics, is a powerful framework for building a compassionate elderly care industry? Explain your answer.
3. What is your personal view of nursing homes? Do you agree with Huang Liangbao that they are a form of abandonment? Why or why not?
4. If you were a nursing home developer, how would you design your homes? What would you look to include and provide for your residents? Explain the reasoning behind your ideas.

Bibliography

China Daily (2015). More elderly Chinese choose to live in nursing homes. *China Daily*. Retrieved on December 14, 2017 from http://www.chinadaily.com.cn/china/2015-10/08/content_22130227.htm.

Fan, Y. (2017). Shanghai's elderly elite flock to luxury nursing homes. *Sixth Tone*. Retrieved on December 14, 2017 from http://www.sixthtone.com/news/1001284/shanghais-elderly-elite-flock-to-luxury-nursing-homes.

Griffiths, J. (2014). Why are so many elderly Chinese dumpster diving? *CNBC*. Retrieved on December 14, 2017 from https://www.cnbc.com/2014/07/16/why-are-so-many-elderly-chinese-dumpster-diving.html.

Lu, J. (2015). 中国式养老, 让更多人有尊严的老去 (Chinese-style elderly care: Let more people grow old with dignity!). *Yicai.com*. Retrieved December 14, 2017 from https://www.yicai.com/news/4648122.html.

Statista Research Department (2021). China smartphone user penetration rate 2013–2019 | Statistic. *www.statista.com*. Retrieved March 28, 2021 from https://www.statista.com/statistics/257045/smartphone-user-penetration-in-china/.

Chapter 15

The Growth of Cockroach Farming in China

Mark Pufpaff and Dennis P. McCann

Abstract

The cockroach farming industry in China has grown without much publicity. However, after a building housing a cockroach farm was leveled in the city of Dafeng, Jiangsu province, under the assumption it was vacant, millions of cockroaches escaped out into the open. Authorities had to work quickly to prevent the swarm of roaches from reaching farming and residential areas. This case breaks open the ethical issues involved in cockroach farming and discusses questions of industry transparency.

Keywords: Cockroach farming, regulation, transparency, corporate social responsibility

15.1 Seeing

Wang Fuming is a cockroach farmer. Yes, a *cockroach* farmer. He owns and operates six farming locations in Jinan, Shandong, an eastern Chinese province on the coast of the Yellow Sea, with an estimated cockroach population of over 22 million and counting. Although Wang may be the largest producer in China, if not the world, he is not alone. Many others throughout the country are getting into the business, seeking a share of the burgeoning market.

Cockroach farming exists as a viable trade primarily because of growing domestic demand for the otherwise unwanted critters by pharmaceutical and cosmetics companies. Pharmaceutical companies desire cockroaches for their alleged medicinal properties, ranging from a treatment for tuberculosis to a remedy for hair loss. Cosmetics companies enjoy them as an inexpensive source of protein and for the cellulose-like substance that resides on their wings, protein and cellulose being pervasive ingredients in many personal care products. The particular breed of cockroach that farmers like Wang are raising is *Periplaneta Americana*, or the "American cockroach", understood to be the only one with such redeeming qualities.

However, this emerging industry was effectively unknown in China until August 10, 2016, when a cockroach farm operated by Yang Pengsheng in Dafeng, Jiangsu Province, was accidentally leveled by a demolition crew under the assumption that the building housing the cockroaches was vacant. When the building crumbled, the cockroaches escaped, which were numbering in the millions. Wang worked with the local government to exterminate the roaches before they reached, en masse, nearby farms and residential areas.

At present, there is little to no regulation governing cockroach farming. The government is allegedly allowing the industry to operate, but on the condition that the activity of the farmers does not draw public attention. The farmers themselves intend to keep a low profile regardless, fearing that if neighboring businesses or apartment building owners find out a cockroach farm is operating nearby, they might try to have the farm shut down. However, the incident involving Yang Pengsheng has shed potentially unwanted light onto this industry, thereby raising managerial questions for those farmers already relying on this trade for their livelihoods.

15.2 Judging

Corporate social responsibility (CSR), a growing trend in China, is a concept that seeks to harmonize a firm's legitimate business objectives, such as earning a profit, with its inherent social obligations, for instance, managing its environmental impact. Though the use of the term "corporate" in CSR may seem to imply that it only concerns large, publicly traded corporations, it actually applies across enterprises of all sizes, from start-ups to multinationals. In light of the growing number of entrepreneurs starting cockroach farms, and the seeming reluctance of the Chinese government to give the industry too much public scrutiny, what might a CSR strategist have to say to one of these entrepreneurs just getting started?

Being in China, CSR, originally a conceptual development from the West, particularly the United States (US), might benefit from acculturation. A kind of "CSR with Chinese Characteristics" could integrate with other historically Chinese approaches to business behavior and strategy, for instance, the notion of "Confucian Entrepreneurship." If CSR had to speak to the average businessperson in China, a cockroach farmer in this case, how might its representatives communicate their message, or deliver its meaning? How might it be practical and relevant, instead of, say, lofty or overly abstract?

To start, it might help to put the principles of CSR within a context distinctly Chinese, for instance, the virtues of Confucian moral philosophy, virtues that most Chinese learn about as they grow up and refer to when speaking about moral concerns. How might these virtues animate a CSR strategy for a cockroach farmer in China?

One issue facing cockroach farmers is a lack of regulation governing the activity of the industry. The government being a stakeholder for all businesses, how would the CSR principle of compliance with the law be managed without any clear legal precedent to work from? In the absence of legal obligation, a cockroach farmer is not thereby free from social accountability, but must rely on a more fundamental, moral discernment of how to operate. Confucian reciprocity, enshrined in the formulation "Do not do unto other what you would not want done unto you", is a strong starting point for moral decision-making. It is also relevant for the establishment of just laws, due to its promotion of fair treatment for all. If a farmer like Wang Fuming wanted to know what limits, if any, there should be to his farming activity, but could not rely on existing regulations as his guide, reflecting on the Confucian virtue of reciprocity could bring such limits to light. If he were a government official in charge of policy making, what would he expect in terms of responsibilities from a cockroach farmer? What might be the chief concerns that would inform the regulatory environment for such farmers? Then, how would the answers to these questions impact the operational strategy of his cockroach farm? This kind of reciprocal thinking can be helpful for entrepreneurs like Wang to anticipate compliance obligations, which are commonly based on public interest, and reduce the risk of being out of compliance as the legal environment develops around the industry.

Another issue is the challenge of location. Where should a cockroach farm be located? Are there any locations that would be inappropriate? The escape of millions of cockroaches, which we could argue might not have happened if Yang Pengsheng's operations had been more transparent, is still a legitimate concern regardless of the degree of transparency, due to the proximity of Yang's farming operation to traditional farms and residential neighborhoods. A core CSR principle is the involvement of all stakeholders in a business's strategy, such as its employees, suppliers, customers, and local community. To take account of their needs and accommodate their legitimate interests in a firm's decision-making process is to express the Confucian virtue of benevolence. A benevolent leader understands that businesses do not exist in a vacuum, are social by necessity, and thereby have to take moral responsibility for the impacts they create. They also understand that businesses are only as strong as the people that support them, namely, their stakeholders, and that by operating in a way that respects the stakeholders' legitimate interests, they are in turn creating a business model that is integrated and sustainable. Cockroach farming requires such stakeholder engagement because operating in secret, void of transparency, and in fear of public reproach, may complicate or even compromise the decision-making of a farm's management. It could also lead to more unintended accidents like that experienced by Yang Pengsheng, who not only temporarily lost his livelihood but also endangered his community, raised the concerns of local authorities, and drew unwanted attention to an industry that, for many, may take some time getting used to.

15.3 Acting

Cockroach farming, due to its increasing profitability and ease of implementation, is only set to grow in China. While the growth of this industry is good and has the potential of providing a comfortable livelihood for farmers across China, it is not without its moral challenges. Being proactive in identifying these challenges, such as those mentioned above, and seeking solutions to them is therefore important. What kind of solutions can you think of?

Would farmers working with the government on appropriate regulations be smart? What advantages might such cooperation bring to the farmer or farmers who involve themselves in this process? Unregulated or improperly regulated industries are inevitable in an innovative business environment. Regulators by necessity must always react to, rather than anticipate, the emergence of new industries. But, a lack of adequate regulation is not an opportunity for unbridled exploitation, as if the only way to succeed in business was by finding and taking advantage of lags in the development of industry regulation. Developing regulatory environments is therefore not an opportunity for exploitation, but an opportunity for collaboration. Business leaders and government regulators need not always be engaged in a game of cops and robbers. They can and should coexist harmoniously. This is why legal compliance is a core principle of CSR strategy.

Do you think that cockroach farmers, instead of playing hide and seek with their stakeholders, particularly their local communities, should embrace a business model that values transparency? Are their fears over the potentially negative reactions of their communities legitimate? Is there really no way to operate that would assuage the possible concerns from local businesses and residents? The real trouble with the escape of Yang Pengsheng's cockroaches, for example, is not necessarily that it happened — accidents are, as they say, a part of life — but that no one knew it *could* happen in the first place. It was an unwelcome surprise, something businesses should never hold the blame for, and something transparent practices seek to avoid. Are we to believe that operating secretly, rather than transparently, even if the nature of the work is distasteful at first, is better for business?

15.4 Discussion Questions

1. What do you think about cockroach farms? How would you feel if one was operating near your home or workplace?
2. How would you advise a cockroach farmer to operate his or her business? What are the opportunities? What are the challenges?
3. Do you think CSR is relevant in China? How would you approach the topic of social responsibility with cockroach farmers like Yang Fuming or Yang Pengsheng?
4. If you are skeptical about the need for transparency in cockroach farming, what would you say about other businesses? Should firms

that manage hazardous waste materials, or other toxic substances, be required to disclose their activities to their stakeholders, especially including members of the communities in which they operate? Why or why not?

Bibliography

Ma, Y. (2013). 农户大棚被拆 百万只蟑螂逃走 (Farmers' greenhouses were demolished and millions of cockroaches escaped). *China Daily News*. Retrieved on August 29, 2016 from https://sjb.qlwb.com.cn/qlwb/content/20120817/ ArticelC09002FM.htm.

Xiao, C. (2014). Cockroaches by the million give Chinese farmer a healthy profit. The National. Retrieved on August 29, 2016 from https://www.thenational.ae/world/cockroaches-by-the-million-give-chinese-farmer-a-healthy-profit1.314861.

Zhao, W. (2012). 养殖场蟑螂外逃扰村民生活 蟑螂养殖成监管空白 (Cockroaches escape from farms and disturb villagers' lives). *www.news.sohu.com*. Retrieved on January 1, 2021 from http://news.sohu.com/20120817/n350861637.shtml.

https://doi.org/10.1142/9789811233654_0016

Chapter 16

How Proya Cosmetics is Leveraging the Power of CSR: For Women, From Women

Mark Pufpaff and Dennis P. McCann

Abstract

Corporate social responsibility (CSR) is a concept with varying interpretations. However, almost always, it involves socially oriented partnerships between corporations and non-profit organizations. This case details a partnership between China's Proya Cosmetics and UN Women. It aims to address the multifaceted issues facing women in China today through fundraising, advocacy, and events. It also discusses what CSR is and whether Proya Cosmetics is embodying its aims.

Keywords: Proya cosmetics, UN women, CSR, gender pay gap, domestic violence, employment discrimination

16.1 Seeing

Gender inequality is a mounting problem in China. From the gender pay gap to employment discrimination to domestic violence, women are struggling to claim the rights they know they have. Let us break down a few of the primary issues, to form the basis for this case study.

16.1.1 *Gender Pay Gap*

In China, according to the World Economic Forum's Global Gender Gap Report 2015, women earned 65% of what men earned for similar work. That means that if a qualified male payroll accountant earned RMB 10,000/month, an equally qualified female payroll accountant would earn, for no other reason than that she is a female, RMB 6,500/month. You would not be in rare company to think that that is not only unfair but unjust, immoral, and should be illegal.

It is important to note, however, that determinations of the gender pay gap percentages in China, as in countries throughout the world, depend on a wide variety of variables which vary across the institutions conducting the research. A good example of how the percentages can differ, depending on the parameters of the research methodology, is from a research report published in March, 2016 by Glassdoor, a job and recruiting website in the United States (US), on the gender pay gap in the US:

> "In the U.S., men earn on average 24.1 percent higher base pay than women in Glassdoor salaries. That amounts to women earning about 76 cents per dollar earned by men. However, once we compare workers with similar age, education and years of experience, that gap shrinks to 19.2 percent. Going further, when we compare workers with the same job title, employer and location, the U.S. gender pay gap is about 5.4 percent."

In China, the gender pay gap percentages also vary, some estimates ranging as high at 54% with others ranging as low as 17%. However, on average there clearly remains a deep disparity in wages earned between Chinese men and women.

16.1.2 *Employment Discrimination*

In 2016, a recent female university graduate named Xiaoyu was denied a local household registration permit (*hukou*, 户口) for full-time work at a research institution in Beijing. The institution had a policy to grant only one *hukou* each year. Instead of Xiaoyu, who had interned at the institute for three months, they granted the *hukou* to a male intern who had only worked at the institute for 18 days. Not only had Xiaoyu passed a rigorous interview process but she also excelled in her work during her internship, having represented the institute on work trips to different areas of the Chinese mainland. Though she acknowledged there may have been other equally if not more qualified candidates, she was disappointed to find out from one of the hiring officials at the institute that her actual qualifications were not taken into consideration. Upon inquiry as to why she did not get the post, she was told the following:

> "We are not discriminating against women; it's just that we need a male employee."

This is not an isolated case. Women throughout China are struggling to be equally considered for jobs they are, on paper, qualified for. It was not a long time ago that "Male Only" and "Male Preferred" conditions were ubiquitous on job postings, and it is still prevalent for women to be automatically disqualified from a job simply for having the intention to get pregnant within a two- or three-year period. Though progress can be claimed, discrimination remains, and without significant legal recourse.

16.1.3 *Domestic Violence*

The Chinese government put into effect their first law prohibiting domestic violence on March 1, 2016. This is great news, but the question lingers as to why it was not done sooner. Official government estimates put cases of domestic abuse, ones where the wife is verbally or physically assaulted by her husband, at one in four women. Unofficial estimates contend that the real number is much higher. Until this law, there was little in the way of legal justice that victims of domestic abuse could claim. Domestic abuse was considered a private (family) matter and outside the jurisdiction of public concern.

Since women had no representation in court, the abuse was enabled to continue unabated, which also prohibited the abusers from being held accountable. However, horrific stories of murders, beatings, and sexual servitude are becoming more and more well known. For example, the murder of 24-year-old Li Hongxia at the hands of her husband, Zhang Yazhou, who strangled her to death in the hospital she was at because of the beatings he had given her earlier. Before her death, she had begun to make known the abuse she was enduring, only to be told by her friends and family that she should not get a divorce and should try to work it out with her husband, all to save "face", the face of her family and the reputation of the small rural village in which she lived.

But, it is changing, if ever so slowly. Women are beginning to vocalize their abuse and people, both in China and around the world, are listening and taking action.

16.2 Judging

Though there are many actors in the fight for women's rights in China, this case study will focus on the role of Proya Cosmetics Co. Ltd. (Proya), with particular attention paid to the function of corporate social responsibility (CSR) in their corporate strategy. A working definition of CSR is the alignment between a corporation's business objectives and their social interests. The case for CSR attempts to establish a real relationship between investments in social causes and increases in corporate profits.

Proya is one of China's largest premium cosmetics companies, with six brands operating under the Proya name and over 1,000 individual products. The company's mission statement is "Beautiful and Better Life" and their products are branded as "Natural and Healthy Skin Care." However, they not only make quality products and benefit from sophisticated and integrated marketing strategies but they also have a heart for social issues and have built a robust CSR strategy to leverage that interest.

In 2013, Proya became the strategic partner of UN Women (United Nations Entity for Gender Equality and the Empowerment of Women). Why? To promote women's rights, which is certainly a worthy cause. But, why would they do that *from a business perspective*? In short, because it is good for the bottom line.

16.2.1 *Why Might Promoting Gender Equality be Good for Proya's Bottom Line?*

It cannot be reiterated enough that CSR is, or at least must be, *strategic*, that is, something that will, or should, advance a given company's business objectives. With this in mind, we have to assume that Proya is partnering with UN Women because somewhere, somehow, they think the partnership will result in the sale of more cosmetics. To anticipate what you might be thinking, this does not mean that their partnership is simply public posturing or that their intentions are insincere. It means that they are not making mutually exclusive their responsibilities to their investors and their service to the common good.

Proya sells cosmetics. Their target market is, generally speaking, women, and particularly the underserved women in China's tier-three and tier-four cities. It is not mere coincidence, therefore, that they are directing their social investments into a partnership that focuses on raising the standards of living and working for women in these cities. If you were a female consumer of cosmetics in, say, Anshan, a tier-four city in Liaoning Province, and knew of Proya's commitment to gender equality and investment in programs that support the employment of women in cities like your own, how would that make you feel? Would you not be the least bit interested in supporting the Proya brand because of this? Proya wants you to say yes. But, they do not only want you to say yes to buying their products; more importantly, they want you to say yes to their mission to serve the needs of underprivileged and discriminated women. The strategic component is that in supporting their mission, you are simultaneously supporting their business. That is the ideal of CSR programming and messaging. That is why promoting gender equality might be good for Proya's bottom line.

16.2.2 *Can CSR Become a Competitive Advantage for Proya?*

It was not long ago that "business ethics" was considered an oxymoron, nothing more than a contradiction in terms. "Leave your ethics at home; we are doing business" is one way to sum up this perspective. "Nice guys finish last" is another. But, why leave your ethics at home? Is there really no value in an ethical business strategy? Is there really no redeeming quality in being a virtuous business professional?

The effectiveness of CSR hinges on its capacity for creating competitive advantage, that is, for discovering new business opportunities hitherto undiscovered or unrealized by anyone else in the marketplace. If a firm figured out how to manufacture a widget for USD 5 less than their competitor, it might be said that they hold a competitive advantage based on price. If another firm boasts the highest quality product, their competitive advantage would be based on quality. But, what if a corporation makes the claim that their competitive advantage is based on their service to the common good, or their being good in general? It might sound odd at first, but that is exactly the strategic claim of CSR initiatives.

When Proya partnered with UN Women, they dedicated themselves to the cause of women's rights in China. Given the history of discrimination against women, not only in China but around the world, few would defend this as a worthless effort. The effects of partnerships like this can be substantial, both internal and external to the firm: internal in the sense that they create solidarity among employees; external in the sense that they attract the interest of competitors and the consumer in the marketplace in general.

If you were L'Oréal, a competitor of Proya, how would you react to their partnership with UN Women and their strategic decision to serve the needs of women? What if they were being praised in the news and experiencing strong word-of-mouth marketing on social media? Would you not feel as if you were missing out on an opportunity, one that they are enjoying the benefits of? Or, what if you were a current female consumer of L'Oréal products? Would you not be tempted to change your loyalty to a firm explicitly and convincingly dedicated to a cause that affects you personally? If nothing else, would you not begin to expect the same from L'Oréal?

These kinds of questions are the ones CSR strategists want companies and consumers to ask themselves. Proya is attempting to pioneer a new way of thinking, a fresh, innovative approach to business growth, one where service and goodness become the standard for winning consumer loyalty and the benchmark for industry performance. They want to move away from the worn-out dichotomy between business and ethics, and transform a so-called contradiction in terms into a necessity in practice.

16.3　Acting

So far, we have argued that CSR strategies can be good for the bottom line and can create competitive advantages. But, there is a difference between the potential for CSR strategy to accomplish these objectives and actually implementing it and managing it so that it does. Let us document some of what Proya has done since the beginning of its partnership with UN Women in 2013. Then, you can decide for yourself.

16.3.1　*September, 2013*

Proya held a press conference in Guangzhou to commence the partnership and donated RMB 3 million to the China Gender Fund.

16.3.2 *November, 2013*

Proya held a fundraising event that included thousands of domestic Chinese and international companies. All funds raised were donated to the Women Employment Equality Project being conducted by UN Women.

16.3.3 *November, 2013*

Proya convened the UN Women Global Forum, where Proya CEO Fang Yuyou led a group of 10 multinational CEOs in signing the Statement of Support for the Women's Empowerment Principles (WEPs), developed by UN Women. Proya was the first private sector company in China to sign the document.

16.3.4 *March, 2014*

The 6th annual WEP meeting was at the UN headquarters in New York City. Fang Yuyou, Proya's CEO, was the only Chinese entrepreneur who was invited and he received positive feedback on Proya's CSR strategies.

16.3.5 *October, 2014*

Proya sponsored "The Enlightenment of Female Leadership and Workplace Diversity to Commercial Development" seminar, jointly hosted by UN Women and CKGSB, and aimed at increasing awareness about the need to protect women's rights.

16.3.6 *November, 2015*

Proya led a group of 38 companies from China in signing the WEPs in New York City, USA.

16.3.7 *December, 2015*

Proya, alongside students from the Beijing Royal School and the Beijing Normal University, supported UN Women's global campaign to end discrimination against women living in China with HIV. Their support was shown through various activities, which were documented and distributed throughout social media channels.

16.3.8 *May, 2016*

Proya, along with other sponsors, helped organize a UN Women advocacy event titled, "International HeForShe Roller Derby Invitational." The event was to promote UN Women's "HeForShe" campaign and to support China's recently passed law aimed at protecting the victims of domestic violence.

16.4 Discussion Questions

1. Why is gender equality an issue in China?
2. From a business perspective, do you think it was smart for Proya to partner with UN Women?
3. What do you think of the achievements of the Proya/UN Women partnership, listed in the ACTING section of the case? Do you think it is impactful? Could/should they do more? If you were Proya, what kind of work would you want to carry out with UN Women?
4. Do you think the partnership with UN Women will be good for Proya's bottom line and/or result in a competitive advantage?
5. Do you think that CSR partnerships are sincere in their social intentions? Is it truly possible to do good (be profitable) by being good (socially active)?
6. If you were a competitor of Proya in China, what would your response be to their partnership with UN Women? Would you care? Why or why not?
7. If you were a consumer of cosmetics in China and knew about Proya's partnership with UN Women, how would you feel? Would that influence your buying behavior or cause any shift in your brand loyalty? Why or why not?

Bibliography

Sohu.com (2016). 河南25岁孕妇在医院做流产期间遭丈夫掐死 (A 25-year-old pregnant woman in Henan was strangled by her husband during an abortion in the hospital). *Eastday.com*. Retrieved on August 12, 2016 from http://xyq.163.com/2015/zt/juqing/25ji.html.

Women and Nature International (2016). PROYA partnered with UN Women in 2013 and became the first Chinese company to sign on to the WEPs. *News from Women and Nature International*. Retrieved on August 12, 2016 from https://www.womenandnature.org/newsroom/.

World Economic Forum (2015). The Global Gender Gap Report 2015. *World Economic Forum*. Retrieved on August 12, 2016 from http://www3.weforum.org/docs/GGGR2015/cover.pdf.

Xinhua News Agency (2016). 我们只是需要男生" 女性求职遭遇"隐性歧视" 维权难 (We just need boys! — Women face "hidden discrimination" in seeking employment). *News.ifeng.com*. Retrieved on August 12, 2016 from https://hope.huanqiu.com/article/9CaKrnJVBOP.

Chapter 17

Are Tobacco Companies Charitable Institutions?

Dennis P. McCann and Mark Pufpaff

Abstract

The new Charity Law of the People's Republic of China prohibits using charitable donations to publicize tobacco products but does not define the penalties for violating this provision. There are other products carrying health and safety risks for Chinese people, such as alcohol, but the law does not forbid these. The case discusses this law and the question of whether this ban should be extended to the manufacturers of other ostensibly harmful products.

Keywords: Charity, corporate responsibility, environment, society, philanthropy

17.1 Seeing

One of the more intriguing aspects of the new Charity Law of the People's Republic of China is that it specifically prohibits "using charitable donations to publicize tobacco products in violation of the law." It then goes on to generalize the prohibition: no one shall "use charitable donations or any other methods to publicize products and matters prohibited from being publicized by laws" (Article 41, in the Chapter on "Charitable

Donations"). The Charity Law does not specify any other products, and does not define the penalties for violating this provision.

The largest of the tobacco companies, China Tobacco, is a State-Owned Enterprise (SOE) manufacturing over 900 brands, whose revenues contribute significantly to funding the government through taxes. Despite the widespread warnings about the health risks, over 60% of Chinese men are estimated to be smokers, with 1.2 million deaths attributed to smoking annually. While China ratified the World Health Organization's Framework Convention on Tobacco Control in 2005, the tobacco companies have found ways to get around the restrictions on advertising their products through ostensibly philanthropic activities. One particularly controversial initiative is insidiously named "Hope", a project in which tobacco companies have provided financial support to at least 100 rural primary schools in China. Under the banner of "Hope", Chinese children have been encouraged to take up smoking, as if it were a normal part of an adult lifestyle. Those who inserted Article 41 in the new Charity Law clearly felt the need to prevent such harmful activities.

17.2 Judging

But, is it wrong for the government to use the Charity Law to restrict the access of tobacco companies to their potential customers? There are other products that also carry various degrees of risk to the health and safety of Chinese people. What about alcoholic beverages? What about choppers, knives, and other household utensils that often become weapons of choice in resolving domestic disturbances? Should those who manufacture them also be prevented from organizing or contributing to philanthropic activities? Why single out tobacco for specific mention in the new Charity Law?

17.3 Acting

When the *Beijing Review* in 2015 asked the question, "Should Tobacco Companies Be Prevented from Donating?", the responses were mixed. One observer called for "zero tolerance for donations", leaving "no room for advertising." Another noted that since "the aim of tobacco companies…is to showcase their social responsibility, promote themselves, and grab a larger market share", they should be banned. On the contrary, someone else thought that tobacco companies should find other legal ways to contribute to the common good. For instance, instead of funding philanthropic activities, they could pay higher taxes, enabling the government to do more for the people. Another asked whether all charitable donations should be subject to the same standard to ensure that their donations are "clean". Only one respondent felt that allowing tobacco companies to donate to charities should be encouraged, in light of the benefits from their contributions.

17.4 Discussion Questions

1. What do you think should be done? Should the ban on donations be enforced against tobacco companies? If so, how so; if not, why not?
2. Should the ban be extended to the manufacturers of other ostensibly harmful products?
3. Should the government allow donations from tobacco companies, but find other more effective ways of discouraging the consumption their products?

Bibliography

Daily Economic News (2011). 中国以烟草品牌命名希望小学超过百所 (More than 100 Hope Primary Schools are named after tobacco brands in China). *Sohu.com*. Retrieved on June 1, 2016 from http://news.sohu.com/20110107/n278720545.shtml/feed/atom/.

Ifeng.com (2007). 千亿烟草业高利税 中国每年120万人死于吸烟 (100 Billion Tobacco Industry High Profits and Taxes — 1.2 million people die from smoking every year in China). *News.ifeng.com*. Retrieved on June 1, 2016 from http://news.ifeng.com/c/7fYWxpoeHga.

The China NGO Project (2016). Charity Law of the People's Republic of China. Retrieved on June 1, 2016 from https://www.chinafile.com/ngo/laws-regulations/charity-law-of-peoples-republic-of-china.

Chapter 18

The "Green Collecting" Movement

Mark Pufpaff and Dennis P. McCann

Abstract

"Green Collecting" is a movement in favor of art pieces that use sustainably sourced materials. In China, the movement has put a lot of attention on the use of ivory — derived from the tusks of elephants — in the creation of various kinds of collectibles. As awareness has grown about the unsustainability of using ivory in art, TRAFFIC, a wildlife trade monitoring network, and WWTX, a Chinese-based trading platform for collectibles, have collaborated to hedge against the further exploitation of elephants for their ivory. This case outlines their partnership and how corporate social responsibility animates their mission.

Keywords: "Green Collecting", corporate social responsibility, ivory, collectibles, sustainability

18.1 Seeing

Corporate social responsibility (CSR) could loosely be defined as the alignment between a company's social or environmental interests and their strategic objectives. This alignment is important because CSR is something other than corporate philanthropy, which is oftentimes independent of a company's strategic objectives. When alignments of this kind are achieved, it can set an industry standard or begin a precedent that is truly transformative. This case will detail the CSR strategy of China's largest online antique and collectibles company, named Wen Wan Tian Xia (WWTX), and why their partnership with an organization named TRAFFIC, a wildlife trade monitoring network, could be considered a benchmark for future companies to model.

18.1.1 *What is "Green Collecting"?*

Green collecting represents a commitment by collectors of art to source items from artists who use sustainably sourced materials in their work. Examples of sustainable materials would include wood, stone, porcelain, ceramics, amber, and nuts. It is simultaneously a commitment against the use of animal-based materials, specifically African elephant tusk (ivory), which are unsustainable on both legal and humanitarian grounds.

18.1.2 *Why does "Green Collecting" Matter in China?*

Historically, China has been in the ivory carving and trading business for thousands of years. Ivory is widely considered to be a cultural heritage product and a prize for collectors and connoisseurs of art. However, in 1989, CITIES (Convention on International Trade in Endangered Species of Wild Fauna and Flora) imposed an international trade ban on ivory, due to the reckless poaching of elephants, particularly in Africa, during the 1970s and 80s. Though this ban had initial effects in reducing demand and production worldwide, and in stabilizing wild elephant populations, it was not able to curb the acquisition and sale of ivory completely.

In 2008, however, CITIES approved the controversial one-off sale of over 102 metric tons of government stockpiled ivory from South Africa, Botswana, Namibia, and Zimbabwe to China and Japan, 62 tons going to China. The reason behind the sale was to combat a recent rise in illegal elephant poaching in Africa and revive a centuries-old handicraft. In hindsight, it had the opposite effect. Since then, demand for ivory products in China has skyrocketed, causing a rampant increase in illegal elephant poaching in Africa and what some are calling an "extinction crisis."

The government has recently issued a ban on the importation of raw ivory, ivory carvings, and ivory hunting trophies, effective until 2020. However, it still allows the resale of ivory products bought before 1989, when the CITIES international trade ban was enacted, and will continue to sell the stockpile of ivory bought with the approval of CITIES in 2005 to anyone in China with proper certification. Though the government is taking action, many feel that only an outright ban on the importation, exportation, and resale of ivory and ivory products will save the dwindling elephant populations in Africa, currently being illegally poached by the tens of thousands each year, resulting in elephant mortality far exceeding their birth rate.

The emergence of "Green Collecting", therefore, is timely. The commotion concerning the use of and demand for ivory and other protected animal products, such as rhinoceros horn, does not necessarily mean that China's rich history of art marking and collecting is somehow intrinsically disordered. To the contrary, it is a distinct and beautiful part of Chinese culture. The "Green Collecting" movement understands and affirms this, and has no intention of reducing demand for antiques and collectibles per se. Its aim is to refocus consumer attention away from the material and toward the craftsmanship. For example, Jin Zihe, an artist in Beijing, reported at 7th China Art Handicrafts Expo in Beijing in December, 2015, that his studio implemented a policy of rejecting wildlife products as carving material. In his own words,

> "It's a new era for carving art. Craftsmanship is the key value of art; the material is just a carrier. There are many options to present art; taking a risk to break the law [and use materials such as ivory] is not necessary. If the craftsmanship itself is a treasure, no matter whether it is carved out of wood or stone, it should always be valuable!"

At the event, Jin, and his studio, was one of the thirty well-known businesses in Beijing to commit to the "Green Collecting" value system.

18.2 Judging

18.2.1 *Who is WWTX?*

WWTX is a volunteer-run online platform for people to exchange information on antiques and trade products. Started in 2005, it has grown into China's largest online trading platform for collectibles, having grossed well over RMB 1 billion in annual sales since 2010.

18.2.2 *Who is TRAFFIC?*

TRAFFIC is a wildlife trade monitoring network, established in 1976, to ensure biodiversity conservation and sustainable development in the trade of wild animals and plants. They specialize in the following:

> "Investigating and analyzing wildlife trade trends, patterns, impacts and drivers to provide the leading knowledge base on trade in wild animals and plants;
>
> Informing, supporting and encouraging action by governments, individually and through inter-governmental cooperation to adopt, implement and enforce effective policies and laws;
>
> Providing information, encouragement and advice to the private sector on effective approaches to ensure that sourcing of wildlife uses sustainability standards and best practice;
>
> Developing insight into consumer attitudes and purchasing motivation and guiding the design of effective communication interventions aimed to dissuade purchasing of illicit wildlife goods."

In China, they have worked with major ecommerce companies to forge agreements prohibiting the sale of ivory on their platforms. For example, on October 14, 2016, in Hangzhou, China, TRAFFIC signed a strategic memorandum of understanding (MoU) with Alibaba Group as a sign of their collective commitment against illegal animal trading practices.

18.2.3 *Why did WWTX Partner with TRAFFIC?*

In 2010, WWTX was labeled "the largest wild animal product trading center in Asia", particularly for the sale of ivory, both legal and illegal in origin. Even though the company was not explicitly promoting the sale of ivory and, by extension, the illegal poaching of elephants in Africa, they were seen in that light because their trading and information website did not specifically exclude those involved in such activities. The negative public image resulting from this omission needed to be set aside. The company therefore changed its strategic objectives by aligning them with a social interest everyone in the firm could support. In other words, they adopted a CSR strategy. Internally, WWTX began its strategic transformation by committing itself to a policy in which the trading and exchange of information regarding ivory and ivory-based products would be prohibited on its website. Externally, it began to cooperate with organizations such as TRAFFIC and government agencies that were making inquiries as to what it knew about the ivory that had exchanged hands through its platform.

Soon after, WWTX partnered with TRAFFIC to promote what would later be called "Green Collecting." However, in the beginning, it took the form of growing public awareness by dialoguing with its consumers and stakeholders about the dangers of sourcing, carving, and selling animal-based products and producing regular reports on the beauty and integrity of carvings made out of sustainable materials, such as wood, stone, amber, porcelain, ceramics, crystal, and even large tree nuts. The dialogue and outreach apparently has shown positive returns. Chi Wei, CEO of WWTX, said in an interview with the *Global Times* in June, 2016, that he has noticed a dramatic decrease in the conversation about ivory both on the website and in his personal circles. Further, a brief tour of their website (www.wwtx.cn) also confirms this alleged progress.

The partnership with TRAFFIC was the logical next step in advancing WWTX's new CSR strategy. It allowed WWTX to remain competitive by promoting solutions to a social problem related to their business. They united social responsibility with their corporate objectives.

18.2.4 *What has the Partnership Accomplished so far?*

The "Green Collecting" campaign was launched by TRAFFIC at an event hosted by WWTX, the 6th China Art Handicrafts Expo. At the event, WWTX and TRAFFIC both expressed their intentions in the development of the campaign. Zhang Sheng, Behavior Change Program Manager for TRAFFIC, stated the following:

> "The survival of many endangered wild species has been seriously threatened by growing consumer demand for and illegal trade in their products. TRAFFIC encourages green collecting, whereby collectors pay close attention to the cultural value of artwork, but avoid those items that would cause reputational damage."

Gou Sen, Operations Manager for WWTX, expressed similar commitments:

> "As the leading collectibles company, we are aware of our corporate social responsibility and actively support 'green collecting', which we hope to see widely adopted by industry insiders and collectors, alongside a refusal to consume illegal wildlife products."

Also at the event were 22 craftsmen who performed a live demonstration, carving art pieces out of porcelain, crystal, and amber. Examples are provided below:

The demonstration was led by Liu Xiangqian, owner of the Small Furnace Art Studio, who was awarded the "Public Welfare and Social Responsibility Advocate Pioneer" certificate for his efforts in promoting "Green Collecting" practices. In response, Liu said the following:

> "China has a rich heritage of collecting, and today's collectors should focus on the intrinsic artistic and cultural value of the artwork and not the material from which it is derived. Ivory is only one medium — artistic carving and its place in traditional culture can be inherited in many ways. We would rather leave wildlife to co-exist with our descendants than leave our descendants with evidence of wildlife killing."

WWTX and TRAFFIC have also collaborated on other events, such as the "Green and Elegant Collecting" event, which was held in Beijing in January, 2015, and the 7th China Art Handicrafts Expo, held in Beijing in December, 2015.

18.3 Acting

CSR is a business concept that is sometimes viewed with skepticism. There have been high profile business scandals from companies claiming a serious and committed CSR strategy. Volkswagen AG is one such example, where its public image as a socially conscious and environmentally responsible corporation was contradicted by the fact that it cheated on emissions tests and sold millions of cars under the false promise of being "green."

But, does the existence of such scandals undermine the strategic and ethical viability of CSR strategy as such? The example of WWTX and TRAFFIC would suggest not. It suggests what business ethics has always affirmed, namely, that there are ways of conducting business that are both financially profitable for the company and morally good for all its stakeholders.

It is yet to be seen how the partnership will continue to develop over time, or what strategic directions the leadership team at WWTX have in mind as they advance their CSR objectives, but it is encouraging to know that CSR can and should be a central concern for companies in China, especially ones operating in an industry under scrutiny. Perhaps WWTX has set a precedent for China's other firms to live up to.

18.4 Discussion Questions

1.   What is "Green Collecting"? Do you think it is a viable solution to the problems inherent in the ivory trade?
2.   Do you think WWTX's decision to partner with TRAFFIC was a good one? Why or why not?
3.   Do you think the concept of CSR has strategic value? Why or why not?
4.   If WWTX continued to allow or promote the sale of ivory on its website, do you think they would be acting unethically? Why or why not?
5.   Do you think the poaching of animals like elephants for nothing other than their tusks is unethical? Why or why not?
6.   If you were Chi Wei, how would you direct WWTX going forward? What would be your strategy for advancing its current commitment to "Green Collecting"?
7.   If you were running TRAFFIC's China office, what would be your next steps in your partnership with WWTX? How would you foresee the partnership developing over time?
8.   The Chinese government has recently issued a ban on ivory imports. How valuable do you think the "Green Collecting" campaign is, in light of that ban?

9. Do you think the "Green Collecting" campaign, or ones like it, will eventually change consumer behavior for good? Or, is something like a total ban, implemented and enforced rigorously by the government, the only way to stop the inflow of ivory into China?

Bibliography

Convention on International Trade in Endangered Species of Wild Fauna and Flora (2008). Ivory auctions raise 15 million USD for elephant conservation. *Press release — Convention on International Trade in Endangered Species of Wild Fauna and Flora (CITES)*. Retrieved on August 1, 2016 from https://cites.org/eng/news/pr/2008/081107_ivory.shtml.

The Wildlife Trade Monitoring Network (2015a). 绿色收藏, 文化传承和生态保护的平衡 (Green collection, cultural heritage and ecological protection balance). *Traffic — The Wildlife Trade Monitoring Network*. Retrieved on August 1, 2016 from http://www.trafficchina.org/node/221.

The Wildlife Trade Monitoring Network (2015b). 30 位文玩商家承诺"拒绝非法野生物贸易 (30 merchants promised to "reject illegal wildlife trade). *Traffic — The Wildlife Trade Monitoring Network*. Retrieved on August 1, 2016 from http://www.trafficchina.org/node/246.

Part 5

Food and Product Safety

Chapter 19

Nongfu Spring Bottled Water Standard Dispute

What is the Role of Public Relations in Crisis Management?

Helen Xu, Dennis P. McCann, and Mark Pufpaff

Abstract

Product quality scandals are a major issue in China. Not only do they erode public trust and consumer confidence but they also can destroy the image of a company, even an entire industry. Enter the role of public relations as it relates to crisis management. This case will detail a dispute involving Nongfu Spring Company (Nongfu) and the *Beijing Times*.

Keywords: Food safety, public relationship management, trust, Internet, social media

19.1 Seeing

On April 10, 2013, Nongfu, one of China's largest bottled water manufacturers and the top selling brand, found themselves faced with a public relations crisis after the *Beijing Times*, a Beijing-based newspaper and part of the People's Daily Group, accused them of failing to meet national standards for drinking water. The article reads as follows:

> "On its bottles' label, Nongfu Spring quotes DB33/383-2005, namely the Zhejiang (provincial) standard, but not the updated national standard, despite its products being available nationwide."
>
> "The local standard, namely DB33/383-2005, was issued by Zhejiang Bureau of Quality and Technical Supervision, at the same time, Nongfu Spring is the only enterprise representative who participated in its promulgation."
>
> "For example, the permitted amount of toxic arsenic shall be less than 0.01 mg/liter according to the national standard GB5749, while the allowed maximum amount is 0.5 mg/liter that claimed in the Zhejiang standard and followed by Nongfu Spring."

Media problems for Nongfu had actually started several weeks prior in March 2013, when the *21st Century Business Herald* — at the time a prominent business newspaper which has since been shut down after investigations revealed the newspaper extorted hundreds of millions of RMB (tens of millions of USD) from Chinese companies — published a report accusing Nongfu of selling bottles of water with unknown substances inside. It also reported that the water in question was sourced from Danjiangkou, a city in China's northwestern Hubei Province, which was allegedly covered in household garbage. Nongfu, responding through its Weibo account, said that its products met national standards for drinking water and that any trash in the area was not affecting the water sources.

Then, just weeks later, Nongfu was again confronted with substandard product quality accusations. After the initial posting on April 10, the *Beijing Times* posted another article on April 12 quoting Ma Jiaya, the Secretary General of the Committee of Healthy Drinking Water:

> "The water standard of Nongfu Spring is even worse than tap water. Any bottled water meets the bottom line of the national mandatory standard GB5749; if not it would be in violation of national food safety law."

From April 10 until May 2, the *Beijing Times* followed up with nearly 70 articles — a suspiciously high number — criticizing Nongfu for their apparent lapse in quality control. As a result of this bombardment of negative press, an online survey on the *East Money* website portal, published shortly after the dispute began, claimed the following:

> "86.9% of respondents said they would not buy Nongfu Spring water any more [and] 69% of respondents said they believe the criteria for Nongfu Spring's bottled water is lower than ones for tap water."

Though public opinion, based on the above survey, was not in Nongfu's favor at the beginning of the dispute, the company responded to the *Beijing Times* attacks immediately and uncompromisingly. They defended their products as safe for consumption and in accord with all standards for drinking water in China. They even went so far as to accuse one of their competitors, *C'estbon* Food & Beverage (Shenzhen) Co. Ltd. (C'estbon), a subsidiarity of China Resources Holding Company, of colluding with the newspaper and instigating the reports, a practice not without precedent in China. In support of their claims to innocence, they noted that the Health Bureau of Zhejiang Province, where Nongfu is headquartered, conducted product quality tests in response to the *Beijing Times* allegation. *China Daily* reported the following:

> "Nongfu Spring, a major domestic bottled-water producer that faced questions about its water quality, has received support from the Zhejiang provincial government, which released test results that confirmed the company's products are safe to drink, *People's Daily* reported on May 9.
> According to the Health Bureau of Zhejiang province, random checks on four batches of Nongfu Spring bottled water from its six production sites on April 11 by the quality watchdog of Hangzhou, capital of Zhejiang province, showed they all passed tests and met national mandatory standards for bottled drinking water. The announcement from the East China province, where Nongfu Spring Co is based, clarifies the recent dispute on water standards adopted by one of China's biggest bottled-water producers."

The *China Daily* report continued, highlighting the words of Zhong Shanshan, Chairman of Nongfu, and Zhou Xiaolin, a quality control official in Zhejiang province:

> "Zhong Shanshan, chairman of Nongfu Spring, said in a news conference on May 6 in Beijing that the company has adopted both national

standards [GB5749] and DB 33/383, the standard set by Zhejiang, and that the national standards are mandatory for all bottled-water enterprises, which is why they are not labeled on its products. He also said that wherever there is a discrepancy between the standards, the company has followed the stricter one.

Zhou Xiaolin, an official with Zhejiang's top quality authority, confirmed to *People's Daily* that all bottled-water producers in the province have been following mandatory national standards. Zhou said the quality authorities in Zhejiang tested 19 batches of bottled water from Nongfu Spring from 2009 to 2012, and all met both local and national standards."

Furthermore, during a press conference on May 6, Zhong Shanshan continued to defend Nongfu of any wrongdoing. He claimed that the nearly 70 articles from the *Beijing Times* attacking Nongfu were indicative, if not conclusive proof, of the fact that they were operating from a serious bias rather than, say, an honest call for justice. He was also supported at the hearing by a Zhejiang media outlet, which drew public attention to the potential unreliability of the *Beijing Times* source of information about Nongfu. Lastly, Zhong announced that Nongfu, even though there was no convincing evidence of any product quality violations, would temporarily suspend selling a core product, its barreled water, in Beijing, in accordance with a mandate from the government, for the safety of its consumers there.

One day later, on May 7, providing another rebuttal argument against any alleged negligence in their water bottling operations, a 2005 article from the *People's Daily* was discovered linking the *Beijing Times* to a mineral water company named De Yi Yuan. The fact that the newspaper owned a bottled water company, many felt, was significant and revealed a profit motive behind the slandering of Nongfu's name. Public opinion about the water company, which was originally negative, in response to this apparent conflict of interest at the *Beijing Times*, changed to a more positive tone, according to a research report by *Danwei*, a service of the *Financial Times*, that tracked the progression of social media responses associated with the dispute between Nongfu and the *Beijing Times*.

Nonetheless, the *Beijing Times* remained obstinate in their allegations against Nongfu, eventually goading the company to file a lawsuit against the newspaper for defamation. Nongfu stated the following confidently, in accordance with the content of the *China Daily* article above:

> "The (bottled-water) product quality is always higher than any existing national drinking water standard, and is far superior to the tap water standard... Anyone who accuses our quality standard of being lower than tap water has severely damaged our reputation."

The amount of damages claimed was RMB 200 million (USD 32.8 million), according to Lu Nengneng, a reporter for the *Shanghai Daily* who was following the court case. The *Beijing Times* in turn countersued, demanding a "public apology and [a] token compensation of 1 yuan."

19.2 Judging

How are we to interpret this scandal in terms of Nongfu's public relations and crisis management strategy? On the one hand, we have the *Beijing Times* claiming that Nongfu has failed to meet national standards for drinking water. If the newspaper's intentions went no farther than attempting to uphold the rule of law through judicious reporting, then we should consider them worthy of their trade. But, there is evidence they were operating from ulterior motives, given the fact that they provided no evidence, outside of their own testimony, of any wrongdoing by Nongfu. On the other hand, we have Nongfu who, perhaps not surprisingly, fervently defended the integrity of its products. And, they remained consistent in their defense. They cited successful water quality tests from the Health Bureau of Zhejiang Province; they stated that the publishing behavior of the *Beijing Times* was questionable at best; they pointed to the possibility of their competitor *C'estbon* colluding with the newspaper to account for the suspicious amount of negative press; and they were even supported by the fact that the *Beijing Times* apparently owned a water bottling company themselves, revealing a potential conflict of interest rooted in deep-seated financial incentives.

Are we to then take this as a case of successful public relations management? Did Nongfu do all it could have done? Could they have done more? Did they make any mistakes?

19.2.1 *Responding to The Core Problem — Public Interest*

Nongfu spent a lot of energy in back and forth media battles with the *Beijing Times*. Though a prompt and proper response to the newspaper's allegations was necessary to establish their claim of innocence, could they have been more proactive in addressing the needs of consumers, namely, the question of whether Nongfu's water was safe to drink? According to sentiments from netizens and the Chinese blogosphere, many felt they might have spent too much time in a war of words. For example, Zhang Bin, a loyal customer of Nongfu, commented the following:

> "I'm running short on patience of this mouth water battle, I just want to know the conclusion whether I can drink Nongfu Spring water or not."

Zhang was not alone. Another example was Shen Zhiyong, CEO of Xinqiao Public Relations Company, who identified the main issue for Nongfu as

> "whether or not there [was] any impact on public health after [people] drank [Nongfu Spring] water. In other words, [did] the water [that] complied with Zhejiang local standard [also] meet the regulation requirements of national standard?"

These sentiments seem to suggest that Nongfu was sluggish in addressing this core problem. But, what about the water quality tests from the Zhejiang authorities, which concluded that Nongfu's water was, in fact, safe to drink? Should they not have immediately absolved Nongfu of any further criticism?

Perhaps the reason was because, even though the tests were initiated on April 11, the results were not published by the *People's Daily* until May 9. That is a lapse of almost a full month, a month where any number of people might have consumed Nongfu products. Imagine if the result of the tests were negative instead of positive? Where Zhang and Shen's responses to the scandal seem to be legitimate, therefore, is regarding the apparent delay in Nongfu's provision of concrete evidence. In other words, they wanted more than just verbal assertions of Nongfu's innocence. And, the faster the better.

19.2.2 *Communicating a Defense — What to Say and How to Say It*

Everyone respects the man or woman who is cool, calm, and collected under pressure. Likewise, in crisis management, no matter the complexity of the circumstances, leaders are expected to keep calm and take control of the situation, cutting out the noise and focusing on the essentials. In other words, they should avoid acting impulsively, or emotionally, without consideration of the potential consequences.

With this in mind, how are we to understand Nongfu's accusation of *C'estbon* Food & Beverage as conspiring with the *Beijing Times*? Here is what they wrote on their official Weibo account, shortly after the April 10 article:

"We have reason to believe that recent reports targeting Nongfu Spring were created by *C'estbon* Food & Beverage (Shenzhen) Co., Ltd."

Was that the right or wrong thing for Nongfu to say? Was that the right or wrong point to focus on? Though it was not inherently irresponsible to publicly blame *C'estbon* — especially if they did, in fact, collude with the *Beijing Times* — Nongfu did not bring forward any evidence to back up their accusation. This raises questions about the effectiveness of such an approach to managing the crisis, as well as the reliability of the statement in the first place. If Nongfu cannot prove *C'estbon* colluded, what good does it do to accuse them? Would that only serve to further complicate the situation? Might that not end up causing more problems than it was intended to solve?

19.2.3 *Consequences — How Public Relations Affects the Bottom Line*

Recall that Nongfu was required by the government to cease selling their barreled water in Beijing, a key market for them, resulting in an economic blow. In 2012, this product generated RMB 4.2 million (USD 639,299) in annual sales, and was estimated to increase to RMB 5 million (USD 751,546) in 2013. Though the embargo on barreled water sales in Beijing was mandated in light of the scandal, Nongfu responded vigorously in a statement by Zhong. He said that if given a choice between accepting a "loss to our customers" and being forced to "lower our head to media attacks... we believe justice and dignity are more important than money." In other words, Zhong is attempting to rise above the dispute by accepting a financial loss as the unfortunate consequence of the behavior of the *Beijing Times*. Sometimes, as they say, "the only way to win is to quit", or in Nongfu's case, detach from the media war and temporarily leave the Beijing market.

Regardless, Nongfu suffered a financial hit. Even though they still ranked within the top 500, number 465, in the 2015 China Top 500 Private Enterprises report, their year over year growth rate has significantly slowed since the scandal. For example, from 2011 to 2012, their annual growth rate was over 30%, whereas after the scandal in 2013, it declined to single digits. We are left to speculate on the exact reasons for the growth rate drop, but their public relations strategy, in response to the scandal, might have played a significant role in how they were viewed by the public thereafter.

19.3 Acting

Public relations is a delicate business, especially during crises. Effective strategies are invaluable, but they need not be inauthentic. Public relations, in other words, is not just an efficient lie or a clever cover-up. It is a method of public communication and management that understands the needs of those involved, prioritizes them accordingly, and acts courageously to fulfill them. With this in mind, how might you have managed this crisis if you were Nongfu?

If you were Nongfu Spring Co...
A good starting point would be to adopt a strict policy of honesty and truthfulness. Only responses that can be communicated sincerely and backed up with evidence should be put forth, unlike, for instance, Nongfu's apparently unfounded claim against *C'estbon* Food & Beverage. Even if Nongfu is right to make such a claim, if they cannot support it, what good does it do?

Another important principle is timing, or the "Golden 24 Hours." The first 24 hours is of crucial importance for guiding public opinion and properly positioning a company in response to whatever crisis might be unfolding. For example, the water quality tests from the Health Bureau of the Zhejiang Province were initiated shortly after the dispute began, but the results were not made public until almost a month later. Could Nongfu not have responded in more immediate ways that would have initiated quicker action toward a satisfactory resolution, for instance, the publishing of a video-taped public visit to a water source or processing operation or a public test of their water quality in a major city like Beijing? Anything to show people that Nongfu was not willing to wait too long before presenting concrete evidence as to their innocence.

Particularly important is the effective use of media resources. According to the information available, it seems like Nongfu communicated with the public primarily by way of their official Weibo account, issuing short and sharp retorts against the *Beijing Times* and *C'estbon*. Was that the most effective use of the breadth of media technology available to corporations today? They could have used different media for different communications, for instance, Weibo and WeChat for short, to-the-point updates, newspapers for the publishing of product quality test results, and Youku for videos of their quality control operations and interviews with relevant personnel. Impactful public relations communication is an art that considers everything from tone to length to the kind of media channel used to distribute the messaging toward its intended audiences.

A final consideration would be the inclusion of the government in seeking a solution, and making such collaboration a part of Nongfu's public relations strategy. For example, China has over 5,000 food safety and hygienic control standards, promulgated and enforced by different levels of the government across the country. Pioneering an effort to consolidate and simplify the standards and their enforcement in order to proactively prevent future disputes like this one could yield vast benefits for all involved, especially Nongfu's customers.

19.4 Conclusion

Crises are not necessarily a barrier to business development; in fact, they can advance it, but only if the crisis is managed well. In China, many business leaders fear public relations because it means being under public scrutiny. But, if it is taken seriously, and prepared for in advance, companies like Nongfu and many others might find that crises are not only surmountable but also an opportunity to establish good relationships among stakeholders and society as a whole.

19.5 Discussion Questions

1. What is public relations? Why is it important?
2. Do you think Nongfu reacted responsibly to the accusations from the *Beijing Times*? Why or why not?
3. If you had to write a crisis management policy for Nongfu, what would it say? And why?
4. Granting that the *Beijing Times* did have ulterior motives for defaming Nongfu, what would be the most appropriate response from Nongfu? If you were Zhong Shanshan, how might knowledge of the *Beijing Times'* conflict of interest affect your public relations strategy?
5. What are the responsibilities of investigative journalists in reporting stories in which their parent company may have a financial stake? Should such stories be reported with a disclaimer making transparent the media outlet's conflict of interest? Why or why not?

Bibliography

Lu, N. (2013). Nongfu Spring sues over articles on water quality. *Shanghai Daily*. Retrieved on August 17, 2016 from https://archive.shine.cn/Business/consumer/Nongfu-Spring-sues-over-articles-on-water-quality/shdaily.shtml.

Wang, Q. (2013). 农夫山泉,一次杀敌一千,自损八百的公关 (Nongfu Spring trying to kill a thousand enemies at a time with self-defeating public reponses). *SocialBeta*. Retrieved on August 17, 2016 from https://socialbeta.com/t/nongfu-spring-publicrelation-management-2013.html.

Xinhua (2013). Bottled water scandal highlights food safety challenges. *China Daily*. Retrieved on August 17, 2016 from http://www.chinadaily.com.cn/business/2013-04/13/content_16399136.htm.

Zhao, L. (2013). Nongfu Spring accuses Beijing Times of defamation. *China Daily*. Retrieved on August 17, 2016 from http://usa.chinadaily.com.cn/china/2013-11/05/content_17080627.htm.

Chapter 20

Expired Meat, Anyone?
Shanghai Husi Food Company Ltd.

Mark Pufpaff, Helen Xu, and Dennis P. McCann

Abstract

In 2014, Shanghai Husi Food Company Ltd. (Husi) was found guilty of supplying reprocessed and expired meat to their western fast food clients operating all over China. The company lied about production and expiration dates and provided false guarantees about the storage life of their products. Many Western fast food clients such as McDonalds and Starbucks were affected by the scandal. The case discusses the scandal, whistleblowing, and food safety issues in the People's Republic of China.

Keywords: Food Safety, meat, consumption, production, suppliers

20.1 Seeing

Food safety is a serious issue in China. A survey published by the *China Youth Daily* in March, 2015, revealed that 77% of those Chinese citizens polled stated food safety as their top "Quality of Life" concern. This is significant, to say the least.

In 2014, Shanghai Husi Food Company Ltd. (Husi), a subsidiary of the United States-based OSI Group (OSI), was investigated for and eventually found guilty of supplying reprocessed and expired meat to their western fast food clients operating in China, lying about production and expiration dates, and providing false guarantees about the storage life of their products. Corporations such as McDonalds, Yum! Brands, and Starbucks were among those who were drawn into the limelight of the scandal.

The scandal went public due to undercover journalists working at a local news station named Shanghai Dragon TV, and a whistleblower named Wang Donglai, who was an employee at Shanghai Husi from 2009–2013 and claimed that the firm forced him to forge expiration dates on their meat products. As the practices of Husi began to gain exposure, government regulators launched formal investigations.

In immediate response to these accusations, OSI, at a July 2014 press conference in Shanghai, stated that it would investigate thoroughly its entire operations in China, replace its management team at Husi's Shanghai location, and build a physical quality control center in Shanghai itself. However, in a February 2016 press release protesting the verdict arrived at by the Shanghai Jiading District People's Court, OSI expressed outrage and plans to appeal, claiming that the verdict was unjust and based on distorted facts and indifference to preexisting Chinese laws and precedence.

The fallout of the verdict resulted in 10 arrests with corresponding fines and prison sentences, corporate fines of RMB 1.2 million (USD 182,000) for each of Husi's Shanghai and Hebei branches, and the suspension of operations at the Shanghai location. On the corporate side, the scandal forced OSI to terminate the employment of over 300 Husi factory workers.

The response from Husi's clientele was unsympathetic:

"We have stopped using all food material provided by the company [Shanghai Husi] and some of our restaurants nationwide [China] may halt serving some products." — McDonalds Corporation

"We have launched an investigation into the supplier [Husi] and have a zero-tolerance policy for any supplier's violations of laws and regulations [they subsequently ordered Kentucky Fried Chicken (KFC) and Pizza Hut's China locations to stop sourcing meat from Husi]." —Yum! Brands

However, a public survey, carried out after the scandal became known, revealed that 78% of respondents believed that these corporations had prior knowledge of Husi's product quality problems.

20.2 Judging

Food safety is important because people's health is at risk. As consumers, we want to put our trust in the quality of the food, meat or otherwise, that we are buying. We want to associate food brands with integrity and a commitment to standards of excellence. For something as fundamental as nourishing ourselves, we need to have confidence that those providing for these needs are acting in our best interest. When food safety scandals occur, like the one surrounding Husi, a critical breakdown of trust results. To reiterate what those polled by the *China Youth Daily* emphasized, nothing less than our *quality of life* is at stake. In the Husi food safety scandal, there are two questions this case aims to reflect upon:

20.2.1 *What is the Responsibility of a Manager?*

A Chinese commentator stated that the scandal was the result of poor management, of a deficiency in the oversight of Husi's meat processing operations. This is an important observation because a manager, if nothing else, is responsible for knowing the work ethic of their team and the integrity of the products they are producing. At Husi, whether the management team intentionally ordered their teams to process, package, and sell expired meat or they simply were not aware that this was happening, they are still responsible for the results. In regard to the former, incompetence is never an excuse for allowing unethical behavior.

Likewise, a manager is responsible for acting ethically. In other words, they need to comply with industry standards, national laws, and internal company policies. They also need to respect the rights of their stakeholders, be they employees, customers, suppliers, local communities, or national government. If Husi's management encouraged the relabeling of expiration dates in order to generate revenue from outdated products, they were failing to protect the interests of those invested in their operations.

One might ask, however, what reason there is for a business to respect the rights of their stakeholders? Is there any morally binding reason to do so? What if it comes at the expense of profits or fulfilling quotas? What if it means closing a branch office or firing a team of employees? These are legitimate (and difficult) questions, to be sure.

One answer to these difficulties may lie in the wisdom of Catholic Social Teaching, in particular Pope Benedict's presentation of the relationship between rights and duties in *Caritas in Veritate*, published in 2009. In this encyclical, he states that rights presuppose duties, and that if we are guided by our duties, we will not only respect the real rights of each other in society but put a limit on the rights that one may claim for oneself (for example, profit maximization is not a right). In other words, our moral duties should inform our decision-making, for our duties help determine our rights.

In business, then, it would be a manager's moral duty to respect the rights of their stakeholders. It is likewise their ethical responsibility to uphold company policy, national laws, and industry standards. When Husi compromised the quality of their products by mixing expired and fresh meat, they violated one's right to clean food. When they falsified the expiration dates on their products to generate additional revenue, they violated OSI's company policies. Even though Husi might have gained profits in the short term by neglecting these duties, the difficulties resulting from their action give a good example of what can happen long term. One of the hallmarks of ethical business practice is that it is sustainable.

20.2.2 *What is the Responsibility of an Employee?*

It is important to note that one of the reason's the Husi scandal became public was because of a whistleblower. A whistleblower is an employee who reveals to a relevant authority, internal or external to the company, the existence of suspicious or outright illegal behavior in the operations of their firm.

Is whistleblowing, among other things, the responsibility of an employee? What if it is generally frowned upon in a given culture? Or what if it might jeopardize an employee's job security? How difficult would it be to "blow the whistle" on a friend or colleague whom you admired?

The idea that employees can (or do) have a responsibility beyond the fulfillment of their job descriptions is not very common in business thinking. Most of the focus is on employee performance, innovation, and their ability to fulfill or exceed expectations. To say that part of an employee's responsibility is to report unethical company behavior to relevant authorities seems almost contrary to the interests of a business. Who wants their employees looking out for unethical behavior, anyhow? That would only give a company a poor public image, right? But this is exactly what a company needs and an employee needs to do.

When Wang Donglai reported the alleged business practices of Husi, namely, forcing him to forge expiration dates in order to sell expired product, he was identifying a serious problem, one that needed to be fixed. It is contrary to OSI's interests to have a subsidiary selling expired meat. It is likewise contrary to the interests of Husi's clientele, for instance, McDonalds or KFC, to continue sourcing meat from a substandard supplier. Even though Husi had a right to expect the loyalty of their employees, they forfeited that right when they chose to engage in unethical business practices. Wang acted responsibly in publicly revealing the behavior of Husi. He enabled justice to be served.

There are of course many cases of employees accusing companies of doing things they never actually did. But, the point here is to show how whistleblowing, even if it seems contrary to the demands of employment, can be an important responsibility for an employee.

20.3 Acting

20.3.1 *How did Husi's Clientele Respond?*

Fast food chains such as McDonalds and KFC have long been under scrutiny for the quality of their ingredients. In recent years, due primarily to growing concerns about the health risks involved in eating fast food as a regular part of one's diet, these multinational chains have made efforts to change and adapt to the demands of their consumers. From their branding to their suppliers to their food storage policies, progress has certainly been achieved.

However, much of this progress is still perceived suspiciously, as the public survey mentioned in the "SEEING" section indicates. When food safety scandals emerge that involve fast food chains, those suspicions are confirmed, regardless of whether the chain was directly involved or not. In the case of Husi, McDonalds and KFC were not directly to blame for Husi's negligence, but the fact that they were sourcing meat from them does not contribute well to their public image. They have to go immediately into damage control. As one Chinese netizen exclaimed, after hearing of the scandal,

> "It made me sick... I've eaten so many McNuggets!" — Chinese netizen

It is likely these sentiments are felt among China's many McDonalds regulars. However, these fast food chains still enjoy a strong brand loyalty in China. As one customer stated during a meal at a KFC location in Beijing,

> "Today, you can't find 'clean' food anywhere [in China]. KFC's meat is not safe, but supermarkets may also sell expired meat too. It doesn't matter to me. I'll still choose KFC to grab a bite to eat." — KFC customer in Beijing

Though this customer may be exaggerating in his analysis of the meat industry in China, there is still the necessity for McDonalds, KFC, and the rest of the brands affected by the scandal to respond appropriately. Their decision to stop sourcing meat from Husi was certainly prudent, especially due to the fact that there are so many domestic competitors seeking market share. It was also the right course of action in terms of rebuilding customer trust, repairing damage to their international brand image, and showing that they respond to these kinds of situations seriously and without excuses.

20.3.2 *How did OSI, Husi's Parent Company, Respond?*

The verdict, as described in Section 20.1, was harsh: 10 arrests, corporate fines, the suspension of business, and the termination of employment for over 300 Husi factory workers. OSI received the verdict after 17 months of litigation. It is interesting to note the tone of their official press releases before and after the verdict.

Before the verdict:

> "We have confidence in China's legal system and believe that the judicial authority will come to a fair and reasonable judgment with full respect to the facts and laws." — Press Release, September 30, 2015
>
> "OSI Group will continue to cooperate fully and in good faith with the authorities. We support the government's consistent application of the country's food quality and safety laws." — Press Release, August 29, 2014

After the verdict:

> "After seventeen months of legal proceedings, detainment of Husi employees for as long as seventeen months, a harmful smear campaign

driven by state-owned media, as well as the denial of entry of press and senior OSI leaders to all court proceedings, the court of jurisdiction has reached an unjust verdict. We have made every effort to follow firm instructions to silently cooperate on the advice it would lead to a fair conclusion. However, we can no longer accept injustices against our people and our reputation.

Sensationalized media reports from Dragon TV led to a raid on the Shanghai Husi plant in July 2014. Dragon TV made false and incomplete accusations that ignored facts and Chinese law. After an actual investigation was completed, all authorities involved have recognized that this case has never been about food safety.

The verdict is inconsistent with the facts and evidence that were presented in the court proceedings. Additionally, OSI will consider pursuing a suit against Dragon TV for its role in harming the reputation and business operations of the company through intentional falsification of press reports." — OSI Press Release, February 1, 2016

The difference in tone certainly creates suspicion that an injustice was done in this case. That OSI was seemingly compliant with the requests of the Chinese authorities and transparent about the scandal on their own website is evidence that their discontent is not unfounded.

It is absolutely inexcusable to sell expired meat, falsify expiration dates, and lie about a given product's shelf life. However, if the sentiments from the KFC customer above have any weight, are we not to be suspicious that the Chinese media, and perhaps even the legal system as a whole, might be ignoring the condition of food safety in domestic companies in order to discount the integrity of foreign brands? Is it possible that favoritism is being shown to local competitors at the expense of their international counterparts?

Also in 2014, a similar food safety scandal was revealed at a Walmart location in Shenzhen. Chinese media responded with a flurry of reports discussing the issue and exposing the Walmart brand to public criticism. Investigations were launched, both internal to Walmart and externally from local authorities, only to find that the claims, which ranged from cooking with long expired oil to selling worm-infested rice, were unfounded and inconclusive. Even though the fallout was different from the Husi scandal, one wonders whether the almost exclusive attention put on international competitors by the Chinese media is strategic and intentional.

20.4 Discussion Questions

1. If you were the CEO of OSI Group, how would you respond to the Shanghai Husi Food Company Ltd. scandal? What action would you take? Do you think their reaction to the verdict is justified?

2. If you were the manager of Husi's Shanghai operations, what would your response be to the scandal? What do you think would be your responsibility? Would you be at fault?

3. Why do you think the scandal occurred in the first place? What might cause a company to allow such behavior? What could be done to avoid it in the future?

4. If you were McDonalds or Yum! Brands, how would you respond? Do you think their responses were enough? What else could they do, if anything? What actions would you take to repair their brand image?

5. As a business leader or potential business leader, what do you think are the important lessons to be taken away from this case?

Bibliography

Benestad, B. (2009). Pope Benedict XVI's Caritas in Veritate. *Josephinum Journal of Theology* 16(2).

China Daily (2014a). Husi faced unethical practice claims in 2013. *China Daily*. Retrieved on March 3, 2016 from http://usa.chinadaily.com.cn/business/2014-07/26/content_17930861.htm.

China Daily (2014b). Shanghai vows harsh punishment after food scandal. *China Daily*. Retrieved on March 3, 2016 from http://www.chinadaily.com.cn/china/2014-07/28/content_17934263.htm.

Food Safety News (2014). Chinese Walmart Store Being Investigated for Food Safety Violations. *Food Safety News*. Retrieved March 8, 2016, from http://www.foodsafetynews.com/2014/08/chinese-walmart-store-investigated-for-food-safety-violations/.

Xinhua (2014a). Expired meat firm sacks 340 employees. *Xinhua*. Retrieved March 8, 2016 from http://news.xinhuanet.com/english/china/2014-09/22/c_133663054.htm.

Xinhua (2014b). Meat scandal shakes China's fast food industry. *China.org.cn*. Retrieved on March 3, 2016 from http://www.china.org.cn/china/2014-07/22/content_33026671.htm.

Xinhua (2015). Food safety top concern in China. *China Daily*. Retrieved on March 3, 2016 from http://www.chinadaily.com.cn/business/2015-06/19/content_21050938.htm.

Chapter 21

IKEA's Belated Recall in China
No Excuses on Product Safety Issues, Right?

Helen Xu, Dennis P. McCann, and Mark Pufpaff

Abstract

In 2016, IKEA, the world-renowned Swedish furniture manufacturer, recalled some of its adult and children's chests and dressers in US and Canada. But, despite the fact that IKEA also sold the same more than a million times in China, the products were not recalled there. Even if the company has more than 20 stores in the country, Chinese law did not force a recall. This case discusses the difference between legal and ethical decision-making at IKEA and asks whether ethical decisions are of importance in the People's Republic in China.

Keywords: Product safety, IKEA, consumers, recall, society

21.1 Seeing

IKEA Group, a Swedish manufacturer founded in 1943, is today one of the most successful multinational firms. It sells everything from ready-to-assemble furniture to appliances to home accessories and operates 276 stores in 25 countries, including China (with 37 more stores operating as franchisees in 17 additional countries/territories). Part of IKEA's success has come from its effective localization strategies, customized and implemented in all of its locations outside of Sweden. This case will

177

explore how localization strategies, particularly the one used in China, affect managerial decision-making in the face of a product safety crisis.

On June 28, 2016, the United States Consumer Product Safety Commission (CPSC) announced that IKEA would be making a major recall of its adult and children's chests and dressers in the United States (US) and Canada. The announcement reads as follows:

> "The U.S. Consumer Product Safety Commission (CPSC), in coopera-
> tion with IKEA North America of Conshohocken, Pa., is announcing the
> recall of all chests and dressers that do not comply with the performance
> requirements of the U.S. voluntary industry standard (ASTM
> F2057-14).
>
> The recalled children's chests and dressers are taller than 23.5 inches
> and adult chests and dressers are taller than 29.5 inches. The 29 million
> [US] units [and 6 million Canadian units] of recalled chests and dressers
> include: MALM 3-drawer, 4-drawer, 5-drawer and three 6-drawer mod-
> els and other children's and adult chests and dressers.
>
> The recalled chests and dressers are unstable if they are not properly
> anchored to the wall, posing a serious tip-over and entrapment hazard
> that can result in death or serious injuries to children."

The impetus for the recall occurred after the death of a child who was crushed by an IKEA dresser that fell over. This is not the only fatality associated with this category of IKEA products. Five other children since 1989 have died in a similar fashion.

After the CPSC decided that IKEA was not in compliance with US product performance standards, IKEA proactively began the recall. They not only recalled all available products for sale in US and Canadian stores but they also offered two options to consumers with already purchased units. The CPSC announcement continues:

> "Consumers should immediately stop using any recalled chest and
> dresser that is not properly anchored to the wall and place it into an area
> that children cannot access. Contact IKEA for a choice between two
> options: refund or a free wall-anchoring repair kit.
>
> Consumers are entitled to a full refund for chests and dressers manu-
> factured between January 2002 and June 2016. Consumers with chests
> and dressers manufactured prior to January 2002 will be eligible for a
> partial store credit.

Consumers can order a free wall-anchoring repair kit. Consumers can install the kit themselves or IKEA will provide a one-time, free in-home installation service, upon request. Consumers can reorder the kits throughout the life of their chest and dresser."

Though the response to this recall was generally positive in the US and Canada, showing that IKEA was cooperative with authorities and transparent to the public, regulators and consumers in China in particular were upset. Why?

Despite the fact that IKEA had sold 1.66 million of the same chests and dressers in China since 1999, they did not initiate a recall of these products. The risk was the same. The danger was the same. But, there was no recall. When questioned by the Chinese authorities about this, IKEA stated that they did not intend to recall the products or extend the same offers (refund, partial refund, free wall-anchoring kit) to Chinese consumers because the chests and dressers in question allegedly met China's national performance standards.

After receiving sharp criticism from Chinese authorities and the public, however, IKEA did eventually go through with a recall of its 1.66 million danger-prone chests and dressers sold there since 1999.

21.2 Judging

IKEA has a significant presence in China. As of the end of 2015, it was operating 20 stores throughout the country, generating sales of RMB 10.5 billion (USD 1.58 billion). China is one of IKEA's fastest growing markets and it shows no sign of slowing down its expansion strategy. It is also one of China's most successful multinational firms.

In light of this, how are we to interpret IKEA's decision not to proactively recall the 1.66 million chests and dressers it had sold in China, when it was already in the process of recalling 35 million of the same units from the US and Canada? Let us break down two major issues:

21.2.1 *Was IKEA Using the Law as an Excuse not to Recall in China?*

Judging by the fact that IKEA initiated the recall in the US and Canada because of legal pressure from the US, it shows that they were using the law as the standard for deciding where to recall their products. Since there was no legal pressure coming from China concerning the performance standards of the products and the risks to Chinese consumers, IKEA had no intention of recalling the 1.66 million products sold there. Only when China criticized them for applying a double standard did IKEA act.

The difference between what is legal and what is ethical is of importance here. China has a developing legal system. Though it is strengthening with each passing year, there are still many ways to take advantage of its growing pains. As mentioned in the SEEING section, IKEA enjoys an effective localization strategy, one that has been particularly successful in China. However, localizing operations does not imply that a firm like IKEA can neglect its moral responsibilities merely because there will not be any legal repercussions. Fairness is a universal value. If IKEA's products were found to be dangerous in the US and Canada, they were dangerous in China too. If they were recalled in the US and Canada, should they not have been simultaneously recalled in China as well?

That said, are not the regulators in China equally responsible? Are they not exhibiting a general lack of concern for the safety of their own people by not being proactive and holding companies and their products to higher standards? Product recalls are notoriously few in China, and not for lack of personnel or oversight agencies in the Chinese government. Since such recalls are more often than not country-specific precisely because of differences in standards and laws, are not China's regulators as much at fault as IKEA in terms of protecting consumers from dangerous products?

21.2.2 *Are Product Safety Standards only Concerned with the Laws of a Given Market?*

IKEA has a concern for safety. This has not been their first product recall, nor will it be their last. They report each recall to the public and on average manage these situations efficiently. But, what does a concern for safety exactly mean? Is the safety of a product determined solely by whether it passes local market standards? It would not seem so, due to the fact that, in the case of IKEA at least, the same product is sold in each market, regardless of differing legal standards across countries. In other words, IKEA does not produce a lower-quality product for a country with lower product performance standards. If the product quality is constant across markets, should not the safety standards also be constant? Moreover, should not the response to a product safety crisis, like the one concerning IKEA's adult and children's chests and dressers, be a world-wide response, instead of a country-specific one?

The decision to recall in the US and Canada but not in China calls into question IKEA's judgment when dealing with product recalls that involve the same products sold in different countries.

21.2.3 *What Role did the Chinese Public Play in IKEA's Decision to Begin a Recall in China?*

Lao Zhang, a Chinese netizen, posted the following comment on Weibo after IKEA announced their recall in China:

> "IKEA is finally recalling the killing furniture in China... Is it because no accidents happened in China so far or our life is not valuable?"

Lao was not alone. While the regulatory environment is incomplete in China, public awareness of consumer rights and product safety issues is growing. As a result, the outpouring of anger and resentment toward IKEA's initial response is understandable. In light of the Chinese public's concern, the question remains as to exactly why IKEA quickly reversed itself and ordered the recall in China. If they were on solid legal ground, meaning they were not in violation of any regulations, why then order the recall? One commentary in FORTUNE made this observation:

> "Ikea's regulator in China, the General Administration of Quality Supervision, Inspection and Quarantine of China (AQSIQ), was guarded in its language announcing the Ikea recall, saying yesterday that, "after the meeting with AQSIQ, Ikea China submitted their recall plan."
>
> It appears the regulator was reacting to angry online consumers — just as Ikea was — instead of proactively dealing with a dangerous product."

This may also explain why the product recall was not extended to the European Union, for example, where IKEA was safe in terms of product regulations, but was hit with little in the way of public outcry.

If it is true that IKEA's decision to recall in China was due to public sentiment, it presents an important managerial challenge. How should you, as a manager, handle product recalls in view of their long-term impact on your firm's reputation? Should you rely on the law as protection and justification for not recalling a product, in order to save money? Or should you anticipate potential consumer unrest and dissatisfaction, and perhaps the shifting of brand loyalty, and recall products across all markets without question?

21.3 Acting

It is important to note that IKEA did in fact recall 1.66 million adult and children's chests and dressers from China. They offered free wall-anchoring kits and refunds, the same as what was offered to consumers in the US and Canada. Though there are arguments for IKEA acting irresponsibly and unwisely in this case, it is undeniable that they did exhibit a healthy degree of transparency and honesty. The question is what might they have done to avoid the criticism from China and the resulting public relations mess in the first place?

If you were IKEA...
While IKEA can certainly be acknowledged for admitting to the dangers of their adult and children's chests and dressers, what would be the benefits of having recalled their products in China, and anywhere for that matter, proactively?

First, a proactive recall would be honored by the Chinese government and respected by the Chinese consumer marketplace. This kind of relationship building would maintain a good public image and give them leverage when combatting intellectual property rights (IPR) issues and working with local governments to expand their operations to new cities.

Second, a proactive recall might result in a wake-up call for the Chinese government and regulators. There is a big gap between Chinese product performance standards and those of the US and Canada, the countries who made possible the recall in China. If IKEA were to work with government regulators in China in setting product standards based on their experience in other countries, rather than taking advantage of the current lack thereof, they might set an example worth imitating and give themselves a strong competitive advantage.

21.4 Conclusion

Localization is important for success in foreign markets. But, it is not a means of exploitation in countries with developing legal infrastructures. Product safety is something integral to the growth of companies like IKEA. A lackadaisical or short-sighted approach toward resolving instances requiring product recalls will only advance and deepen the problem. The outrage from the Chinese public should be considered a lesson learned for IKEA. The fact that their product was challenged as unsafe is unfortunate, but the fact that they listened and responded is commendable.

21.5 Discussion Questions

1. The IKEA China case suggests that sometimes being in compliance with the law is not enough to ensure that a company fulfills the first principle of business ethics, "Do No Harm!" When the law is not enough to ensure that all stakeholders are adequately protected, what should be done?
2. If you were the CEO of IKEA China, what would your response to the recall in the US and Canada have been? Would you have pushed for a recall in China too? Why or why not?
3. If you were the spokesperson for IKEA China, how would you have engaged the public? What would your message have been? How would you have communicated it? Was the recall enough to rebuild trust and assuage the anger of the Chinese public?
4. If you were Vice President of Marketing for IKEA, would your messaging change in light of product recalls such as these? How would you balance the fact that product recalls happen with your pledge to product safety?
5. If you had to write a product recall policy for IKEA, what would it say?
6. Conversely, do you think that China's regulators should be held accountable for IKEA not proactively recalling their products in China? Why or why not?
7. What, finally, are the responsibilities of a product safety regulator in the consumer marketplace?

Bibliography

Mo, H. (2016). IKEA denies recall of drawers in China, to announce final decision today. *Ecns.cn*. Retrieved on July 21, 2016 from http://www.ecns.cn/cns-wire/2016/07-11/217682.shtml.

United States Consumer Product Safety Commission (2016). Following an additional child fatality, IKEA recalls 29 million MALM and other models of chests and dressers due to serious tip-over hazard; consumers urged to anchor chests and dressers or return for refund. *United States Consumer Product Safety Commission*. Retrieved on July 21, 2016 from https://www.cpsc.gov/Recalls/2016/following-an-additional-child-fatality-ikea-recalls-29-million-malm-and-other-models-of.

Wang, X. (2016). IKEA recalls drawers deemed dangerous. *China Daily*. Retrieved on July 21, 2016 from http://www.chinadaily.com.cn/china/2016-07/13/content_26068273.htm.

Chapter 22

Combating Toxic Products in China: Concerned Parent Turned Responsible Entrepreneur

Mark Pufpaff and Dennis P. McCann

Abstract

Product safety is a concern in China. From the quality of the material inputs used in production to the degree of compliance by manufacturers to existing safety standards, companies have responsibilities to consumers in the way their products are created. When such responsibilities are skirted or ignored, consumer confidence goes down and the search for alternatives begins. To understand which brands are trustworthy and which are not, Wei Wenfang started a company named DaddyLab, which tests the toxicity of stationery and other products used by children in primary school. This case discusses the concept of responsible entrepreneurship and whether Wei embodies its characteristics.

Keywords: Responsible entrepreneurship, product safety, consumer welfare

22.1 Seeing

Wei Wenfang started DaddyLab in 2015, a Zhejiang-based non-profit turned hybrid quality control company that tests everyday children's products, particularly school supplies, for dangerous levels of toxic chemicals.

The idea for the company came after Wei became concerned about the odor of a brand of textbook plastic wrap he was buying for his three-year-old daughter for primary school. Having worked in various quality control positions throughout his career, his sensitivity to matters of product toxicity was high and he became immediately suspicious of the plastic wrap. He decided to have it tested. The results confirmed his suspicions:

> "Wei…bought all the plastic wrapping paper he could find in Hangzhou and drove 650 kilometers to the National Supervision and Testing Center of Fine Chemicals in Taizhou for analysis. One week later, the results showed that large amounts of phthalate and polycyclic aromatic hydrocarbons (PAHs) were detected among the seven kinds of wrapping paper. Both chemicals have raised health concerns, with a recent study suggesting that long-term exposure to PAHs could lead to decreased immune function, kidney and liver damage, and breathing problems, while phthalates, which act as binding agents in materials and can improve the elasticity of plastics, have been linked to behavioral problems and asthma."

Upon receiving the results, Wei publicized them through WeChat, China's dominant social media application, and eventually influenced his daughter's primary school to stop requiring students to use that brand of plastic wrap. Although Wei was pleased at this outcome, he soon realized the potential magnitude of the problem, namely, that all kinds of school-related products could be harmful to children.

DaddyLab was thus founded to discover toxic items through product testing methods, field requests from worried parents about which chemicals are and are not harmful, and consult the public on which products being sold in China meet international safety standards. Being a concerned parent turned responsible entrepreneur, Wei's motivation for DaddyLab is the health and well-being of his daughter, and all children throughout China and the world. In his own words,

> "If parents knew that their children were being exposed to these risks, they would find it completely unacceptable. Like the old saying goes, I'm thinking of children all over the world as if they were my own."

His company motto, "Love, not profit, is the key to our success," perhaps sums up his intention for DaddyLab best. However, the company aims to be more than just a good intention.

Product testing is an expensive endeavor. It apparently cost Wei RMB 10,000 just to test the plastic wrap his daughter's primary school was requiring her to buy. Now, with a physical lab lined with items for inspection, including pens, pencils, erasers, rulers, rubber stamps, glue, and much more, the sustainability of Wei's business model is an ongoing challenge. However, after investing over RMB 1 million of his own funds to start DaddyLab, Wei now uses a crowdfunding approach to acquire the cash necessary to test a given product.[1] Each product tested by Wei and his team has been funded by parents invested in finding out whether it is safe for their children to use. Since its inception, DaddyLab has been inundated with product inspection requests from parents across China, many of them from middle-class families in tier-one cities like Beijing, Shanghai, Guangzhou, and Shenzhen who are eager to support Wei's work. Wei's crowdfunding model, which he facilitates through WeChat, has enabled him not only to do the work he feels is contributing to a better life for children in China but also to expand his company.

With a current staff of 17 and counting, working across functions such as product testing, information technology, e-commerce, marketing, human resources, and finance, Wei has successfully grown his company while fulfilling his promise — to be a reliable source of product safety information — to those invested in the company. But, to compensate for the burden of sourcing funding for each product inspection, Wei also built a sales department for DaddyLab, which sells products through an online storefront — all imported to date — that the company has approved as safe for use by children; it generated RMB 250,000 in its first month of operations, effectively transitioning DaddyLab from a non-profit organization to a hybrid enterprise, with both fundraising and revenue-generating dimensions. In developing such a storefront, Wei is not only acting as a brand ambassador and retail outlet for companies selling products already

---

[1] Crowdfunding is process by which entrepreneurs of any kind can source funding from the public at large. They can launch crowdfunding campaigns on dedicated, online crowdfunding platforms or create their own homegrown crowdfunding initiatives through social media. Oftentimes, the entrepreneur will promise donors an outcome for their contribution; examples would be musicians promising donors a copy of their album once printed, or authors a copy of their book once published. Crowdfunding is an alternative to traditional fundraising in that it has a grassroots quality, allowing individual citizens, as opposed to foundations or philanthropic organizations, to contribute on a mass scale. Though the amount of each donation is on average small, it is the quantity of contributions that makes crowdfunding a legitimate fundraising technique for entrepreneurs.

in compliance with international product safety standards but also as a de facto accountability mechanism for government regulators to bring non-compliant domestic companies and manufacturers up to standard.

Wei publicizes all his work through WeChat. In its official account, which anyone is free to access and browse, DaddyLab publishes the results of its product tests and provides information on the company. It has a following of at least 120,000.

22.2 Judging

Should we consider Wei a hero, a modern manifestation of that ancient archetype of the *Junzi*, the virtuous man or woman whom Confucius taught was able to rise above mere self-interest and act from a genuine concern for the good of society? Perhaps, given the public's anxiety about product safety issues in China, especially as these relate to their children's health and safety. But, is there not more to Wei's story that simply smoothing over anxious discontent and restless concern?

Wei has tied socially conscious intentions and strategic business practices together in a unique business model, one that shows how business can be a force for good. DaddyLab is attempting to move beyond simply being compliant with Chinese law. Wei and his team are committed to transforming the entire meaning of what it is to be compliant in China, namely, that it is not just government regulators to whom a business has a responsibility, but the entirety of the consumer marketplace, who are now demanding even higher standards than those which are outlined in law. Wei is illustrating how, at least in theory, the public and private sectors can mutually support each other, how bottom-up, grassroots movements can align with top-down policy implementations and work together for the good of society. Although it is unclear whether these kinds of transformations and collaborations will ever become the norm, does not the DaddyLab business model wield the potential to do so?

What started as his own concern, namely, the quality and safety of consumer products for children, has become the concern of parents all across China. The idea that a business can of itself be an empowerment mechanism for widespread service to society is certainly not novel, but it is important. That DaddyLab received such an outpouring of crowd-funding support for its work is indicative of the power of business innovation. Wei found a way to tap into the latent concerns of parents nationwide, by developing a platform that they could act through. Is there any other way to define empowerment?

Wei is also working to evolve what it means to be a consumer in China. DaddyLab's online store, which is committed to selling only products that meet international standards, is sending a clear message to companies that the integrity of their products matters, perhaps even more than their aesthetic appeal, price point, or ease of use. That it generated a revenue of RMB 250,000 in its first month is telling of the need for trust-worthy consumer options in China, and of the desire of consumers to support products they perceive as safe. Perhaps *mei ban fa* (没办法), the Chinese expression for "nothing can be done", is seeing its sunset hour in China's consumer culture.

Lastly, being a non-profit, DaddyLab's crowdfunding activity is historically unprecedented in China, since non-profit crowdfunding is only a recent — as of 2015 — and slowly emerging trend within the Chinese crowdfunding ecosystem. But, Wei has shown that crowdfunding is no less effective for non-profits as it is for for-profit organizations in China, a promising development for the sector and potential light bulb for those would-be social entrepreneurs searching for a viable means for getting their ideas operational. Is not DaddyLab helping to shape a new paradigm in the way non-profits interact with the increasingly widespread Chinese consumer public?

22.3 Acting

Given the potential of DaddyLab's business model and mission, and the initial success Wei and his team have experienced to date, is there any-thing left to worry about? DaddyLab, whether they know it or not, have committed themselves to strict standards of operational excellence. This commitment is perhaps best understood by an examination of the implicit business values DaddyLab has exemplified to date:

1. Financial transparency: DaddyLab has set a precedent of financial transparency, having been open from the start about communicating with the public about their expenses, revenues, and funding. This is an important precedent to uphold going forward, especially in terms maintaining funding for DaddyLab's product testing work. If you have done nothing wrong, you have nothing to hide, right?

2. Honest reporting: Wei has been honest and forthcoming in his product safety reports. He publishes his work on DaddyLab's official WeChat account, which anyone can view and follow. He communicates violations explicitly and does not seem vulnerable to any conflict of interest, for example, submitting to the demands of a company with an interest in targeting and scandalizing the products of a competitor, regardless of whether they were compliant or not. Dishonesty is the surest way to become untrustworthy, and for DaddyLab's industry, trust is everything.

3. Benevolence: In his work, Wei has thus far embodied the Confucian value of benevolence. He shows a deep concern for the health of children in China and has enshrined this concern in his company motto: "Love, not profit, is the key to our success." Working from an impulse of benevolent concern for the well-being of others is crucial for remaining steadfast against temptations toward corruption. Care for others is a mission that can be infinitely shared without diminishing returns.

22.4 Discussion Questions

1. How would you define the term "Responsible Entrepreneurship"?
2. Do you think DaddyLab's business model is smart? Are hybrid organizations like DaddyLab uniting the best of the non-profit and for-profit business strategies?
3. Is there anything morally wrong with making money from doing good for society? Why or why not?
4. If you were advising Wei and his team on a three-year expansion plan for DaddyLab, what would be your strategic recommendations?

Bibliography

Ren, L. (2016). 魏文锋: 愤青老爸的突围 (Wei Wenfeng: The Breakthrough of an Angry Young Dad). *Sina.com.cn*. Retrieved on October 30, 2016 from http://finance.sina.com.cn/meeting/2016-10-25/doc-ifxwztrt0415403.shtml.

Yang, S. (2016). — 位"愤青"老爸的突围 (The Breakthrough of An Angry Young Dad). *Shanghai Observer*. Retrieved on October 30, 2016 from https://www.jfdaily.com/news/detail?id=10886.

Zhang, W. (2016). 老爸"魏文锋: 与"毒书皮" "毒跑道"作战 (Dad Wei Wenfeng: Fighting "Poison Book Cover Up" and "Poison Traces"). *Tencent News*. Retrieved on October 30, 2016 from https://news.qq.com/a/20160914/004630.htm?_k=jnjlaz.

Chapter 23

Food Safety in China

Mark Pufpaff, Helen Xu, and Dennis P. McCann

Abstract

China is a country of over one billion people. All of those people need to eat every day. And, not only eat but eat well. Unfortunately, over the past decade, a series of high-profile food safety scandals have deteriorated the country's confidence in the quality of its food. People are skeptical about everything from meat to lettuce to cooking oil. What can be done? Many, who feel the food industry is too far corrupted, say *"mei ban fa"* (没办法), or "nothing can be done."

However, all hope is not lost. There are entrepreneurs and innovative business leaders who are taking strong action to counter this poor public perception of China's food industry. They see this social problem as a responsible business opportunity and are setting a new precedent in farming practice in China.

Keywords: Food safety, social business, agriculture

23.1 Seeing

In Sydney, Australia, it was reported that over 3,000 Chinese expatriates were buying local infant milk formula and selling it on Chinese ecommerce platforms in 2015, each allegedly earning over USD 100,000 every year. In April 2013, customs police in Hong Kong announced a two-day "anti-smuggling operation" that resulted in the arrest of 10 people and the seizure of almost 220 pounds of baby milk formula illegally transported into the Chinese mainland. Also in 2013, German supermarkets experienced an unprecedented increase in the demand for infant milk formula, driven primarily by Chinese tourists on shopping sprees. Over a half dozen countries in Europe and Asia are experiencing shortages in baby milk formula, due to increasing demand from Chinese travelers. Why the craze over buying baby milk formula from abroad, now appropriately dubbed "white gold"?

In 2004, at least 50 infant deaths throughout China were linked to drinking counterfeit milk formula, which was completely lacking in the nutritional makeup needed for proper growth. In 2008, six babies died and a total of 296,000 babies and toddlers became ill due to drinking milk formula contaminated with melamine, a toxic compound that is illegal for use in food products. In short, Chinese people do not trust domestic milk formula.

The meat industry in China suffers from similar perceptions. In 2012, consumers reported finding pork that glowed blue in the dark. Investigations revealed it was contaminated with phosphorescent bacteria. Although food experts at the Shanghai Health Supervision Department stated that the pork was still safe to eat after properly cooking it, consumers remained skeptical. In 2013, Chinese authorities arrested over 900 people for selling fox, mink, and rat meat marketed as mutton meat in Jiangsu Province and Shanghai. In 2015, over 100,000 tons of smuggled meat, some of it allegedly over 40 years old, was confiscated during a nationwide food safety campaign spanning 14 provinces and regions.

Likewise, for vegetables. In 2011, 12 people were arrested for selling toxic bean sprouts in Shenyang, a city in northeastern China. The sprouts reportedly contained high levels of toxic chemicals, including sodium nitrate and urea, and dangerous antibiotics. The fruit and vegetable industry in general is riddled with criticism regarding the indiscriminate use of synthetic farming chemicals, including pesticides, herbicides, and fungicides.

Although these scandals are all isolated, they are merely manifestations of a common conviction that food safety issues are pervasive throughout China and that the majority of the violations are never reported, to the expense of public health and awareness. Regardless of the frequency of the violations, however, it is clear that there can be no

tolerance, ethically or legally, for such behavior. It is an atrocious violation of human dignity to put a person's health secondary to corporate
profits and nothing short of outrageous that such negligence should be
allowed in an industry that is as necessary as food.

What can be done? It is simple. People are beginning to create their
own solutions. Xue Ling, in an interview with the *China Daily*, says that
growing her own vegetables on her balcony in Beijing "is the only way to
keep [her] food, at least the vegetables, clean and safe." The desire for
ownership over the growing process, Xue continued, is becoming popular
in Beijing; so popular, in fact, that she started her own company selling
equipment for urban farming, and sales are growing quickly. Zhang
Guichun of Beijing and Peng Quigen of Shaoxing, Zhejiang province,
have taken matters further and started their own rooftop farms, growing
everything from medicinal herbs used in Traditional Chinese Medicine to
rice and watermelons.

The aim of these urban farmers is clear: to build trustworthy food
chains. No conception of the common good includes questionable, let
alone downright dangerous, food products. The current sentiment in
China is that centralized industrial and factory farming are entirely
untrustworthy. From the growing of crops and raising of animals to
the processing and distribution of final products, adherence to standards of excellence is rare at best. Even organic farming, which is
growing in popularity and accounts for over 1.6 million hectares of
currently cultivated farmland in China, is viewed with reserve. Many
are cautious to put their faith in the ministerial bodies certifying the
farms. Seeing, in this sense, is believing. If they can go to the farm
and see the operations, consumer confidence in the quality of the
farm's products increases. However, with rumors of fake organic
certification labels being sold on the Internet and used by "organic"
farmers, coupled with the lack of a rigorous approach to regulating
and inspecting so-called organic farms, consumer adoption has been
relatively slow.

The idea that should emerge from this is that China is in the middle
of a serious struggle. Growing consumer unrest has led to political policy
reform, increased government regulation, and long-term commitments to
sustainable agriculture. However, prevailing sentiment is strong and it is
unclear whether government intervention will be enough to rebuild a broken system. More and more, the Chinese people themselves are taking
matters into their own hands.

23.2 Judging

Just how important is the food industry? Do we ever stop to think about how much we depend upon farmers? The amount of trust that is implicit in the exchange of goods between consumers and producers is astounding. We are, in a very real way, entrusting them with our lives. It is true that the majority of people, especially those living in cities, have become increasingly disconnected from the process of growing, raising, harvesting, and slaughtering the plants and animals we eat each day. In our supermarkets, we walk down aisles of seemingly endless food products that have little resemblance to what we would typically envision as produced on a farm. We would not know how they were produced if our lives depended on it. That would not matter, of course, if those producing the products could be trusted in their processes and messaging. But, when trust deteriorates, as we have seen in China, all the attractive packaging and savvy marketing slogans in the world cannot save it. The outrage of consumers in China, in response to the revolving door of recent food scandals, is as righteous as it is necessary. Injustice can only survive in silence.

But, what exactly are people in China so upset about? Could we not say they are just overreacting? Pesticides are not really *that* bad, right? As long as the animals grow, their living conditions do not *really* matter, right? Should not people just calm down?

A basic reason for consumer discontent in China is the lack of alternative options. When corporate scandals occur, consumers should be able to respond by transferring their loyalty to a more reputable brand; the ability to change brands is how consumers hold producers accountable to their promises. However, China's history of food scandals, and the lack of trustworthy alternatives, has had the effect of suffocating people into accepting a "*mei ban fa*" attitude. When there is nowhere to go, it does not much matter which way you turn. In other words, the dependence that consumers have on farmers and the rest of the supply chain is life-giving only when it is based on trust. Where there is no trust, there is no such thing as food safety.

In light of this, is it any wonder that Chinese citizens are starting to grow their own food? Is it any wonder that more inclusive, transparent methods of farming are cropping up throughout the country? Imagine you are a mother raising a family. If you had the capacity to ensure your children ate clean food by growing your own, would you even hesitate in buying a farming kit from someone like Xue Ling? Would you even hesitate in starting a rooftop farm, perhaps in cooperation with your neighbors, to have control over the growing process of your food, thereby ensuring your family is eating healthily?

Another reason people are upset is the absence of transparency. When someone buys *bok choy* at their local grocery store, there is little in the way of information about its origins. In other words, people are relying on a farm they do not know, farmers they have never met, and farming methods they have not had the chance to approve. In the wake of China's food scandals, this lack of transparency has resulted in nothing but skepticism. Consumers are more and more looking for assurances about the sources of their food. In response to this desire, community support agriculture (CSA) has been welcomed with open arms across China. Originally conceptualized and implemented in Japan, CSA is built upon transparency between producer and consumer. Consumers commit to buying food from a producer, or group of producers, for the duration of a given growing season. They typically pay in advance, at the start of a season, and receive predetermined amounts of fresh, seasonal food on a regular, usually weekly, basis. This creates shared risk, where farmers are not in danger of losing their livelihoods if a given harvest is below expectation, and consumers are encouraged to support the farmers to increase the chances of a good yield. Oftentimes, as CSA farms are localized by design, consumers directly participate in the growing and harvesting process. It is also typical that they visit the farm periodically to commune with the farmers, or go there to pick up their weekly portion of vegetables, eggs, or meat. This interaction between buyers and sellers is what builds the community aspect of the CSA farming model. It has also had the effect of enabling Chinese people a glimpse back into their rich agricultural history. In fact, many CSA farms provide education courses, empowering city dwellers to return to their families in the countryside and develop CSA farms of their own. This not only reunites formerly separated families, but restores and enriches the farming culture in China's smaller villages, providing economic growth and fostering solidarity.

Everyone wishes food scandals would not happen. However, once they have, it is comforting to know some people see them as an opportunity to reorient a troubled industry back toward the common good.

23.3 Acting

Shi Yan founded Shared Harvest in Mafang village, Eastern Beijing, in May 2012. She describes the farm as a "public-interested, service-oriented social enterprise… producing local, seasonal and organically-grown veggies and other food products." Based on the CSA model, Shared Harvest strives to build community by connecting urban consumers to rural producers. Being membership-based, the farm welcomes the active involvement of its customers in everything, for instance, planting seeds, nurturing plant growth, and harvesting yields. This model has appealed to the urban populations in downtown Beijing, and the farm is growing in scale and popularity.

Shared Harvest has two farming locations, in the Tongzhou and Shunyi districts of Beijing, and over 500 members. They also cooperate with many schools — supplying them with fresh food and helping them to build and maintain their own gardens — farmers markets, and restaurants — including the prestigious Conrad Beijing. They have received positive news coverage locally and internationally and are frequently visited by those curious to learn how they operate. During one such visit, Steven Schwankert, a representative from *The Beijinger*, a popular media outlet for Beijing locals and expatriates, commented on the freshness and diversity of the vegetables grown at the farm.

Alongside the integrity of their products and their strong reputation is their educational agenda. Creatively named "Earth School", Shared Harvest, like many CSA farms, provides educational opportunities for urban consumers interested in learning how to farm organically and inclusively. Liu Yueming, a biologist trained in Beijing, is one such example. After learning the CSA model, she returned to her hometown to care for the family farm and be closer to her aging grandfather and son, whom she supported from afar in Beijing. She has since grown their farm's member base from 20 to nearly 400, the majority of them from local communities. She also sends surplus produce to farmers markets committed to sourcing food exclusively from CSA farms. Slowly but surely, the CSA model is creating a reliable alternative food market and is rebuilding trust in China's food chain.

Alesca Life, a startup from Beijing, has innovated a new approach to urban farming. Co-founder and CEO, Young Ha, left his job at Dell in search of a creative response to rising food security concerns. The result was unprecedented in China. By modifying old shipping containers with hydroponic growing systems and outfitting them with advanced software controls, he and his team created "smart urban container farms." These containers are nearly completely run on software, designed to require no more than two hours of physical labor each week. Each container has stacks of growing trays, using nutrient solutions and LED lights to grow the greens. The hydroponic approach to farming uses no pesticides or herbicides and claims to be more water and land efficient than traditional methods.

Currently, the company is selling container farms to local Beijing hotels and restaurants keen on serving trustworthy organic greens to their customers. However, Young has indicated that the firm's intention is to begin selling directly to consumers. It would be a variation of the food truck model, where strategically placed containers could serve fresh, organic salads to working professionals for lunch or dinner.

23.4 Conclusion

Both CSA farming and urban farming, among other models, are increasing popular throughout China due to widespread food safety concerns. By remaining local and transparent, these producers have begun to rebuild trust in China's food chains and are providing a legitimate alternative to consumers worried about the integrity of their food.

23.5 Discussion Questions

1. What is factory farming? Do you think it is good for society?
2. What is urban farming? Do you think it is an encouraging trend? Do you feel it can or will have a large impact on city life?
3. Have you ever grown your own food? If yes, what was your experience like? If no, would you ever consider doing so?
4. What would be your approach to farm management? What would be your ideal size for a farm? How would your strategy differ across product lines, for example, fruits, vegetables, dairy, and meat?
5. How would you define farming ethics? If you had to develop a code of ethics for a farm, what would it say?

Bibliography

Qbaobei.com (2013). 奶粉限购 (Milk powder purchase restrictions). *Qbaobei. com*. Retrieved March 28, 2021 from http://www.qbaobei.com/qbaobeiweek/ershijiuqi/Index.html.

Sohu.com (2013). 香港10人违规带奶粉被捕 (10 Hong Kong people arrested for illegal milk powder). *News.Sohu.com*. Retrieved from http://news.sohu.com/20130302/n367563504.shtml.

Sun, Y. (2013). Approach brings people back to farms. *China Daily*. Retrieved from http://usa.chinadaily.com.cn/china/2013-07/14/content_16773035.htm.

Zheng, J. (2012). Balcony farmers are taking root. *China Daily*. Retrieved from http://www.chinadaily.com.cn/life/2012-06/25/content_15521007.htm.

Chapter 24

Organic Farming in China

Mark Pufpaff, Helen Xu, and Dennis P. McCann

Abstract

Organic farming is a development in agricultural practice that emerged in response to concerns about large-scale industrial farming or so-called agribusiness. As we shall see in this case study, the widespread use of synthetic chemicals, growth hormones, and Genetically Modified Organisms (GMOs) in industrial farming has come under heavy criticism in recent years. The industry has been scrutinized from many angles, including consumer health, sustainability, entrepreneurship, and business ethics. However, industrial farmers engaged in these practices have defended themselves and their behavior, presenting their own research aimed at assuaging anxiety about the risks associated with eating food produced under these conditions.

Nonetheless, the organic farming movement is international and gaining momentum, with much of the progress being pioneered through agricultural entrepreneurs. This case study will compare the organic farming movement in China and the United States (US) and provide examples of industry entrepreneurs.

Keywords: Food safety, agriculture, environment, organic

24.1 Introduction

24.1.1 *What is Organic Farming?*

Organic farming is a farming method that produces organic food products. To be organic, plants or livestock must be grown or raised according to particular standards. These standards apply from "farm to table", that is, from the sourcing of seed or feed to the processing or packaging of final products.

In the production of vegetables or fruits, for example, an organic farm would be prohibited from using synthetic fertilizers and pesticides, sourcing seeds treated with fungicides, applying growth hormones, or using GMOs. Raising livestock would require that the animals have a "natural" lifestyle, meaning they have exposure to fresh air, direct sunlight, and space to exercise. Their feed would also have to be organic, without the use of pesticides, herbicides, or fungicides, and not enhanced with GMOs.

Organic farmers also innovate methods for maintaining high-quality soil, the prerequisite for high-quality crops. Strategies such as crop rotation can prevent soil-borne plant diseases and weed growth. Contour plowing can protect soil from erosion and companion planting can mitigate crop damage from insects.

The logic of organic farming aims to understand the relationships within nature. For instance, biological pest control is a natural alternative to using pesticides. Likewise, natural fertilizers such as compost, manure, and bone meal are alternatives to using sewage sludge or biosolids. Organic farming, therefore, seeks to create and maintain cycles of production that are not dependent on synthetic interventions.

24.2 Seeing

24.2.1 *Organic Farming in China*

Understanding the emergence of organic farming in China is tantamount to recognizing the negative impact China's history of food safety scandals has had on consumer confidence. In a 2014 survey conducted by the Beijing-based research company, Horizon Research and Horizonkey, 80% of the over 3,000 participants indicated that they were upset about food safety in China. Asked about which part of the supply chain they found most untrustworthy, 58% of the respondents stated "Production and Processing", while 25% stated "Planting and Breeding." Concerns over other supply segments, for instance, "Wholesale and Retail", were negligible in comparison.

As these statistics reveal, trust is a major issue in China's food sector. As Yu Chung-cheng, an organic vegetable farmer outside Beijing, said, "Scandals have destroyed people's trust in vegetable dealers." However, he sees organic farming and its proliferation as a way to rebuild trust, as openness and transparency are hallmarks of the movement. For instance, organic farms surrounding Beijing and Shanghai are all open to the public, where visitors can freely walk around, observe the operations, and even converse with the workers themselves.

Countering scandals and changing consumer perceptions is a slow and arduous process, especially in China. The fact that the majority of distrust there concerns the "Production and Processing" and "Planting and Breeding" supply chain segments is telling. For organic farmers in China, how can distrust be avoided or overcome in these areas? When customers ask, as many have according to Yu, "Are your organic vegetables real or not?", what is there to say?

Mahota Farm, a 43-acre organic farm outside Shanghai, is certified by the Organic Food Development Center (OFDC). The OFDC has the strictest requirements and is the most well-known and respected of all China's organic certification bodies according to Tom Chen, Senior Manager of Agriculture at Mahota. It is also the only certification body in China to be accredited by the International Federation of Organic Agriculture Movements (IFOAM), a non-profit organization that works with international institutions, such as the United Nations, and governments to promote organic food. The choice to become certified by the OFDC was strategic. Even though Mahota underwent a two-year conversion period, preparing their plots and processes to accommodate OFDC's organic standards for operation, they felt it was worth it. Consumer trust is paramount. Being able to label their products as certified organic by the OFDC brings them one step closer to overcoming widespread customer skepticism.

The regulatory environment for properly labeling organic food products is developing. At the ministry level, the Certification and Accreditation Administration (CNCA) oversees and enforces organic food laws. The China National Accreditation Service (CNAS), an affiliate of the CNCA, is in charge of accrediting certification bodies such as the

OFDC, who in turn certify organic farms like Mahota. Each level in the accreditation and certification process is held accountable by the one above it, the top level (CNCA) being held accountable by public sentiment, as expressed in research surveys such as the one described above. A solid structure of accountability is important, especially if the organic movement in China is meant to reconcile the vast gap between buyer expectations and product quality.

However, problems certainly exist. In 2011, there were reports that fake organic food labels could be purchased on Alibaba's ecommerce retailer Taobao for next to nothing. Even though the organic market is growing, problems like these need to be addressed in real time to build confidence in the movement. The CNCA responded by creating ostensibly irreproducible organic food labels, fit with the Chinese organic food emblem, the certification body logo, and a unique 17-digit code by which produce can be tracked back to the production location, producer, and certifier.

Food safety is the heart of the organic movement in China. Fred Gale, a USDA economist and China agricultural expert, stated, "In other countries it's [the organic food movement] mainly an environmental movement, whereas in China it's mainly motivated by food safety fears and wanting to avoid pesticide residues." Zhou Zejiang, President of IFOAM Asia agrees: "People are still worrying about food safety. In this case, they see that there is a special product [organic food] prohibiting the application of chemicals and GMOs and they think this their salvation."

24.2.2 *Organic Farming in the United States*

Until the 1920s, all agriculture was organic, in the sense of using natural means to treat soil and control insect damage. The modern organic movement, therefore, is more of a renaissance than a revolution. In the US, behind the arguments against industrial farming is a sincere desire to realign farming practices with the self-sufficient processes of nature itself. Wendell Barry, a US environmental activist, stated that

> "An organic farm, properly speaking, is not one that uses certain methods and substances and avoids others; it is a farm whose structure is formed in imitation of the structure of a natural system that has the integrity, the independence and the benign dependence of an organism."
> — Wendell Barry, "The Gift of Good Land"

In 1939, a Swiss chemist named Paul Hermann Müller developed dichlorodiphenyltrichloroethane (DDT), a highly efficient insecticide. After observing its effectiveness in combating insect-based diseases such as malaria and yellow fever, it was quickly adopted for use in agriculture. DDT is recognized as the origin of chemical-intensive farming methods and the reason for the subsequent decline in organic approaches to agriculture.

In the US, from the mid-20th century onward, industrial farming exploded and the use of synthetic chemicals, let alone growth hormones, GMOs, and biosolids, has become ubiquitous. Food products derived from industrial farming operations now dominate the consumer marketplace.

The modern organic farming movement in the US developed against this backdrop. Unlike China, where the organic food industry developed primarily in response to consumer fears about food safety, in the US and in Europe, it developed progressively, resisting the use of synthetic agricultural inputs *in principle*. Organic farming began as an agricultural concept in the 1930s, was organized as a movement by the 1960s, and emerged as a full-blown industry in the 1990s. There are several reasons why the movement has had this particular trajectory.

First, in 1962, Rachel Carson, a US marine biologist and conservationist, published a book titled *Silent Spring*. In it, she criticized the use of synthetic pesticides and highlighted their real and potential environmental effects. Her book raised public awareness in the US about the issue and ushered in a sense of environmental concern that has only grown in intensity.

Second, a series of food scandals attributed to the use of chemical inputs has progressively eroded public trust in the safety of such methods and garnered momentum for the marketization of organic produce. For example, in 1989, the US Environmental Protection Agency (EPA) banned a chemical ripening agent known as daminozide, or Alar. It was originally used to regulate the growth of fruit, particularly apples, but after research publicly revealed it as a possible human carcinogen, it was prohibited for use in agriculture of any kind.

Third, the global trend toward environmental sustainability and responsibility in general has naturally included the agricultural industry. In the US, the emergence and proliferation of organic urban farming, farming cooperatives, and farmers markets has developed into a formidable alternative to industrial farming products while supporting the localization of organic agriculture. A good example is the Central Co-Op in Seattle, Washington. They support local organic, non-GMO farmers and hold a strong commitment to promoting sustainable agriculture as a whole.

With the emergence of organic farming as an industry, especially in terms of its contrast to conventional farming, the United States Department of Agriculture (USDA) developed an organic seal. Even so, the organic movement has mixed feelings about this certification. Some say its requirements are not stringent enough. Others that its reporting requirements and financial costs are restrictive.

Regarding the latter, Goldfinch Gardens, a small organic farm in North Carolina, is one of many who have forgone getting USDA certified. Benjamin McCann and Cedar Johnson, co-owners of Goldfinch, stated their concerns:

> "There are many reasons not to certify a small farm like ours. The record keeping requirements are burdensome. The annual fees are prohibitive. The National Organic Program (NOP) seems to best represent large organic farms and the food industry rather than small family farms marketing locally. It doesn't offer any marketing advantage when our relationship to our customers is personal." — Goldfinch Gardens Website, "Blog" Subsection

Unlike China, certification is not seen as a necessary prerequisite to operating successfully in the US. The fact that Goldfinch has operated for years without a certification is testament to the spirit of the movement, namely, that is it motivated by principle. Also indicative of the movement is its emphasis on personal relationships. The farmers themselves know their clients and anyone can visit their farm to learn about its operation. Many, including Goldfinch, offer apprenticeships and educational opportunities to those interested in learning about organic farming. The same cannot be said of industrial farms.

However, certifications do provide a safety net of accountability for a farmer's customers. McCann continued,

> "I have been uneasy with the total lack of accountability that our choice gives our customers and the farming community. As the local food movement has grown, the number of small organic farms that have forgone certification has grown. Very few Asheville area direct market organic farms are Certified Organic. How is a customer to know how

their food is grown or what practices the farmer uses? You are always welcome to visit the farm and ask us any questions, but that takes time and you need to know what to look for. We appreciate the trust that has been shown, and we have always striven to live up to it, but we shouldn't be setting our own standards." — Goldfinch Gardens, "Blog" Subsection

Goldfinch has since applied to become Certified Naturally Grown (CNG). McCann finds the CNG more appropriate for small farms due to its certification model, "which relies on peer inspections, transparency, and direct relationships." Paired with its relevance for smaller farming operations is its adherence to "robust organic practices." As stated in the CNG website,

"...CNG is tailored for direct-market farmers producing food for their local communities. CNG enables them to get credit for their practices while offering accountability to their customers." — CNG Website

Again, in contrast with China, where the different certifications are ordered hierarchically according to prestige, the different US certifications each serve a particular purpose, depending on the type and size of a given organic farm. In the case of Goldfinch Gardens, this distinction is to their advantage.

24.3 Judging

The old story about the tortoise and the hare is relevant for exploring the relationship between organic and conventional farming.

The tortoise is symbolic of organic farming. Throughout the early to mid-20th century, organic farming, like the tortoise, has been eclipsed, and some may say bullied, by the dawn and widespread adoption of conventional agriculture. This eventually led to a "challenge" by organic farmers, implying that they were ready to stand by their methods and defend their relevance in meeting the needs of contemporary society. Like the hare, conventional farmers shrugged off any notion of a serious threat to their market dominance. Also, like the hare, they began to lose their way as the 20th century drew to a close, only to find that the tortoise was slowly but surely gaining ground on them, without any signs of stopping.

The steady growth of the organic industry, and the parallel increase in demand for organic products, has brought into question the necessity of conventional farming approaches. Real dialogue and serious research about how organic farming can accommodate global demand while promoting sustainable agriculture and contributing to economic development has led to ever-greater public awareness and begun to reorient the trajectory of the food industry. For instance, the emergence of branding techniques centered around terms such as "all natural", "free range", "cage free", "no preservatives", and "locally sourced" are all offshoots, in varying degrees, of the organic farming movement.

The hare is symbolic of conventional farming. The industry can be characterized as having pursued synthetic solutions to natural problems. Like the hare, it made quick progress. But, over time, unlike the tortoise, conventional farmers found themselves in a predicament. In the United States, for example, commodity crops and petroleum production are heavily subsidized. The subsidization of petroleum in particular has become controversial, due to its being a finite fossil fuel. As conventional farming uses heavy inputs of pesticides, herbicides, and fungicides, all of which are derived from petroleum, it has become unclear whether the industry could sustain itself without government subsidies, since the cost of those inputs would be much higher without it.

This is just one example of the many difficult questions that conventional farmers face. However, the ideal of the organic farming movement is not without its critics. Rampant urbanization and a growing lack of knowledge about farming in general among citizens worldwide, some say, have created a potential ceiling to the development of the industry. If organic farming is to replace conventional farming, how many more organic farmers would there need to be in the world? Is it realistic to expect such an increase in agricultural careers? Another question is whether organic farming can scale without losing its essential principles? Can the industry, like the tortoise, win the race while remaining consistent in its approach?

The story of the tortoise and the hare provides a black and white contrast. However, some say both sides will eventually need to compromise and cooperate to address the evolving needs of the global populace. Perhaps the hare could help the tortoise by giving it a push. Likewise, the tortoise might help the hare by providing it a leash.

24.4 Acting

Below are a few examples of entrepreneurs in China and the US who are contributing to the global organic movement.

24.4.1 *Entrepreneurs in China*

Gou Yingda, the 20-year-old CEO of Ye Nong You Pin Technology, an Internet-based company linking organic farmers with urban consumers in Xinbin county, Liaoning province. His business model is unique, renting the usage rights of farmland to consumers for an annual fee. Gou hires and pays farmers to work each plot, monitors the cultivation of the crops to ensure the yields are organic and high quality, and facilitates the delivery of the produce to the consumer after the harvest. In Gou's words,

> "Our company aims to optimize farm inputs, as farmers know the market prospects before they grow crops, improving efficiency and reducing pollution."
>
> "We pledge to provide organic food with no pesticide residue, and aim to become China's top agricultural brand." — Gou Yingda, *China Daily* Interview, April 2015

Gou's intention to integrate information technology with organic agricultural techniques is admirable, as he is aiming to leverage the best of contemporary technological developments with the tried and true principles that have governed organic agricultural practice in China for thousands of years.

In terms of social responsibility, Gou stated that he created his online agribusiness platform because he feels he can help poor farmers increase their income while providing a trustworthy way for urban consumers to eat healthier food.

Verdura is a specialty grower of herbs and microgreens just outside of Shanghai. They pledge against the use of pesticides and herbicides and have created processes that reduce waste, recycle water, and minimize negative impacts on the environment. Their grow systems are innovative, using a combination of hydroponics, aquaponics, and conditioned soil. From their website,

> "Hydroponics is a form of applying soil-less, nutrient solution culture to plant roots. Hydroponics comes from the Greek roots hydro (water) and ponos (work), which means: "Let the water do the work." Our hydroponics plants are a closed-loop system fed with natural vitamins and minerals to stimulate growth. We control growth factors, such as temperature, light, humidity, and hygiene, for optimal results year-round."

"Aquaponics is a combination of aquaculture (raising fish) and hydroponics (growing plants in nutrient water without soil) in a symbiotic, integrated system. The fish waste provides the organic nutrients for the plants and the plants naturally filter the water."

"Conditioned Soil reuses all the peat moss, vermiculite, perlite, and coconut coir that we use to grow microgreens. Instead of throwing it away, we combine it with our compost to recondition the soils top layer for healthy growing of some of our larger greens and edible flowers."
— Verdura Website, "How We Grow" Subsection

Their approach to agriculture has been well received and they have an increasing customer base in Shanghai. Their commitment to sustainable operations, aimed at minimizing negative impacts on the environment, and their desire to "connect people back to where their food is grown" are a model for future developments in this sector.

24.4.2 *Organic Industry Entrepreneurs in the United States*

The Windy City Harvest Youth Farm is an organic urban farm and youth development program in the city of Chicago, Illinois. It employs local teenagers from low-income communities and provides educational and personal development opportunities. The aim is to grow fresh, sustainable produce, distribute it to local markets, increase awareness about the benefits of sustainable agriculture, and provide opportunities for the underprivileged. In their own words,

"The teens in this program come away with real-world work experience, a great deal of learning, and the ability to make a positive impact in their communities. While weeding, watering, planting, and harvesting, they learn about being part of a team. And they take pride in shaping the farm from the ground up." — Angela Mason, Associate Vice President of Urban Agriculture

Boot Camp Farms is an 80,000 square foot urban farm in Bridgeport, Connecticut. Alongside producing organic food by way of an extensive hydroponic growth system, they provide jobs and training for war veterans. On average, the farm produces 800,000 pounds of organic produce each year and employs more than 40 full-time employees.

Their mission is aligned with the spirit of the organic movement throughout the US:

> "Our sustainable, state of the art, controlled environment farms will allow us to accelerate the process of creating large scale American local agriculture, so all of us can eat healthy foods at an affordable price. Because of the yield advantage achieved by growing 12 months in a controlled hydroponic environment, we can and will help to ensure the existence of local farms by using best sustainable agriculture practices." — Boot Camp Farms Website, "Mission" Subsection

As these entrepreneurial examples indicate, organic farming is developing with a sense of social responsibility and a view of the common good.

24.5 Discussion Questions

1. How would you define sustainability? How important is agriculture in your definition?
2. Can the organic farming industry support the needs of growing global populations? What if it cannot?
3. If you were a farmer, would you start an organic or conventional farm?
4. Do you think the use of synthetic chemicals in agriculture is morally wrong? What about GMOs? If so, do you have any evidence to support your conclusion?
5. Do you think organic agriculture will or could replace conventional agriculture in the future?
6. Do you think synthetic chemicals are harmful to the environment in terms of soil, water, and air pollution? What evidence do you have to support your conclusion?
7. Should the agricultural industry continue to support the use of chemicals that require large inputs of fossil fuels, particularly petroleum? On what basis would the search for alternatives make sense? From a business point of view? From a moral point of view?
8. What are the responsibilities of farmers to their stakeholders? Does organic farming fulfill them? Conventional farming?
9. What do you think are the long-term effects of organic farming? Of conventional farming?

Bibliography

He, D. and Wang, H. (2014). Dissatisfaction with food safety pervasive, survey finds. *China Daily*. Retrieved on March 24, 2016 from http://www.chinadaily.com.cn/china/2014-07/25/content_17920201.htm.

Ma, D. (2015). Post-95 entrepreneur aims to bring China's agriculture online. *China Daily*. Retrieved on March 24, 2016 from http://www.chinadaily.com.cn/china/2015-04/29/content_20575431_2.htm.

Palmer, X. (2015). Organic food in China. Retrieved on March 24, 2016 from https://www.smartshanghai.com/articles/wellbeing/organic-food in-china.

Yangtse Evening Post. (2011). 不少"有机蔬菜"是假冒的 (Many organic vegetables are counterfeit). *News.ifeng.com*. Retrieved on March 24, 2016 from http://news.ifeng.com/c/7fZxdMU7sCQ.

Part 6

Chinese Suppliers/Production

Chapter 25

Do Intellectual Property Rights (IPR) Always Matter?

How an IPR Violation Created a Flourishing "Taobao Village"

Mark Pufpaff, Helen Xu, and Dennis P. McCann

Abstract

Taobao is an online platform on which users can sell their products within China and all over the world. Many Chinese villagers use this opportunity and produce products to be sold on the platform. The problem is that they ignore international Intellectual Property Rights and produce and sell products that resemble brand products from all over the world. The case discusses the developments of the so-called Taobao Villages, the protection of property rights in China and foreign manufacturers' responses to these challenges.

Keywords: International Property Rights, trade, suppliers, poverty, production

25.1 Seeing

Since 2009, across the rural countryside of China, historically agrarian and relatively poor villages are seeing an economic transformation through developments in ecommerce infrastructure. Taobao, an online

213

marketplace for buyers and sellers operated by Alibaba Group, is leading this development. For sellers, Taobao is a platform where anyone anywhere in China can set up an online store and sell their goods to the nation, or even to a worldwide consumer base. To villagers in rural China, this created an unprecedented opportunity which they fully embraced. The result? The creation of what has become known as the "Taobao Village."

But, what is a "Taobao Village" and how is such a status achieved? Alibaba Group's research arm, AliResearch, has defined it as follows:

"A 'Taobao Village' is a cluster of rural [Internet retailers] within an administrative village where:

1. residents got started in e-commerce spontaneously, primarily with the use of [the] Taobao Marketplace;
2. total annual e-commerce transaction volume is at least RMB 10 million (USD 1.6 million);
3. at least 10% of village households actively engage in e-commerce or at least 100 active online shops have been opened by villagers."

The first "Taobao Village[s]" were founded in 2009, and since then have grown dramatically. Here are some snapshot statistics from AliResearch's annual reports on this trend:

2013

# of Taobao Villages: 20
# of online shops from rural villagers: 15,000
# of jobs created (estimated): 60,000

2014

# of Taobao Villages: 211
# of online shops from rural villagers: 70,000
# of jobs created (estimated): 280,000

2015

# of Taobao Villages: 780
# of Taobao Villages in "impoverished regions": 176
# of online shops from rural villagers: 200,000

25.2 Judging

If the availability of ecommerce in rural China has provided widespread economic benefit to the otherwise financially disadvantaged, and provided opportunities to those lacking options for meaningful work, are there any ethical issues worth arguing about? It depends.

Sun Han, for example, single-handedly transformed his village of East Wind, "a traditional village, [where] people tilled the fields and raised pigs", into a hub for furniture manufacturing. How did he do it? In a report by *National Public Radio* (NPR),

> "The transformation of East Wind village began about 400 miles away in Shanghai, where Sun Han stumbled into an IKEA one day.
>
> "I saw a lot of IKEA furniture," says Sun, standing in his factory amid the whir of sawing machines and the shriek of packing tape being stretched across cardboard boxes. "I felt their structure [IKEA's furniture] was very simple, and the prices were pretty high. I thought if I produce and sell them, the profit would be pretty high."
>
> Sun bought a bookshelf and found a factory to copy it."

The point of interest is the fact that Sun Han bought an IKEA bookshelf, had it copied at a Chinese factory, and then began selling it himself, without the permission of IKEA. In other words, he violated IKEA's intellectual property rights (IPR).

In doing so, he has become quite successful and is beginning to transition his business model from imitation to innovation. The NPR report continues,

> "As for Sun Han, the man who knocked off IKEA, he's now trying to build his own furniture brand. He remains grateful to Taobao. Without the ecommerce platform, he says, East Wind village never would have changed."
>
> "Young people would have kept moving to the cities and not coming back," he says. "The village would have been just old people and kids."

The effects of Sun's decision have been significant. His furniture manufacturing company is now only one of over 600 operating in the village, resulting in a massive increase in East Wind's standard of living.

However, this is not the end of the story. IKEA works hard to protect its IPR worldwide. It also deserves to have these efforts respected. When merchants like Sun Han illegally copy a company like IKEA's designs for their own personal profit, no matter their intentions, they are engaging in a form of theft. IKEA, their investors, and their stakeholders all lose in proportion to the success of the counterfeiter. Every counterfeit sale is tantamount to stealing profits rightly due to IKEA, robbing returns from IKEA's investors, and diminishing the overall impact of the firm in the communities in which it exists.

It is true that IKEA is a profitable company. Their 2015 net profits cleared over USD 3.9 billion, a 5.5% increase from 2014. It is likewise true that prior to copying IKEA's designs, Sun Han and the East Wind community were relatively poor and relegated to farming as their only means of income. But, does this disparity justify Sun Han stealing IKEA's designs?

This situation is reminiscent of the Robin Hood philosophy, where stealing from the rich was supposedly justified because the spoils were distributed among the poor. But, on what basis is it permissible to steal from the rich, or in this case, a profitable company like IKEA? Even though villagers like Sun Han may struggle financially, does that entitle them to disregard the rules of fairness when competing in the marketplace? Does that justify breaking the law?

The problem that can arise is the opening of a floodgate of counterfeit activity. In 2011, for instance, in the Chinese city of Kunming, the capital of Yunnan province, a company named 11 Furniture effectively built a furniture store to model the exact appearance, both inside and out, of an authentic IKEA store. From the size and color scheme to the layout and design of their products, it was for all intents and purposes an exact replica. What would be the effect if IKEA simply shrugged it off and ignored it? Would it not encourage others to do the same, or similar? IKEA China made the following statement:

> "Inter IKEA Systems B.V, the worldwide franchisor and owner of the IKEA Concept, sees it as very important to protect the intellectual property rights.
>
> We have reported it [the fake store in Kunming] to Inter IKEA Systems B.V and they are dealing with this matter together with their legal counsel. The best thing we can do to prevent such stores from opening up in the future is to open more stores and make the IKEA products available to more people."

The Chinese government is likewise clear on the legal implications of IPR violations. In Article 5 of the Anti-Unfair Competition Law, effective as of December 1, 1993, it states the following:

> "A business operator shall not harm his competitors in market transactions by resorting to any of the following unfair means:

(1) counterfeiting a registered trademark of another person;

(2) using for a commodity without authorization a unique name, package, or decoration of another's famous commodity, or using a name, package or decoration similar to that of another's famous commodity, thereby confusing the commodity with that famous commodity and leading the purchasers to mistake the former for the latter;

(3) using without authorization the name of another enterprise or person, thereby leading people to mistake their commodities for those of the said enterprise or person; or

(4) forging or counterfeiting authentication marks, famous-and-excellent-product marks or other product quality marks on their commodities, forging the origin of their products or making false and misleading indications as to the quality of their commodities."

If IKEA turned a blind eye, or the government simply overlooked IPR violations, what kind of marketplace would be the result? How would companies compete? What value, or lack thereof, would that bring to consumers? Though it might restrict opportunities for people like Sun Han in one sense, in another it is meant to protect people like him and others who are looking for innovative means to make a living through entrepreneurship. The only condition is that they make such a living by competing honestly.

25.3 Acting

Why is IPR, defined as the protection of corporate or individual property rights by way of patents, trademarks, and copyrights, protected in the first place? According to the World Trade Organization,

"Industrial property [is] protected primarily to stimulate innovation, design and the creation of technology. In this category fall inventions (protected by patents), industrial designs and trade secrets.

The social purpose is to provide protection for the results of investment in the development of new technology, thus giving the incentive and means to finance research and development activities."

Stimulating innovation and investment in research and development is directly opposed to the intention of Sun Han, which was nothing more than imitation. Though there was an economic transformation in the village of East Wind, and the community achieved the title of a "Taobao Village", it is questionable whether we can all truly rejoice.

25.4 Discussion Questions

1. Was Sun Han acting unethically? Do you think his choice to copy IKEA's designs is a form of theft? Why or why not?
2. If IKEA was to find out about this, should they file a claim against him? Would it be an act of charity to overlook this, in light of Sun Han's benevolence toward the people of East Wind?
3. The knockoff IKEA store in Kunming is still operational. Even though the Chinese government may have laws protecting domestic and international IPR, do you think they are effective? Why or why not? What might be the reason why the store has not been closed down?
4. What if Sun Han did not realize he was violating IKEA's IPR? Would he be morally responsible then? Now that he does realize the problem, should he try to negotiate some kind of settlement with IKEA that might also benefit the people of East Wind? What might he propose to make things right for all parties?
5. Is there ever a time when the "ends" justify the "means", that is, when illegal or unethical behavior is carried out for a morally good reason? Can you think of examples worth discussing?
6. The entire "Taobao Village" movement is beginning to make a serious impact across all of rural China. Assuming Sun's case is not unique, how should brand name companies, like IKEA, respond? How much should they care? Should they care at all? How far should they go to protect their IPR? Is there any reason why IKEA and other established enterprises might not collaborate with entrepreneurs like Sun Han in order to further the development of more and better "Taobao Villages"?

Bibliography

AliResearch.com (2016). Research Report on China's Taobao Villages (2015). *www.aliresearch.com*. Retrieved on May 21, 2016 from http://www.aliresearch.com/en/Reports/Reportsdetails?articleCode=20805.

Anti Unfair Competition Law of the People's Republic of China (2021). Retrieved March 28, 2021 from https://www.wipo.int/edocs/lexdocs/laws/en/cn/cn011en.pdf.

Langfitt, F. (2014). The Alibaba Effect: How China's eBay Transformed Village Economics. *National Public Radio*. Retrieved on May 21, 2016 from https://www.npr.org/sections/goatsandsoda/2014/09/11/347481629/alibaba-and-taobao-how-china-s-ebay-transformed-a-rural-village.

Chapter 26

"Fake Goods Are Better Than the Real Deal"?

Dennis P. McCann and Mark Pufpaff

Abstract

In 2016, Jack Ma, China's richest man, mentioned publicly that he thinks that fake good are better than the original ones. This comment started a discussion on production processes in China, the protection of property rights, and how foreign manufacturers of brand products are affected by them. The case discusses these issues from various perspectives.

Keywords: Internet, suppliers, International Property Rights, fraud, suppliers

26.1 Seeing

Jack Ma may only have been talking with his investors, but the whole world was listening. What they heard him say is best captured in CNN's headline story: "Alibaba's Jack Ma: Fake goods are better than the real deal" (*CNN Money*: June 14, 2016). Was this another "Gotcha!" story? Had Jack Ma inadvertently revealed that his much publicized commitment to high standards of business ethics, his attempt to model an ideal of "Confucian Entrepreneurship" was itself a fake? Surely, his enemies, particularly those high-end manufacturers, like Gucci, who had protested Alibaba's joining the International AntiCounterfeiting Coalition, thought so. Their efforts helped press the Coalition into suspending Alibaba's membership, which itself was a major concern prompting Jack Ma's statement to his investors. So now, out of his own mouth, they had words proving they had been right about him all along. The problem was not fake goods, but an entrepreneur whose business ethics was also fake.

But, before we haul Jack Ma off to a public struggle session as an enabler of fake goods and fraudulent marketing schemes, in all fairness we should make sure we have understood what he actually said and why he said it. Here is what he said at that meeting of Alibaba's investors: "The problem is that the fake products today — they make better quality, better prices than the real product. The exact factories, the exact raw materials, so they don't use the name." He was describing the challenge faced by Internet marketing platforms like Alibaba's Taobao, created by the widespread practice of outsourcing production of name brand luxury goods to Chinese factories. Here is how it works. Outsourcing means contract manufacturing, in which the Chinese contractor produces goods according to specification for a name brand company, usually headquartered overseas. Problems arise when the contractor then uses the same equipment and materials to produce products similar to the brand name, but for sale at steep discounts. This surplus production, which ranges from complete fakes — items masquerading as genuine with the luxury brand name attached — to "copycat" products that resemble the luxury brand item but are marketed under a little-known label, may be both lucrative and questionable legally for the Chinese contractors; however, for the brands being knocked off, it is hard to prevent given the complexities of global supply chain manufacturing and marketing. Often, the labels are deceptively similar to luxury brand names, but are sold at such steep discounts that no sophisticated shopper would confuse them with the genuine article.

While counterfeit goods may be illegal, copycat products may not be. A fake purports to be something that it is not, for example, an item falsely branded identifying it as a genuine Rolex watch. However, if you are accosted by a street vendor, say, in Hong Kong, hawking "genuine fake Rolexes" — or if you would find such items on Taobao or eBay — you should know that what the vendor has for sale, at best, is a copycat product and not the real thing. The vendor's "genuine fake Rolexes" may or may not turn out to be what Jack Ma described as a "fake product." It may have been produced at a factory that produces genuine Rolex watches, or then again, it may not. Just how different the fake may be from the genuine in product quality and reliability you may not learn until after you've bought it and tried it out. As the old saying goes, "You pays your money; you takes your chances...."

Jack Ma's remarks on the high quality of "fake products" was meant to defend Alibaba's marketing platforms against the accusations of luxury brand manufacturers who are convinced that these platforms enable counterfeiting schemes that are costing them millions of dollars. Their sense of outrage had already forced the Anti-Counterfeiting Coalition to suspend Alibaba's membership, despite Jack Ma's well-documented efforts to suppress, if not actually eliminate, the marketing of fakes on his platforms. His remarks were hardly a defense or endorsement of "fake products", but an explanation of why it is so hard to prevent their sale. He attempted to describe, without endorsing, "a new business model" in China, namely, contract manufacturing that provides an opportunity for ambitious contractors to profit at the expense of the companies that are outsourcing production through them. Given the ambiguities of Chinese law governing intellectual property rights, "fake products" can only be stopped if they involve a direct violation of the original product's trademark or brand label. A handbag that looks like Gucci, made with material that feels like Gucci, and has a design that is similar, if not identical to Gucci, might be a copycat, but unless it bore the Gucci label, instead of, say, "Gubbi," or "Gummi", it cannot be excluded from the marketplace.

The international furor created by his comments to Alibaba's investors, however, prompted Jack Ma to reiterate his policy of "zero tolerance for those who rip off other people's intellectual property." In his view, Alibaba remains "100% committed to leading the fight against global counterfeiting, online and offline." To underscore the sincerity of his commitment, he noted that for every request demanding that a company violating Alibaba's rules be removed from its platforms, Alibaba had "proactively removed eight thanks to heavy investments in technology and staffing for its anti-counterfeit work." He defended Alibaba as a company that runs on "a culture of trust."

26.2 Judging

Should Jack Ma be given the proverbial "benefit of the doubt" when it comes to the credibility of Alibaba's anti-counterfeiting practices?

How far should he be expected to go in honoring intellectual property rights, without jeopardizing Taobao's own business plan, and thus undercutting his support from investors and other stakeholders? At one point in his remarks, Jack Ma seemed to accept the inevitability of fakes due to "human instinct." Struggling to become "the world's leading fighter against counterfeits" involves struggling to overcome this instinct. But, which instinct? For what?

Deciphering his understanding of the struggle against counterfeit goods may take us well beyond considerations of Alibaba's collective self-interest. Jack Ma also remarked how Alibaba is hurt by unchecked commerce in counterfeit goods: "Every fake product we sell, we are losing five customers.... We are the victims of that. We never stop fighting." If Alibaba is losing five customers, it must mean that they feel cheated for some reason. This is understandable in the case of someone who thinks they are buying a real Gucci bag or a genuine Rolex, but are misled by the counterfeit brand label attached to the product. Such trade based upon an intent to deceive the customer is likely to turn them away. But, what are customers to think when they are offered such items at a 90% discount from their official list prices? Can I blame Jack Ma, if acting on my desire to save money — call it "greed", if you will — I buy the fake and pass it off to others as genuine, trying to impress them with my generosity, or my magnificence, or my prowess for making good deals? The human instinct that Jack Ma is struggling with is not unique to people in business. It is as much a flaw in their customers, suppliers, employees, and government regulators, all of whom bear some responsibility for the proliferation of fake goods. Trying to get something for nothing, or next to nothing, is all too human and all too common. After all, why are companies with high-end brand names outsourcing their production to China? Are they not playing the same game? It could be argued that if they really wanted to suppress fake goods, they should have dispensed with outsourcing and manufactured their products at home.

Such considerations inevitably lead us to the question of moral leadership. The "culture of trust" that Alibaba seeks to promote is closely linked to Jack Ma's personal claim to represent an ideal of Confucian entrepreneurship. What kind of moral leadership should we expect of a Confucian entrepreneur? A follower of Confucius is committed to discerning the Way, or the cultivation of virtues, that will sustain the common good, depicted in the Chinese Classics as the ideal commonwealth (*Datong*), in which social harmony can be achieved and sustained. Discerning the

Way becomes possible when one knows and honors the basic distinction between a *Junzi* and *Xiaoren*, that is, between a moral leader and, literally, the little people who know and act upon nothing higher than their own immediate self-interest. Both *Junzi* and *Xiaoren* seek happiness, but the *Xiaoren* understands happiness as nothing higher than his or her own satisfactions. The *Xiaoren*'s all-consuming question is "What's in it for me?" The *Junzi* knows that this question is deceptive, for happiness comes only through following the Way, that is, cultivating the virtues that build upon all that is good, noble and promising in human nature and conforming them to the objective moral order. To become a Confucian entrepreneur means conducting business in a way that is consistent with the Way, the objective moral order. It means, for example, foregoing all deceptive business practices, all forms of cheating customers, suppliers, employees, and other stakeholders, even if it may be advantageous in the short term. A Confucian entrepreneur knows that marketing counterfeit goods is contrary to the Way, for one can profit from such practices only by exploiting the vulnerabilities of others.

A Confucian entrepreneur well understands that, despite the basic goodness of human nature, most of us tend to be *Xiaoren*. We tend to favor our own interests at the expense of others. All too often, we rationalize our greed as nothing other than "business as usual." Moral leadership, and its exercise, is therefore exceptional and truly difficult. None of us escapes the pervasiveness of what Jack Ma called "human instinct." But, at the same time, a Confucian moral leader in business knows that genuine goodness or benevolence is attractive to others. If I struggle to realize that ideal, others will follow. This is what he means by Alibaba's commitment to create "a culture of trust." How else can we explain the success of his Internet marketing platforms, like Taobao? Jack Ma's contribution is to realize that successful commerce depends on trust. If buyers and sellers cannot trust one another, or the third-party broker that brings them together, there will be no trade, no exchange, and thus no profit for any-one. If a marketing platform is rigged, so that cheaters — counterfeiters and the like — can get away with cheating their customers, eventually the platform will collapse, surely as soon as customers can find another more credible and reliable way of doing business. A Confucian entrepreneur thus must struggle against any and all forms of corruption that will under-mine his or her capacity for doing good business. Therefore, it makes sense for Jack Ma to struggle against the proliferation of fake goods in Alibaba's market platforms. His commitment, at least, is credible.

26.3 Acting

But, what more should Jack Ma do? As a Confucian entrepreneur, he believes that leading by good example is far more effective than trying to deter counterfeiters through government-sponsored campaigns threatening them with punishments. But, leading by good example means doing more than making speeches in support of the Anti-Counterfeiting Coalition. We now know what more Jack Ma thinks Alibaba is already doing. His marketing platforms are self-regulating, that is, he has invested heavily in verifying the vendors who use them as well as the legitimacy of the products they are selling. If his managers suspect that a vendor is marketing an item illegally, that is, offering fraudulent products, they will investigate and the vendor will be suspended. At least, that is how it is supposed to work. But, a few years ago, Alibaba discovered that some of its managers were accepting bribes from vendors seeking to register businesses on their marketing platforms. When Jack Ma discovered what was going on, he put a stop to it, and the managers were fired. Nevertheless, the incident suggests that even when a *Junzi* tries to create a "culture of trust", he or she must be vigilant all the time against *Xiaoren* — both inside and outside the organization — trying to corrupt it for their own gain.

It is hard to see how Jack Ma can make good on his claim to moral leadership without addressing the need to thoroughly educate everyone involved in Alibaba's operations as to their responsibilities within his "culture of trust." This has always been the Confucian Way. The proposition is that persuasion rather than coercion will prove more effective in achieving compliance within such a culture. Perhaps Taobao should offer mandatory classes in best business practices, not only to its managers but also to vendors using its platforms. Perhaps the lessons should give hope to entrepreneurs using Taobao's platforms, by showing them how other companies have made the transition from copycatting popular brand name products to innovating high-quality products of their own design and manufacture. One such success story is the Taiwanese computer hardware and electronics company, ASUS, and there are many others. What may be persuasive, in short, is an appeal to the enlightened self-interest of Alibaba's customers and various stakeholders. Jack Ma's insights into the progress that Chinese contract manufacturers have made were not meant as an endorsement of cheating in any form. But, it does contain an appeal that points the Way forward. If you have come this far, why not take the next step toward creating your own brand name?

26.4 Conclusion

Respecting intellectual property rights, as Jack Ma has often insisted, is a serious challenge. Alibaba claims to have "zero tolerance for those who rip off other people's intellectual property." But, what is intellectual property, and what is the extent of valid rights claims about it? Should marketing platforms like Taobao be held morally and legally responsible for the violations of intellectual property rights allegedly committed by vendors using their platforms? Are the complexities of supply chain management in a global economy increasingly reliant upon ecommerce a legitimate excuse for Taobao not doing more to prevent the marketing of "fake goods"? The controversy that erupted internationally over Jack Ma's comments indicates that these issues are hardly resolved. At the same time, a closer look at what he said and did not say should alert us to the fact that not all fake products are alike. Some really are meant to rip people off, both consumers and brand name producers, while others are copycats with varying degrees of quality. Should some be tolerated, while others are prosecuted to the full extent of the law? On what grounds would you distinguish these? Finally, under the circumstances outlined in this case study, what can "zero tolerance" possibly mean? Good business ethics — Confucian or otherwise — urges us to "Do no harm." Is "zero tolerance" the most effective way to achieve compliance with that imperative?

26.5 Discussion Questions

1. What would you do, if you were in Jack Ma's situation, to assert Alibaba's leadership in the anti-counterfeiting movement?
2. Do you think it is fair to exclude Chinese vendors, who have been accused of selling "fake goods", from access to Taobao and other ecommerce platforms? Why? Why not?
3. Suppose you are shopping for a present to give to one of your loved ones. You want to impress them, so you are looking to buy a luxury brand name watch or handbag. You know where you can get one, perhaps a fake, at a 90% discount. Would you consider buying such an item? Why? Why not?
4. Do you think that the managers at Taobao, who accepted bribes from vendors registering to use the platform, should have been fired for their actions? Why? Why not?

5. Do you think that firing such managers is appropriate, when the company claims to be building a "culture of trust"? Why? Why not?
6. Do you think that Chinese copycatting can be defended by arguing that China is poor and the West is rich? Does that make it OK to counterfeit Western luxury goods? Why? Why not?
7. Would you cheat on an entrance exam, if it would make the difference in getting admitted to the kind of graduate program you need to get ahead in your career? How does your personal attitude toward cheating carry over into how you react to the controversy over Jack Ma's remarks on "fake goods"?

Bibliography

Northrup, L. (2016). Alibaba founder Jack Ma: No, I didn't mean that counterfeit goods are better than originals. *Consumerist*. Retrieved on July 4, 2016 from https://consumerist.com/2016/06/23/alibaba-founder-jack-ma-no-i-didnt-mean-that-counterfeit-goods-are-better-than-originals/.

Sina.com (2012). 阿里查受贿处理淘宝员工27人 (Alibaba accepted bribes — 27 employees involved). *Tencent*. Retrieved on July 4, 2016 from https://finance.qq.com/a/20120609/000505.htm.

The Telegraph (2016). Alibaba's Jack Ma: Fakes are often better than the real thing. *Telegraph Reporters*. Retrieved on July 4, 2016 from https://www.telegraph.co.uk/business/2016/06/14/alibabas-jack-ma-fakes-are-often-better-than-the-real-thing/.

Chapter 27

Rip Curl and Supply Chain Transparency

Mark Pufpaff and Dennis P. McCann

Abstract

International supply chain management is an involved enterprise. There are a lot of moving parts, all of which need to work harmoniously together for the production of goods to happen effectively and on time. This case discusses a situation where Rip Curl, an Australian designer of surfing sportswear, was outsourcing production to a factory in China that was in turn subcontracting to a factory in North Korea, an unauthorized country for the production of Rip Curl apparel.

Keywords: Supply chain, China, North Korea, Rip Curl, subcontracting, Rules of Origin

27.1 Seeing

Rip Curl, an Australian designer of surfing sportswear, found itself in a whirlwind of media condemnation in February, 2016, after a video[1] and collection of photos surfaced of factory line workers in North Korea

---

[1] The video showed factory laborers in rows working behind sewing machines and related tools. None of the workers looked at the person shooting the camera. No questions were posed to the workers and there were no interviews with floor managers.

producing the firm's 2015 winter line of products. As news reports suggested, the video and photos contained evidence of Rip Curl's products being produced under conditions of "slave labor", a descriptor routinely used by North Korean defectors. But, that was not the only issue. The media diatribe also accused Rip Curl of selling its products with a "fake" label, namely, one that stated their apparel was "Made in China" instead of North Korea. This latter claim, evidenced by a photograph of the tag of a finished product in the factory, occasioned two potential scenarios. One, Rip Curl was attempting to hide from its consumers that it was manufacturing its apparel in North Korea, a country commonly regarded as having a devastating history of human rights abuses. Or two, the firm was simply not aware that its chosen manufacturer in China was outsourcing some or all of Rip Curl's work order to North Korean factories.

The video and photos were taken by visitors to North Korea, whom the local government was showing the Taedonggang Clothing Factory — which is close to the country's capital of Pyongyang. Although it is unclear whether the video was shot illegally, the photographs, and particularly the one of the "Made in China" label — shown below — were taken secretly by Nik Halik, an Australian businessperson.

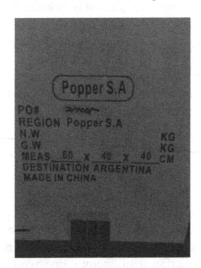

After noticing the "Made in China" labels, Halik stated he was shocked and felt that Rip Curl's customers should know where their apparel was being made. He and others with what they felt to be incriminating evidence sent their materials to Fairfax Media, who subsequently launched an investigation and eventually confronted Rip Curl about it. Rip Curl's official response to the accusation was as follows:

> "We were aware of this issue, which related to our Winter 2015 Mountain-wear range, but only became aware of it after the production was complete and had been shipped to our retail customers. This was a case of a supplier diverting part of their production order to an unauthorized subcontractor, with the production done from an unauthorized factory, in an unauthorized country, without our knowledge or consent, in clear breach of our supplier terms and policies. We do not approve or authorize any production of Rip Curl products out of North Korea.
>
> We are very sorry that Rip Curl has breached the trust our customers put in us to make sure that the products they wear cause them no moral concern. That's our responsibility to you and we have let you down on this one. All our suppliers know that our terms of trade prevent them diverting production to non-certified factories and we do undertake factory inspections and audits to try to prevent this happening. In this case, we took immediate action to discipline the supplier for his breach and we are increasing our inspections and audits."

27.2 Judging

What are the ethical issues involved in this case? We have an issue of human rights abuses at a North Korean factory manufacturing Rip Curl apparel. We have the alleged mislabeling of the country of origin, where the firm's goods were produced. We also have the question of whether Rip Curl knew their Chinese manufacturer was outsourcing all or some of the production of their 2015 Winter line to North Korea. Let us unpack it point by point.

Media reports on this scandal claim that those who were working in the Taedonggang Clothing Factory were undergoing slave-like labor conditions, such as forced labor, long hours, little or no pay, and minimal time off. Non-compliance with these conditions, however unjust, would typically result in the dissenting worker being removed from the factory and sent to an actual labor camp, where conditions were oftentimes worse. Although there is no evidence outside of the media's interpretation of the video and photographs to corroborate their description of the conditions, it presents a difficult situation for Rip Curl. Being accused of producing their apparel in a factory that subjects its workforce to such conditions is not only bad for the firm's brand reputation but it is also morally problematic. This latter point has a number of implications. First, just because a given factory is willing to exploit their workers, does not make it morally permissible for a company to manufacture its products there. Likewise, even if the legal environment of a given country does not require their textile factories to pay their employees a fair wage, this does not automatically provide a moral justification for foreign companies like Rip Curl to use them. The phrases "Just because it is legal, doesn't mean it is ethical" and "Just because you can, doesn't mean you should" come to mind. Second, it is helpful to have a moral test for determining whether a given business decision is an ethically sound one. For example, the principle of reciprocity in Confucian thinking, which states, "What you do not want done to yourself, do not do to others" (*Analects* 15:23, 6:28), is one such standard. Applied here, Rip Curl's leadership would make their decision to produce their apparel at a given factory if, in reflection, they themselves would feel reasonably comfortable working in such a factory. Third, it enables exploitative factory owners to continue subjecting their workforce to the plight of slave-like working conditions. By manufacturing at one of these factories, Rip Curl implicitly would be condoning the behavior of the factory leadership, silently telling them that the way they are running their operations is okay, just as long as they produce according to the firm's requirements.[2] In other words, Rip Curl's outsourcing activity would be a signal to the market that it condones the preexisting conditions at the factory and, as a result, removes any incentive for the factory to clean up its operations.

Mr. Halik's photograph of the "Made in China" label on apparel being produced in North Korea looks, on the surface, like an exercise in deceit on behalf of Rip Curl. Why would "Made in China" be on a jacket label being produced in North Korea?

The core of the labeling issue is whether Rip Curl was in violation of any relevant trade laws. Media reports condemned the firm for selling their apparel with so-called "fake" labels. But, is that the case? Perhaps not. Rules of Origin (ROO)[3] is a term that describes the criteria for

---

[2] This third point is of course dependent upon Rip Curl's leadership knowing about the conditions and intentionally remaining indifferent to them.

[3] ROO regulations are to determine the country a product was produced in. There is no universal set of ROO regulations, and they often fluctuate among countries over time as economic relations between trading partners change. The implications of having a product

determining where a product is manufactured. If it is manufactured in China, the product would be labeled "Made in China." However, ROO regulations also allow for a certain percentage, which varies across industries and product lines, of the manufacturing process — either in terms of the actual production or the sourcing of materials — to involve foreign countries and still qualify as being "Made in China", for example. In other words, the Chinese factory's decision to subcontract some portion of Rip Curl's product order to North Korea may not have been illegal. The legal question would be what percentage was subcontracted. However, given that the percentage in the textiles industry can range to upwards of 40% of the final product, there very well may not have been any legal foul play in this case. This would, then, render media accusations on this issue exaggerated at best.

To the point about whether Rip Curl knew its Chinese contractor was subcontracting some or all of its work order to North Korea, we may first look at the firm's official response. It stated, "This was a case of a supplier diverting part of their production order to an unauthorized subcontractor, with the production done from an unauthorized factory, in an unauthorized country, without our knowledge or consent, in clear breach of our supplier terms and policies. We do not approve or authorize any production of Rip Curl products out of North Korea." This argues that Rip Curl did not know about the subcontracting being undertaken by its contracted factory in China. It also makes it clear that Rip Curl's policy is that its products are never contracted to North Korean factories. Taken together, this suggests that something was amiss in the fact that its jackets and other apparel were being produced there. It reveals a possible breach of contract on behalf of the Chinese factory. It also reveals a lapse in due diligence on the part of Rip Curl. Either way, it raises the issue of supply chain transparency.

---

manufactured in one country and not another primarily has to do with import and export duties. In this sense, there are two kinds of countries: preferential and non-preferential. Preferential countries, as the name suggests, have low, if any, duties. Non-preferential countries, contrariwise, have higher duties. Thus, there is a financial incentive for countries to manufacture in preferential countries, to ensure they have labels indicating that their products were made there — a given label tells customs officials what duties, if any, are to be imposed upon importation. ROO regulations are relevant to this case because of the media accusations lodged against Rip Curl, claiming it was selling its apparel with "fake labels".

Rip Curl not knowing that their Chinese contractor was outsourcing some or all of the production to North Korea, a country the firm has stated it does not "approve or authorize" production in, is not an excuse for allowing it to happen. This fact they certainly acknowledge, given their apology: "We are very sorry that Rip Curl has breached the trust our customers put in us to make sure that the products they wear cause them no moral concern. That's our responsibility to you and we have let you down on this one." But, they go even further. They not only apologize but also describe the action they took thereafter: "In this case, we took immediate action to discipline the supplier for his breach and we are increasing our inspections and audits." If they have done as they say, should we not commend them for their efforts to increase their supply chain transparency and restore trust with their consumer base?

27.3 Acting

What are we to make of Rip Curl's response to the scandal? To recall, the first part of their response included an explanation on what happened, namely, that the Chinese factory subcontracted some or all of its Rip Curl work order to North Korea. It also included a statement that condemned the Chinese factory's decision to subcontract, especially to North Korea, as contrary to Rip Curl's policy. The second half of the statement began with an apology, informing their customer base that they understand their responsibility to ensure they sell products produced under ethical and legal conditions. They then state that all their contract factories, which would include the one under discussion in this case, know, presumably by way of their work order contract, that subcontracting to non-certified factories is prohibited. They close with a commitment to and an affirmation of the action taken, namely, to correct any errors in misunderstanding between Rip Curl and its contract factories and to tighten up its own due diligence in ensuring compliance throughout the manufacturing process.

By most accounts, this is a good response. It is descriptive, apologetic, and focused on a constructive resolution. Given that reporting on the scandal stopped almost as soon as it began — no new media reports on this issue have arisen as of March, 2017 — it seems reasonable to trust that Rip Curl has done what it said it would do: institute better governance over its overseas manufacturing contracts and ensure greater supply chain transparency. What do you think?

27.4 Discussion Questions

1. What are the moral issues of this case? Please list and explain them.
2. Why might Rip Curl have as a policy that none of their apparel manufacturing can be carried out in North Korea? What reasons do you think the company might have for such a restriction?
3. Do you think it is a moral problem if a corporation uses the cheapest manufacturing option, regardless of the working conditions of the factory? For example, if you were Rip Curl and you could dramatically cut your manufacturing costs by outsourcing production to North Korea, but knew that their factories were exploitative, would you do so? Why or why not?
4. What do you think of the media's claim that Rip Curl's products contained "fake" labels? Should Rip Curl have addressed this claim in its official response, given the Rules of Origin issues involved?
5. Do you think that Rip Curl was right to apologize to its customers? Does their apology imply they knew about the outsourcing to North Korea and are now embarrassed about it? Or does it imply they did not know about the outsourcing, but wish they did? What do you think?
6. Supply chain transparency is the idea that a corporation should have nothing to hide in the process of producing its goods. Do you think Rip Curl had a transparent supply chain in this case? If so, how so? If not, why not?

Bibliography

Devonshire-Ellis, C. (2016). Rip Curl's North Korea scandal is actually a China Rules of Origin issue. *China Briefing*. Retrieved on March 16, 2017 from http://www.chinabriefing.com/news/2016/02/22/40672.html.

Logan, N. (2016). Aussie clothing company Rip Curl apologizes for clothes made in North Korea. *Global News*. Retrieved on March 16, 2017 from https://globalnews.ca/news/2533629/aussie-clothing-company-rip-curl-apologizes-for-clothes-made-in-north-korea/.

McKenzie, N. and Baker, R. (2016). Surf clothing label Rip Curl using 'slave labour' to manufacture clothes in North Korea. *The Sydney Morning Herald*. Retrieved on March 16, 2017 from https://www.smh.com.au/business/surf-clothing-label-rip-curl-using-slave-labour-to-manufacture-clothes-in-north-korea-20160220-gmz375.html.

Chapter 28

Black Hearts, Black Lungs: Courting Disaster in China's Coal Mines

Dennis P. McCann and Mark Pufpaff

Abstract

In August 2007, waters from an adjacent river flooded some of the tunnels of the Zhangzhuang mine near the city of Xintai. 172 miners were trapped in the mine and died. The flooding was caused by heavy rain and not by problems within the mine and was labeled as a natural disaster. Since China had just introduced a new set of regulations mandating payment of 200,000 yuan to the families of workers killed in industrial accidents, the question of whether the incident was a natural disaster or an industrial accident became significant for the families of the workers killed. The case discusses this incident and presents questions on labor safety, corporate responsibility and the current situation of mine workers in China.

Keywords: Environment, labor relations, production, supplier

28.1 Seeing

Would you categorize coal mining accidents as natural disasters? In at least one instance, a government official tried to do so, when waters from an adjacent river flooded some of the tunnels of the Zhangzhuang mine near the city of Xintai in August 2007. "The disaster was caused by heavy rain, not problems within the mine, so it was decided that this was a natural disaster," Civil Affairs Minister Li Xueju said, during a news conference in Beijing. "Sometimes the alert system may not be timely or accurate enough. They did not imagine the rain would be so heavy and they did not imagine that the river bank would leak."

When aggrieved family members of the miners who drowned in the flooding angrily dismissed the so-called "natural disaster" excuse as a cover-up, and threatened reprisals against both the company and the government, the Chief of the State Administration of Work Safety, Li Yizhong, admitted that poor planning and inadequate safety procedures were also to blame for the confirmed deaths of 172 miners trapped in the accident. "The root (problem) is some local authorities and companies have failed to take sufficient action to tackle safety loopholes and build a sound early-warning mechanism.... Although extreme weather and natural disasters were factors in the recent accident, it also reflects deep problems in safety systems."

The dispute over the meaning of "natural disaster" is not insignificant, since China at the time had no universal system of compensation for victims of such events, but did have a new set of regulations mandating payment of 200,000 yuan to the families of workers killed in industrial accidents. The new regulations were meant to establish financial incentives for mine owners and operators to comply with occupational safety standards, such as those which Li Yizhong conceded had not been implemented at the Zhangzhuang mine. Nevertheless, attributing the accident to a "natural disaster" falls into a pattern of "lies and fraud" that, alas, has been all too typical in China's coal industry.

After a similar accident killed 57 miners in Zuoyun County near Datong City, Shanxi Province, in May 2013, *CSR Asia Weekly* published an analysis revealing the pattern of illegalities that had become commonplace, particularly in privately owned coal mines:

"Mine owners made workers mine in areas they were not authorised to mine, exceeded production quotas (based on limits set by the authorities) by up to ten times, and employed more workers than could safely be accommodated underground. Signs of flooding in days just before the accident were ignored by managers who ordered miners to stay on the job. Rescue equipment was substandard."

The "Black Hearts" — as they have become known in the Chinese blogosphere — who carried out these policies, hoping to maximize profits, calculated that they could get away with them because not only were they bribing local government officials but the miners they hired were usually migrants from western China who were desperate for a job and had little or no local support network if things went wrong. The pattern also included falsification of accident reports, clandestine removal of the bodies of victims to other jurisdictions, and paying money to silence the victims' family members.

Death from working in a coal mine comes in many forms, some swift and others slow. Gas explosions, undetected because of a failure to use basic mine safety equipment, are probably as big a killer as the flooding of tunnels that is likely to occur any time there are torrential rains. The rains themselves, of course, are part of a pattern of increasingly severe weather resulting from the deterioration of the natural environment, for which coal mining is partially responsible. While sudden death through water or fire — according to Chinese government statistics recording the number of coal mine accidents — seems to be diminishing from year to year, the mortality rates for miners suffering from black lung disease are on the rise. It is hard to imagine a slower and more painful death than that caused by coal workers' pneumoconiosis (CWP). Yet even as the number of deaths attributed to accidents has decreased, the number of miners diagnosed with black lung disease has increased, and not surprisingly so, since the effects of trying to breathe in an active coal mine are cumulative and slowly evolving. China's National Health and Family Planning Commission has labeled it the most common occupational disease, reporting that in 2013, 750,000 people were treated for it, with 60% of these having worked in the coal mines. Other estimates of its extent range far higher. The NGO "Love Save Pneumoconiosis (LSP)" claims the number is more like 6 million. As the LSP reports, "symptoms of the disease include coughing, chest pain, shortness of breath and bronchitis. Patients can lose their ability to walk because of breathing difficulties, with extreme cases leading to death."

But, what about workers' compensation? Surely the victims of black lung disease have received assistance. According to statistics reported by the LSP, however, "only 19 percent of the 6 million coal workers suffering from pneumoconiosis had received compensation as the result of legal proceedings as of the end of 2014." All too typical are the complaints of workers who have either been told that their employers have no money for compensation, or have been forced to sign agreements for partial payouts that waive their rights to as much as 70% of the mandatory minimum. Wang Baosheng, a coal miner from Leping in Jiangxi Province, was working at the Zhaojiashan coal mine in 2012 when he was diagnosed. Angry and dissatisfied over the firm's excuses for delaying his workers' compensation, Wang and his fellow workers sued the mine owners for the 6 million yuan they were owed, only to have a local court dismiss their case, since they had signed waivers in exchange for a much smaller lump sum payment. Later, the court's decision was overturned and the waivers were declared invalid, paving the way for what may turn out to be a very slow legal process, the outcome of which is highly uncertain. Coal mine operators typically evade their responsibilities through a number of stratagems, including refusal to sign the required certification that the employee contracted the disease on the job, hiring workers without contracts who thus have no legal basis for making any claims against the firm, and declaring that the firm has no money to pay compensation if the workers' claims are eventually upheld. Of course, many victims of pneumoconiosis die before their cases are resolved, thus relieving the mine owners of their legal liabilities.

Why then would anyone choose to work in a coal mine? The simple answer is that it pays well, or at least pays better than other jobs that unskilled laborers might obtain. One study indicated that coal miners make six times the monthly salary of a cab driver, who may receive 1000 yuan a month for his work. People working as coal miners are typically men, often migrants from other provinces in western China who are desperate to support their families. The Black Hearts of the coal mine operators exploiting them know that such men will put up with horrendous working conditions, so long as the pay is good enough to send regular remittances home. The Black Hearts' attitude seems to be that workers lives do not matter; that they are expendable, just another commodity to be used up in a relentless pursuit of maximizing profits. China's elaborate (and impressive) set of laws and regulations governing laborers, their rights and responsibilities, has little impact on the Black Hearts' calculations, since local officials usually can be paid off to look the other way as safety standards and other procedures are routinely violated. Can working in a coal mine ever be made safe? Can coal miners ever expect to be paid fair wages and the other benefits owed them, so long as the whole industry seems mired in an apparently impenetrable thicket of corruption?

28.2 Judging

Does a person cease to be human when he or she signs an employment contract? Can we ignore the plight of coal miners, as if they were victims of a "natural disaster", simply because they freely signed an employment contract? "You made your bed, now lie in it. You have no one to blame but yourself." Or so the old saying goes. Do coal miners deserve anything more than our indifference? We sit comfortably at our desks, in libraries, or in front of computer screens, white collar workers under no threat of black lung disease, with not the slightest chance that a gas explosion will topple the roof under which we carry on our activities. So, maybe we pray, "Thank God, I wasn't born to be one of these." And then turn to *Facebook* or some other favorite diversion, to hide from ourselves the truth about our indifference to the sufferings of others.

But, maybe you are not so lucky or so privileged. What if you are the son or daughter of a coal mine owner or operator? Your family's business makes it possible for you to be here, enjoying the lifestyle of a 21st century student, living in a safe and secure bubble, kept out of harm's way, at least for now. But, suppose you are called home, and now you must carry on the management of your family's coal mine. After all, it was that eventuality that prompted your parents to pay for your university education. Once you get settled, you soon discover that your family's prosperity rests on shaky grounds. Far from setting a good example to other mine owners and operators, your family has engaged in all the practices that you have learned put their workers' lives at risk of death, dismemberment, and disease. So far, your family has been lucky. There have not been any major accidents, and the firm has enjoyed good face for your parents, for all their managers, and the community at large. The faces of the miners emerging from the tunnels down below, at the end of their workday, may be blackened, and weary, but the workers are not complaining, so why should anyone else be worried?

If you ever come to that day, when the challenge of managing a coal mine rests squarely on your shoulders, or when you have accepted responsibility for advising a coal mine operator, what would you do? If you felt the need to try improving things at the coal mine, where would you begin? Especially when your friends, and your relatives, might think you are crazy for even trying? As your uncle said to you, toward the end of a heated argument, "If it isn't broken, don't fix it!" But, what if it is broken, not just the safety equipment and the workers' compensation scheme, not just your family's firm but the entire industry, and the system that supports it? Where to begin?

To make a fresh start, we need a new attitude. We may have learned that the first principle of business ethics is "Do No Harm". But, now that you have begun to learn — or fear that you may discover — that since there is a lot of harm happening, maybe doing no harm is simply not enough. Why should a business be held to such a low level of expectation? Is there not something more positive that we could aim for? In the old days, everyone was urged to "Serve the People". Whatever happened to that spirit? We know that history has given us all too many reasons to be cynical about it. But, the slogan was not just for cadres signing up for government jobs. Serving the People means contributing to the common good of all. This is what all businesses should be aiming at. After all, coal mining, in principle, contributes to the common good by enabling China to meet its growing energy needs — heating homes in winter, supplying power to our factories, schools, hospitals, and government services, generating electricity to enhance all our activities — while maintaining the lowest possible cost. Mining China's vast supplies of coal has always been seen as preferable to importing foreign oil, or investing in alternative sources of renewable energy, at least until recently. So, we must admit, that coal mining is a legitimate business, for it does contribute to the common good.

But, like all such businesses that are in high demand, it can and will be corrupted by Black Hearts who can see no further than opportunities for exploitation. The era of economic reform saw the deregulation of basic industrial production processes, with the expectation that markets would become more efficient by enabling private enterprises to compete with the traditional state-owned enterprises (SOEs). One of the unintended consequences of deregulation, however, was that all too many private owners and operators discovered that they could maximize profits by systematically ignoring safety regulations, bribing local officials, and paying whatever fines might be imposed were an accident to happen. Apparently, corrupting the system for their own personal gain was the Black Hearts' business plan. If this situation is ever to be turned around, we must face the fact that such a business plan cannot contribute to the common good. In fact, it has just the opposite effect. Coal mines that engage in illegal (and immoral) business practices make a profit only by shifting the true costs of their activities onto others who cannot fight back. Like the miners they endanger on a daily basis, like the environment they degrade, like the families they impoverish by destroying the health of the workers trying to support them.

If you inherited a coal mine, or advised someone who ran one, you would face a stark choice: If our business plan can only succeed by corrupting the regulatory system, defrauding our workers of wages and benefits, forcing them to put their lives and their health in harm's way, then we must either get out altogether, or find a very different way of doing business.

The question we started with has yet to be answered: Does a person cease to be human when he or she signs an employment contract? By now, we should know that it must be addressed not just to coal miners but also to the owners and operators of coal mines, indeed to all of us who benefit from the energy supplied by them, however remote our activities may be, however clean our occupations and lifestyles. Do I cease to be human when I take up employment, either as a worker or as an owner or manager? Human dignity is inherent, a seed to be cultivated in Confucian tradition, a God-given gift in Christian tradition. In all wisdom traditions, it is recognized as universal, meaning that all human persons enjoy it, as well as the rights and responsibilities it confers, and that it cannot be bought or sold or temporarily set aside. No conceivable employment contract can legitimately override it. All must respect it, if there is to be any genuine progress toward the common good, or the ideal commonwealth (*Datong*) envisioned by the Confucian classics. If human dignity cannot be waived away, then no employer can waive away the rights and responsibilities — including the right to adequate safety procedures and appropriate health care — that are meant to sustain it. Freedom of contract is no excuse for tolerating labor conditions that systematically reduce workers to expendable commodities. Any mine owner or operator who would try to hide behind such a lame excuse would rightly be subject to shaming as a Black Heart. Black Heart disease is a choice; black lung disease is not.

28.3 Acting

Given the systemic corruption that has enabled Black Heart mine owners and operators to succeed, it is clear that the policies and actions of no one individual or company are likely to transform the situation, without the assistance of many other groups and state institutions.

Rather than allow this to become yet another excuse for inaction, those willing to show leadership in transforming China's coal industry should focus on what they can do to improve the situation. Here are some possibilities:

- Obey the law: While this is the minimum requirement, it entails adopting a cooperative and constructive attitude toward government regulation of the coal industry, complying with all directives, while supporting officials at all levels who are trying to carry out their duties honestly and fairly. If all owners and operators were to obey the law, the problem of corruption would disappear, and the way would open to focusing on whatever other solutions are needed to reduce the likelihood of mining disasters.

- Support investigative journalism: Abandon the code of silence by which Black Heart owners and operators are protected from the public's demands for accountability and transparency. There are positive signs of a general improvement in journalistic ethics in China, as reporters and investigators seek to make their own contribution to the common good. Learn to regard journalists as allies in the struggle to achieve accountability. If you have nothing to hide, you have nothing to lose.

- Compete for best reputation for safety in your industry: Do you reward workers for using safety equipment properly? Do you encourage safety by publicizing the number of days running that have been accident-free? Have you attempted to learn all you can about innovations in safety equipment and procedures that reduce the risk of underground accidents? Usually, these can save you money, especially when their cost is compared to the costs incurred when an accident happens.

- Cultivate good relationships with your stakeholders: Have you considered who your stakeholders are? Who are your investors, your suppliers, your customers, as well as the regulators who certify your compliance with the law? What is your standing in the court of public opinion? If you are dependent on the good will of your investors, or the bankers who loan you the capital to sustain your business, what are you doing to convince them that transparency is in your mutual interest, that investing in technologies improving the miners' health and safety is to their benefit as well as your own? How can transparency be made to work for your suppliers and customers? If they knew the truth about your policies and actions, would you be able to retain their loyalty and support?

- Become an employer of choice in your community: An employer of choice is one whom workers at all levels actually want to work for. Everyone knows that coal mining is a dirty and hazardous business. But surely in your community, working for some coal mine operators is preferable to working for others. It is possible to outperform your competitors in attracting good workers at all levels. What can you do to become an employer of choice? How would you redesign work routines, safety procedures, and health maintenance policies, specifically to attract good workers? Do you really think that paying the highest wages, or offering the greatest opportunities for overtime work, will inevitably make you an employer of choice? Do you have enough faith in your workers to try implementing policies that address their real needs?

- Implementing housing and other social benefits: If your workers live in company housing, what is their experience of life in your care? Is there any provision for their social needs, like recreational facilities, participation in social clubs, access to communication with family back home, opportunities to visit nearby cities and towns? If you take respect for human dignity seriously, you cannot ignore the impact — positive or negative — of living under your roof, so to speak. Perhaps the day is almost over when living in company towns is the normal or preferred way for workers to live. But, if your company is still providing housing for its employees, then these issues must be addressed. Any progress you make in improving living conditions for workers will not only help make you an employer of choice but it will also improve productivity in the mines.

The idea behind these suggestions is to trigger a virtuous circle of improvements. Instead of remaining trapped in a vicious circle in which it becomes nearly impossible not to be identified with Black Heart mine owners and operators, you should begin to plot a virtuous circle that will demonstrate moral leadership in an industry that desperately needs it. Some of these suggestions are relatively low cost to implement, but they do require a change of attitude and an entrepreneur's willingness to try new things. Others may be costlier initially, but promise great rewards in the long term. Where you begin is up to you; but, it is imperative that you start somewhere.

28.4 Conclusion

Government statistics tell the story of steady improvements in the safety of China's coal mines. For the past dozen years, the trend has been moving in the right direction, with usually fewer and fewer deaths from coal mine accidents reported. In March 2015, the State Administration of Work Safety (SAWS) reported 931 deaths from coal mine accidents, marking the death toll dropping below 1,000 for the first time. This marked an 86.7% decline from the toll of some 7,000 reported in 2002 (*Xinhua*). The difference may be explained in terms of two other trends, namely, that coal production is declining in China and that the government has sustained a major crackdown on illegal mines — privately owned and usually smaller mines that heretofore had successfully evaded regulation thanks to the corruption of local government officials. No doubt, the downward trend in coal mine deaths is itself a reflection of the partial success of the national government's ongoing campaigns against corruption. More good news can be found in the level of concern expressed in China's increasingly influential blogosphere, and the resurgence of investigative journalism, which recognize that turning a blind eye to the sufferings of coal miners brings shame to all of China, not only internally but also internationally.

While some may doubt the reliability of the government's statistics, viewed over time, they present an encouraging picture. They suggest that coal mine owners and operators, as well as the miners who work for them, should no longer feel that courting disaster is an irresistible fate. If things are now moving in a positive direction, all the more reason for those who would exert moral leadership in China's coal industry to seize the opportunity to commit themselves to doing good while doing well. Becoming a Black Heart need no longer be the inevitable risk of managing a coal mine. Being condemned to a slow death through Black Lung disease need no longer be the inevitable outcome of working in a coal mine. What can you do to help?

28.5 Discussion Questions

1. What do you know about coal mines? If your family owned and operated one, how would you explain it to your friends and classmates?
2. Do you think coal mine owners and operators should be given the benefit of the doubt when they claim that they cannot afford reliable

safety equipment or other improvements designed to reduce the chance of accidents?

3. If heavy rains cause a coal mine to flood, resulting in the drowning of several miners, do you think the managers who refused to shut the mine down in time can reasonably attribute the cause of their deaths to "natural disaster"?

4. Do you think coal mine owners and operators bear responsibility when their workers contract black lung disease? What if the company's health care workers indicate that the miners suffering pneumoconiosis also smoked cigarettes, cooked over wood fires, and engaged in other activities that might impede the proper functioning of their lungs? Would that make a difference in your opinion? If so, how so; if not, why not?

5. Given the fact that coal miners make a lot more money than unskilled workers in other industries, for example, taxi cab drivers, do you think they have no right to complain when accidents happen, given what they knew of the risks involved in the jobs they signed up for?

6. What is human dignity? How, if at all, does it translate into policies protecting the rights of workers and the responsibilities of their employers?

Bibliography

CCTV.com (2006). 山西大同透水事故井下被困矿工升至57人 (The number of trapped miners in the flooding accident in Datong, Shanxi rises to 57). *CCTV. com*. Retrieved on June 1, 2016 from http://www.cctv.com/program/qqzxb/ 20060522/101829.shtml.

Xinhua News (2007). Flooded mine traps 172 in Shandong. *China.org.cn*. Retrieved on June 1, 2016 from http://www.china.org.cn/english/China/ 221290.htm.

Xinhua News (2015). Coal mine accident deaths drop to 931 last year. *Xinghua News*. Retrieved on June 1, 2016 from http://english.www.gov.cn/news/ top_news/2015/03/10/content_281475069137907.htm.

Yuen, Y. (2015). Coal miners suffering from black lung disease fight for compensation. *Global Times*. Retrieved on June 1, 2016 from http://www. globaltimes.cn/content/907788.shtml.

Part 7

Environmental Issues/Pollution

Chapter 29

Bike-Sharing is Caring?

Mark Pufpaff and Dennis P. McCann

Abstract

Bike-sharing, the ability for a person to rent a conveniently located bicycle for a short-term purpose, has grown quickly in popularity since the industry began in 2014. Bicycle units have become ubiquitous throughout cities in China, with both positive and negative effects. This case details the emergence of the industry, the major players, the effects of industry competition, and the environmental impacts. It also challenges readers to reflect on and discuss strategic questions concerning the future of the industry.

Keywords: Bike-sharing, sharing economy, ofo, Mobike, environmental responsibility, waste, sustainability

29.1 Seeing

Bike-sharing schemes have been around in one form or another since the 1960s. However, with the advent of the Internet and digital technologies such as smart phones, paired with the emergence of the so-called "Sharing Economy", bike-sharing schemes have taken on an unprecedented form. This case will track the development of the bike-sharing industry in China, and focus on *ofo* and *Mobike*, the country's two leading bike-sharing companies.

First, let us provide some context. What is the "Sharing Economy"? A preliminary definition is as follows:

"A sharing economy is an economic model in which individuals are able to borrow or rent assets owned by someone else."

There are a number of prominent examples of what this model looks like in the form of a business. One is China-based *Didi Chuxing*, which covers a host of transportation-related services. One of its core offerings, *Didi Taxi*, is a platform by which anyone with a private vehicle can use it to provide taxi services to interested patrons. Another example is US-based Airbnb, a company that allows private home owners or apartment renters to offer their spaces to travelers visiting their cities for a fee. In practice, it turns one's home or apartment into a temporary hotel.

Both *Didi Chuxing* and Airbnb are examples of platforms that enable the sharing of private assets within the consumer marketplace. A common feature of all such companies operating within the "Sharing Economy" is that their services are facilitated through smartphone applications, through which interested consumers may contact them.

Bike-sharing schemes in China, although similar in practice and commonly considered as part of the "Sharing Economy", are different in one important feature. Instead of enabling private bike owners to share their bicycles with those interested in using them, both *ofo* and *Mobike* own the bicycles that are shared in the consumer marketplace. This decision most likely had to do with the nature of the asset as bicycle rentals would be harder to manage by private owners, and their strategy for making the available bicycles recognizable and accessible to the consumer marketplace — identifying generic-looking privately owned bicycles — would be harder due to a lack of branding.

For this reason, it has been argued that bike-sharing in China is more similar to traditional bicycle renting, given that industry players actually own the assets. That the rental process takes place digitally as opposed to at a brick and mortar location does not necessarily change the nature of the business model. It also does not alter the fact that bikes are being rented, as opposed shared for a fee. When a *Didi Taxi* driver shares her or his private vehicle with someone in need of a ride, that is arguably different in kind from a businesswoman renting an *ofo* bicycle located near her apartment to get to work. The strategic relevance of this important difference will be discussed in Section 29.2.

In the meantime, let us introduce our competitors:

29.1.1 *ofo*

ofo was founded in 2014 by Dai Wei, then a Ph.D. student at Peking University in Beijing. It has grown into a "unicorn", the name given to start-ups who reach a USD $1 billion valuation. According to its website, *ofo* "developed the world's first 'non-docking' bike-sharing platform operated by a mobile application. [*ofo's*] platform combines the concepts of the sharing economy and smart appliances to overcome the 'last mile of travel' challenges of people in urban areas." By non-docking, they mean there is no centralized docking area. Instead, bicycles can be picked up and dropped off anywhere that allows bike parking. The approved areas for parking bikes are typically determined by the city in which *ofo* is offering its services. By smart appliances, *ofo* means that its bicycles are findable, unlockable, and can be paid for through its smartphone application. Given below is an image of what one of their bikes looks like:

These bikes can now be found sprinkled throughout many cities in China and even around the world. They claim on their website to have in circulation over 6,500,000 bicycle units and boast over 100,000,000 registered users.

29.1.2 *Mobike*

Started in 2015 by founders Hu Weiwei, Wang Xiaofeng, and Xia Yiping, *Mobike*, like *ofo*, is "a bike sharing service to fulfil urban short trips — anytime, to any legal parking destination — by combining innovation and today's IoT (Internet of Things) technology." Beyond providing an affordable means of transportation, their stated mission is to "reduce congestion, and our cit[ies'] carbon footprint…*Mobike* improves the quality of city life." All of their bike units come outfitted with a Quick Response (QR) code, which can be scanned using the *Mobike* smartphone application, and a Global Positioning System (GPS) that allows users to find those nearest to their locations. Once scanned, the bike is unlocked and ready for use. A picture of one of their bikes is shown below:

Mobike has over 5,000,000 bicycle units in operation across over 100 cities globally.

With these companies introduced, let us review the state of the industry. In short, it is exploding. According to *Mobike* CEO Davis Wang, "Right now, [*Mobike*] is transporting more people than taxis in China in many cities. And in some cities, for example in Chengdu, we are transporting more people than the subway. So *Mobike* is becoming one of the major transportation platforms in many of the cities in which we operate." Bike-sharing's popularity has surprised those both inside and outside of

China. The explosion of the industry has led to an environment of hyper competitiveness. Both *ofo* and *Mobike*, along with some 70+ smaller competitors, are all racing for market share. An incredible number of these bright colored bicycles, each color representing a different brand, are being seen throughout cities across China. Investors are flocking to get in on the phenomenon, thereby lifting the value of these companies sky high. Local governments are scrambling to figure out how to manage the massive influx of bicycles to their cities, many of which were not built for high-volume bicycle use. At quick glance, the industry appears pretty chaotic. However, most view it as sustainable, with its current problems being more akin to growing pains than actual barriers to development. For example, Jeffrey Towson, a Professor at Peking University, had this to say about the industry:

> "[Bike-sharing is] still a very good business, but doesn't have the awesome economics of *Didi*, Uber, and Airbnb. Of course, these are still early days and their business model is still changing. Many of the most successful businesses such as Google and Facebook didn't really figure out their business models until later. They were a consumer phenomenon at the beginning."

29.2 Judging

What are we to make of the bike-sharing industry? Does its development raise any strategic questions, or even moral questions?

Let us begin by discussing the branding and market positioning of *ofo* and *Mobike*. Joe Xia, Founder and Chief Technology Officer (CTO) of *Mobike*, said this in an interview:

> "*Mobike* is indeed part of the sharing economy…[but] first, I think we need to rethink the concept of sharing economy."

Does anything strike you as strange about this statement? The first part is an affirmation that *Mobike* — and by extension the industry at large, given the homogeneity of the business model across competitors — is part of the sharing economy. Perhaps he is interested in positioning his company this way because the sharing economy has produced a number of incredibly successful start-ups, and has permanently revolutionized the tourism and transportation industries, to name just two. Having *Mobike* perceived by investors and the general public as something other than a traditional bicycle rental company seems advantageous for a couple of reasons. One, there is a lot of hype around companies breaking into the sharing economy ecosystem. This hype helps small companies get known and achieve scale. Two, there is a lot of investment capital available to companies in the sharing economy. According to a worldwide research study conducted by Deloitte, as of 2015, USD $12 billion in start-up capital had been invested in a relatively small number of firms — for example, USD $2.7 billion had gone to Uber, a ridesharing company similar in kind to *Didi Taxi*, alone. This amount is only set to grow, and has already far surpassed the investment capital that was and is available to social start-ups like Facebook and Twitter.

The second part of Xia's statement, however, raises some questions. What exactly does he mean by "we need to rethink the concept of sharing economy"? Why would we need to do that? Does it not betray an acknowledgment that *Mobike* and company are not, strictly speaking, a part of the sharing economy? Or, is he simply indicating that not all sharing economy business models will be in lockstep with the pioneers of the industry? At the very least, Xia is arguing defensively. There may be a couple of reasons why.

First, bike-sharing in China is hyped to the max. Its popularity has surprised everyone. At present, everyone is talking about it, investing in it, and using it. The hype, it may be argued, is driving the investment behavior. And, the ease of access to investment capital is skyrocketing the valuation of *ofo* and *Mobike*. But, as mentioned above, and as any knowledgeable investor would know, the profitability of the industry is of paramount importance. Currently, it is speculated that most companies — including *ofo* and *Mobike* — are running on negative operating margins. There are serious lingering questions as to how, without mass consolidation — through mergers and acquisitions — the industry will begin to turn a profit. Economies of scale do not seem to have the same advantages in the bike-sharing industry as they do in other industries, given that scale does not necessarily create a superior service, drastically reduce the per unit cost structure of the bicycles produced (it is estimated that per unit costs are actually rising as *ofo* and *Mobike* grow, due to the race to innovate new marketable bike-selling points, rather than falling), or increase the amount of revenue generated per unit produced. Moreover, the barriers to entry into the industry are low. To put it rather bluntly, anyone with a couple of hundred thousand RMB can order a thousand bikes and distribute them across a local neighborhood.

Second, capital is readily available. *ofo* and *Mobike* are well funded, and are enjoying easy access to further investment dollars. But, given the industry's razor-thin, if not completely negative, operating margins, it is questionable whether such capital will last indefinitely. Xia may be trying to forestall the drying up of investment capital by branding the company as something revolutionary and disruptive, as opposed to merely a digitalized iteration of a traditional business model, namely, bicycle renting. If investors begin to see that the hype is merely that, the future of firms like *ofo* and *Mobike* may be compromised, at least in their present form.

That said, *ofo* and *Mobike* may very well have pioneered something revolutionary in the bicycle rental sector, and it is just taking time for the sustainable players to fortify their market positions and the less competitive players to close shop. It is clear that the industry is different from traditional bike rental companies, and not just in terms of its adoption of digital technology. Introducing the non-docking system, where bikes can be parked anywhere deemed legal by the local city government, is new. Such a system could be massively disruptive to traditional bike rental shops, effectively driving them out of business due to the ubiquity of dock-less bicycle units.

Morally speaking, there are two important areas to discuss:

1. Reducing waste: *ofo* and *Mobike* are competing primarily by distributing as many bicycle units as possible in whatever markets they are operating in. The brand that is seen most by prospective consumers is deemed the winner. This has created a number of problems. The most pressing is that management of this massive number of bicycles is near impossible. Preventing units from being stolen or vandalized, ensuring bikes are parked legally, and inspecting bike units for routine wear and tear are all difficult. Bike-sharing companies have a responsibility to the communities in which they operate to offer a service that will not become a burden to local residents, businesses, or governments. The fact of "Bicycle Graveyards", where damaged and illegally parked bicycles are collected, is evidence that the number of units in circulation and their lack of oversight have combined to become a burden on communities. It commits city resources to cleaning up illegally parked units and finding spaces to store them before

disposal. It has created congestion on sidewalks not reserved exclusively for bike-riding. It has increased the potential rate of accidents, given that city streets in China, since the advent of the motor vehicle in China, have not been built with a thriving bicycle-riding community in mind. All this is to say that *ofo* and *Mobike*, while providing a service people are certainly using, create unintended consequences in terms of their impact on diverse stakeholders.

2. Encouraging responsible usage: If bike-sharing companies are facing a governance issue, their users are facing a responsible usage issue. Complaints abound from bicycle retailers, bicycle repair shops, taxi drivers, security personnel, motorists, pedestrians, and neighborhood families concerning carelessly discarded bicycle units. Such complaints and sentiments have issued different reactions. Some, called "Bike Hunters", have reacted constructively, citing patriotism and commitment to traditional moral values, by searching the streets, both alone and in teams, for vandalized and illegally discarded bicycles. Vandalized bikes are reported to the corresponding company for fixing, while illegally parked bicycles are brought to legal parking areas. They view this work as a civic duty, one that is meant to shine forth the honorable character of the Chinese people. Others, however, have taken a different approach. There are a number of viral videos of, along with media commentary about, disgruntled citizens toppling legally parked bicycles and vandalizing illegally parked units in protest against how careless they feel the industry — both firms and users — has been in respectfully introducing their service to the cities in which they operate. Both of these reactions are part of a wider debate that has developed about the state of public morality in China. Who knew dock-less bike-sharing, which is now being talked about domestically as one of China's four great modern inventions — the others being their high-speed rail system, Alipay, and the e-commerce ecosystem, reminiscent of the original "four great inventions", namely, gunpowder, the compass, papermaking, and printing — would become the springboard for such a conversation?

29.3 Acting

What might the leaders of the bike-sharing industry in China want to consider going forward?

First is profitability. The race for market share, currently underway, is important. But, it has created a price war, a supply of bicycle units in excess of demand, and a visible waste problem. These are problems that can be alleviated through the development of a more refined business model. In supply chain terms, pivoting from what seems to be a "push" strategy — where demand is forecasted — to a "pull" strategy — where demand is responded to — may be helpful. There are a couple of reasons why. "Push" strategies are good for products where market demand is known with relative certainty, and where economies of scale are significant for cost reduction. This does not seem to be the case for bike-sharing. Given the unexpected growth trajectory of the industry to date, and the future effects of its development yet to be seen, forecasting demand with even relative accuracy may be a near impossible task. Also, as mentioned above, economies of scale are not having the cost-reduction effects for bike-sharing companies that they have had for firms in other industries. Strategically, this means that there is little incentive, at present, to grow as big as possible as fast as possible. A more calculated growth strategy, rooted in an accurate understanding of market demand, would help to raise profits, reduce excess production and waste, and hedge against over-leveraging in terms of debt and investor repayments.

Second is sustainability. China is a world leader in many areas of sustainability, from renewable energy investments to green financing. Its future development plans are permeated with sustainability and environmental initiatives. Although a more or less recent response to international trends, China's international and domestic commitments in this area should be taken seriously. It would be unwise for business leaders in new industries to be complacent about their environmental impacts. Having *ofo* and *Mobike* bicycles going to landfills, or being found in lakes and rivers, is not only bad for the image of the industry but it also puts them in conflict with the priorities of the government. Aligning their business strategies with the government's intention to create an "Ecological Civilization" is not only smart business but also contributes to the common good. It enables businesses and the government to work together on a common mission with common objectives. Win-win strategies should be the priority.

29.4 Discussion Questions

1. Do you think bike-sharing is part of the "Sharing Economy"? Why or why not?
2. In your view, what are the moral issues facing the bike-sharing industry in China? How would you resolve them?
3. What is the environmental impact of innovative businesses like *ofo* or *Mobike*? If they are contributing toward mitigating some forms of environmental pollution, should they be given a free pass when they fail to address other problems created by their business?

4. Do ostensibly social businesses, claiming legitimacy as part of the "Sharing Economy", have any responsibilities to address the externalities — social, economic, and environmental — generated by the success of their business models?
5. Strategically speaking, how would you manage the future development of *ofo* or *Mobike* (pick one)?

Bibliography

Deloitte (2015). The sharing economy: Share and make money — How does Switzerland compare? *Deloitte Report*. Retrieved on October 16, 2017 from https://www2.deloitte.com/content/dam/Deloitte/ch/Documents/consumer-business/ch-cb-shared-economy-shareand-make-money.pdf.

Kun, L. (2017). Opinion: Is China's bike-sharing cycling off a cliff of hype and greed? *CGTN.com*. Retrieved on October 16, 2017 from https://news.cgtn.com/news/3d636a4e306b6a4d/share_p.html.

Sohu.com (2017). 摩拜单车CEO王晓峰: 摩拜单车的思考与经验 (Wang Xiaofeng, CEO of Mobike: Thougts and Experiences of Building Mobike). *Sohu.com*. Retrieved on October 16, 2017 from https://www.sohu.com/a/195576089_649849.

Chapter 30

Coal Mining and the Shift Toward Clean Energy in China

Dennis P. McCann and Mark Pufpaff

Abstract

Consistent with its COP21 (Conference of Parties, 21st annual meeting) agreements, creating a United Nations Framework on Climate Change, China recently announced a three-year suspension of new permits for coal mine operations. At the same time, China has made major investments in developing renewable energy sources, and now leads the world in wind and solar power generation. It has also begun to ramp up its efforts to develop nuclear power. The search for alternatives, of course, means a shift away from carbon-based fossil fuels like coal and oil whose use generates the emission of the so-called "greenhouse gases", thought to be responsible for global warming. This case discusses China's motives in the global climate debate.

Keywords: Environment, safety, coal, climate

30.1 Seeing

In December 2015, representatives of 195 nations gathered in Paris to sign the "COP21" (literally, "Conference of Parties, 21st annual meeting") agreements, creating a United Nations Framework on Climate Change. The comprehensive agreements focused on five major objectives:

> "Mitigation — reducing emissions fast enough to achieve the temperature goal; A transparency system and global stock-take — accounting for climate action; Adaptation — strengthening ability of countries to deal with climate impacts; Loss and damage — strengthening ability to recover from climate impacts; and Support — including finance, for nations to build clean, resilient futures."

Prior to the COP21 meeting in Paris, Presidents Barack Obama of the United States of America and Xi Jinping of China had met in Washington, DC, in September 2015, to pledge their personal support and leadership on behalf of the agreements, establishing common ground that most observers felt would be crucial to the success of the COP21 effort to contain global warming to an average 2°C by the end of this century. The 2° threshold is estimated by climate scientists to be the highest global temperature increase that can be absorbed without unleashing catastrophic and irreversible damage to the planet's ecosystem.

If COP21 is to be implemented, it will require a significant restructuring of the energy policy in both countries. Nevertheless, there are important signs that China is prepared to fulfill its promises. Much of the impact will fall on China's coal industry, which leads the world in the production of coal, and its consumption to meet China's increasing energy needs. Even so, over the past ten years, China has moved to close down illegal coal mines and restrict small operators unable to meet regulations intended to safeguard the safety and health of the people working in the mines. The result, according to government statistics, has been a dramatic decrease in the number of deaths attributed to coal mine accidents, as China for the first time has reported less than a thousand deaths annually. While moving in the right direction, such figures also suggest just how far China has yet to come, compared to the safety records of other major producers.

Consistent with its COP21 pledges, China recently announced a three-year suspension of new permits for coal mine operations. At the same time, China has made major investments in developing renewable energy sources, and now leads the world in wind and solar power generation. It has also begun to ramp up its efforts to develop nuclear power. The search for alternatives, of course, means a shift away from carbon-based fossil fuels like coal and oil whose use generates the emission of the so-called "greenhouse gases", thought to be responsible for global warming. The realization of the full extent of the problem caused by reliance on fossil fuels comes at a time when the environmental and social costs of air and water pollution are increasingly evident. Coal mining, for example, is not only dangerous but is also dirty and debilitating. Black lung disease is on the rise among China's mine workers, compounding the cost of pollution cleanup with the cost of ongoing medical treatment for those affected. When all the costs are recognized, it is clear that coal can no longer be counted on as China's path to cheap and abundant energy.

30.2 Judging

China's willingness to exercise leadership in the world's struggle to mitigate climate change is surely encouraging to all, especially the young, who may live to see the turn of the 21st century. But, China's commitment, not surprisingly, is probably based as much on calculations of national security as it is on an altruistic concern for mitigating climate change. As the costs, both environmental and social, of reliance upon coal as the major energy source begin to exceed any conceivable benefit from it, it is merely a matter of collective self-interest to shift China's energy policies in a cleaner, more sustainable direction. Nevertheless, with positive responses now underway and with reasonable expectations for what is yet to come, it is clear that China's national self-interest now coincides with everyone's need to address the problem of climate change. But, what are we to make of that? The English poet and playwright, T.S. Eliot, in *Murder in the Cathedral*, had Thomas Becket, the victim targeted for assassination, exclaim, "The last temptation is the greatest treason. To do the right thing but for the wrong reason." Can China's shift away from a coal-based energy policy be dismissed as merely doing the right thing but for the wrong reason? Is there ever such a thing as the wrong reason, when what is being done is so clearly right?

Ethics, among other things, is the study of such conundrums. If my motives for doing something are not pure, should the verdict on my actions be negative regardless of the good achieved through them? The makers of public policy, the Obamas and Xis of this world, are by no means the only ones who must wrestle with such dilemmas. Entrepreneurs and business managers typically face the challenge of achieving as much good as possible in any given situation, even as their motives for doing so may be challenged by others. Bill Gates, for example, may be allocating a vast amount of his fortune to philanthropy, but — so the accusation goes — he is only doing it to enhance his own power, or the good reputation of the company he founded, namely, Microsoft. If entrepreneurs and business managers think they can wait to make a decision until everyone's motives are clear and the outcomes are unmistakably positive, they may miss opportunities and risk never accomplishing anything. An ethic of responsibility, where one is prepared to act when neither are the motives pure nor the consequences fully known, may give us a better way forward than the kind of moral absolutism that Becket refused to compromise in an act of "treason."

Demonstrating moral leadership in business, as well as in politics and government, requires a sense of responsibility. Moral leaders must act to achieve whatever good is possible at the moment, even while knowing that the choices they make are less than perfect, and may carry downside risks of negative consequences that cannot be avoided if anything is to be done at all. Mitigating climate change, reducing air and water pollution, and working to create a clean environment for all are all noble goals, and we are right to embrace them; but, actually making progress toward them may create additional problems along the way.

30.3 Acting

It is certain that as China's coal industry shrinks, there will be those who will bear the brunt of the negative consequences of this shift. Investors, if they are not wise enough to read the writing on the wall, are likely to lose money on their coal mine investments. But, their suffering will be relatively minor compared to the pain of unemployment or underemployment and other betrayals and breaches of contract that the coal miners will have to endure as they are laid off or have their wages cut, and other benefits suspended, for lack of funds.

Under the circumstances, it is not surprising that pundits are now debating whether China's coal mines are a "sunset industry", that is, one that has peaked and faces a future with diminishing returns. The sun sets as the need diminishes for the industry's products, as the markets shift to other, cheaper, more efficient alternatives. Since China still leads the world in coal production, it may be premature to designate coal mining as a sunset industry. But, if the nation actually succeeds in meeting its goals for reducing carbon-based emissions over the next twenty-five years, coal mining will have become as obsolete as the horse-drawn cartage became for our grandparents. It just makes sense to begin responding to the likely consequences of the shift away from coal and other fossil fuels.

We know that millions of workers will face the prospect of unemployment. What does China plan to do about this? Typically, managing a sunset industry requires cooperative planning involving both government agencies and NGOs, as well as businesses. Hiring decisions need to be thought through, on the assumption that fewer workers will be needed in the long term. Unfunded liabilities for pensions and health benefits for current workers will have to be addressed, even as the companies that employed them seek bankruptcy protection. Efforts to restore environments seriously compromised by mining activity will have to be developed. In short, the cost of achieving a cleaner, more sustainable energy future must include provision for those who have had their livelihoods disrupted as a result of the shift underway.

30.4 Conclusion

China's attempt to exercise leadership in the global effort to mitigate climate change is admirable, and ought to be supported by all who love China and regard themselves as friends of the earth. Nevertheless, like all such major shifts in economic policy, the processes of change will impose sacrifices on many who are not in a position to protect their own interests, the first of which are the miners who may be left behind as the nation moves to cleaner and more sustainable energy policies. The claim of moral leadership requires a positive response to their plight, even as the country moves forward on other fronts.

30.5 Discussion Questions

1. Why is climate change a moral issue? If it is man-made, who bears responsibility for it? What should be done about it?
2. If addressing a problem like climate change is a moral imperative, how should our responses be managed to balance the needs of all stakeholders? Should policy planners be concerned to address the suffering of those whose livelihoods will be disrupted because of shifts in China's energy policy?

3. Does the recognition of mixed motives inevitably cancel the good intended in a particular policy or action? Are actions done out of self-interest inevitably less moral than actions done with pure motives or perfectly good intentions?
4. In managing a sunset industry, bankruptcy proceedings may eventually be part of the challenge. In any bankruptcy, of course, all stakeholders will be pressuring management to get back what they think they are owed. If management is forced to choose between compensating investors for their losses and maintaining their commitment to the workers' pensions or health plans, which should it pick? Are the losses of one group of stakeholders more compelling than the losses of another group? How so?
5. Is there a good way to manage a layoff? If workers must be terminated, or have their hours reduced or their wages cut, is there any good way to do this? If you were a manager and had to downsize a company, how would you do it? What would be your priorities? Is there any reason why investors' interests should be preferred to workers'? Or vice versa?

Bibliography

UNFCCC (2016). Report of the Conference of the Parties on its twenty-first session. *United Nations Framework Convention on Climate Change Resource*. Retrieved on February 10, 2016 from https://unfccc.int/resource/docs/2015/cop21/eng/10.pdf.

Xinhua (2015a). Coal mine accidents, deaths continue to decline. *China Daily*. Retrieved on February 10, 2016 from http://www.chinadaily.com.cn/china/2015-09/25/content_21977824.htm.

Xinhua (2015b). Xi meets Obama on ties ahead of UN climate conference. *China Youth International*. Retrieved on February 10, 2016 from http://en.youth.cn/RightNow/201512/t20151201_7370278.htm.

Chapter 31

Takeout Trash — The Environmental Impact of Food Delivery in China

Mark Pufpaff and Dennis P. McCann

Abstract

Each day, China's food delivery platforms process 57 million orders. Every order is delivered in a food container leading to an enormous amount of plastic bags, containers, and disposable chopsticks consumed and disposed every day. Food delivery has led to serious waste problems. The case looks at different perspectives on this problem and asks what can producers, platforms, and consumers do to decrease garbage in food deliveries.

Keywords: Environment, food safety, garbage, sustainability

31.1 Seeing

400 million. That is the amount of food delivery orders processed each *week* by China's leading food delivery platforms — *Baidu Waimai, Ele. me,* and *Meituan Waimai.* Each *day,* that is over 57 million orders. While economically speaking this may bode well for delivery companies, local restaurants, and food suppliers, environmentally speaking it means something quite different. It is estimated that among each of the three aforementioned companies, more than "65 million food containers, 20 million pairs of disposable chopsticks, and 20 million plastic bags" are consumed

every *day*, with little if any of it being recycled or otherwise sustainably disposed of. It is likely, when carry-out and other types of takeout orders are taken into account, these numbers are even higher. By a large margin, China leads the world in the amount of takeout food it consumes. The industry — valued at RMB 166 billion as of 2016 — has grown 800% since 2011, with little sign of stopping.

It also leads the world in the amount of household waste it generates. According to the World Bank, China generates some 520,000 tons of household waste every day, a large percentage of this waste being from food delivery. This is almost 1/3 more than India, and more than twice that of the United States. Such consumption behavior has not come without consequences. According to *Sixth Tone*,

> "Food delivery waste is a microcosm of China's worsening pollution problem. The nation's cities are besieged by mounting piles of garbage, while the country's creaking waste management systems struggle to keep up.
>
> Cities are growing incapable of controlling the waste their inhabitants produce. In 2016, reports of trash dumping across provincial borders drew widespread public attention. In an effort to cut costs, more than 20,000 tons of waste produced in Shanghai were quietly dumped on Xishan Island in nearby Suzhou, Jiangsu province.
>
> Even more serious is the plastic waste dumped directly into the ocean, causing virtually irreparable harm to aquatic ecosystems. According to data published in the journal *Science*, China is the No. 1 offender, responsible for almost one-third of all oceanic plastic waste. Pollutants ingested by fish are making their way back up the food chain and into humans, leading to increased risks of cancer and birth defects."

Compounding problems is that a lot this waste is not recyclable (let alone biodegradable). It is doomed for the landfill, or worse if it is illegally disposed of. That said, it is important to note that it is not as if China's government is void of regulation on this front. Article 6 of the Environmental Protection Law of the People's Republic of China states the following:

> "All units and individuals shall have the obligation to protect the environment. Local people's governments at various levels shall be responsible for the environmental quality within areas under their jurisdiction.

Enterprises, public institutions and any other producers/business operators shall prevent and reduce environmental pollution and ecological destruction, and shall bear the liability for the damage caused by them in accordance with the law. Citizens shall enhance environmental protection awareness, adopt low-carbon and energy-saving lifestyle, and conscientiously fulfill the obligation of environmental protection."

While this certainly obliges most, if not all, of Chinese society to work toward environmental ends, and serves as an attempt by the government to orient public morality to include sustainability-related objectives, it leaves open the question of enforcement. In light of the negative externalities resulting from the growth of China's food delivery and takeout culture, enforcement indeed is a question in need of attention, especially because the lack of it has real consequences for the future of the country.

31.2 Judging

Sustainable development is a concept that concerns just that, the future of a given country and, ultimately, the world. In 1987, the United Nations published a report titled *Our Common Future* — also known as the Brundtland Report — from which emerged perhaps the simplest and most enduring definition of the term "sustainable development":

"Sustainable development is development that meets the needs of the present without compromising the ability of future generations to meet their own needs."

Drawing from this definition, the question of consumption takes on a dual meaning. While it is necessary to consume for our own needs, it is likewise necessary to consume *in a way* that does not lessen the ability for future generations to do the same. In other words, all consumption decisions, however seemingly small and insignificant, have societal effects, and cannot be made without generating moral consequences. When the question of consumption is viewed in this way, our decision-making must be tempered by and oriented toward that which is, at the very least and to the extent possible, not destructive to society. Although it is easy to view any one or another consumption decision as morally neutral, given how quickly they are often made and how routine they often are, it is tougher to deny the moral insignificance of individual consumption decisions when they are considered *en masse*. For example, when *Meituan Waimai* uses "20 million pairs of disposable [wooden] chopsticks" as part of their daily order fulfillment, it is estimated that some 6,700 mature trees are felled; extended across a full year of business operations, that amounts to 2.5 million mature trees. These numbers represent just one of many such delivery platforms. Given that each pair of chopsticks corresponds to one takeout meal ordered, each person ordering a meal is contributing to the felling of mature trees in China (or wherever they may source their timber, if it not produced domestically). If such trees are being felled at a rate faster than they are being grown, then ordering takeout food from *Meituan Waimai* is an unsustainable consumption decision, and would be at odds with the fulfillment of the ideal outlined in the Brundtland Report.

That said, consumers are not the only ones that must assume the consequences of their decisions. Businesses, and the people who run them, must also make decisions that have societal consequences. If the only takeout options available to consumers are unsustainable ones — in other words, ones that use unsustainable material inputs or generate externalities that cannot be mitigated or otherwise offset in some way — then businesses are making it harder for China to develop sustainably. Using plastic bags, tubing, and containers — usually made from low-density polyethylene — for takeout orders, knowing that China's recycling infrastructure is still developing, that many consumers will not consider the environmental impacts of the trash they dispose of,[1] and that the enforcement of plastic bag bans[2] has been ineffective at best, businesses such as *Baidu Waimai* are neglecting their responsibility to manage their environmental impact. Given the obligations outlined in Article 6 of the Environmental Protection Law, this would be, technically speaking, in defiance of law.

Moreover, as businesses exist and operate in society, and form an integral part of local communities, they have inherent social responsibilities.

---

[1] According to a 2,000+ person survey conducted by the *China Youth Daily* in May 2017, 71.6% of those polled stated they are unaware of the environmental impacts of their consumption decisions.

[2] The State Council officially banned the production and consumption of plastic bags that are thinner than 0.025 millimeters on June 1, 2008. Although one of the global pioneers in banning such bags, it has made comparatively little progress in actually weeding out the production and consumption of them due to lax enforcement and avoidance of responsibility among government bodies.

What they provide to the consumer marketplace is, in turn, what the consumer marketplace has to choose from. Therefore, what they offer and how they offer it matter, not only legally but also morally. This is the basis for what is known as Corporate Social Responsibility (CSR), the idea that a business has a moral duty to work toward sustainable ends — whatever that might mean or look like for a given firm — so as not to exploit manpower, indiscriminately use up limited resources, or pollute carelessly. The avoidance of harm to society is only one half of the CSR equation, however. The other half is service-oriented. It involves strategically giving back to the communities in which a business operates. Such work includes employer-sponsored volunteer hours for employees, partnerships with relevant non-profits, and philanthropic activity. The most successful companies in the CSR space have achieved an alignment between their social goals and their strategic business objectives. Firms in China, including those in the food delivery industry, can and should embrace such CSR strategies, as this would encourage better consumption behavior on behalf of the public and support the government's social agenda.

While the morality of production and consumption decisions by individual consumers and producers is important, there is a cultural dimension to be considered as well. Underlying the growth of the takeout industry in China, at least in part, is a growing obsession with convenience. Ordering takeout to be delivered to a consumer's doorstep is much easier and faster than going grocery shopping, cooking a meal, and then cleaning the dishes afterwards. In other words, the convenience of ordering takeout, despite the effects the fulfillment of such convenience is having on society and the environment, is being prioritized over more laborious, albeit more sustainable,[3] forms of dining (e.g., cooking at home). However, personal convenience is not necessarily in line with the goals of sustainable development. While *Ele.me* may enable people to fulfill their own needs quickly and satisfactorily, the method of fulfillment may not be contributing to the ability of future generations to do so in the same way or to the same degree. As Chen Ronggang of *Sixth Tone* put it,

"If we continue to saddle the environment with the remains of our quick-and-easy takeout hot pot, our environment will, one day, bite back."

---

[3] While generally considered more sustainable than eating out or ordering delivery, home cooking can be done in an unsustainable and wasteful way (e.g., by bagging groceries in plastic bags and buying food in unsustainable packaging).

31.3 Acting

What can consumers and businesses do to comply with the Chinese government's Environmental Protection Law and align with the vision of sustainable development defined in the Brundtland Report?

Nielsen, a global marketing research firm, published a report in 2014 called the Global Survey on CSR. They found that 55% of online consumers were willing to pay more for products and services being offered by companies with a social and/or environmental mission. Similarly, a Cone Communications Social Impact Survey found that 89% of consumers in the US would switch brands — assuming similar quality and price points — to support one with an explicit social mission. While this is good news, and indicates the potential of businesses and consumers to work together toward social ends, many consumers who express such sentiments and intentions in surveys oftentimes do not act accordingly. This is sometimes called the "attitude-behavior gap." The explanation as to why this gap exists, at least in part, surrounds price and quality. Consumers almost invariably choose products that either match their budgets or fulfill their quality expectations, regardless of whether the firm supplying the product has a social mission. While this is reasonable consumption behavior, it leaves a lingering contradiction between how consumers would like to consume and how they actually consume. This has two significant implications.

One, consumers are not, as they say, "practicing what they preach." However, before moralizing over their alleged hypocrisy, it is important to understand the context in which consumers make their consumption decisions. As mentioned earlier, businesses determine the range of product and service options available for consumers to choose from. They also are responsible for the degree of transparency they provide to the public, say, concerning their sourcing methods and the kind of material inputs they use in production. While consumers have an obligation to conduct a certain amount of due diligence, so as not to support immorally run or incompliant firms, they are pragmatists first. Consumers will buy and use what works and satisfies their needs. If it happens to fulfill a social goal in the process, all the better. CSR is therefore not about "purifying the intentions" of consumers so that they will patronize social businesses on principle, but about accommodating consumers' altruistic impulses by enabling them to buy products or services — at their desired price point and quality level — that simultaneously support their social interests. This is the basis for social innovation.

Orienting existing product lines to align with a social objective (for example, Unilever is committed to 100% sustainably sourced palm oil by 2019 — as of 2017, they were at 50%) is one way to close the "attitude-behavior gap" of consumers without requiring that consumers even change brands. Social entrepreneurs should see the attitude dimension as a competitive advantage against larger firms that may take longer to transform their product lines. Thus, it is important to note that having a social mission alone is not enough to attract consumers, at least according to the rationale behind the "attitude-behavior gap." While consumers may readily admit they would — in a perfect world — support socially conscious businesses, price and quality are what ultimately matter. But, that is not to say that social businesses cannot have high-quality and/or competitively priced products. Quite the contrary. They can and should. The point is that businesses cannot rely exclusively on having a social mission, however well branded and communicated, for sales. The true value of a social mission lies in the value it adds to an already excellent product or service.

For companies like *Baidu Waimai*, *Ele.me*, and *Meituan Waimai*, there are a number of opportunities that they could respond to, even proactively. In the *China Youth Daily* survey referenced above, 40% said environmental education should be strengthened and 86.4% said they would support stronger environmental regulation on businesses — particularly in the use of plastic bags. Takeout delivery platforms should not assume that these numbers will not rise, or that consumers will continue current consumption habits despite changing or evolving attitudes. Companies should see the data as an opportunity to begin pushing out educational material on how they are addressing environmental concerns related to their operations. They should also see it as a way to anticipate, or even work with, the government in either drafting new environmental regulation or enforcing current regulation. Such efforts should be handsomely rewarded.

31.4 Discussion Questions

1. What are the moral issues involved in this case? List and explain them.
2. Do you think consumers have a responsibility to choose sustainable or socially oriented brands? Why or why not?
3. What is the role of government regulation in shaping markets for sustainable and socially innovative products and services?

4. Do you think it would be smart for firms to adopt a social dimension into their business strategies? Why or why not? Do they, in fact, have a moral obligation to do so?

5. If you were to advise any of the three major food delivery platforms in addressing their environmental impacts, what would be your recommendations?

Bibliography

Chen, R. (2017). The mountains of takeout trash choking China's cities. *Sixth Tone*. Retrieved on November 2, 2017 from http://www.sixthtone.com/news/1001003/the-mountains-of-takeout-trash-choking-chinas-cities.

Cone Communications (2017). Cone communications social impact survey. *www.conecomm.com*. Retrieved on November 2, 2017 from https://www.conecomm.com/2017-cone-communications-csr-study-pdf.

NielsenIQ (2014). Doing well by doing good. *NielsenIQ Report*. Retrieved on November 2, 2017 from https://www.nielsen.com/us/en/insights/report/2014/doing-well-by-doing-good/.

Qu, Q. (2017). Plastic pollution continues due to lax enforcement of govt ban. *Global Times*. Retrieved on November 2, 2017 from http://www.globaltimes.cn/content/1063915.shtml.

The National People's Congress of the People's Republic of China (2021). *The Environmental Protection Law of the People's Republic of China*. Retrieved on March 28, 2021 from http://www.npc.gov.cn/wxzl/gongbao/2014-06/23/content_1879688.htm.

Chapter 32

China's Beef Industry and Its Environmental Impact

Helen Xu and Dennis McCann

Abstract

China is the world's third-largest beef producer after the United States and Brazil. Despite this, China is not complying with the environmental measures that have been adopted elsewhere by the beef industry. Current Chinese regulations and standards covering the negative impact of the meat industry are scarce; research studies measuring the impact of current policies on air pollution have a focus other than the beef industry, such as thermal power, metallurgy, and iron and steel production. The case discusses the current situation of meat production in China and its effect on the environment.

Keywords: Environmental impact, GHG emissions, grain fed vs. pasture fed beef production, environmental responsibility, the "Silent Stakeholder," consumers' choices

32.1 Seeing

In 2007, a research team from the University of Tsukuba in Japan found that meat production generates greenhouse gases and other pollutants. The researchers, according to the *Animal Science Journal*, found that the "the total contribution of 1 kg beef production to greenhouse gas (GHG)

emissions and warming potentials were 36.4 kg of carbon dioxide equivalents, 340 g of sulfurous dioxide equivalents, 59 g of phosphate equivalents and 169-megajoule of energy, respectively." This combination of elements poses a serious threat to the ecosystem of rivers and lakes despite regulatory control laws[1] and the penalties that govern environmental water quality and effluent standards.

According to researchers from the American Environmental Working Group in 2011, "ruminants are the worst offenders, with lamb generating 39 kg of carbon dioxide equivalent for each kilogram of meat, and beef generating 27. Then come pork (12), turkey (11) and chicken (7). Plants are all lower, ranging from potatoes (3) to lentils (1)." The term ruminant, in this context, refers to "mammals that can acquire nutrients from plant-based food by fermenting it in a specialized stomach before digestion, principally through microbial actions." These findings are supported by a study published by the US National Academy of Sciences showing that beef production "requires 28, 11, 5, and 6 times more land, irrigation water, GHG, and reactive nitrogen than the average of the other livestock categories, for example, dairy, poultry, pork, and eggs." Gidon Eshel, research professor at the Bard Center for Environmental Policy, who led the study, explained that the easiest way to make one's diet more sustainable was without question to reduce beef whenever possible. This accords with Prof. Mark Sutton of the UK's Centre for Ecology and Hydrology, who observed that "governments should consider these messages carefully if they want to improve overall production efficiency and reduce the environmental impacts. But the message for the consumer is even stronger. Avoiding excessive meat consumption, especially beef, is good for the environment."

Given these findings, other than abolishing the beef industry outright, how else can the challenge of environmental pollution in beef production be addressed? According to a study conducted by Meat & Livestock Australia (MLA), effective measures have been carried out in the past 30 years to reduce the environmental impact of black cattle, measures which include the genetic selection of animals, increases in survival rates, and expansions in lot feeding. Since the early 20th century, the Australian government has been troubled by the fact that most of the meadows for cattle grazing have been either overloaded or rendered unproductive due to overuse, as the *Jingjiao Daily* reports. Given this situation, both the government and local

---

[1] The Water Pollution Prevention and Control Law, 1971 and the Livestock Excrement Law of Japan, 2004.

factories have committed themselves to improving production practices and the efficiency of irrigation water. Moreover, they paid more attention to the protection of vegetation and tree planting methods so as to maintain the sustainability of meadows, and thus provide more grazing areas for cattle. For example, rotational grazing, with a grazing period of 5–6 years for each meadow plot, is a sustainable way to keep grassland in a healthy condition. As a result of these practices, the Australian government has reported "a 14% reduction in GHG emissions intensity; a 65% reduction in consumptive water use for beef production; land occupation for grazing per unit of production was down 19%; while land use emissions were estimated to have decreased by 42%." Stephen Wiedemann, the co-author of the MLA study, argued that their research findings indicate that "the practices actively pursued by the industry, such as a focus on productivity and herd management, have resulted in dual benefits by reducing environmental impacts per kilogram of product, at the same time as improving productivity."

Although China is the world's third-largest beef producer after the United States and Brazil, these studies have not received a lot of attention, nor is China complying with the measures that have been adopted elsewhere by the beef industry. Current Chinese regulations and standards covering the negative impact of the meat industry are scarce, one of the only ones being the *Discharge Standard of Water Pollutants for the Meat Packing Industry*, which came into effect back on July 1, 1992. Research studies measuring the impact of current policies on air pollution have a focus other than the beef industry, such as thermal power, metallurgy, iron and steel production, and the chemical and machinery industries. So far, the environmental impact of the beef industry remains a low priority.

32.2 Judging

What are the moral issues involved in this case?

We have a growing body of research indicating with increasing certainty that the beef industry as a whole is a net negative in terms of environmental impact. This impact has to do with the creation of GHG emissions, the destruction of carbon sinks — for example, rainforest lands — to create additional pastures for cattle grazing, and more. However, does that leave everyone, from cattle farmers to slaughterhouses to distributors to consumers, complicit in whatever long-term — and perhaps irreparable — damage the industry is causing? Let us discuss three areas of moral concern.

First, the producers: The supply chains that support the beef industry are varied and complex. From the raising of beef cattle to the feed for their diets to the packaging of products for sale in grocery stores, the industry touches an immense number of stakeholders worldwide. Given its reach into the international economy, the beef industry is unlikely to simply dissolve itself for fear of causing any further environmental damage. Too many jobs, livelihoods, lifestyles, corporate interests, and political gains are involved. More incrementally, however, there *are* ways the industry can address the environmental concerns it is being confronted with.

For example, reducing GHG emissions — carbon dioxide and methane, primarily — by altering the diet fed to cattle. Cattle produce an average of 49 kg of methane per head per year. That number can be reduced by cultivating low- to moderate-fiber pasture feed. High amounts of fiber result in more digested energy being released as methane,[2] instead of being metabolized and, so to speak, kept inside. Ancillary to this is that cattle are slaughtered as young as possible. There is already a financial incentive to do this, but the environmental impact is also noteworthy. Cattle that live shorter lives produce less methane. Thus, having pasture feeds that are high in digestibility — that is, capable of maximizing the energy derived from meals — will grow cattle to slaughter weight faster than pasture feeds that are too high in coarse and fibrous inputs.

Another is to continue, to the extent possible, the move away from grain-fed beef production and toward pasture-fed beef production. The reason is both environmental and strategic. Grain-fed production uses significantly more fossil fuel than pasture-fed production, given the logistics and management involved in grain production, which needs to then be transported to cattle farms. Pasture-fed production circumvents that activity, and thus reduces the amount of GHGs produced in the feeding of cattle. Strategically, given the finiteness of fossil fuels, as such resources diminish, the cost to use them in production will increase; this of course depends upon demand and the yet to be seen developments in technology, developments that may altogether move us away from fossil fuels, or at least severely limit their need in the international economy. Nonetheless, we can still say that those production systems that use the

---

[2]Methane is produced by microbes in the rumen. This is an undesirable loss to the animal, as it represents a loss of energy, part of the feed that the animal has failed to utilise.

least amount of fossil fuel per kilogram of product produced *now* will have the greatest long-term advantage if or when finite resources become scarcer.

Second, the consumers: It would be a rather peculiar state of affairs if, whenever research suggested that consuming a particular product was contributing to an undesirable outcome, everyone just stopped that buying that product. Consumer psychology is deeper than that. Values-based consumption is only one of many factors that make up the decision-making process of consumers. Others include one's environment — what one sees in the behavior or perspectives of family, friends, movie stars, media personalities, etc. — personal experience, financial situation, and emotional disposition. Furthermore, values-based decision-making also has a lot to do with which values resonate enough with the most people to effect the change desired. For example, if you had the capacity to reach the entire population of China with one message about the environmental dangers of beef production, what would your message be? What values-based, or other, message would you communicate? Is the environmental angle the most effective? What about animal rights? Or the healthiness of plant-based alternatives? When you think about it, there is no easy answer, because each consumer is different and influenced in different ways and with different messages.

Does that mean that efforts to embed and cultivate an ethic of responsibility within the consumer marketplace are in vain? Certainly not. But, there are conceptual issues to break open. For example, is it possible to have a responsibility to the environment? Is that the same as having a responsibility to your neighbor? Perhaps not at first sight. But, advocates of the notion of the environment as the "Silent Stakeholder", a term suggesting that the natural environment is the "precondition for every corporation's very existence", argue that although silent, the way we treat the environment nonetheless produces effects we must take responsibility for. If that is true, then consumers do have a responsibility to support companies who are responding to the unspoken, if you will, needs of the environment. In the beef industry, this includes companies who attempt to limit their pollution and waste, who innovate sustainable methods of pasture management, who are smart about which kinds of cattle will thrive in particular climates, and so on.

Third, the government: Governments can and should provide the regulatory framework within which producers produce and consumers consume. It has the ability to protect consumers and hold producers accountable. For example, many countries have regulations outlining the framework within which the beef industry is to operate. The table below provides a snapshot of examples of this kind of regulation, and the purpose it is to serve.

Given all of this, are there any concrete examples of producers, consumers, and regulators working together to effect positive change in the way the beef industry operates and impacts the environment?

32.3 Acting

The livestock sector is reported to be responsible for 14.5% of global human-related GHG emissions. The beef industry is expected to take action to manage the challenge of global warming. It is widely acknowledged that Japanese black cattle provide the most expensive beef in the world. However, according to the *Xinhua Net*'s report, the Director of Betsukai (Hokkaido, Japan) was pleased to announce that they had found a way to deal with 200 million tons of excrement, the total discharge of livestock every year. How did they do that? The local authority set up a Resources Recycling Center in response to the challenge. The Center generates electricity by using livestock manure. The manure from 100 cattle can supply 20 families with the electric power they need. This solution not only creates new energy but also protects the environment by realizing the recycling of organic matter.

Beyond Meat, an American food manufacturer established in 2009, is renowned for its numerous investors, including Bill Gates, the co-founders of Twitter, Biz Stone and Evan Williams, the former CEO of McDonald's, Don Thompson, and Leonardo DiCaprio. Beyond Meat caught the investors' attention because its innovative product met their expectations. According to DiCaprio,

> "Livestock production is a major contributor to carbon emissions. Shifting from animal meat to the plant-based meats developed by Beyond Meat is one of the most powerful measures someone can take to reduce their impact on our climate."

According to its website, "The Beyond Burger is the first plant-based burger that is meat-like worldwide." Instead of animal-based meat, genetically modified organisms, soy, or gluten, the Beyond Burger consists of pea protein, yeast extract, and coconut oil. It contains 20 gram of

Country	Release Body	Regulation/Legislation	Purpose
Australia	Meat & Livestock Australia in association with the Australian Lot Feeders' Association and the Feedlot Industry Accreditation Committee	National Guidelines for Beef Cattle Feedlots in Australia (3rd Edition)	The industry's quality assurance system, the National Feedlot Accreditation Scheme (NFAS), requires all accredited feedlots to adhere to the Code of Practice along with all other relevant environmental, animal welfare, and food safety legislation. Under this government and industry managed program, every accredited feedlot is independently audited each year to ensure compliance.
Canada	National Farm Animal Care Council	Code of Practice for the Care and Handling of Beef Cattle	The Code is intended to be used as an educational tool in the promotion of sound animal husbandry and care practices. The Code contains recommendations to help producers and others in the agriculture and food sectors compare and improve their own management practices.
China	Bureau for Environmental Protection in association with General Administration of Quality Supervision Inspection and Quarantine of the P.R.C.	Discharge standard of water pollutants for meat packing industry	This standard is designed to promote production planning and pollution abatement technology, and prevent water pollution.
USA	United States Department of Agriculture (USDA)	The United States Humane Slaughter Act (Federal Meat Inspection Act)	This act authorizes inspectors to analyze the operations of slaughtering establishments to prevent the inhumane slaughter of cattle.
USA	United States Department of Agriculture (USDA)	American Federal Food, Drug & Cosmetic Act	This act indicates the hormones and growth promoters that are federally approved for beef production.

plant-based protein, 25% of the daily value for iron, and 0% cholesterol. Ethan Brown, the CEO of Beyond Meat, came up with his solution to address the following simple question: How can you create meat directly from plants? As Brown indicated in an interview with *Business Insider*, "raising livestock is an incredibly inefficient way of producing protein. It takes a lot of land, energy, and water just to generate one pound of meat from an animal. About 30% of the animal is meat we eat; the rest is not useful. By manufacturing meat, we can simultaneously solve four problems." Since May 2017, different products of Beyond Meat are supplied to the Meat Section of Safeway, a traditional fresh supermarket, and are also sold in the U.S. through two other major supermarket chains, Krogers and Albertsons.

However, not all welcome what they regard as "artificial food." Impossible Foods, another biotechnology company in the U.S. aims at discovering healthy, sustainable new ingredients from nature, while also addressing allegations concerning a possible food safety crisis. A notification announced by the Food and Drug Administration showed that "heme", a type of iron found in red meat, may also be an allergen contained in its Impossible Burger. Impossible Burger is a star product that uses 95% less land, 74% less water, and creates 87% less GHG emission compared to cows. Although the company issued an official statement clarifying that "all products have passed the lab test internally", doubts have been raised about ingredient safety and the product's future.

It is very encouraging and promising to see that more beef companies are aware of their environmental impacts, and who are responding by exploring different and more sustainable methods of production. However, little action has taken place in China to date. It is to be seen how the government responds going forward.

32.4 Discussion Questions

1. What moral issues are involved in this case? Why do they matter?
2. What do you think should be improved by a beef manufacturer in China? If you had to write a policy for a food manufacturer, what would it say?
3. How should the government respond? Should regulations enforced on the beef industry reflect the environmental impact of its production processes? If so, how so; if not, why not?

Bibliography

Boehrer, K. (2014). Study: To cut down on environmental impact, eat less beef. *Huffington Post*. Retrieved January 3, 2018 from https://www.huffingtonpost. com/2014/07/21/beef-environmental-impact_n_5599370.html.

Carrington, D. (2014). Giving up beef will reduce carbon footprint more than cars, says expert. *The Guardian*. Retrieved January 23, 2018 from https://www. theguardian.com/environment/2014/jul/21/giving-up-beef-reduce-carbon-footprint-more-than-cars.

Department of Primary Industries (2007). Responsible, sustainable beef production. Retrieved February 26, 2018 from https://www.dpi.nsw.gov.au/animals-and-livestock/beef-cattle/husbandry/general-management/production.

Eshel, G., Shepon, A., Makov, T., and Milo, R. (2014). Land, irrigation water, greenhouse gas, and reactive nitrogen burdens of meat, eggs, and dairy production in the United States. *Proceedings of the National Academy of Sciences of the United States of America*, 111(33), 11996–12001.

Haspel, T. (2014). Vegetarian or omnivore: The environmental implications of diet. *The Washington Post*. Retrieved January 3, 2018 from https://www. washingtonpost.com/lifestyle/food/vegetarian-or-omnivore-the-environmental-implications-of-diet/2014/03/10/648fdbe8-a495-11e3-a5fa-55f0c77bf39c_story.html.

Huang, F. (2007). 牛肉温室效应大 生产1斤排放36斤二氧化碳 (Beef has a big greenhouse effect — Production of 1 kg emits 36 kg of carbon dioxide). *People.cn*. Retrieved on January 3, 2018 from http://news.sohu.com/ 20070725/n251239221.shtml.

Kowitt, B. (2017). Leonardo DiCaprio is investing in the plant-based food startup beyond meat. *Fortune*. Retrieved January 23, 2018 from http://fortune. com/2017/10/17/leonardo-dicaprio-beyond-meat-investment/.

Mackay, E. (2015). Australia's beef industry reduces environmental impact. *Global Meat News*. Retrieved January 23, 2018 from https://www. globalmeatnews.com/Article/2015/03/30/Australia-s-beef-industry-reduces-environmental-impact.

Rothlin, S. and McCann, D. (2016). *International Business Ethics Focus on China*. Springer: Berlin, Heidelberg.

Stone, M. (2015). How a startup that makes fake meat from plants caught the attention of Bill Gates and the founders of Twitter. *Business Insider*. Retrieved January 23, 2018 from http://www.businessinsider.com/how-a-startup-that-makes-fake-meat-from-plants-caught-the-attention-of-bill-gates-and-the-founders-of-twitter-2015-7.

Xinhua Net Japan Channel (2014). 日本,一百头牛能解决20户家庭用电. *Xinhua News*. Retrieved January 23, 2018 from https://kknews.cc/zh-cn/ world/xobbkg.html.

Chapter 33

China's "Toxic School" Controversy

Mark Pufpaff and Dennis P. McCann

Abstract

After almost 500 children studying at a junior middle school in the city of Changzhou in Jiangsu province became sick with a range of illnesses. Investigations revealed the school had been built on polluted ground. The premises had been formerly occupied by three chemical pesticide factories, which left the ground toxic. After investigations, questions arose as to why the school was built there. This case presents the moral issues involved, including corruption, stakeholder rights, and corporate social responsibility.

Keywords: Education, ground pollution, corporate social responsibility, stakeholder rights, due diligence

33.1 Seeing

The primary and secondary school systems in China are challenging and highly stressful. Take what is at stake in the results of the infamous *gaokao* exam — the college entrance exam taken at the end of secondary school that single-handedly determines the university options of all mainland Chinese students — it is enough to smother a person. The anxiety associated with the *gaokao* is due to the difficulty of attending top domestic universities, where admittance rates are exceedingly low. The responses

285

to these difficulties vary. Some students, deciding to forsake educational opportunities at home, prepare to study abroad for their university degree. Other families enroll their children at private, international primary and secondary schools that they feel might give them an edge when preparing for the *gaokao*, thus increasing their chances of being accepted into a prestigious national university.

All the pressure surrounding the *gaokao* has had some interesting, and perhaps unintended, results, however. In particular, it has created a burgeoning market for alternative education, that is, academic institutions of varying pedagogical philosophies that promise results above and beyond the perceived capacity of state-run institutions. One such example is the Changzhou Foreign Languages School (CFLS), a junior middle school for 14–16-year-old students in Changzhou, Jiangsu, a coastal province in eastern-central China.

CFLS is a privately operated school that many in Changzhou regard as a dream for their students. It is expensive, as most private educational institutions are in China, but not so cost prohibitive that middle-class working families cannot save enough for the tuition, assuming their children are admitted. It is viewed as a stepping stone for studying at Changzhou's top high schools, and hopefully, by extension, China's top universities thereafter, and as a model of education that embraces a more comprehensive approach to learning, as opposed to the rote learning techniques espoused by so many state-run operations.

Beginning in April, 2016, however, many parents began transferring their students from CFLS. In the wake of a China Central Television (CCTV) report, aired nationwide on April 10, 2016, CFLS became the center of an unfortunate controversy. The report described the illnesses of nearly 500 students attending the school at the time, ranging from nosebleeds, dizziness, and headaches to dermatitis, lymphoma, and leukemia. The cause of the ailments, the report continued, was exposure to inordinately high levels of pollution in the soil, groundwater, and air surrounding CFLS. The origin of the pollutants was traced to three chemical pesticide factories having operated adjacent to the school's current location until 2010, when they were relocated. But, the story does not stop here.

In 2012, CFLS began the construction of their current campus, which represented a move from their prior location in an older part of Changzhou. CFLS's new campus location, however, having been previously occupied by the three pesticide production factories, needed to be tested for any prohibitive levels of pollution. Investigations were carried out from 2011–2013. CCTV cited the results, summarized in an article from the *Los Angeles Times*:

"A report after the [three pesticide production] factories were closed about six years ago found extreme amounts of toxic substances in the area around the proposed campus — including chlorobenzene levels 78,899 times the permitted levels in soil and 94,799 times the permitted levels in groundwater, CCTV said. Carbon tetrachloride levels were found to be 22,699 times the national limits. That probe also found elevated levels of lead, cadmium and mercury."

In February, 2016, Gao Yuefeng, Deputy Director of the Changzhou Xinbei District Environmental Protection Bureau, admitted, in a report by Beijing-based media group *Caixin* before the airing of the CCTV report in April, that the results of the 2011–2013 investigation had revealed that while the soil in question was in fact tainted, "by outdated production methods used by the [pesticide factories] and due to lower environmental protection standards in place at that time, ...the level of contamination was not serious." Gao also claimed that at the time of the investigation, the air quality met national standards and boldly asserted that "to be sure, there is no problem with the air *now*."

Commenting on the same environmental report, Gao's reassurances in February, 2016, were in stark contrast to the claims of the report aired by CCTV just two months later.

The 2011–2013 investigation was not the only one performed. After receiving parental complaints in January, 2016, concerning a foul smell at the premises, which was immediately noticeable after the beginning of its first semester of operation at the new campus in September, 2015, CFLS closed for two weeks following an investigation. The investigation, carried out by provincial and Changzhou city environmental authorities, according to *Caixin*,

"found that levels of petroleum hydrocarbons and benzyl chloride in the soil under the closed pesticide factories were above its standards. The [Ministry of Environment Protection] said [provincial and Changzhou city] investigators found 1,500 cubic meters of contaminated soil giving off the pungent smell. The investigation had also unearthed buried solid waste, but authorities failed to give any details about it."

The response to these findings by CFLS was to begin land restoration work, which included covering the contaminated soil with fresh soil and planting trees. However, Zhang Yi, Director of the Shanghai Institute for Design & Research on Environmental Engineering, was quoted by *Caixin* saying,

> "Soil polluted by chemical plants has little capacity to decompose naturally. Simply covering the contaminated layer with clean soil without treating it may even make the problem worse."

But, in spite of such concerns, and after the so-called restoration work, CFLS posted a report just days before students were asked to return to school for their spring semester on February 22, stating that the air, groundwater, and soil were all safe, based on results of a subsequent investigation conducted by a private company the school had hired.

Nevertheless, at the airing of the CCTV report on April 10, everything that CFLS and local governmental officials like Gao had been saying was called immediately into question. Perhaps unsurprisingly, outrage was the response, and not only from the parents of the victims. Condemnations from all over China poured in over social media and microblogging websites. There were three areas of concern.

One area focused on the fact that CFLS began the construction of its new campus seven months before the 2011–2013 investigation was complete. We are left to speculate as to why due to a lack of information. But, it would not be unreasonable to assume that starting construction would be dependent upon clean results. That they started early raises serious questions as to both the integrity of the investigation and the relationship between CFLS and the local governmental bodies in charge of approving construction permits.

Another area focused on the testimony of former employees of Jiangsu Changlong Chemicals Company (JCCC), a subsidiary of Shenzhen Noposion Agrochemicals Company, one of China's largest pesticide producers. Xu Lixiong, one of the former employees who spoke to Caixin, said that JCCC regularly and indiscriminately discharged chemical waste into a nearby river that linked up with the Yangtze River, Asia's longest river, and buried unknown amounts of hazardous waste 8–10 meters below the ground in the area where the school is currently located. This was done, Xu said, to save time and money. Though we do not know exactly why Xu came forward or whether his testimony can or will eventually be corroborated, it nonetheless stands to reason that his admissions and the results of the environmental tests done on the site in question are generally supportive of the same conclusion, namely, that foul play was involved in the construction of CFLS's new campus.

A third concern was raised by the nature of the illnesses of the students themselves. Though no absolutely conclusive link between the pollutants and the students' ailments has been made, the fact that students began showing signs of illness after the school opened at their new campus in September, 2015, and their conditions only worsened until the CCTV report in April, 2016, is evidence that the attempts by CFLS and local governmental officials like Gao to assuage concerns are suspicious at best. Pan Xiaochuan, a Professor of the Public Health School at Peking University, was paraphrased in a *China Daily* article as saying,

"the high number of students being diagnosed with diseases and conditions in such a short space of time should be connected with the heavy pollution levels."

Though CFLS and local government officials in Changzhou have remained obstinate in their position that the environmental conditions at the school are safe, many, including students, parents, netizens, and even the national government, are not convinced.

33.2 Judging

It is unclear exactly why CFLS chose to relocate their new campus to a plot of land previously inhabited by large-scale chemical production factories. Common sense would certainly put up immediate red flags. But, whatever the reason, the decision was a major one, and not without serious risks. Whether they knew it at the time or not, CFLS was committing themselves to a responsibility that extended far beyond the self-interest of the school.

This case is far from conclusive on questions of corruption, bribery, kickbacks, collusion, or other kinds of backdoor business behavior. But, the evidence pointing in the direction of these kinds of practices is significant. For example, why would construction of the campus begin seven months prior to the completion of the environmental report that was supposed to determine whether the project would be approved for construction in the first place? That the report eventually approved the project, which was already underway, rather than absolving CFLS of suspicion, further confirms the likelihood of foul play. Indeed, why else would such a large number of students all be coming down with illnesses related to exposure to toxic chemicals if the toxicity levels in the air, soil, and groundwater around CFLS were at or below national standards?

Regardless, that these questions are even being asked brings into view considerations of corporate social responsibility (CSR) and basic business ethics. The first principle of business ethics is "Do No Harm." CFLS is in trouble because it is being claimed that they did do harm, and a lot of it. Students are sick. Parents are distraught. Netizens are furious. The education system has suffered a serious blow. Questions of poor government oversight are ubiquitous. What happened?

When CFLS decided to build on a site with preexisting environmental hazards, they promised their stakeholders, however implicitly, that they were prepared to be held accountable for ensuring the new campus was safe. This responsibility not only extended to the students who would frequent the premises each day but also the staff who entrusted their careers to CFLS, and the parents who paid the tuitions necessary to keep CFLS operational. When they were accused of failing to fulfill this responsibility, however, they adopted a policy of denial. Even if they are as innocent as they claim, was there not a better course of action? Was there not a way for CFLS and Changzhou's local government officials to respond to the problem in a way that would have been inclusive and constructive instead of divisive and destructive?

In CSR strategy, there are two principles that stand out as relevant in interpreting and understanding this case. One is the involvement of a firm's stakeholders in realizing its business objectives. There is no issue with CFLS wanting to make a profit. In fact, making a profit is a necessary part of operating a sustainable business. It is also testament to a well thought through and strategically implemented business plan. But, it does not imply maximizing profits through any means necessary, which oftentimes involves ignoring the responsibilities that a company owes to some or all of its stakeholders. Therefore, involving the participation of a company's stakeholders in the process of working toward its business goals ensures that the achievement of such goals is a win-win across the board. If CFLS had honestly and transparently involved their stakeholders, ranging from their students to their local communities to the relevant government agencies, in the process of realizing their desire to relocate to a questionable location, would they not have avoided the scandal? If they involved in the relocation decision those who are now condemning them for it, would not that ensure that all relevant interests would be accounted for in the implementation of the project?

Another CSR principle is for a company to act in giving back to their local communities. CFLS had ample opportunity to do this, and do it well. Not only could they have invested in a treatment project that would clean up contaminated soil and groundwater but they could have subsequently pioneered further gentrification of the area. They could have acted as a model worthy of imitation for other businesses. They could have improved the livelihoods of those living around the contaminated site by reducing the risk of pollution-related illnesses or environmental degradation. It is true that not all businesses can or should give back on such a scale. But, would not a broad commitment to giving back whenever possible dispose a company, such as CFLS, to make decisions based on the best interests of those in their immediate communities? Would it not likewise hedge them against pure self-interested schemes aimed at nothing more than profit maximization?

33.3 Acting

The old saying "It can only go up from here!" is perhaps relevant, assuming CFLS has hit rock bottom with the nationwide report aired by CCTV. But, how exactly should the leadership at CFLS turn this scandal around? What are the challenges they face, and how might they overcome them?

First, they are facing widespread distrust. Everything they say from here on out will be received with immediate skepticism. Giving excuses is useless. Continuing to deny any wrongdoing is perhaps even worse. What the public wants is accountability. They also want to see action. A good response to situations like this is engagement. If CFLS engaged directly and respectfully with those affected by the scandal, namely, the sick students and their parents, listened to their concerns, and asked for their feedback on what CFLS could do to make things right for them, progress would begin to be made. It would show the students and parents that CFLS cares about their well-being and is willing to invest in an inclusive solution. It also shows that they are taking ownership of the scandal, regardless of their level of culpability.

Second, they are most likely facing immediate decisions over whether to close the school until a solution is realized. Keeping the school open and requiring that students continue attending class could only make things worse. On the contrary, closing the school could result in mass student transfers away from CFLS, due to parents not wanting their children to take a break in their education. However, part of the responsibility is accountability and accepting the consequences of one's actions. Playing it safe and closing the school would at the very least prevent further illnesses or the worsening of existing ones. It would give time for the leadership at CFLS to decide on an appropriate course of action. It would allow them space to involve the stakeholders necessary for implementing and carrying out a proper response. Remember, "Do No Harm" is the first principle of business ethics, or in the case of CFLS, "Do No Further Harm."

33.4 Discussion Questions

1. What is environmental responsibility? Why is it important?
2. Given the details of this case, do you think pollution is a moral issue? Why or why not?
3. Do you think the three pesticide factories that contaminated the area around CFLS's new campus should be held responsible for the illnesses of the children attending school there? Why or why not?
4. What was the responsibility of CFLS in choosing (if they had a choice at all) the location for their new campus, given that it was contaminated? Are they obliged to inform the public about the dangers?
5. If you were advising CFLS, would you have suggested they go ahead with their relocation plans? Why or why not?
6. If you were the director of CFLS, how would you manage this crisis?

Bibliography

China Daily (2016). 500 students sickened at school built on toxic site. *China Daily*. Retrieved on August 5, 2016 from http://www.chinadaily.com.cn/china/2016-04/18/content_24617459.htm.

Makinen, J. (2016). Hundreds of Chinese kids fall ill from toxic chemicals at school, state TV reports. *Los Angeles Times*. Retrieved on August 5,

2016 from https://www.latimes.com/world/asia/la-fg-china-school-toxic-20160419-story.html.

Zhang, Y. (2016). New Jiangsu school grapples with plot of toxic land across street. *Caixin*. Retrieved on August 5, 2016 from https://www.caixinglobal.com/2016-03-04/new-jiangsu-school-grapples-with-plot-of-toxic-land-across-street-101011827.html.

Part 8

Corporate Governance/Corruption

Chapter 34

JPMorgan Employment Bribery: A Case of Family Matters and Employment Ethics

Mark Pufpaff and Dennis P. McCann

Abstract

In November, 2016, JPMorgan Chase was found to have an internal program called "Sons and Daughters." It prioritized hiring the children of high-ranking political officials and business executives in China and Hong Kong SAR as a means of doing business. They were fined for bribery by the Securities and Exchange Commission for violating the Foreign Corrupt Practices Act. This case discusses what is and is not proper hiring protocol, the Confucian notion of *guanxi*, and provides an imagined scenario for discussion and debate.

Keywords: Human resources, employment ethics, bribery, *guanxi*

34.1 Seeing

Hiring managers have a difficult job. Not only do they have to interview, analyze, and make decisions based on limited information about and experience with their potential hires but they also have to remain as objective as possible in the selection process, to ensure each candidate is fairly considered.

However difficult, if not impossible, it is to achieve perfect objectivity in selecting employees, there are certain hiring practices that raise serious ethical concerns. Fairness, both within the hiring process itself and in the way firms recruit for competitive advantages in the marketplace, is a standard worth honoring, and one that should form the basis of discussion about what is and is not permissible in terms of employment ethics.

In November, 2016, JPMorgan Chase (JPMorgan), an investment bank based in New York, NY, was fined USD 246 million by the Securities and Exchange Commission (SEC) in the United States for violating the Foreign Corrupt Practice Act (FCPA). The reason for the fine? The bank had an internal program to hire the children and relatives — 222, at least — of high-ranking political officials and business executives in China and the Hong Kong Special Autonomous Region (HKSAR) for purposes of maintaining existing or gaining new business contacts.

At first sight, this may seem more strategic than morally problematic, but it was revealed that JPMorgan was hiring them without regard for their qualifications, and ordering that their applications bypass the rigorous screening process usually espoused at the bank to ensure top-rate hires. In other words, JPMorgan was hiring the unqualified, or at least untested through standard interview methods, sons, daughters, and relatives of decision makers in China and HKSAR for no other reason than to leverage them to win business. The actual, everyday contributions of these hires to the advancement of the company's objectives were of secondary importance, if not completely irrelevant.

According to the SEC, this program, internally referred to as "Sons and Daughters", generated at least USD 100 million in revenues. Andrew Ceresney, Director of the SEC Enforcement Division stated the following:

> "JPMorgan engaged in a systematic bribery scheme by hiring children of government officials and other favored referrals who were typically unqualified for the positions on their own merit. JPMorgan employees knew the firm was potentially violating the Foreign Corrupt Practices Act (FCPA), yet persisted with the improper hiring program because the business rewards and new deals were deemed too lucrative."

Having allegedly hired "the friends and family members of executives at three-quarters of the major Chinese companies that it took public in Hong Kong" — as of December, 2015 — and provided them with "well paying, career-building JPMorgan employment" without undergoing the firm's "normal hiring practices", the bank was admittedly operating in contrast to their code of conduct, particularly their so-called "decision tree":

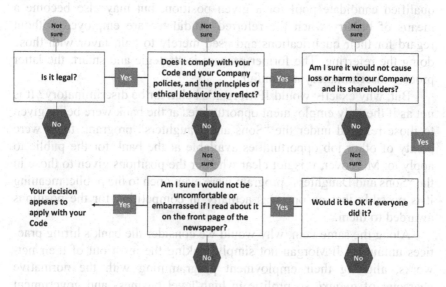

In a public statement concerning the scandal, Brian Marchiony, JPMorgan's spokesman, stated the following:

> "We're pleased that our cooperation was acknowledged in resolving these investigations. The conduct was unacceptable. We stopped the hiring program in 2013 and took action against the individuals involved. We have also made improvements to our hiring procedures, and reinforced the high standards of conduct expected of our people."

34.2 Judging

Employment ethics is a field that aims to delineate what is acceptable and unacceptable in terms of hiring practices and explores the professional responsibilities of hiring managers and Human Resources (HR) department heads in upholding standards of excellence.

While it is common for companies to allow for internal referrals and candidate endorsements from employees, as a natural part of the recruiting process and desire to find candidates aligned with their corporate culture and stated operational values, such allowances are not intended to compromise the quality of fairness presupposed within the employment environment. In other words, referrals can be a viable way to increase the qualified candidate pool for a given position, but may also become a means of bribery when the referred candidates are employed without regard for their qualifications and used merely to gain favor with those doing the referring. The former process is strategic and smart, the latter process discriminatory and unfair.

But, why exactly would JPMorgan's behavior be discriminatory? It is not as if the only employment opportunities at the bank were being given to those referred under the "Sons and Daughters" program; there were plenty of other job opportunities available at the bank for the public to apply to. Moreover, it is not clear whether the positions given to those in the "Sons and Daughters" program were even open to the public, meaning it is possible that no one was actually in competition for the positions awarded to them.

Along the same vein, why would we consider the bank's hiring practices unfair? Is JPMorgan not simply making the most out of their networks, aligning their employment programming with the normative character of *guanxi*, so prolific in high-level business and government dealings in China and the HKSAR? Should not JPMorgan actually be commended for their savviness in networking and relationship building, and rewarded — perhaps to the tune of USD 100 million — for leveraging such activity more effectively than any of their competitors?

With these counter positions in mind, ask yourself what you would expect if you were a general applicant for a position at JPMorgan. Would you not expect to know of all their hiring programs, all open positions, and the requirements for applying and interviewing? Is a degree of transparency not expected, so that each applicant feels they have an equal opportunity to apply for and be offered a position? Would knowing that the hiring process was inherently fair not encourage you to apply, even empower you to find innovative ways of presenting your credentials in order to stand out? It would be reasonable to answer these questions in the positive. But, what if the "Sons and Daughters" program was advertised on JPMorgan's website? What if you read that the children and relatives of high-ranking government officials and corporate executives had their own special referral program, where referees bypassed the extensive screening processes everyone else had to submit to and were given jobs they were not necessarily qualified for? Would that not be discrimination, on the basis of family status and position?

Likewise, if you were a competitor of JPMorgan. Fair competition, where companies strive for market share based on competitive advantages developed within an agreed-upon legal framework and grounded in basic business values, is critical for creating a marketplace that is honest, transparent, and accountable. It is reasonable to compete for top talent in an industry; creativity in recruiting is crucial to becoming an employer of choice. But, turning hiring practices into vehicles for bribery is opposed to creativity, and destroys the integrity of the competitive game. Everyone appreciates good sportsmanship. No one likes a cheater.

34.3 Acting — For Discussion

Here is an imagined situation that might have occurred when JP Morgan's "Sons and Daughters" program was still in force:

You were recently promoted to program manager at JPMorgan's Hong Kong office. It will be a significant increase in responsibility, as you will now have to manage a team of 10. However, you are excited and have confidence that you can build and sustain a productive team. Having worked at JPMorgan for some years as an analyst before your promotion, you have seen and experienced the pressure on employees to perform, and the need for managers to ensure that their teams achieve consistently high rates of success from quarter to quarter. Unfortunately, you have even seen some employees fired for underperforming. You know that, as Program Manager, you must set expectations early and act decisively if any of your team members are lagging in productivity.

As you get settled into your new position, you begin to plan for the year ahead. One area where you plan to focus is digital banking, and making Chase Business Banking and Commercial Banking more visible and accessible to your portfolio of clients. You know that these are high-value service lines for JPMorgan and plan to add one more employee to your team to increase your outreach to prospective customers. You discuss your plan with your manager and get approval to move forward.

As you are preparing your job description for posting on JPMorgan's recruitment website, your manager informs you that they are assigning to your newly opened position a new hire from their "Sons and Daughters" program. You are baffled. "This doesn't make any sense," you say to yourself, "I haven't even interviewed him!" You had heard of the program before, but were unaware of how it was used in practice. You questioned whether it was aligned with JPMorgan's code of conduct, which boasts being an equal opportunity and affirmative action employer. Given your new responsibilities and desire to make a good first impression as a Program Manager, however, you choose not to raise an issue with your manager and thank her for finding a candidate.

As your new employee, named Liu Wei, arrives for his orientation, you learn about his background. He is the son of a high-ranking government official in mainland China, one whose family is heavily influential in the financial services industry and has contacts in the top rungs of the central government. You also learn that his family has ties to a major food wholesaler in Hong Kong, one that JPMorgan had recently taken public on the Hong Kong Stock Exchange. Although these facts make you uneasy, as you begin to wonder about the real reason he was hired, you start to really worry when you review Mr. Liu's academic and professional background and realize that he had studied marketing at university and that his only experience in financial services had been as part of an investment fund team at his school. In other words, he had very little financial services experience. "How could he have been hired," you blurt out in a fit of anger in your office, "he is completely unqualified!" You decide to discuss the situation with your manager.

You knock on your manager's door and ask if you could have a word with her. She agrees and you sit down. You say, "As much as I appreciate you finding Mr. Liu to take the newly opened position on my team, after reviewing his credentials, I have concluded that he does not fulfill the requirements for the job." Your manager says quickly from behind her computer, "While that may be true on paper, you could train him to become competent in doing the job, right?" You reply, "Perhaps, but I would prefer to hire a candidate through our regular recruiting processes, so that I am sure to get an employee who is qualified and who I am confident will produce for us." Your manager puts her pen down and leans back in her chair. She replies, "You know that Mr. Liu is the son of a highly influential government official in mainland China, and was referred to our "Sons and Daughters" program by his father. If we do not hire him, it may damage our relationship with Mr. Liu's father, and cost us business contracts in China." There is an awkward pause in the office. She continues, "We appreciate you taking Mr. Liu as part of your team and expect that you will treat him well and overlook any of his deficiencies for the good of the company's prospective business dealings." She stands up and walks out, leaving you behind. You are speechless.

You decide to go outside and get a coffee. As you sit and drink, you realize the complexity of your situation. On the one hand, you feel a strong moral obligation to reject the hiring of Mr. Liu, and take a stand against the hiring of unqualified candidates. As Program Manager, you are accountable for the productivity of your team, and having an unqualified team member is a severe hindrance to your success. On the other hand, you value your job and do not want to compromise your recent promotion by immediately confronting your manager. She did, after all, confirm that she knew Mr. Liu was unqualified. Perhaps if your team underperforms because of Mr. Liu's lack of skills, you will not be held accountable. You begin to sweat. Your phone beeps with a notification that your boss wants you to return to continue discussion about Mr. Liu.

What should you do?

34.4 Discussion Questions

1. Do you think JPMorgan's "Sons and Daughters" program was discriminatory? Why or why not?
2. Do you think JPMorgan's "Sons and Daughters" program compromised fair competition in the marketplace? Why or why not?
3. Do you think the SEC was accurate in labeling the "Sons and Daughters" program a vehicle for bribery? Why or why not?
4. If you were a corporate recruiter, what policies of standards would you hold yourself accountable to?

Bibliography

Levin, N. (2015). JP Morgan hires were referred by China IPO clients. *Financial News*. Retrieved on December 13, 2016 from https://www.fnlondon.com/articles/jp-morgan-hires-were-referred-by-china-ipo-clients-20151201.

Morran, C. (2016). JPMorgan Chase to pay $264M to settle corruption allegations for hiring friends, family of government officials. *Consumerist.com*. Retrieved on December 13, 2016 from https://consumerist.com/2016/11/17/jpmorgan-chase-to-pay-264m-to-settle-corruption-allegations-for-hiring-friends-family-of-government-officials/.

Sweet, K. (2016). JPMorgan Chase to pay $264 million in Chinese bribery case. *OnlineAthens*. Retrieved on December 13, 2016 from https://www.onlineathens.com/business/2016-11-17/jpmorgan-chase-pay-264-million-chinese-bribery-case.

Chapter 35

Box Office Fraud: Popcorn, Soda, Candy, and Corruption

Mark Pufpaff, Helen Xu, and Dennis P. McCann

Abstract

China's movie industry has developed over the past decades without a number of setbacks. Despite this, China is the second largest movie market in the world. Its competitiveness often leads to unethical behavior in the industry. One major scandal shook the industry when a film distributor, Beijing Max Screen, inflated ticket sales to boost the performance statistics of the movie. The case discusses the scandal, looks at different players in the movie business in China, and asks how to increase business ethics in this particular industry.

Keywords: Fraud, Internet, competition, corporate governance

35.1 Seeing

Everyone loves going to the movies. In China, this fact has never been truer than over the past five years. Record-breaking box office sales have made China the second largest movie market in the world. In 2015, ticket sale revenues rounded off at USD 6.8 billion, an impressive 49% increase from 2014, and up from USD 1.51 billion in 2010; in February, 2016 alone, box office sales reached USD 1.05 billion. Demand for domestic movies is also increasing, with notable films such as *Monster Hunt* and

Lost in Hong Kong having grossed USD 380 million and USD 250 million to date, respectively. Stephan Chow's *The Mermaid* has passed the sought-after USD 500 million threshold for a single territory (China) to become the first Chinese film to enter the penthouse suite of other top-grossing films such as *Star Wars: The Force Awakens*, *Avatar*, *Titanic*, and *The Dark Knight*. The infrastructure development associated with the emergence of the movie industry in China is likewise remarkable, with film-related distribution networks extending well beyond top-tier cities, such as Beijing and Shanghai, to second- and third-tier cities. Cinemas are becoming ubiquitous and demand is only set to grow. "May the force be with you", indeed.

However, just as a child does not mature without occasional "growing pains", so the Chinese film industry has not developed without its share of setbacks. Most recently, *Ip Man 3*, part of the Ip Man trilogy, has been at the center of controversy. During opening weekend, *Ip Man 3* grossed over $70 million. But, just as quickly as some people gasped at its success, others found themselves choking on allegations of fraud.

What happened? The film's distributor, Beijing Max Screen, inflated ticket sales to boost the performance statistics of the movie.

How did Beijing Max Screen do that? There were several ways. First, they manipulated the screening schedules on mobile ticketing applications. According to the *Hollywood Reporter*,

> "Several of China's top mobile ticketing apps — which is how over 70 percent of Chinese movie tickets are now bought — showed sold-out *Ip Man 3* screenings running every 10 minutes until 3 a.m. at some cinemas, an impossibly frequent schedule."

Second, they bought discounted tickets to their own film and coordinated the fake screenings, dubbed "ghost screenings", in an attempt to justify the ticket sales. According to the Chinese news outlet, *Xinhua*,

> "Beijing Max Screen, the film's distributor, admitted to having bought RMB 56 million (approximately USD 8.6 million) worth of the tickets itself, and the conspirators fabricated more than 7,600 screenings of the film that they claimed generated RMB 32 million (approximately USD 4.9 million) in ticket sales, said the film bureau under the State Administration of Press, Publication, Radio, Film and Television in a statement released late on Friday."

Authorities stated that three mobile ticketing sites were reprimanded, along with 73 theaters. Beijing Max Screen was ordered to suspend distribution activity for one month.

However, why would Beijing Max Screen want to inflate the sales numbers of *Ip Man 3* in the first place, especially because the film was expected to perform well anyway? Besides trying to further position themselves as the go-to distributor for film launches in China and attempting to create additional interest in the movie by ensuring an above average opening weekend, *Variety* reports,

"In the case of "Ip Man 3" there was a clear incentive to inflate the figures. The chairman of Max Screen is Shi Jianxing, who is also chairman of Hong Kong-listed firm ShiFang, which in turn has a contract that gives it 55% participation in the theatrical *revenues*, not net profits, of "Ip Man 3" in mainland China."

In other words, the higher the revenues of *Ip Man 3* in mainland China, the greater the financial reward for ShiFang. As both Beijing Max Screen and ShiFang are directed by Shi Jianxing, the investment by Beijing Max Screen in buying tickets to their own film and its efforts in organizing the "ghost screenings" were intended to return far higher profits for Shifang based on their contractual relationship. And so, the plot thickens.

This is only the most recent scandal involving fraud in China's movie industry. Other instances have involved theaters selling hand-written tickets in order to hide, and subsequently embezzle, revenue. Many state that this kind of activity is inevitable in an industry where growth and expansion far outpace developments in regulatory oversight; however, others counter by saying the capacity for responsible governance is present, but is simply suffering from poor implementation.

35.2 Judging

How are we to interpret these scandals? Let us work through two hypothetical scenarios.

If you were a...
Mid-level manager at Beijing Max Screen charged with coordinating the ghost screenings on ticketing apps and cinemas, how would you feel? Suppose you would receive a bonus for carrying out your work quietly.

Would that justify intentionally deceiving the industry marketplace and government authorities? Should you allow financial incentives to determine your behavior, even if you may otherwise find it morally wrong? Assume your job security would be at risk if you reported this behavior to the relevant authorities. Does keeping your job take priority over upholding your ethical commitments?

Say you had to organize a team of employees to assist you in this task. Even if you might be okay with carrying out this kind of work by yourself, and for your own personal benefit, how would your decision-making change if you knew you would be putting your employees at risk? Mid-level managers can sometimes find themselves between a rock and a hard place. They are accountable to their superiors while being responsible for their employees. If your superior is asking you to do something you suspect is unethical, is the mere fact that he or she is your superior enough to neglect your responsibility to act in the best interest of your employees? Do you have an obligation to remain accountable to a boss who is asking you to lie or violate the law? At what point are you justified in saying "No"?

If you were the…
CEO of a competitor of Beijing Max Screen, what would their activity look like to you? Naturally, film distributors want to distribute top-selling films. How far would you go in order to acquire the distribution rights of a given film? If you noticed a number of distributors inflating the box office sales figures of the movies they distributed, are you morally justified in doing the same thing? As the CEO, do you have a responsibility to stand against "business as usual" if you notice it is steeped in corrupt business practices? How would you avoid the temptation of assuming you could carry out the fraudulent behavior more effectively and secretively than Beijing Max Screen? Competition is good when the business environment is ethical and properly regulated, but can be destructive when the prevailing standard rewards whoever can hide their iniquities most efficiently.

The legal repercussion of Beijing Max Screen's activity was a one-month suspension of distribution activity. In a public response to this penalty, the company stated,

> "As a company entering the film market, we are eager to make a contribution to Chinese film, but we lacked a deep understanding and familiarity with the relevant regulations. The company solemnly pledges to learn from the experience and comply with the rules."

However, there were no fines, no arrests, and no replacement of top management. What does that say to you and other competitors? Is the upside of inflating box office figures worth the risk of a mere one-month suspension? Worth having to submit a short, relatively lackluster, and perhaps even inauthentic response to the press? As a CEO, are you responsible to act ethically even if the regulatory environment does not provide enough incentives to do so? Leaders are leaders because of their character. They are attractive because of their integrity, their moral consistency, their reliability, their transparency. The position of CEO is only a position. It can as easily be occupied by a villain as by a hero. However, villains are not leaders. They are liars masked as leaders. How important is it to you to uphold your personal virtue as a CEO, to avoid the temptation to lie and deceive as a strategy for gaining market share or beating your competition for movie distribution bids? Why might that commitment be good for business in the long run? How might it make your company an industry benchmark? How would you feel if you knew the success of your firm was due merely to corruption?

The difficulty in interpreting events like this is that we rarely understand fully that real people actually decide to do these things; we tend to see news events as before-and-after scenarios. The company was good one day, bad the next; we miss the intermediate deterioration that must happen for such a transformation to occur. It is uncommon to seriously enter into the psychology of corruption, to literally feel the play of influences that a person goes through when they finally, usually against their better judgment and supported by a myriad of excuses and justifications, decide to act unethically. Confessions from two Chinese officials convicted of corruption provide examples of the how the temptations of corruption lead otherwise honest people to lose sight of their responsibilities:

"I am unworthy of my mother, this organization, and society. If I could do it all again I would rather give up my life than abuse the law. I hope other cadres will use me as a warning and that other corrupt officials can learn from my mistakes." — Zhang Yin, former vice chair of the CPCC in Xuzhou, Jiangsu province

"I'm so sorry that I worked more than 30 years at the NDRC (National Development and Reform Commission), with the trust of the leaders and my comrades, and smeared a black mark on my workplace...I am completely and bitterly remorseful." — Liu Tienen, former deputy of the National Development and Reform Commission

These confessions tell an interesting story. The sorrow these officials expressed after their convictions is testament to the way corruption blinds people into thinking their actions have no effects, effects, which, if they had understood them beforehand, would have deterred their activity from the start.

Being a manager is difficult. Being a leader is hard. We may want to avoid the assumption that corrupt people are weak and that we, the onlookers, would never succumb to such petty temptations.

35.3 Acting

If it is clear that the behavior of Beijing Max Screen is not only ethically wrong but also illegal and ultimately bad for business, then what can be done in order for firms to avoid acting similarly? Zuo Heng, associate researcher for the China Film Art Research Center, stated that

> "It's the capitalists' nature to seek flaws in the system to maximize profits. Only when the laws and regulations are more predictable and preventive can such scams be eradicated."

However, is it as simple as regulating the market? Are there any management dilemmas to overcome? Or leadership temptations to avoid?

First, the movie industry in China is growing rapidly. There are particular difficulties associated with competing in an environment like this, a so-called sunrise industry. The most glaring difficulty is a lack of regulation. There will inevitably be loopholes that can be taken advantage of. As a manager or CEO, it is important to recognize this and establish ethical codes of conduct that take precedence over any existing legal frameworks, however ambiguous or easily exploitable they may be. Acting from firm ethical commitments will create a culture within your firm that bases decision-making on whether it is compatible with your code of ethics, not whether it is currently allowable within an evolving legal framework.

Second, emerging industries will eventually saturate and reach a plateau in terms of growth rate. Therefore, it is prudent to strategize in the long term. In directing your firm, you might be able to get away with short-term, profit maximization schemes early on, as the industry finds its identity. But, once industry best practices are discovered and benchmark companies emerge, fly-by-night strategies will fail to gain the necessary traction and market share to compete sustainably. Why not strive to be a leader in your industry, like Jack Ma and Alibaba Group in ecommerce or Pony Ma and Tencent in social media? These leaders have committed their companies to long-term strategies and obliged themselves to operate responsibly in the public limelight. They are not showing interest in quick money schemes, but desire to be examples for their industries and employers of choice among their competitors.

Third, find your niche early and stick to it. Do not behave like anxious drivers in bad traffic, who switch lanes every time another one starts moving. Avoid chasing the fast lane when you can lead in your lane. Different industry sectors are profitable at different times. Part of managing a firm is being consistent in your strategy. Constantly chasing profits will inevitably lead you to cutting corners, which can eventually destroy your brand image and even result in the closing of your operations. Good management, like heroic leadership, is not dependent upon whether you are distributing the highest grossing films or operating within the most popular movie genres. It consists in doing business with integrity, no matter what the external conditions are.

35.4 Conclusion

The Beijing Max Screen scandal is the latest example of an industry that is still finding its moral foothold. It is clear that the competitive environment is fierce and that major players are looking for any competitive edge to exploit. This creates a myriad of difficulties for management. But, they are not impossible difficulties; they can be overcome. Examples like Beijing Max Screen are not simply an excuse to condemn, but an opportunity to learn. The movie industry in China is one that is good for society and good for the economy. It is up to the managers of today and the managers of tomorrow to ensure that it does not end up creating chaos instead of enjoyment.

35.5 Discussion Questions

1. What is fraud? What about Beijing Max Screen's behavior was fraudulent?
2. If you were Donnie Yen, the star of the film *Ip Man 3*, how would you respond publicly? What would you say if asked about the scandal?

3. If you were Shi Jianxing, how would you respond to the public? Would you apologize? Is there a responsible or irresponsible way of apologizing?
4. What do you think of the punishment the Chinese government gave to Beijing Max Screen? If the punishment was too lenient, as some commentators have stated, what kind of message might that send to the firm's top management?
5. Do you think Beijing Max Screen's public statement to the press was authentic? Or was it just a formality to appease those following the scandal? Does it reflect a genuine intention to amend their behavior?
6. If fear of punishment is not a strong enough incentive to deter companies like Beijing Max Screen from acting fraudulently, what would be?
7. How can the government effectively incentivize firms in the film industry away from corrupt practices? What incentive structure, or accountability structure, would overcome the temptations toward corruption?

Bibliography

Brzeski, P. (2016). China punishes 'Ip Man 3' distributor over box-office fraud. *The Hollywood Reporter*. Retrieved on May 24, 2016 from https://www.hollywoodreporter.com/news/china-punishes-ip-man-3-876963.

Lang, B. (2016). Box office hits record, but number of frequent moviegoers drops 10%. *Variety*. Retrieved on May 24, 2016 from https://variety.com/2016/film/news/box-office-hits-record-but-frequent-moviegoers-down-1201751770/.

Lin, W. (2016) Mainland movie market in the throes of a 'capital feast'. *China Daily*. Retrieved on May 24, 2016 from http://www.chinadaily.com.cn/hkedition/2016-06/21/content_25782162.htm.

Xinhua (2016). China monthly box office surpasses North America's. *China Daily*. Retrieved on May 24, 2016 from http://www.chinadaily.com.cn/culture/2016-03/02/content_23708602.htm.

Chapter 36

China's Crackdown on Ponzi and Pyramid Schemes in Finance

Dennis P. McCann and Mark Pufpaff

Abstract

After China's stock market experienced serious turbulence in 2015, the number of Peer-to-Peer (P2P) start-ups and schemes where lenders and borrowers, in theory, could deal with each other directly increased. The benefits of these new businesses seemed obvious, financial intermediaries with their rules and regulations are eliminated, no time-consuming credit worthiness checks, and it got easier for small businesses and individuals to get loans.

However, one of the largest players in the field, *Ezubao*, was accused of running a Ponzi scheme. The case discusses the scandal, explains the concept of a Ponzi scheme, and asks how the Chinese government can protect investors in the future.

Keywords: Fraud, Internet, investments, Ponzi scheme, finance

36.1 Introduction

When China's stock market suffered through a period of extreme turbulence over the summer of 2015, it was not surprising that investors — especially small investors who had just watched a chunk of their life savings evaporate into thin air — would be eager to find some other way to make money off their dwindling financial assets. At the time it may have seemed providential that Peer-to-Peer (P2P) schemes had begun to flourish, promising savers a new method for putting their nest eggs to work. With China's government promoting ecommerce and innovation in Internet-based financial services, the P2P start-up industry provided a solution to the many bottlenecks that choked the flow of capital through the established banking system. "Peer-to-Peer", apparently, meant exactly that: eliminate financial intermediaries with their rules and regulations, their time-consuming creditworthiness checks, and their biases against issuing loans to small businesses and individuals, and instead set up a platform where lenders and borrowers, in theory, could deal with each other directly. Lenders could do their own risk assessment, and borrowers could make a fresh start at establishing their credit. What could possibly go wrong?

36.2 Seeing

The initial response to the ready availability of P2P lending platforms was just short of overwhelming. The platforms flourished as part of the social media culture that exploded with the advent and proliferation of "smart phones", which enabled innovative techniques for raising and pooling capital, such as "crowdfunding", and promised — indeed, often guaranteed — a rate of return well above what could be earned by bank deposits or conventional investments in stocks and bonds. Small savers and investors found such promises hard to resist, given the ways in which they generally had been excluded from reaping the rewards of China's new prosperity. Flushed with success, the P2P platforms evolved toward providing a full range of financial services. They became directly involved in raising capital, and allocating investment funds, making participation in the expanding financial markets even easier for ordinary people. The stock market collapse over the summer of 2015 only served to increase the demand for P2P investments. As one entrepreneur put it, "We couldn't get the funds we needed from the bank. Peertopeer turned out to be the best alternative."

But then, something happened in the wake of the general contraction in financial values. Certain problems in the P2P platforms became glaringly exposed.

One of the largest of these, *Ezubao*, was accused of running a Ponzi scheme. Founded in 2014 by the legendary wunderkind, Ding Ning,

Ezubao attracted nearly RMB 60 billion from more than 900,000 mainland investors. Besides the guarantee of irresistible rates of return (usually in a range of 9–15%), Ding would accept deposits as low as one yuan, while persuading investors that his company was prospering through showy displays of wealth intended to project "a positive company image" and an effective advertising campaign featured on China's state-run *CCTV*. By December 2015, it had become apparent that *Ezubao*'s alleged business plan was unsustainable, and investigators soon exposed its fraudulent basis. The firm's "risk controller" admitted to *Xinhua* that "*Ezubao*'s operators made up as much as 95 per cent of the projects listed on its website and used funds from new investors to pay old debts," a strategy recognizable as a Ponzi scheme. As a result, by Chinese New Year 2016, at least 21 people had been arrested, the Ministry of Public Security had established a website for victims to document their losses as investigators continued efforts to follow the money trail, and a new set of regulations for Internet finance was issued by the China Banking Regulatory Commission (CBRC).

It soon became clear that *Ezubao* was not the only P2P platform to cross the line into fraudulent activities. As the government's crackdown gained momentum, an outfit called "the Kindness Exchange" (*Shanxinhui*) was accused of running a scam that, in the name of raising funds to help the poor, was cheating its members. *Shanxinhui* promised returns as high as 50% to poor members, while rich investors earned 10–30%. It also offered "bonus payments" to those who recruited new members, who at the time it was exposed as a fraud numbered five million. When the government froze some RMB 100 million of *Shanxinhui*'s assets in July, over a thousand demonstrators took to the streets of Beijing to protest against the crackdown. Apparently fearing that their deposits would disappear in the wake of the "Kindness Exchange's" collapse, they defended the firm for its good intentions and the good results that they had personally enjoyed. While most of the demonstrators were released after a reeducation program focused on "the rule of law", some 67 were detained on criminal charges for participating in an "illegal assembly."

36.3 Judging

What is a "Ponzi scheme" and why is it both immoral and illegal? A Ponzi scheme is a fraudulent business plan that pools deposits ostensibly for purposes of investment. Promises are made, usually for high returns, but the funds deposited are not managed as investments. Deposits come in, as new investors are recruited, and the money is used to pay off previous investors. The scheme can be sustained, at least for a while, so long as new investors are continuously recruited to supply sufficient funds to cover the firm's obligations to previous investors, plus, of course, whatever may be the cost of the operations and the profits taken by the perpetrators of the scheme. The Ponzi scheme collapses when the firm is unable to attract enough new recruits to cover its obligations. While such schemes are very hard to detect so long as the promised payments are made, they often raise suspicions especially among investors who regard their rates of return as unsustainable. An experienced and honest investment advisor knows that, as the old saying goes, if a thing seems too good to be true, it probably is too good to be true. An investment scheme guaranteeing rates of return dramatically higher than average over extended periods of time is either managed by a genius with an infallible crystal ball, or it is fraudulent and to be avoided at all costs.

P. T. Barnum is falsely revered for observing, "There's a sucker born every minute." Alas. People, even very rich people knowledgeable in the ways of finance, have been known to fall for Ponzi schemes. The infamous Bernie Madoff, now serving a 150-year sentence in a US federal penitentiary, is living proof that Ponzi schemes can work — but only up to a point. If there is no real investing going on, there are no risks taken, but also no rewards, and thus no profits generated for distribution among the investors. Eventually, when the scheme is exposed, someone — indeed, countless someones — will be left holding an empty bag. Those at the end of the line, the most recent recruits to the scheme, will be left with nothing. A Ponzi scheme is immoral, because it is a fraud based on deliberate deception. Depositors hand over their money, trusting that it will be invested and will earn the return that has been promised to them. It is hard to imagine an experienced investor knowingly participating in a Ponzi scheme; even if they could countenance the deception involved, they would realize the scheme is inherently unstable and likely to be exposed at any time, with catastrophic consequences.

The illegality of Ponzi schemes in China should also be crystal clear. Ponzi schemes are one of a number of "illegal fundraising activities" forbidden in the Criminal Law of 1997. Recently, China revised its laws to cover especially the forms of fraud perpetrated through P2P lending platforms and other online financial services. The draft rules issued by the State Council in August 2017 specify the nature of the crimes and the penalties for them, including fines and forfeiture of income illegally obtained through such schemes. The draft rules make it clear that the State Council's intervention is based on a concern far deeper than fear of social unrest. What is at stake is the basic integrity of China's financial system, particularly as it experiments with the wave of innovation opened up by the advent and widespread adoption of social media.

36.4 Acting

In the wake of the government's crackdown against Internet-based financial fraud, P2P lending schemes generally have suffered through severe contractions, whose consequences are not yet fully understood. Some observers predict that perhaps 90% of existing P2P platforms will cease operations in the near term. Does that mean that P2P lending will disappear in China? Should it? Despite the panic evident among some lenders as well as borrowers using these services, it is not the government's intent to abolish P2P lending platforms, but to regulate them effectively so that they can perform their limited but indispensable service in China's "new economy". The emerging regulatory framework evident in the draft rules published by the China Banking Regulatory Commission in August 2016 regards P2P platforms as "intermediaries, matchmakers between borrowers and lenders":

> "Under the planned rule, online platforms shouldn't take deposits from the public, pool investors' money, or guarantee returns. It also rules out peer-to-peer sites distributing wealth-management products and limits their use for crowdfunding."

The intent, in other words, is to restrict P2P platforms to their original purpose, on the assumption that their service as matchmakers between borrowers and lenders can still be undertaken both legally and profitably. As Hu Eryi, head of P2P001.com, observed in welcoming the new rules,

> "The newly released CBRC regulation will make up for the long-term lack of standards, information, intermediaries, and risk monitoring and early warning systems in the P2P lending sector. It's a milestone for the

development of the sector and will become a necessary prerequisite for its standardized development."

As in other areas where China's "new economy" is subject to regulation, the intent is to achieve accountability through transparency, guided minimally through clear and consistent efforts at compliance based on mutual trust and cooperation. Those who appreciate the benefits of the rule of law for expanding China's social and economic development can only applaud this effort to root out the Ponzi and Pyramid schemes that have marred the evolution of its innovative P2P platforms. Here, as elsewhere, there is really no need to throw out the baby with the bathwater.

36.5 Discussion Questions

1. What is a Ponzi scheme, and why is it considered fraudulent? What is fraud, and why is it considered both immoral and illegal? If you were an investor with savings to invest, and wanted to get good returns for your investment, how would you protect yourself against being victimized by Ponzi schemes and other forms of financial fraud?
2. P2P platforms are made possible through advances in digital technology. As with so many forms of social innovation, they challenge us to rethink the role of free choice — or personal responsibility — in market transactions, and whether the government still has a role in regulating these transactions. Do you think P2P platforms should remain free of government regulation? If government regulation is necessary, what do you think should be its purpose and limits?
3. Investors with small amounts of savings were attracted to P2P platforms because they promised to allow them to make gains on their capital more or less equal to what investors with large amounts of capital were getting. In choosing to invest in P2P platforms, were these small investors simply being greedy? When some of them were victimized in Ponzi schemes, did they get what they deserved in losing some or all of their capital? Why? Why not?
4. What should be our moral judgment on P2P platforms? Since some investors have been victimized by them, should they be abolished? Alternatively, if P2P platforms are no better than conventional financial institutions in eliminating the possibility of fraud, should they be

tolerated as social innovations? Should frauds committed through them be regarded as part of the price of progress?

5. In business, as in other areas of human activity, should evil be tolerated that good may come of it? Do the good consequences of social innovations like P2P platforms outweigh the evil, that is, the harms done to investors victimized by the frauds sometimes enabled through them? Should such considerations be taken into account when the government is formulating policies for regulating them? If so, how so; if not, why not?

Bibliography

Cntv.cn (2015). New rules on online P2P lending amid rampant fraud. *The State Council of the People's Republic of China.* Retrieved on 26 October 2017 from http://english.gov.cn/news/video/2015/12/30/content_281475263385723.htm.

Jiang, X. (2016). 'Milestone' regulation formulated to standardize P2P lending companies. *The State Council of the People's Republic of China.* Retrieved on 26 October 2017 from http://english.gov.cn/state_council/ministries/2016/08/25/content_281475425466368.htm.

Noronha, K. (2017). China: Dozens detained in Beijing at pro-charity protest. *International Business Times.* Retrieved on 26 October 2017 from http://www.ibtimes.co.uk/67-demonstrators-detained-beijing-after-pyramid-scheme-protest-1632153.

Ren, D. (2017). China regulators warn that 90 pc of peer-to-peer lenders could fail in 2017. *South China Morning Post.* Retrieved on 26 October 2017 from http://www.scmp.com/print/business/china-business/article/2072177/china-regulators-warns-90-pc-peer-peer-lenders-could-fail.

Reuters (2015). China's P2P lenders offer relief to small entrepreneurs. *South China Morning Post.* Retrieved on 26 October 2017 from http://www.scmp.com/print/business/banking-finance/article/1813850/chinas-p2p-lenders-offer-relief-small-entrepreneurs.

Zhou, X. (2016). China's HK$59 billion online Ponzi scheme: Who started it, how did it happen and now what? *South China Morning Post.* Retrieved on 27 October 2017 from http://www.scmp.com/print/news/china/money-wealth/article/1908096/chinas-hk59-billion-online-ponzi-scheme-who-started-it-how.

Chapter 37

China's Expired Vaccine Scandal: Entrepreneurship Run Amok?

Dennis P. McCann and Mark Pufpaff

Abstract

This case describes how a Chinese entrepreneur started a business by buying up discarded vaccines and reselling them to hospitals and clinics. The entrepreneur, Pang Hongwei, was convicted once, but could still continue her activities very quickly turning it into a multi-million dollar business. Only in 2016 did the Chinese authorities put an end to this and arrest more than 300 business people and government officials involved. The case discusses the scandal and asks what responsible entrepreneurship is.

Keywords: Product safety, corporate governance, supplier, production, consumers

37.1 Seeing

We have all heard the old saying, "If at first you don't succeed, try, try again!" Pang Hongwei, a pharmacist in Shandong Province, had an idea for an innovative business. She would buy up supplies of vaccines about to be discarded by other wholesalers and resell them for a profit to hospitals and clinics that needed them immediately. If she did it right, she could negotiate a steeply discounted price with the wholesalers, for whom the vaccines were worth next to nothing, and then resell them for whatever the market would bear — a market made up of medical facilities that otherwise might not be able to secure a supply of the much-needed vaccines. All her enterprise would require would be a warehouse for storing the vaccines — which she could rent cheaply enough in Jinan — and a network of distributors who could generate sales by visiting her potential customers and convincing them that her "just-in-time" delivery service was, as they say, just what the doctor ordered.

She had tried this once before a few years earlier, but had run afoul of the law. There were, as inevitably there seem to be for all innovative businesses, irregularities that caught the attention of the authorities. The vaccines were not properly refrigerated, either in storage or in special delivery vans. And, a close check revealed that the vaccines were past their expiry date, the date the original pharmaceutical manufacturers had indicated, beyond which they should not be sold or used. But, these are mere technicalities, are they not? Whoever pays attention to expiry dates? Those who do are usually looking for a way to get a better price, a leverage point for additional savings. Now, be honest. When was the last time you threw away anything in your pantry or your refrigerator simply because the label indicated it was beyond the expiry date? If there is no harm done, when opening and cooking a can of beans beyond its expiry date, why would there be any harm using vaccines that had expired? If someone complained, you could offer them a discounted price; but, why throw out something that still could be sold for a profit? Waste not; want not, as my mother — and possibly Pang's — would say.

The government, however, took a dim view of her business model, and Pang was convicted in 2009 of illegally trading in vaccines and sentenced to three years in prison. Inexplicably, the sentence was suspended (in effect reducing it to five years' probation), which enabled her to start up her business once more in 2011. After some dramatic initial success, Pang — now working with her daughter — was once again discovered selling the illegal vaccines in 2015, worth RMB 570 million (USD 88 million). This time, the authorities tried to determine the extent of her sales network, pursuing for arrest some 300 suspects, operating in 23 of China's 34 provinces and administrative units. More importantly, they attempted to trace the illegal vaccines, in order to prevent the use of those that remained on the shelves of the hospitals, clinics, and other dispensaries that had purchased them. Since they needed the public's cooperation in locating the suspect supplies, reports on Pang's illegal operations were finally released to the news media a year later in March, 2016. The result was an explosion of public anger and fear that may yet seriously compromise China's private and public health programs of immunization.

The outrage, naturally enough, begins with the concerns of parents for their children. According to the *New York Times*, 18 April 2016, "Why didn't we learn about this sooner? If there's a problem with vaccines for our kids, we should be told as soon as the police knew. Aren't our children the future of the nation?" Others placed the vaccine scandal in the long line of recent catastrophes affecting the safety of China's foods and medicines. According to *The Politic*, 15 May 2016, "We have already tolerated melamine, poisonous capsules, Sudan Red, plasticizer, gutter oil, clenbuterol, milk with melted leather, poisonous ginger, rice with cadmium and expired meat...How is that such a big country like ours cannot guarantee the safety of our children?" Much of the anger was directed against China's government regulators, whose reassurances — supported by World Health Organization (WHO) representatives — that the illegal vaccines were unlikely to cause harm directly were regarded, at best, as lame excuses.

While the illegal vaccines distributed by Pang may not have been harmful as such, they were likely to be ineffective because they had been stored and transported without refrigeration and had aged beyond the expiry date. Despite such reassurances from regulators, the public reaction to the scandal seems to have precipitated a sharp — hopefully short term — decline in children's vaccinations. Some parents are either refusing to have their child vaccinated, or postponing it until they can be sure that it is safe. The government thus has had to warn the public of the dangers of an "anti-vaxxer campaign" which would only make things worse (*China Digital Times*, 23 March 2016). Public opinion was moving quickly from protest against Pang's activities toward supporting campaigns — such as those seen in the USA and Europe — rejecting all forms of vaccination.

What are we to think of this? Is Pang just another entrepreneur, out to make a fast buck, on the basis of what she thought was an ingenious business plan? Or is she a predator who brazenly put innocent people's lives at risk in order enrich herself and her family? Should we praise her for her entrepreneurial spirit or condemn her for her callous disregard of human life?

37.2 Judging

We hear a lot these days about "responsible entrepreneurship." But, what might that mean in this case? As someone trained in the field of pharmacy,

Pang should have known about the importance of expiry dates on various medicines and health products. She should have known that risks of using vaccines beyond their expiry date could be serious. Even if no direct harm was done, the person vaccinated was not likely to get the immunization that the vaccine was designed to give. The person vaccinated would, in effect, remain vulnerable to serious illness. If a given person fell ill, and the illness were contagious, for example, it would also mean that anyone in contact with that person would also be at risk. We know this from studying the effects of anti-vaccination campaigns in other parts of the world. Diseases once considered extinct — such as whooping cough — have been known to resurface when enough children in a particular locale are no longer vaccinated. Should Pang be held responsible for such outbreaks, were they to occur, because parents no longer trusted the government's reassurances about vaccination?

Of course, it could have been worse. What Pang did was to sell vaccines beyond their expiry date. Rather than simply dispose of them, as a pharmacist would know to do, she hit upon a way of making money — lots of money — from them. But, they were real vaccine products, not counterfeits. There had been other episodes in China where fake vaccines concocted of harmful substances had been sold, causing illness and even death among those who used them. Pang was not a counterfeiter. But, can we justify her actions, and regard her as an entrepreneurial hero for the boldness of her business plan and her skill in organizing a sales network that achieved extraordinary results in a relatively short period of time? She may have been an entrepreneur; but where was her sense of responsibility?

Adding the word "responsible" to the word "entrepreneur" suggests a qualification: A distinction can and ought to be made between entrepreneurs who are responsible and those who are not. What might be the difference? Surely, it is not just a distinction between those who get caught doing something wrong and those who do not. Pang got caught, but why is what she did irresponsible? It is often said that rules are meant to be broken. Because they are innovators, entrepreneurs are more likely to break the rules than most other people. They must learn to think outside the box, try something new, imagine a product or service that may not yet be readily available, or design and implement a business plan that has not been tried before. They must take risks in order to earn big rewards. Pang, it seems, shares these traits with all entrepreneurs. So, what did she miss that led her astray?

What does it mean to be responsible? Confucius may give us the most useful clues, on this as in so many other things. When asked by Zigong, the disciple who was a merchant,

> "Is there any one word that could guide a person throughout life?", Confucius answered: "How about '*shu*' [reciprocity]: never impose on others what you would not choose for yourself?" (Analects XV.24).

This, of course, is the so-called "Golden Rule", which is the cornerstone not only of Confucian ethics generally but also of Confucian entrepreneurship in particular. Assuming responsibility means becoming responsive to the needs of others, as well as one's own. It means anticipating those needs, foreseeing the impact of one's actions, and avoiding those actions that are likely to cause harm to others, even when there is no rule explicitly forbidding them. Assuming responsibility means following the path laid out in the "Five Constant Virtues" (*wǔ cháng* 五常):

> "Benevolence (*rén*仁), righteousness (*yì* 义), propriety (*lǐ* 礼), wisdom (*zhì*智) and fidelity (*xìn*信)."

A responsible entrepreneur, like any responsible person, comes to realize that these are interrelated and form a seamless garment. We wear it like a second skin, and through them we learn to act responsibly.

Marketing vaccines that are unsafe because they are beyond their expiry date and improperly handled in storage and distribution is wrong, not only because it is illegal, but more importantly because it turns away from the path laid out by each of the five virtues. Benevolence is lacking when an entrepreneur's business plan ignores the risks that it imposes on others for the sake of making a profit. Righteousness is lacking when an entrepreneur confuses innovation with disrespect for law and order. Propriety is lacking when rules designed to protect one's customers and other stakeholders are deliberately broken. Wisdom is lacking when an entrepreneur is unable to foresee the harmful consequences of one's actions on others, especially when such actions undermine the prospects for a harmonious society. Fidelity is lacking when the pursuit of wealth overrides all moral constraints, and the entrepreneur's actions no longer reflect any sense of personal integrity. Pang's actions, interpreted in light of these virtues, are just the opposite of what one would expect from a responsible entrepreneur. She should have known better. With her skills and training, what need was there to engage in illegal and irresponsible behavior in order to make a living?

37.3 Acting

Once Pang was detained by the authorities and her sales network disrupted, China had another mess to clean up. Public confidence in the government's immunization programs had to be restored. Parents had to be reassured that vaccination was a safe procedure with great health benefits for their children. But, in order to achieve these goals, the government had to respond with reforms that would actually address the problems revealed by Pang's highly successful operation.

It was fortunate that the vaccines marketed by Pang were exclusively from the second tier of a two-tiered system of immunization. Tier One consisted of mandatory vaccinations, whose supplies were exclusively under government control, such as the vaccines against polio and measles, which were available free of charge. Tier Two, however, consisted of vaccinations stipulated as optional in China, for example, vaccines for rabies, influenza, and hepatitis B — which patients must order and pay for through their health care providers. Money could only be made from these Tier Two vaccines, for their supply chain was largely in private hands and products were distributed through market transactions. Since vaccines in this second tier were Pang's target of opportunity, the government's reform efforts focused on preventing further abuses in the Tier Two distribution system. So it is that "health and drug officials promised to tighten vaccine purchase rules to stamp out under-the-counter trade." A representative from the WHO in Beijing judged that "the proposed changes were promising and would mean clinics would not have to rely on selling patientpaid vaccines for their upkeep" (*New York Times*, 18 April 2016).

A far more difficult challenge may be restoring people's confidence in the government's ability to protect their health and safety. While the proposed reforms within the vaccine supply chain may be sufficient to prevent others from copying Pang's misbegotten scheme, the public's weariness over the pervasive corruption plaguing almost all aspects of the health care system, as well as food safety and other issues upon which the quality of their lives depends, suggests that the government must find new ways to regulate China's markets and implement needed reforms. As one Chinese netizen suggested,

> "The government's usual playbook for handling such incidents: 'Always 'inferring from one example,' always 'patching up after the damage is done,' always 'promising to punish with due severity' and always paying attention after the problem 'becomes big.' Is there any use? What does the government watchdog do?'" (*The Politic*, 15 May 2016)

At the very least, the public seems to be demanding greater transparency and accountability across the board. But, how is that to be achieved in China today? What do you think should be done to prevent episodes like the recent vaccine scandal?

37.4 Discussion Questions

1. What is an entrepreneur? What does it mean to embody the ideal of "Responsible Entrepreneurship"?
2. What is "Confucian Entrepreneurship"? Will a return to Confucian values among China's business communities make a difference in the way we respond to crises like the vaccine scandal?
3. What is your position on Pang and her innovative business plan? Would you consider her a successful entrepreneur? If so, how so; if not, why not?
4. Do you think that business conditions would improve generally if entrepreneurs could be convinced to practice the "Five Constant Virtues" (*wǔ cháng* 五常)?
5. Do you think that "consumer confidence" in the health care industry would improve if entrepreneurs sincerely embraced Confucian values?
6. What are the responsibilities of government regulators in the vaccine crisis? What should they have done and when should they have done it?
7. Did they make a serious error in not disclosing the problem to the public when they first knew about it? Why did they wait a year before informing the public? Do you think it is likely that children might have been harmed by their silence? Why or why not?

8. Do you think that targeted or piecemeal reforms in supply chain management will be enough to prevent future scandals, like the vaccine crisis reported here? If not, what else do you think should be done? How would you envision the reforms, if you were a government regulator charged with managing the distribution of vaccines in China?

Bibliography

Connor, N. (2016). £61 million deadly vaccines fraud uncovered in China. *The Telegraph*. Retrieved on August 9, 2016 from https://www.telegraph.co.uk/news/worldnews/asia/china/12199887/61-million-deadly-vaccines-fraud-uncovered-in-China.html.

Dong, Y. (2016). "I Wish I Could Strike You With Thunder": China's vaccine scandal reveals a culture of corruption. *The Politic*. Retrieved on August 9, 2016 from https://thepolitic.org/i-wish-i-could-strike-you-with-thunder-chinas-vaccine-scandal-reveals-a-culture-of-corruption/.

Xinhua (2016). Premier vows no leniency in vaccine scandal. *China Daily*. Retrieved on August 9, 2016 from http://usa.chinadaily.com.cn/china/2016-03/23/content_24045131.htm.

Chapter 38

Huishan Dairy: Got Stock?

Mark Pufpaff and Dennis P. McCann

Abstract

China Huishan Dairy Holdings Co Ltd. was accused in December, 2017 of accounting fraud and embezzlement by a US-based short selling investment firm named Muddy Waters. The accusations were based on on-the-ground investigations into the integrity of Huishan's financials. Not a few months after Muddy Waters published their findings, Huishan's stock price dropped 85% in 90 minutes. This case analyzes Muddy Waters' research findings, Huishan's operational inconsistencies and suspicious executive behavior, Huishan's response to Muddy Waters' research, and the morality of fraud and embezzlement.

Keywords: Accounting fraud, embezzlement, short selling, investigative research

38.1 Seeing

On March 24, 2017, China Huishan Dairy Holdings Co Ltd. (Huishan) saw an 85% drop in its share price on the Hong Kong Stock Exchange. The drop resulted in a massive loss of approximately USD 4.1 billion in market capitalization for the firm, and marked one of the largest ever drops in the exchange's history. All this within a few trading hours. Why?

Muddy Waters Research LLC[1] (Muddy Waters), an investment research firm, published a report on December 15, 2016, stating that Huishan's financial worth was "close to zero". The report states the following reasons:

"Since at least 2014, the company has reported fraudulent profits largely based on the lie that it is substantially self-sufficient in producing alfalfa.[2] We found overwhelming evidence that Huishan has long purchased substantial quantities of alfalfa from third parties, which gives us no doubt that Huishan's financials are fraudulent."

Self-sufficient alfalfa production was stated to be essential to Huishan's industry-leading gross profit margin, given that none of their competitors claim to grow alfalfa at self-sustaining levels. They claimed on their IPO prospectus in 2013 that their alfalfa production farms were in close proximity to their feed-processing subsidiaries and cow farms, thus lowering logistics and transportation costs and avoiding the markups associated with sourcing alfalfa from third-party suppliers. That Huishan was sourcing most, if not all, of its alfalfa from third-party suppliers is evidence that their stated profit margins, from at least 2014 (but perhaps as far back as 2011), were fraudulent.

"We believe Huishan has engaged in capital expenditures fraud related to its cow farms. We estimate that Huishan has overstated the spending on these farms by RMB 893 million to RMB 1.6 billion. The primary purpose of the capital expenditures fraud is likely to support the company's income statement fraud."

Given Huishan's fabricated profit margin claims, which gave the impression the firm was more profitable than it actually was, it began to exaggerate capital expenditures for the construction of new cow farms to account for the lack of profits. In their 2013 IPO prospectus, they reported

---

[1]In Chinese, Muddy Waters is taken from an old Chinese proverb, "浑水摸鱼", meaning "muddy waters make it easy to catch fish". This proverb animates the firm's mission to hold firms accountable through investigative research and informs its investment methodology, namely, to short companies they foresee as unsustainable.

[2]"Alfalfa is a protein and vitamin rich grass that boosts milk yield and protein content, a key determinant in the selling price of raw milk."

an average new farm construction cost of RMB 45.2 million, covering land, construction, machinery, and equipment. However, although Huishan's capital expenditure reporting is vague and scarce, Muddy Waters estimates that in 2014 and 2015 the firm was reporting an average of RMB 89 million for each farm built; in 2016, that average increased to RMB 107 million. Not only is this significantly higher than Huishan's stated average but Muddy Waters' investigators who visited a majority of the firm's farm locations (35 in total) also discovered that many were incomplete or not started at all.

> "Chairman Yang Kai appears to have stolen at least RMB 150 million of assets from Huishan — the actual number is quite possibly higher. The theft relates to the unannounced transfer of a subsidiary [Liaoning Muhejia Livestock and Technology Co., Ltd.] that owned at least four cattle farms to an undisclosed related party. It is clear to us that Chairman Yang controls the subsidiary and farms."

This suggests that Yang used proxies[3] to transfer Huishan assets to Muhejia, which he owned, a process that began in April, 2014. He did this by setting up a separate subsidiary named Huishan Investment Fuyu Shenyang Farming Company (Fuyu), which constructed the cattle farms in question. Once constructed, the Fuyu assets were transferred to a then newly established (as of December, 2014) third-party entity named Liaoning Fuhan Farming Company Ltd. (Fuhan Farming), 100% owned by an individual named Wang Bing. Wang and Fuhan Farming are suspected of being the proxies for Yang to hide the transfer of assets to himself, given that Huishan's 2015 financial reports do not disclose "any consideration[4] [shares] received for the disposal of the [Fuyu] subsidiary". To reinforce this suspicion, it was reported that Muhejia still owned the Fuyu farms after the alleged transfer,[5] indicating that Wang and Fuhan

---

[3] "A proxy is an agent legally authorized to act on behalf of another party."

[4] "Consideration shares may be offered as non-cash consideration by a buyer in a transaction. The shares offered may be common voting shares, non-voting shares, or preferred shares with the right to preferential dividends. The issuance of consideration shares is common by public company buyers, since the value of the shares can easily be determined."

[5] This is based on Muddy Waters' investigative reports, based on interviews with Fuyu personnel, visits to Fuyu farms, and interviews with Muhejia salespeople.

Farming never took ownership of them. In short, Yang is suspected of using shareholder dollars to build the Fuyu farms, and Wang and Fuhan Farming as a front to move the Fuyu assets from Huishan's ownership to his own.

However, Yang is not the only executive to show suspicious behavior at Huishan. Fast forward to March 21, 2017, and we have reports that Yang's wife, Ge Kun, who was responsible for the firm's treasury, had gone missing — she was last seen in Hong Kong. Her mysterious disappearance came after Ge reportedly failed to make a number of bank payments to Huishan's creditors, *eo ipso* creating a flurry of anxiety about the financial wherewithal of the firm. Shortly thereafter, four independent directors, which comprised part of Huishan's audit committee, resigned in tandem, all citing "other commitments" as their rationale. Then, as stated above, on March 24, Huishan's share price plummeted by 85%. Yang, who owns Champ Harvest Ltd., a majority shareholder in Huishan, sold 250.9 million shares that day, evidence that even the Chairman's faith in the firm was failing.

It is also reported that after Yang found out about the failed bank payments on March 21, he went to the Provincial government of Liaoning and negotiated with 23 of his creditors to roll over their existing loans with Huishan, to give the firm more time to assess its financial stability. However, after the share price drop on March 24, it is unlikely many of them would have continued to back Huishan. There is good reason why. Huishan is accused of serious white collar crimes, including accounting fraud and embezzlement.

38.2 Judging

Let us take a step back. What is happening in this case? There are two problem areas in need of further reflection: one, the accusation of accounting fraud, where Huishan was fabricating profits by overstating its profit margins; two, Yang's embezzlement of Huishan assets through a third-party proxy set up as a legal workaround.

In moral terms, accounting fraud is synonymous with lying. Huishan was lying to its shareholders, its creditors, and the regulatory agencies charged with oversight of its industry. In the act of overstating its profit margins, based on a bogus claim of being self-sufficient in alfalfa production, Huishan was intentionally deceiving the public for its own gain.

This is unfair business practice. For example, when investors voluntarily bought shares of Huishan under the impression that their financial situation was as reported, they inherited an unforeseen risk, namely, that Huishan's shares were artificially propped up, and would eventually fall. In other words, investors began at a loss, because they invested based on false information. Huishan's creditors likewise faced a challenging situation. They lent Huishan money based on fabricated financial data. They too inherited an unforeseen risk, namely, that if Huishan's fraudulent activity were found out, and their stock plummeted, they would not have the financial assets left to pay off their debt, interest, or principal. This seems to have happened, and explains why Yang immediately met with 23 of his creditors to ask for a rollover, which would extend the time available for Huishan to pay back its debt. Huishan also compromised its standing with government regulators in mainland China and the authorities governing the Hong Kong Stock Exchange. Both mainland China and Hong Kong have strict regulations concerning accounting fraud and financial manipulation.

MAINLAND CHINA:

In fulfilling accounting practice, companies and enterprises may not commit any of the following acts:

- arbitrarily changing the verification standards or computation method for their assets, liabilities and creditor's rights, and falsifying the statement of their assets, liabilities and creditor's rights by false statement, over-statement, no-statement or under-statement;
- false statement of or concealing their incomes, delaying or anticipating the verification of their incomes;
- arbitrarily changing the verification standards or computation method for their expenses and costs, and falsifying the statement of their expenses and costs by false statement, over-statement, no-statement or under-statement;
- arbitrarily adjusting the computation and distribution method for profits, conjuring up false profits or concealing profits; or
- any other act violating the provisions of the State's unified accounting system.[6]

---

[6]Accounting Law of the People's Republic of China, Chapter III: Special Provisions on Accounting Practice of Companies and Enterprises, Article 26.

HONG KONG:

A person commits an offense if he makes any fraudulent misrepresentation or reckless misrepresentation for the purpose of inducing another person:

- to enter into or offer to enter into:
  - ○ an agreement to acquire, dispose of, subscribe for or underwrite securities; or
  - ○ a regulated investment agreement; or
- to acquire an interest in or participate in, or offer to acquire an interest in or participate in, a collective investment scheme.

A person who commits an offense under subsection (1) is liable:

- on conviction on indictment to a fine of USD 1,000,000 and to imprisonment for 7 years; or
- on summary conviction to a fine at level 6 and to imprisonment for 6 months.[7]

Embezzlement, a close cousin to fraud, is synonymous with theft. It is the wrongful and undeserving appropriation of monetary assets from an organization for one's own benefit. In Yang's case, he is suspected of embezzling some RMB 150 million in assets from Huishan. Such an amount cannot be stolen with ease. Much secrecy and cover up is involved, as is clear from how Yang seems to have done it. He set up a subsidiary (Muhejia), which he owned. He then set up a different subsidiary (Fuhu), which built the farms. Lastly, he contracted, or more likely colluded, with Wang to create Fuhan Farming. Fuhan Farming bought the farms from Fuhu, but never took ownership, as they were found to be operating under Muhejia's, and by extension Yang's, control. It was, then, a plot by Yang to transfer assets from Huishan to himself without formally notifying the relevant authorities or Huishan's shareholders. Why is this wrong?

A central concern is one of ownership. If I stole your computer, which you paid for, why might you be upset? The primary reason would be because it is *yours*, and not mine. In other words, it is an ownership issue. Your claim to own the computer is justified by the voluntary transaction you engaged in to buy it. Since I was not part of that voluntary transaction,

---

[7] Securities and Futures Ordinance, Part IV: Offers of Investments, Section 107.

I am not entitled to ownership, and thus not allowed to take it from you without your consent. The same principle applies to Yang because Huishan is a public company with shareholders. Shareholders, including Yang, are "owners" in the corporations they hold shares of. Thus, if Yang takes corporate assets without public disclosure, he is stealing some portion of what rightfully is owned by all of Huishan's shareholders.

38.3 Acting

How did Huishan respond? In December, following the Muddy Waters investigative research report, Huishan stated that the report was "groundless" and contained "obvious factual errors". In other words, they said the report was not a reflection of reality and that Huishan was not in any legal or financial trouble. Was this wise?

For the sake of argument, let us say the leadership at Huishan knew the accusations of the Muddy Waters report were true. Is there any justification for rejecting such accusations? There are a couple of reasons why we might say no. One, they are lying, and they will have to keep lying indefinitely until a public scandal forces them to admit their wrongdoing. The problem with lying in circumstances like this is that it limits any kind of creative, solution-oriented response. If an alcoholic never acknowledges her alcoholism, sobriety is impossible. There are many ways to get sober; there is only way one to remain an alcoholic. This analogy is not unrelated to Huishan's decision to reject the accusations against them. They restricted their options by doubling down on "business as usual" and not coming clean. Of course, publicly admitting they fabricated their profit margins, for example, would not bode well for Huishan in the short term, but it would allow them to creatively discern a constructive response. Another aspect of this is the lack of foresight into what the fallout of their admission would be. It could certainly be a worst-case scenario, where their stock plummets, they are delisted from the Hong Kong Stock Exchange, their creditors pull their loans, and their consumers switch brands — in other words, yes, it is entirely possible that Huishan could go out of business. But, perhaps not. Perhaps they only have to deal with financial fines, or a delisting, or a downsizing of their firm. Maybe Yang would have to step down as Chairman, a common practice for corporations caught in corruption scandals. In short, perhaps frankly acknowledging the accusations made against them would not be the worst-case scenario. That, at least, seems a better bet than forcing the worst-case scenario by pushing the lie to the end, resulting in a full-blown scandal.

Two, Huishan provided no facts to justify their rejection. The truth matters, especially in the financial marketplace where data largely inform investor confidence and behavior. Muddy Waters went through months of investigation, and produced a report complete with data, interpretation, photographs, interviews, and analysis. They make a strong, evidence-based argument to support their conclusion that Huishan's public worth was "closer to zero". If Huishan is going to reject their findings wholesale, it would behoove them to ground their response in countervailing evidence. Since Muddy Waters is not only a research organization but also an investment firm, they have an interest in maintaining the credibility of their position on Huishan. Huishan, who is at the mercy of the financial markets given their listing on the Hong Kong Stock Exchange, has a lot to lose. Merely rejecting Muddy Waters' conclusions seems to have only served to create further anxiety concerning their financial solvency and subjected them to more intense scrutiny. The original accusation certainly matters. But, Huishan's response matters just as much, or more.

The fallout from Huishan's stock crash on March 24, 2017 occasioned a much more urgent and less dismissive response. First, the company filed a missing person report for Ge Kun, Yang's wife; she is still missing. Yang, the controller of Champ Harvest, has pledged nearly his entire portfolio of shares to secure loans. Huishan has also acknowledged that they have missed payments on a loan secured on October 25, 2015, from a combination of banks, namely, Hong Kong Shanghai Banking Corporation (HSBC), China CITIC Bank International Ltd., Hang Seng Bank Ltd, Bank of Shanghai Hong Kong Ltd., China Merchants Bank Co Ltd., and Chong Hing Bank Ltd. The loan in question has two tranches,[8] valued at USD 180 million and 20 million, respectively. It seems that now, as worry is mounting among Huishan's creditors, and they have already hemorrhaged the majority of their market capitalization, they are adopting more straightforward, non-deflective language in communicating their next steps. Is it too little, too late?

---

[8] "Tranches are pieces, portions or slices of debt or structured financing. Each portion, or tranche, is one of several related securities offered at the same time but with different risks, rewards and maturities."

38.4 Discussion Questions

1. What moral issues are involved in this case? Please list and explain them.
2. Muddy Waters has a vested interest in the price of Huishan's stock falling. Can we legitimately trust their report and conclusions concerning Huishan's financial condition? Why or why not?
3. If you were Yang, acting on behalf of Huishan and its shareholders, how would you have responded to the Muddy Waters report?
4. Given the details of this case, if Huishan did falsify their financial records, what do you think their reasons were? Can you think of any moral or legal justification for falsifying financial records?
5. Given the details of this case, do you think Muddy Waters' accusation that Yang embezzled RMB 150 million in corporate assets is accurate? Why or why not?
6. Please review the regulations quoted in the JUDGING section. Do you think Huishan has violated these regulations? If so, how so? If not, why not?

Bibliography

Chen, J. (2017). Tranches. *Investopia.com*. Retrieved April 13, 2017 from http://www.investopedia.com/terms/t/tranches.asp.

China National People's Congress (2021). Accounting Law of the People's Republic of China. *Website of the National People's Congress of the People's Republic of China*. Retrieved March 28, 2021 from http://www.npc.gov.cn/npc/c30834/201711/b0743587142d470bbb692705ed1570a5.shtml.

Costa, S. and Nishizawa, K. (2017). Huishan dairy, muddy waters target, sinks 85% in Hong Kong. *Yahoo!Finance*. Retrieved on April 14, 2017 from https://sg.finance.yahoo.com/news/huishan-dairy-plummets-91-erasing-040542737.html.

Divestopia.com (2017). Consideration Shares. *Divestopia.com*. Retrieved April 13, 2017 from https://www.divestopedia.com/definition/750/consideration-shares.

Ren, S. (2016). Muddy waters shorts China Huishan dairy. *Barrons*. Retrieved on April 14, 2017 from https://www.barrons.com/articles/muddy-waters-shorts-china-huishan-dairy-alfalfa-fraud-worthless-1481859996.

Tarver, I. (2015). Proxy. Retrieved April 13, 2017 from http://www.investopedia.com/terms/p/proxy.asp.

Chapter 39

The Ethics of Short Selling: The Case of Muddy Waters Research LLC

Mark Pufpaff and Dennis P. McCann

Abstract

Short selling, in short, is legal betting against the continued growth of a publicly traded firm. It predicts that, for one reason or another, the stock price of a given firm will decrease, thus benefitting the investor holding the short position. The company Muddy Waters was founded by a short selling expert named Carson Block,[1] who made a name for himself and his firm by allegedly discovering fraud at a number of publicly listed Chinese companies through investigative research. Once discovered, Muddy Waters would publish a research report summarizing their findings. The case describes two cases in which the company applied this business model to Chinese companies and asks whether it is ethical to profit from another's losses and whether investors should be allowed to invest in the failure of a firm.

Keywords: Short selling, fraud, finance, corporate governance

---

[1]Carson Block is an American investor. However, before founding Muddy Waters Research, he lived and worked as an entrepreneur in China for a number of years. One of his primary businesses was a self-storage facility, which incurred various hardships since its opening. Block views China as one of the hardest places to do business in the world.

39.1 Seeing

What is short selling? According to *Investopedia*, it is defined as follows:

> "Short selling is the sale of a security that is not owned by the seller, or that the seller has borrowed. Short selling is motivated by the belief that a security's price will decline, enabling it to be bought back at a lower price to make a profit. Short selling may be prompted by speculation, or by the desire to hedge the downside risk of a long position in the same security or a related one. Since the risk of loss on a short sale is theoretically infinite, short selling should only be used by experienced traders who are familiar with its risks."

Short selling, in short, is legal betting against the continued growth of a publicly traded firm. It predicts that, for one reason or another, the stock price of a given firm will decrease, thus benefitting the investor holding the short position. They do this by "selling" a given company's shares — which they do not own — at the current market rate, and then buying them back at a lower rate, thus profiting from the difference. This type of investing is not only difficult but also risky. If, for example, an investor shorts a stock, but the stock rises, then the investor, if he wants to cap his or her losses, must buy back the stock at a price higher than what he or she originally paid for it, resulting in a loss.

Who is Muddy Waters Research (Muddy Waters)? According to their website,

> "Muddy Waters, LLC is a pioneer in on-the-ground, freely published investment research. Muddy Waters peels back the layers, often built up by seemingly respected but sycophantic law firms, auditors, and venal managements. We pride ourselves on assessing a company's true worth, and being able to see through the opacity and hype that some managements create. Our research approach is to combine diverse talents, including forensic accountants, trained investigators, valuation experts and entrepreneurs, many of whom have hands-on experience running businesses in the U.S. and emerging markets.
>
> Muddy Waters produces three types of research product: Business fraud, accounting fraud, and fundamental problems. Business fraud reports focus on issuers that have massively overstated their revenues.

Accounting fraud reports cover real businesses that boost profits through fraud. Fundamental problem reports discuss opaque businesses that have serious fundamental problems that the market does not yet perceive."

Muddy Waters was founded by a short selling expert named Carson Block. He made a name for himself and his firm by allegedly discovering fraud at a number of publicly listed Chinese companies through investigative research. Once discovered, Muddy Waters would publish a research report summarizing their findings. These reports would detail their investigation, and argue for why they felt that the firm was worth less than the current market valuation. They would also indicate that they, themselves, had taken a short investment position on the company, expecting that the stock would drop in the near future.

There are two cases to briefly examine. One is Sino-Forest Corporation (SFC), a Chinese forest plantation operator formerly listed on the Toronto Stock Exchange, which was investigated for fraud by Muddy Waters in 2011, and later filed for bankruptcy in 2012. Before Muddy Waters began its investigation, SFC was worth around USD 6 billion in market capitalization. After Muddy Waters published its research into the company, the stock price dropped 82%, losing billions of dollars in market capitalization and causing investors to dump their positions at massive losses. One such investor was John Paulson[2], who alone lost USD 720 million. Muddy Waters claimed SFC was nothing more than a "multibillion dollar ponzi scheme" and that the firm was far overvalued. It is unclear exactly how much money Muddy Waters made from their short position on SFC, but it is sufficed to say it was substantial.

Another case is China Huishan Dairy Holdings (Huishan), a Chinese dairy company. Muddy Waters, for months, investigated the company after identifying it as a potential fraud. Similar to the report produced about SFC, Muddy Waters published a scathing report about the worth of Huishan Dairy, claiming its market value was "close to zero". This prompted concern among investors, and initiated independent investigations into the claims made by Muddy Waters. Not four months after the publishing of the original research report, Huishan's stock price — it was listed on the Hong Kong Stock Exchange — dropped 85% in just a few hours, losing some USD 4.1 billion in market capitalization. Again, Muddy Waters had taken

---

[2] John Paulson is an American investor. He made a name for himself by using credit default swaps to bet against the 2008 subprime mortgage crisis, making massive gains.

a short position at the time of the publication of their research, and stood to make, and most likely did make, windfall profits after the stock price plummeted.

These cases are meant to draw out the method by which Muddy Waters makes their money.

39.2 Judging

What are the moral issues involved in short selling? Are there any? What about the business model of Muddy Waters? While we may welcome a reduction in fraud among publicly traded companies, in China or otherwise, should such firms be actively targeted by companies seeking to profit from their demise?

The most common objection to short selling concerns market manipulation, the practice of heavyweight investors — hedge funds, for example — manipulating the price of a stock to their benefit. The primary way they do this is, if they own an adequate amount of stock in a company, by selling the stock while simultaneously taking a short position on it. Because of the amount of stock sold by the hedge fund, the stock price drops, whereby they benefit from their short position. Such a selloff can also have, and often does have, a ripple effect across the market. Other hedge funds or wealth investors may sell as well, *eo ipso* driving the price lower. The problem here is that the stock volatility is not necessarily reflective of the activity of the stock issuing company itself. In other words, the company in question has not, for instance, released poor financials, flopped on a product release, or failed to complete an important merger or acquisition, activity that would reduce investor confidence and incite a stock price drop. Instead, a wealthy investor with a lot of leverage in the market could manipulate the price downwards to ensure a profitable short selling investment outcome.

However, such market manipulation is not always done with clean hands — some say it cannot be done with a clear conscience at all. Coined "short and distort", there is the practice of investors spreading unfavorable rumors about a given publicly traded company in which they have a short position, either through private networks or through the press, to encourage a mass selloff of that company's stock. The investor who initiates the proliferation of such rumors benefits from increased paranoia about the firm; however, the firm, which is undeserving of the bad press, and their investors, who would otherwise have kept their investment positions in the company, both lose.

Muddy Waters is in the business of causing allegedly fraudulent firms to collapse. The means by which they accomplish this is their research reports, which present target companies as essentially worthless, as was clear from the language used in the publications on SFC and Huishan. Given their short positions with these companies at the time of publication, there arise conflict of interest concerns. Is Muddy Waters to be trusted to relay honest and objective information about a company under their investigation, given that they have an invested interest in its failure? It would be reasonable to say no. It would be like SFC, after reading Muddy Waters' report, launching an internal investigation into the accusations of fraud and then stating the investigators had not — surprise, surprise — found any wrongdoing. Such evidence of conflict of interest brings into view the real possibility of Muddy Waters using a "short and distort"[3] strategy to affect their desired outcome in the market.

In Muddy Waters' summary description of themselves, they use inflammatory language. For example,

> "Muddy Waters peels back the layers, often built up by seemingly respected but sycophantic law firms, auditors, and venal managements.
> We pride ourselves on assessing a company's true worth, and being able to see through the opacity and hype that some managements create."

Here, they are assuming that whatever company they do investigate, and subsequently publish a report on, will have suffered from layers of cover up, something Muddy Waters is claiming they are able to see through. The following question arises: If they were being objective, or trying to be fair, why use this kind of language to describe those involved in the rise of a publicly listed firm? It seems to create a false dilemma, an unnecessary either/or scenario, where Muddy Waters is presented as the righteous harbinger of justice, while their target companies and the regulators, investors, and analysts who enabling their success are conspirators of the highest order. Again, we return to the problem of conflict

---

[3]The relative inverse of "short and distort" is "pump and dump", where an investor publishes positive, albeit misleading or outright fabricated, news about a company to drive its stock price up, only to dump it when it reaches a certain height.

of interest. How trustworthy are their reports, if they want to brand themselves this way? They attempt to assure us:

> "Our research approach is to combine diverse talents, including forensic accountants, trained investigators, valuation experts and entrepreneurs, many of whom have hands-on experience running businesses in the U.S. and emerging markets."

While that may be true, and those involved in investigative research at Muddy Waters may very well find illegal behavior at the firms they look into, they are unaccountable in terms of the *way* in which they communicate such findings. They could just as easily exaggerate their finding as present them objectively. They could just as easily "fill in the blanks" with conclusions supportive of their accusation as leave such gaps in their knowledge open to interpretation. The problem is not whether Muddy Waters is capable of discovering fraud; there is no serious evidence to think otherwise. The problem is whether what they find is what the public reads. And, that claim is difficult to have confidence in when they have such a clear invested interest in the market reacting one way, namely, dumping stock in whatever company is under investigation.

39.3 Acting

Are there any first principles that should govern the ethics of short selling? Although commonly viewed as just another, albeit riskier and more advanced, form of investing, it raises ethical concerns of the sort not found in traditional buy/sell investment methodologies. If short selling is legal, which it is, a kind of ethical code of conduct is required. Here, are a few principles to get us started:

1. Short selling should be governed by existing insider trading laws. Just as an investor cannot and should not invest in the growth of a firm using insider information,[4] so a short seller should not ensure gains based on insider information about a firm's impending decline in

---

[4] Insider information is confidential information kept confidential for legally appropriate reasons. If the information is disseminated to select persons who can profit from it — through investing — in an uncompetitive way, that is, before its general and legal release to the public, it is insider trading.

value. Such activity is called insider trading, and undermines the logic of competition, which requires equal access to material information by investors, big and small.

2. Short selling should be an honest endeavor. If short selling assumes more risk than traditional buy/sell methodologies, then an investor must be ready to accept the consequences of taking such risks. Higher risk exposure is not an excuse for foul play, whether in the form of spreading rumors, fabricating research, or smearing target firms in the press.

3. Short selling should be non-manipulative. Just because a hedge fund can manipulate a stock up or down by moving their positions to and from it does not mean they should use such leverage to ensure profits from short selling. It creates an unfair advantage, one that smaller scale investors do not have, and corrupts the investment marketplace.

Other considerations may include a cap on the amount an investor can profit from a stock on a downward trajectory, a temporary ban on short selling in all forms during a period of rapid stock price decline, and further enforcing existing regulations against practices such as "naked shorting"[5] and "bear raids".[6]

Muddy Waters became known for discovering fraud where other investors and analysts, and even government regulators, did not. They decided to take advantage of that knowledge and profit from it. This has brought them much criticism, not only from those invested in the allegedly fraudulent companies but also from the companies themselves. Muddy Waters is, in the words of Carson Block, its founder, going to "war" with firms such as SFC and Huishan. But, is it a just war?

---

[5] "Naked shorting is the illegal practice of short selling shares that have not been affirmatively determined to exist. Ordinarily, traders must borrow a stock, or determine that it can be borrowed, before they sell it short." Staff, I. (2003). Naked Shorting. Retrieved May 15, 2017, from http://www.investopedia.com/terms/n/nakedshorting.asp.

[6] "A bear raid is the illegal practice of ganging up to push a stock's price lower through concerted short selling and spreading adverse rumors about the targeted company. A bear raid is sometimes resorted to by unscrupulous short sellers who want to make a quick buck from their short positions." Staff, I. (2013). Bear Raid. Retrieved May 15, 2017, from http://www.investopedia.com/terms/b/bearraid.asp.

39.4 Discussion Questions

1. What is short selling? Please explain how it works.
2. Do you think profiting from another's losses is ethical? Should investors be allowed to invest in the failure of a firm? Why or why not?
3. Based on what you know, do you think Muddy Waters Research is smart and savvy? Or do you find them sneaky and manipulative? Or somewhere in between? Please explain your view of the firm.
4. Do you think short selling should be legal? Why or why not?

Bibliography

Celarier, M. (2017). Muddy waters ends 2016 with a big gain. *Institutional Investor*. Retrieved on May 15, 2017 from https://www.institutionalinvestor.com/article/b1505q7kzxzsyg/muddy-waters-ends-2016-with-a-big-gain.

Costa, S. and Nishizawa, K. (2017). Huishan dairy, muddy waters target, sinks 85% in Hong Kong. *Yahoo!Finance*. Retrieved on May 15, 2017 from https://sg.finance.yahoo.com/news/huishan-dairy-plummets-91-erasing-040542737.html.

Hayes, A. (2003). Naked shorting. *Investopedia.com*. Retrieved on May 15, 2017, from http://www.investopedia.com/terms/n/nakedshorting.asp.

Mitchell, C. (2013). Bear raid. *Investopedia.com*. Retrieved on May 15, 2017, from http://www.investopedia.com/terms/b/bearraid.asp.

Part 9

Society

Chapter 40

The Perils and Possibilities of "Celebrity Philanthropy" in China: No Good Deed Goes Unpunished!

Dennis P. McCann and Mark Pufpaff

Abstract

The catastrophic earthquake that erupted in Sichuan Province in May 2008 left nearly 70,000 dead, over 370,000 injured, and 18,000 missing. Zhang Ziyi, one of China's most acclaimed actresses, was in Cannes, France, for the International Film Festival when the earthquake struck; she responded hastily by making a personal pledge of RMB 1 million yuan, as well as raising USD 500,000 (RMB 3.3 million yuan) in donations for earthquake relief. Despite these efforts, a discussion started on whether celebrity philanthropy was nothing more than a scam and Ms. Zhang came under attack. The case discusses the questions on whether philanthropy always has to be altruistic or can also have other objectives.

Keywords: Philanthropy, natural disaster, charity, celebrity, social media

40.1 Seeing

The catastrophic earthquake that erupted in Sichuan Province in May 2008 occasioned an unprecedented response among Chinese people and humanitarians worldwide, seeking to contribute whatever they could to assist the victims of that disaster. And, there were many victims, indeed: nearly 70,000 dead, over 370,000 injured, and 18,000 missing. Millions of people were left homeless, including most of those who survived in the affected areas. The earthquake, which registered a staggering 8.5 on the Richter scale, drew immediate attention worldwide, particularly focused on the deaths of more than 5,000 school children trapped in hundreds of schools that had collapsed. The parents' grief was especially touching, as so many of the children were their family's only offspring, a consequence of their faithful compliance with the government's "One-Child Policy", enacted in the late 1970s.

Such was the outpouring of support — public and private, domestic as well as international — for the earthquake's victims that many saw in it the hopeful beginnings of a new philanthropic culture in China. The Chinese government, in contrast, for example, with Myanmar's initial refusal of international assistance in response to the devastation caused by Cyclone Nargis earlier that month, appeared to be a model of transparency in reporting the extent of the devastation and accepting the help of anyone capable of responding. Among those who did respond were a number of prominent Chinese citizens, including the internationally acclaimed actress, Zhang Ziyi.

Ms. Zhang, who was in Cannes, France, for the International Film Festival when the earthquake struck, responded hastily by making a personal pledge of RMB 1 million yuan, as well as organizing at the Festival an event alleged to have netted some USD 500,000 (RMB 3.3 million yuan) for earthquake relief and establishing a foundation in her own name to receive donations for the victims. Despite her good intentions, or perhaps precisely because they were so widely and favorably publicized internationally, Ms. Zhang came under attack when — after unrelated allegations accusing her of sexual immorality — the Chinese blogosphere denounced her for failing to live up to her pledges. It was discovered that the amount actually sent by her was RMB 160,000 yuan short of the RMB 1 million yuan promised, and that the event at the Cannes Festival had netted a little under USD 1,500 (RMB 10,000 yuan). There were also reports that the foundation she had set up was not properly registered and ineffective in carrying out its stated purposes. These facts were used to support the idea that celebrity philanthropy was nothing more than a scam, a cheap way of generating favorable publicity by making promises that the celebrities never intended to keep.

Despite Ms. Zhang's assurances to the contrary, and her detailed explanations on the nature of these discrepancies, as well as her effort to make up the shortfall in donations as reported, certain members of the Chinese blogosphere remained implacable in their skepticism, congratulating themselves that if not for their fierce criticism of celebrity philanthropy the pledges would never have been redeemed. Ms. Zhang tried to defuse the situation by submitting to an intensive interview with *China Daily* on March 16, 2016. Besides the explanations and reassurances, she reflected on the ways in which celebrities can go wrong in their philanthropic activities. She was asked, "What qualities do you think are required for doing charity work, besides passion?" She replied, "Besides passion, I think one needs a lot of energy, a professional team and enough knowledge." She conceded that while she had the energy, she did not have "a professional team, or the right approach." Ms. Zhang continued, "I wanted to do something good, but we had our problems, such as my lack of experience, my failure to disclose to the public, my limited knowledge about philanthropy and other reasons…. It was certainly a setback. But I learned something new from it."

Indeed, Ms. Zhang has taken several further steps to improve the effectiveness of her philanthropy. For one, she is working with an international non-governmental organization (NGO), "Care for Children", based in the UK, with an admirable track record of successful projects in China. Through them, she is funding the building of a Children's Center in Deyang, Sichuan province, a project approved by the PRC government in November 2009. Ms. Zhang and her foundation will cover more than half of the RMB 9 million cost estimated for the construction. She is also following up on pledges made by other celebrities to her foundation, in order to secure payment, and has promised to make up for any shortfall in these pledges.

Ms. Zhang remains committed to philanthropic activities. She does not believe it is realistic for celebrities to remain anonymous in their donations. But, they must take responsibility for the promises they make. In her own life and career, she thinks such activities have taken "a very important position": "The achievements I have made today are the result of the many years that my country invested in me. If the country suffers, we have to do our part. You cannot make up the feeling that you have with the country and the people. It is real." She also explained her specific focus for charity: "My interest is in kids, especially disabled children. When I see them — whatever country they come from, I hope I can work for them, to improve their welfare."

40.2 Judging

Personal acts of charity are generally distinguished from corporate philanthropy, inasmuch as the latter is assumed to have some strategic business purpose, while the former are regarded as purely altruistic. Ms. Zhang's initial response to the catastrophic Sichuan earthquake seems to conform to conventional expectations about personal charity. Her critics, however, apparently assume a very different view of "celebrity philanthropy", one that is not only cynical about the personal motives of the rich and powerful but also that regards them as carrying an obligation — precisely because of their success — that goes well beyond, say, the pressure on successful corporations to adopt corporate social responsibility (CSR) strategies. Indeed, Ms. Zhang's comments suggest that she shares their assumptions at least in part. The critics may be saying, "You owe us, so now's the time to pay up." But, how far is that from Ms. Zhang's own admission, "When the country suffers, we have to do our part"? The controversy over "celebrity philanthropy" in China thus seems to blur the distinction not only between personal charity and corporate philanthropy but also between philanthropy and CSR. But, just how useful is it to blur these categories?

Do philanthropic activities cease to be altruistic simply because celebrities are sponsoring or underwriting them? Perhaps the answer to this question lies in exploring our ambivalent attitudes toward celebrity. On the one hand, they are persons who have achieved extraordinary success, becoming public figures whose lives, for better or for worse, have come to play iconic roles in our fantasies and aspirations. It is not accidental that internationally acclaimed actresses like Ms. Zhang are known as "divas", that is, goddesses whose every moment is tracked by worshipful followers, seemingly insatiable in their desire to know literally everything about their lives and loves. On the other hand, celebrities are also hounded by critics eager to discover scandals, as if there were no limits to what such public figures should have to endure, by way of assaults upon their privacy or human dignity.

The proliferation of celebrity culture is but one indication of the growing inequalities that have occurred in China's current era of economic and social reform. Unlike the increasing number of newly rich and powerful Chinese who manage to avoid the limelight cast by celebrity status, China's gods and goddesses live and die in it, waxing and waning like the moon, more an object of people's desires as well as a pretext for focusing their resentments. Celebrities provide critics — like the members of the blogosphere who engaged in a feeding frenzy over Ms. Zhang's philanthropic difficulties — with an easy target, especially in a society that still officially espouses egalitarian ideals even as its inequalities continue to grow.

Perhaps celebrities should regard themselves no longer as individuals worthy of personal respect and humane decency — as if traditional Confucian standards of benevolence still applied to them — but as business corporations, which must advance their own interests through a variety of strategic operations, including public relations management and CSR policies. This apparently is the standard by which the Chinese blogosphere is determined to judge "celebrity philanthropy" for better or for worse. In such a perspective, Ms. Zhang's personal sincerity, her expressions of compassion for the children victimized by the Sichuan earthquake and other catastrophes, is strictly irrelevant, or at least not to be taken at face value. The outcomes of her activities must be carefully measured, and rendered transparent, so that they may become accountable to the public's verdict upon them. As long as they remain in the limelight of public opinion, celebrities, then, must organize their activities as if they were corporations, with a range of stakeholders continually pressing their demands upon them.

Is there a discrepancy between what the celebrity — in this case, Ms. Zhang — promised and what was actually donated? If so, the celebrity must make a full disclosure and, if need be, compensate the recipients for any shortfall. Is there confusion about the philanthropic organizations — in this case, Ms. Zhang's foundation — their supporters, and their pledges? If so, not only must the celebrity make the governance of the organization fully transparent but she must also disclose the donors — naming and shaming them if necessary to get them to fulfill their pledges, while promising to make up for any shortfall should it persist. In short, "celebrity philanthropy" should be regarded as a form of CSR, a part of the corporation's strategy to insure the goodwill of the communities in which it engages in its profit-making activities. Celebrities, no less than business corporations, are involved in activities that can only succeed if and when the legitimate concerns of all their stakeholders have been addressed. From the point of view of the stakeholders, celebrities no less than business corporations owe the communities that support them, and must give back to them, when called upon to do so.

This, or something very like it, is the set of assumptions operative in the Chinese blogosphere's critique of celebrity philanthropy in general and Ms. Zhang's philanthropic activities in particular. As her interview in *China Daily* made clear, in order to preserve her own status as both a revered Chinese diva and an honest philanthropist, Ms. Zhang admitted that she has "learned something new" from the criticisms expressed in the blogosphere concerning her philanthropic work. She has, in short, become more business-like in her approach to philanthropy, having reorganized her foundation, clarified its purposes, developed a collaborative relationship with a well-established NGO, "Care for Children", and made up whatever discrepancies had been disclosed between her pledges of support and the donations actually received. She appears determined to proceed further as a "celebrity philanthropist" by conforming her activities to the legitimate expectations of her critics.

But, we may well wonder at what cost comes this "something new". Must celebrities no longer regard themselves as individual persons, responding freely to the promptings of their own consciences, moved with compassion to respond to the needs of others? Must they set aside their personal feelings, including their own self-esteem and need for mutual recognition, in planning and carrying out their philanthropic desires? While there are all sorts of impositions that fated individuals must learn to endure as they become celebrities, is society right to demand that they alienate themselves still further in order to engage in "celebrity philanthropy"?

40.3 Acting

Is there also something new for all of us to learn, as we reflect on the challenges of "celebrity philanthropy"? As the saying goes, "Once burnt, twice sorry". Some celebrities may decide that the personal ordeal that Ms. Zhang had to go through gives them good reasons to either remain totally anonymous in their charitable activities or forego them altogether. While Ms. Zhang's response rejects both of these options, her story does suggest the lengths to which celebrities must be prepared to go if they are to engage in philanthropy without having it turned against them.

One lesson for all aspiring philanthropists is that good intentions — for instance, Ms. Zhang's apparently sincere "passion" for helping others, especially children in need — are simply not enough to ensure the success of their efforts. Though catastrophes like the Sichuan earthquake cry out for swift response and massive assistance, philanthropists of all stripes — and not just "celebrity philanthropists" — should think through very carefully the interventions they hope to make, their likely impact, and the difficulties they may face in maneuvering through the complex of local, provincial, and state regulations. While making individual chari- table donations may not require much by way of due diligence, anyone hoping to engage in philanthropic activities should seek professional assistance, including the advice of lawyers on how to comply with regula- tions at each level.

Similarly, anyone — including celebrities — seeking to become a philanthropist should consider collaborating with established NGOs, both local and international, who have demonstrated the capacity to address the needs of various stakeholders, both short term and long term. Building relationships of mutual trust, transparency, and accountability through such NGOs is likely to increase the chances of success as well as decrease the philanthropist's vulnerability to unfounded criticism. Given the recent changes in China's Charity as well as Foreign NGO Management laws, philanthropists may look to establish partnerships with local NGOs, since these are clearly to be encouraged by China's national government. There are many organizations, including Rothlin CSR in Action, that offer sup- port to philanthropists seeking to identify suitable local partners and build collaborative relationships with them.

Finally, those who are moved by the sufferings unleashed by cata- strophic events should ready themselves for action even before such things happen. No one can predict with certainty the timing of the next big earthquake or flood or other natural disaster. What we can know is that such events will occur, and that we ought to be prepared to respond to them. Philanthropists, therefore, should support planning for disaster relief well in advance of any specific disaster. Such planning may help shorten the delay in delivering assistance, to the immediate benefit of those who are victims of such catastrophes.

Compassion such as Ms. Zhang felt on hearing the news from Sichuan, to be sure, is absolutely indispensable; and, as we know from Confucian tradition, compassion is natural, even spontaneous. What must be cultivated, however, is the wisdom that understands the need to prepare in advance for such events. What can be done now, what resources can be organized now, in order to meet the peoples' needs when disaster strikes, as it surely will, sometime in the future?

40.4 Discussion Questions

1. Do you think that "celebrity philanthropists", like Ms. Zhang, should be given the benefit of the doubt, at least with regard to their intentions of helping others in need?

2. Do you think that celebrities and their activities, including their philanthropic activities, are fair game for investigative journalists hoping to discover scandals or forms of corruption to be exposed and punished?

3. In light of what we have learned about "celebrity philanthropy" in China, what reforms do you think should be attempted to prevent scandals, like Ms. Zhang's, in the future?

4. Are there any limits that members of the Chinese blogosphere should observe in covering the lives of public figures like Ms. Zhang? Do celebrities have a right to privacy, or do they forfeit any such consideration when they step forward into the limelight?

5. Does reading about what happened to Zhang Ziyi make it more or less likely that you will make a personal donation or support philanthropic activities as the need for them arises in China?

Bibliography

China Daily (2016). Interview with Zhang Ziyi. *China Daily*. Retrieved May 26, 2017 from http://www.chinadaily.com.cn/china/2010-03/16/content_9594056.htm.

qq.com (2010). 章子怡被疑捐款"注水" 汶川地震捐款少给16万? (Zhang Ziyi "Filling Water" suspected of donation — 160,000 less donations for Wenchuan earthquake?). *Tencent*. Retrieved May 26, 2017 from https://ent.qq.com/a/20100130/000171.htm.

Quality Magazine (2008). Off-topic: Digital sensors uncover earthquake victims. *Quality Magazine*. Retrieved May 26, 2017 from https://www.qualitymag.com/articles/85695-off-topic-digital-sensors-uncover-earthquake-victims.

Chapter 41

Singles' Day in China: What's Not to Love About Big Business?

Mark Pufpaff and Dennis P. McCann

Abstract

Singles' Day, a Chinese tradition which was started in 1993 in Nanjing University, has developed from a party of single students into one of the biggest mass consumption events on the planet. The case discusses the moral, social, and environmental implications of this event in which a billion boxes are sold in China every year.

Keywords: Consumption, Internet, social media, society

41.1 Seeing

In 1993 at Nanjing University, the tradition of "Singles' Day" began. It was celebrated on 11/11 (November 11), a date symbolic of singlehood because of its four "ones". Single people from both sexes would celebrate by partying together and attending blind date events and related activities for bachelors and bachelorettes. While originally confined more or less to Nanjing during the decades of the 1990s, it has since spread rapidly throughout China, and has garnered much international attention.

In its current form, Singles' Day in China is mostly known as a day of mass consumption, similar to Black Friday and Cyber Monday in the United States. China's largest online retailers prepare discounts on a vast range of products, while consumers standby ready to take advantage of the savings. Revenues from Singles' Day sales have been steadily increasing year over year since 2009, with 2017 being no exception. Alibaba alone, through Tmall and Taobao, generated a record-breaking USD 25.4 billion in revenue, processed 256,000 transactions per second (1.48 billion transactions in total), and delivered over 700 million orders through its logistics affiliate, Cainiao. JD.com came in second, having generated USD 19.14 billion in sales. For comparison, Black Friday and Cyber Monday generated a combined USD 11.63 billion, less than half of what Alibaba by itself generated on Singles' Day.[1]

These numbers are, to be sure, staggering. Joseph Tsai, Alibaba's Co-Founder and Vice Chairman, accurately stated in an interview that "on Singles Day, shopping is a sport, it's entertainment." While such a description may very well be true, given the amount of product moved over a mere 24-hour period, it does reveal a trend that a growing number in the environmental and cultural fields find disconcerting.

41.2 Judging

There is increasing concern about a culture of materialism and consumerism in China. While not an altogether recent development, Singles' Day is more and more being seen as the apotheosis of capitalistic influence, marked by ceremonies glorifying the ever-increasing amount of purchases.

Originally, Singles' Day was a non-commercial celebration. No events. No media. No hype. No shopping. Although there was gift-giving involved, and the patronage of dining or drinking establishments, it was primarily just single men at first, and then single women a couple of years later, getting together to celebrate their singlehood as a way of overcoming the relative stigma attached to not being married. With the rise of Alibaba, however, and the popularity of its online retail platforms Taobao and Tmall, the company leveraged the rather minor consumer dimension of Singles' Day and turned it into the world's largest shopping day. For example, in 2009, there were only 27 domestic merchants who formally

---

[1] Although the population in the US is ¼ that of China, their middle-class populations are closer — 109 million (China) compared to 92 million (US) — the demographic seen as the primary driver in sales days such as Singles' Day, Black Friday, and Cyber Monday.

participated in Singles' Day by offering product discounts on Alibaba's platforms; in 2017, there were over 1 million, both domestic and international. But, is this really a trend to be worried about? Alibaba Group President Michael Evans put it this way:

> "It's not that we need Singles Day...it's [just] the opportunity for merchants and consumers to have fun and engage in something that's really exciting. It's the opportunity for consumers to explore and find new brands and new products."

No harm, no foul, right? But, others, like the BBC's Taiwan correspondent Cindy Sui, see in Singles' Day a more ominous threat to traditional Chinese values and principles. She writes the following in the wake of Alibaba's record-breaking Singles' Day sales:

> "But whatever happened to the traditional Chinese values I was raised on — thriftiness, frugality, and getting by with what you have? They have been shoved aside. At least by some well-to-do and [the] increasingly wasteful middle-class urban dwellers. Some people have become so hooked on materialism that they have become credit card slaves, owing huge debts. At the stroke of midnight, when the world's biggest online shopping event came to an end, the staggering sales figure on Alibaba's website was a sign of just how much China has changed."

Although rather pessimistic in tone, Sui's reminiscence about traditional Chinese values echoes what Chinese President Xi Jinping emphasized in positive terms in 2014, during his keynote speech at the International Conference in Commemorating the 2,565th Anniversary of Confucius' Birth and the Fifth Congress of the International Confucian Association:

> "Confucianism, along with other philosophies and cultures taking shape and growing within China, are records of spiritual experiences, rational thinking and cultural achievements of the nation during its striving to build its home. These cultures have nourished the flourishing Chinese nation."

Implicit within his affirmation of Confucianism is an emphasis on promoting social harmony through ethical behavior rooted in Confucian values — filial piety (孝, *xiào*), reciprocity (恕, *shu*), benevolence (仁, *jen*), righteousness (義, *yi*), and ritual propriety (禮, *li*) — virtues seen as essential to filling the moral void left by a decline in socialist values and the rise of materialistic and capitalistic forces in Chinese society. The recognition of such a cultural change is also prevalent internationally. Sébastien Billioud, co-author of *The Sage and the People*, a book about the role of Confucianism in contemporary Chinese society, stated the following in an interview:

> "The promotion of some — not all — traditional culture resources by the authorities can certainly be understood within a context where they intend to fight against a number of social problems: the cult of money, unbridled individualism, moral anomie and corruption...[however] everything does not [have to] come from the top...you have within society [a] powerful counter-current nourished by aspirations for other sets of values — the religious revival under all its forms, the Confucian revival [and] the increasing commitment of segments of the population, especially the youth, in all sorts of non-governmental organizations exemplify this trend."

Taken together, it seems that the forces of materialism and consumerism are rising simultaneously with a revival of traditional, cultural, and philosophical values. But, can they coexist harmoniously? Before tackling that question, let us outline the discussion of another issue that Singles' Day provoked in China, namely, environmental protection.

The concept of an "ecological civilization" was introduced in 2007, in a report to the 17th National People's Congress. The concept was built upon by President Xi at the Third Plenary of the 18th Central Committee in 2013, who called for "ecological civilization" reforms. Since 2013, China has made significant progress in a number of environmental areas — reductions in coal production, investments in renewable energy, the growing of forests as carbon sinks, etc. — which has rightfully been lauded by countries around the world. However, serious pollution problems continue to exist, mainly in the form of energy production, air, water, and soil pollution, and trash buildup. In the aftermath of Singles' Day, activists have called attention to the environmental costs of such consumption.

One issue is packaging. Singles' Day is estimated to have generated the delivery of over 1 billion boxes of goods. Each box is made of cardboard, secured with tape, and stuffed with plastic wrap. It is estimated that some 2 million trees are required to produce 1 billion cardboard boxes, let alone the raw materials needed for the plastic inputs. Given the perspective from activists that a majority of the products consumed on Singles' Day would not be consumed otherwise — in other words, they are needlessly produced — these environmental costs are likewise unnecessarily incurred.

Another issue is recycling. It is estimated that China recycles at most 20% of its paper and cardboard products.[2] The rest is trash, and headed for the landfill. While recycling, or the lack thereof, is an issue that would exist even if Singles' Day did not, many view Singles' Day as needlessly exacerbating an already serious problem in China.

A third issue is emissions. A study conducted post-Singles' Day 2016 found that 52,400 tons of carbon dioxide emissions were produced on that day alone, derived from the manufacturing of products and packaging, and the transportation and delivery of orders. Without evidence of much change in the sustainability of such processes from the previous year, the carbon footprint from Singles' Day 2017 is likely higher.

Given this, is Singles' Day in conflict with President Xi's vision of an ecological civilization? Or more broadly, is capitalism doomed to be ever an adversary of those interested in environmental protection? Perhaps; perhaps not.

41.3 Acting

If we take Singles' Day as the symbolic manifestation of those forces that are good and bad in Chinese society today, that is, as evidence of what capitalistic marketing can achieve and destroy, then the discussion concerns the possible (or impossible) reconciliation of those forces. For example, is Confucianism in necessary or inherent conflict with capitalism? Or is there complementarity, say, through Confucianism's emphasis on hard work, organizational loyalty, self-discipline, and moderation to align production and consumption with the good of society and the welfare of its members?

---

[2] For comparison, the United States recycles 67.2% of its paper products (2016), Australia 87% (2015), and United Kingdom 78.7% (2011).

When addressing these questions, one important distinction is that Confucianism, or any wisdom tradition in China, should not be dismissed out of hand as inherently incompatible with capitalism, or the economic order in general. In fact, far from being hopelessly adversarial, it can and should be fully integrated. One example of how this has been done is the *rushang* (儒商), or Confucian entrepreneur. Such a person strives to animate their business behavior by way of Confucian values — such as the five virtues stated in the JUDGING section. Confucian entrepreneurship, then, at once acknowledges the value of capitalism as a means for private citizens to earn while at the same time tempering the means only toward those outcomes which align with the principles of Confucian morality. Confucian entrepreneurship thus seeks to affirm what is mutually beneficial in Confucianism and capitalism, and avoids to the extent possible unwilling compromise or an outright opposition between the two.

Building on this idea, it is also important to distinguish between Confucianism — which is a kind of governance — and capitalism — which is a form of economics — categorically. If Confucianism can animate governance strategies,[3] say for the State, and the State is in charge of providing a reasonable regulatory framework under which capitalism can grow and develop for the good of society, then Confucianism and capitalism can and should be viewed as complementary (or at least potentially complementary) and capable of sharing a similar vision for society. Such a permeation of values throughout a society is important for a number of reasons. Not only can it create Confucian entrepreneurs, for a specific example, but it can also more generally produce good people and responsible citizens. Such people in the Confucian tradition are called *junzi* (君子), or morally refined persons, persons who are capable of acting for others and in view of the good of society. They are contrasted by the *xiaoren* (小人), or a small-minded person, the kind of person who struggles to see beyond his or her own interests, and because of such incapacity rarely if ever considers the consequences of his or her actions on others and the greater society.

---

[3]Important to clarify, however, is that allowing Confucian principles to animate political policy is not the same as theocratic governance, in that the Chinese government would not be leveraging Confucian ritual upon its citizens. It is similar in the Judeo-Christian cultures of the West, in the sense that while politicians may bring their values to bear in how they govern or develop public policy, they do not leverage explicitly Jewish or Christian rituals upon the citizens they represent.

This brings into view the role of values, or the lack thereof, in shaping business culture. It makes a significant difference whether a country's business leaders are *junzi* or *xiaoren*. Capitalism cannot be viewed as impervious to values, given that it does not have an explicit moral creed *per se* and is in practice only a system[4] (albeit an efficient one) that enables particular ends, but in need of values, so as to ensure such a system is not abused for subversive purposes — such as the exploitation of labor, the buying of favors, and so on.

All this said, where does that leave Singles' Day? Should we follow the advice of Matthew Walsh of *Sixth Tone*, who advocated that this should be the last Singles' Day ever, given its environmental costs? Or should we align with sentiments of Alibaba's Michael Evans, and actively participate in the excitement of "explor[ing] and find[ing] new brands and new products"? Or should we merely abstain from Singles' Day, and take recourse back to the frugality and thriftiness of the BBC's Cindy Sui? This case has only introduced the issues involved. We leave it to you to discuss the right way forward.

41.4 Discussion Questions

1. Singles' Day, if nothing else, represents a day of mass consumption. Do you (or should you) view the consumption of goods in moral terms? Why or why not?
2. Joseph Tsai of Alibaba described Singles' Day shopping as "sport" and "entertainment". Do you think this description, paired with the staggering statistics associated with Singles' Day 2017, betrays a dangerous change in China's culture? Why or why not?
3. Given the environmental issues involved, and within the context of the greater climate change debate and China's commitment to building an "ecological civilization", do you think Singles' Day is a net positive for Chinese society? If so, what do you think is good and worth preserving about Singles' Day? If not, why not?
4. Do you think Singles' Day, and the perceived hyper-consumerism some think it represents, is in conflict with traditional Chinese values, Confucian or otherwise? Why or why not?

---

[4] The capitalist system has a number of core characteristics, including private property, voluntary exchange, competition, compensation structures, and price systems.

5. In light of Alibaba's role in establishing Singles' Day as a consumer event, do you view the firm's leadership as exhibiting the qualities of a *junzi* or a *xiaoren*, or a mixture of both?

Bibliography

Li, W. (2013). Systemic protection of the ecological environment. *China Today*. Retrieved December 8, 2017 from http://www.chinatoday.com.cn/english/report/2013-12/18/content_585417.htm.

Reuters (2017a). Alibaba's singles' day sales smash record with $25 billion haul. *Yahoo!Finance*. Retrieved December 8, 2017 from https://finance.yahoo.com/news/alibaba-apos-singles-apos-day-191322983.html.

Reuters (2017b). It's not just Alibaba. JD.com generated $19 billion in sales at its rival event. *Yahoo!Finance*. Retrieved December 8, 2017 from https://finance.yahoo.com/news/apos-not-just-alibaba-jd-095530981.html.

Chapter 42

Samsung's Kowtowing Dilemma

Mark Pufpaff and Dennis P. McCann

Abstract

In October 2016, a photo went viral in which Chinese executives of
the Korean corporation Samsung were kowtowing at a sales meeting in
Heibei Province. The picture created a scandal; online bloggers claimed
South Korean executives "forced" their Chinese counterparts to kowtow
to apologize for product failure with one of their products, the Samsung
Galaxy Note 7. Kowtowing has different meanings in China and in
Korea and debate on the meaning of bowing arose. The case discusses
the scandal and encourages students to reflect on cultural differences and
their effects on business practices.

Keywords: Culture, corporate culture, respect, conflict, product safety

42.1 Seeing

In late October, 2016, a photograph went viral throughout the Chinese
blogosphere, sparking widespread controversy. It consisted of a group of
Samsung China executives kowtowing to an audience of smartphone
distributors at a sales meeting in Shijiazhuang, the capital of China's
Hebei province.

Although at first glance the photograph does not immediately betray
any subversive behavior or messaging, many in the Chinese blogosphere

saw into it what they claimed to be South Korean executives "forcing" their Chinese counterparts to kowtow. This interpretation derived primarily from the Samsung executive in the white shirt leaning over two other executives with his hands on their backs (slightly left of center). Enraged netizens further claimed that Samsung China was pressuring its executives to "beg" — using the kowtowing gesture — their distributors to place additional product orders. As these interpretations proliferated around the Internet, anti-Samsung rhetoric flared up, ultimately resulting in some attempts to incite a consumer boycott of Samsung products.

Important to note, however, is that there has been no official confirmation — as of yet — concerning which of the executives in the photograph were South Korean and which were Chinese, nor any concrete evidence regarding the claims that the Chinese executives were "forced" to kowtow and that the executives were "begging" distributors for product orders. The only response from Samsung states that those present at the Shijiazhuang sales meeting were "deeply moved" by the amount of product orders placed by distributors at the meeting — hinting that they were not "begging" but expressing thanksgiving. A Samsung spokesperson stated the following:

"This was regional stock ordering event for distributors, PR had no knowledge of it beforehand. As we understand it, despite the influence of the Galaxy Note 7 explosions, distributors continued to support Samsung, and booked many orders at the event. This was extremely touching for Samsung's top executives, and in accordance [with] their customs they kneeled to express gratitude towards these distributors. Samsung's China executives were also moved, and they kneeled too."

However, many in the Chinese blogosphere felt differently, and criticized Samsung China for "not treating their employees like humans."

Trouble for Samsung began in August, 2016, when they launched their Galaxy Note 7 smartphone. Almost immediately after the release, there were incidents of the battery exploding while charging. After two product recalls, the Galaxy Note 7 was permanently discontinued pending an investigation — that investigation is ongoing. This product quality crisis reportedly left Samsung in the hole for some USD 17 billion dollars, in sunk costs and lost profits. Samsung, having enjoyed profitable operations in China since it entered the market in 1985, stood to lose out to burgeoning domestic smartphone brands as a result.

The drama surrounding the Galaxy Note 7 is the backdrop for understanding why Samsung China employees would kowtow to their distributors in the photograph. That their distributors were still placing orders for Samsung products (the Galaxy Note 7 notwithstanding) was a testament to their loyalty to the Samsung brand and their confidence in the quality of its other product offerings. However, what was a seemingly innocent cultural expression of gratitude was interpreted by the Chinese public as submitting Chinese Samsung China executives to disgrace, thus spiraling Samsung into a public relations quagmire.

Kowtowing has a long history in China. Originally performed during the dynastic era as an act of supplication by subjects to their masters, or inferiors to their superiors, kowtowing was primarily carried out within the context of religious ceremonies, or situations requiring a high degree of ritualistic propriety. One example was peasants kowtowing before local magistrates in the hope that whatever they were requesting would be granted. Another instance was domestic officials or foreign ambassadors kowtowing before the Chinese emperor to gain favor or blessing. A final manifestation of this practice was the emperor himself kowtowing to the shrine of Confucius, a common occurrence during the Ming Dynasty. All of these examples exemplify an act of submission on behalf of the one doing the kowtowing. Although common during the dynastic era, it has become increasingly rare since the founding of the People's Republic of China in 1949, and is generally considered antiquated, even humiliating.

In South Korean culture, however, kowtowing enjoys a more positive perception. Broadly viewed as a sign of respect and an affirmative expression similar to the various forms of bowing in Japan, it is not uncommon to see it used in particular social settings, religious contexts, and even business environments.

Given the differing perspectives of kowtowing in China and South Korea, it becomes clear why the photograph could have inspired controversy. If the claims of the Chinese blogosphere are accurate — that Chinese executives were "forced" to kowtow and that they were "begging" for product orders — it is no wonder they were upset. However, given the lack of corroborating evidence for these claims, and the counter position of Samsung that the Chinese executives voluntarily kowtowed, there are lingering questions as to whether those in the Chinese blogosphere were overreacting and making unqualified assumptions about the reality behind the gesture.

42.2 Judging

Conducting international business well demands, among other things, an acute sensitivity to the local customs, norms, and practices of the culture one is operating in. That is not to say that doing business domestically does not require such sensitivities — it certainly does, especially in larger countries where subcultures may be significant in different geographic regions — but on an international level, the implications are oftentimes much more drastic.

Were Samsung China's executives wrong to kowtow at their sales meeting at Shijiazhuang, given the historical perception of kowtowing and the rarity of its occurrence in 21st century Chinese culture? While they may not have been wrong in the sense of intentionally causing harm, they did seem to be negligent toward its possible outcomes. Although Samsung is a South Korean firm, that does not mean that South Korean customs, such as kowtowing, which are accepted domestically, will find favor and have the same effect in foreign markets, even ones relatively close in geographic proximity like China. Though we can affirm their intention of showing respect to their distributors, we must question the moral appropriateness of their method. Let us explore two reasons. One is that the act of kowtowing by South Korean executives puts undue pressure to conform on their Chinese counterparts. If the

Chinese executives do not kowtow, they may be viewed as indifferent to the loyalty of Samsung's distributors in China. They may also be judged unfavorably by their South Korean counterparts as rebellious, disrespectful, or embarrassing. At the very least, it creates inconsistencies in what should be a concerted expression of gratitude. A second reason is cultural. Does not Samsung have a responsibility to know how kowtowing is perceived in China? If they understood it as even potentially disgraceful, especially in a society not unlike their own — South Korea — where saving face (*mian zi*, 面子) is paramount for building profitable business relationships, should they not have chosen a more acceptable form of expression?

The Samsung spokesperson stated that its South Korean executives kowtowed after being "deeply moved," and that their Chinese colleagues, steeped in the same feeling, followed their lead. That betrays a potential problem, namely, that Samsung's Chinese employees had no foreknowledge that their South Korean counterparts were going to kowtow. The spokesperson's explanation makes it seem almost spontaneous, as if they were so touched they could not help but prostrate then and there. Whether that is true or not we may never know, but it brings up the issue of preparedness, and how companies managing culturally diverse teams in foreign markets need to have something akin to a code of conduct that all employees are informed about, and that helps guide corporate behavior, especially in formal and public meetings such as the one in Shijiazhuang. Having all relevant employees "on the same page" about cultural expectations and nuances — in this case how to express gratitude — is a moral responsibility, and one that should be taken seriously, lest the door be left open to criticism and backlash of the kind seen in the Chinese blogosphere.

Speaking of the reaction from the Chinese blogosphere, what are we to make of that? How credible are their claims that Samsung China "forced" its Chinese executives to kowtow, thereby exposing them to humiliation, or that their act of kowtowing was nothing more than a form of "begging?" Are their testimonies to be trusted, their interpretations of the photograph relied upon, as we form our moral judgments of this case? Perhaps not. There seem to be two major reasons for being skeptical of them.

One, we are not told how much information they have, nor how the photograph from the meeting was leaked — who took it and who it was given to. We also do not know if they have testimony from one of the

Chinese executives who was there at the meeting, or whether someone in the audience revealed what they witnessed on stage among the executives. If they had reliable testimony from an "insider" that would provide context to the photograph, then we might give more credence to their judgments. But, we do not, and it seems that if someone in the blogosphere had such evidence, that evidence would have been made public, however anonymously, and formed the basis for their accusation. Lacking such evidence, should we not view the outbursts of the blogosphere as nothing more than anecdotal or emotional? Private interpretations of an out-of-context photograph, without any corroborating basis for such an interpretation, should at the very least be questioned. Moreover, an interpretation, like those offered by the Chinese blogosphere, which is not self-evident — for example, it is not self-evident that the man in the white shirt was "forcing" those whom his hands were on to kowtow — should likewise be questioned, if not dismissed altogether. However, from Samsung's perspective, the reaction from the blogosphere cannot simply be disregarded, even if their accusations are far-fetched, as such sentiment can and does influence public perception, and can be picked up and further proliferated by the media if not carefully responded to.

Two, Samsung was already on ice with Chinese consumers after a controversial approach to its Galaxy Note 7 recall in the fourth quarter of 2016. After implementing the recall of the smartphone in several international markets, it continued to sell the Galaxy Note 7 in China. It reportedly assured its Chinese consumers that the batch of units available in China was safe. When one of those units exploded, a wave of fury erupted from the consumer and media marketplaces. Accusations of immoral corporate decision-making on the part of Samsung abounded. An opinion piece from CCTV news encapsulates the sentiment:

> "Samsung Electronics said they wanted to be an enterprise that's favored by the Chinese people, however it's not easy for China to like them. Samsung also wants to be the enterprise that contributed to Chinese society, but contribution requires sincerity instead of arrogance. Samsung made it look like they are fixing their mistakes, but in fact they hold double standards on the recall of its products. With a less than 200 words statement, Samsung excluded China from the markets where Note 7 would be recalled and replaced. Samsung's discriminative policies have caused significant dissatisfaction among Chinese consumers."

Given that the controversy over Samsung's recall strategy was only months before the kowtowing photograph surfaced, one wonder's whether lingering discontent over Samsung's alleged ill-treatment of the Chinese consumer marketplace influenced the blogosphere's interpretation of the photograph. It is at least possible that they saw into the photograph what they wanted to see, namely, the cultural humiliation of Chinese business-people by a foreign enterprise, thereby further weakening Samsung's position in China. The range of responses differed in intensity, but a common denunciation of Samsung and its purported irresponsibility can be discerned. Below are several statements that were posted on *Sina Weibo*, China's major microblogging website:

"Now we can say goodbye to Samsung."

"We bow for our parents, teachers, heroes, martyrs, our virtuous ancestors, what's the purpose of this sort of bowing? I can't accept this in my heart."

"They [Samsung] claim to be a global company, but the management doesn't know about the importance cultural differences?"

"South Korea is a country whose president is controlled by a cult and "eight fairies." If the culture and mindset of its largest economic pillar [referring to Samsung] aren't normal, do you think this country can continue on this course?"

Some microbloggers even referred to Samsung using the derogatory ethnic slur *bangzi* (棒子), a term originally used to describe the children of prostitutes in Korean society.

Regardless of whether clear answers to the above uncertainties will ever surface, it still leaves Samsung with a strategic question, namely, how best to respond to the blogosphere's interpretations of the photograph.

42.3 Acting

Samsung responded to the controversy surrounding the circulated photograph by issuing a single statement, as quoted in the Section 42.1. They publicized this statement through *The Paper*, a Chinese-based news outlet. They also provided similar comment to *The Straits Times*, a Singaporean newspaper. However, that is all we are told of their response. It remains to be discussed whether that was enough.

Samsung is a massive enterprise. It is reasonable to assume they will have critics, and that not every dissenting voice needs to be listened to, or at least addressed formally. But, the scale of a business is not an excuse to be callous in responding to stakeholder outcry. Presumably, many of the microbloggers who were expressing discontent were part of Samsung's target market, given that many, if not most, of them use smartphones to post and comment on issues of interest. Granting this, it is in Samsung's best interest not to ignore them, especially if their criticism is legitimate. However, even if their claims are not true, or at least not overly convincing, as may be the situation in this case, a response is still warranted. Why?

The Chinese blogosphere is presenting a challenge to Samsung, in the form of a taunt. It is analogous to the way a bully coerces a victim into attacking by nagging them endlessly, so that the bully is thereby justified in "self-defending" themselves. If the Chinese blogosphere is the bully and Samsung is the victim, what is the best response? It is reasonable to assume that unless Samsung takes a position, remaining silent is tantamount to admitting guilt. The bully, the blogosphere, will just continue to poke and pry until a reaction is goaded out of the victim, Samsung. But, unlike some victims, who boil over emotionally and act outrageously — to their own disadvantage, to be sure — Samsung has a choice to make. They can fight back aggressively, condemning the blogosphere for spreading lies and unfounded accusations. Or, they can communicate calmly and clearly the facts as they know them, and let those facts stand for themselves. Samsung seems to have done the latter, perhaps to its advantage.

That said, we are working with incomplete information, as discussed in the JUDGING section. Samsung certainly did provide a counter to the claims of the blogosphere, but it did so by utilizing deflective language, without any firm evidence to the contrary. They began their statement by saying, "This was regional stock ordering event for distributors, PR had no knowledge of it beforehand." How are we supposed to interpret this? Does a lack of foreknowledge about the kowtowing activity absolve Samsung PR from their responsibility to learn about it thereafter? Why would they not simply gather the facts after the controversy broke, perhaps by discussing with the executives in attendance, and then formulate a more persuasive statement, one that explains what happened irrespective of whether they knew about the meeting beforehand? The next sentence begins with, "As we understand it…" On the one hand, even if this was meant to plead ignorance of the events, is not PR supposed to speak authoritatively on behalf of the firm? On the other hand, they may be trying to avoid pigeonholing Samsung into a position they do not have full confirmation on, namely, how the executives were treating each other on stage when the decision was made to kowtow. The remainder of the statement is straightforward and informative, but the question remains as to whether it was convincing, given it was their only response.

PR, to be convincing to those who are ready to bury Samsung for cultural indifference, needs to be authoritative in the way it communicates its responses. Any hint of insincerity, cover up, excuse making, or ambiguity can further deepen any wounds already being felt by Samsung's stakeholders. However, being overly forthright or argumentative, especially if the blogosphere does have a "bullying" agenda against foreign firms — known as "soft-power protectionism"[1] — can be counterproductive as well.

Balancing honesty with confidence is difficult. Do you think Samsung's PR did a good job responding to its kowtowing controversy?

42.4 Discussion Questions

1. Samsung's spokesperson issued a brief statement, explaining that their Chinese executives voluntarily kowtowed, and that they did so in response to their distributors having submitted a significant amount of new product orders. Do you feel this response was enough to assuage the criticism coming from the Chinese blogosphere? If so, why do think it is enough? If not, why not?

2. The Chinese blogosphere has an infamous reputation for reacting to news emotionally, and without the complete set of facts. Their responses can be picked up and echoed quickly by thousands, even millions, of other microbloggers throughout China. If you were a public relations professional at Samsung, what would your strategy be

---

[1] Soft Power as a concept was put forth by Joseph Nye, to describe the ways in which nations achieve their goals through attraction, as opposed to coercion (hard power). In terms of protectionism, which is intended to advance one nation's economic interests by making competition hard for foreign enterprises, soft power methods, which may be on display in the Chinese blogosphere's activity in this case, can be used to deflect interest away from foreign firms, and toward domestic enterprises.

in responding to the case at hand? To what degree should you engage with the blogosphere, and how would you go about changing their views, if at all?

3. It is easy to downplay the importance of cultural differences and over-emphasize the role of profit making and mutual benefit in achieving business objectives. "As long as my foreign partner or client is making money, what does it matter how I behave," might be one way to put it. What does this case tell you about the need to respect cultural differences? How would you make a business case for respecting cultural nuances when doing business in foreign markets?

Bibliography

Cosmin, V. (2016). Chinese customers outraged after Samsung execs kneeled to apologize for the Galaxy Note 7 fiasco. *Phonearena.com*. Retrieved February 13, 2017 from https://www.phonearena.com/news/Chinese-customers-outraged-after-Samsung-execs-kneeled-to-apologize-for-the-Galaxy-Note-7-fiasco_id87324.

Kharpal, A. (2016). Samsung acted with 'arrogance' in Note 7 recall in China: *CCTV state broadcaster*. CNBC. Retrieved February 13, 2017 from https://www.cnbc.com/2016/09/30/samsung-acted-with-arrogance-in-note-7-recall-in-china-cctv-state-broadcaster.html.

Tan, A. (2016). Samsung galaxy note 7 US$17 billion fiasco. *RojakDaily*. Retrieved February 13, 2017 from https://rojakdaily.com/news/article/1077/samsung-galaxy-note7-us-17-billion-fiasco.

Chapter 43

Journalistic Ethics in China From Reporting the News to Becoming the News

Mark Pufpaff and Dennis P. McCann

Abstract

Journalism is a noble profession. The professionals working to bring news and event coverage to the general public in a truthful and transparent manner are doing society a great service. However, when such a great responsibility is abused, and erodes the integrity of the profession, justice is called for. This case details the behavior of Chen Yongzhou, a reporter for a newspaper called *New Express*, who was accused of and eventually pled guilty to publishing fabricated articles about a company named Zoomlion for bribes.

Keywords: Journalism, defamation, bribery, Confucianism, five constant virtues

43.1 Seeing

On September 9, Zoomlion Heavy Industry Science and Technology (Zoomlion), a partially state-owned construction machinery manufacturing company in Changsha, Hunan Province, complained to local authorities that Chen Yongzhou, a reporter for the *New Express* newspaper in Guangzhou, Guangdong Province, part of the *Yangcheng Evening News Group* (Yangcheng), had been publishing fabricated articles on the company's financial activities since 2012. As a result, on September 16, a formal investigation into the complaint was launched and Chen was eventually detained on October 18, after police in Changsha allegedly found evidence of corruption.

After Chen was detained, his colleagues at *New Express* defiantly dedicated two front page articles pleading with authorities for his release, which apparently drew support from across the country. They defended his integrity in interviews and acknowledged him as "professionally capable". One reporter publicly mourned his arrest and potential removal from the firm, stating the following:

> "If he's really going to be replaced, it's a great loss to the paper's future development."

The paper also stood behind his articles, which were the basis for his detainment, in a public statement aired on October 23:

> "Based on our investigation and knowledge, Chen Yongzhou has not violated the ethics of news reporting or laws in the coverage of Zoomlion's financial issues."

On October, 26, however, *New Express* went silent. Chen, interviewed live on a news channel of Central China Television (CCTV), confessed that he had received bribery payments for the publishing of 14 fabricated articles aimed at undermining Zoomlion's financial integrity. He said "middlemen" unaffiliated with *New Express* provided the articles, and that he was paid to publish them without submitting the content to any kind of fact-checking process. In fact, Chen admitted he did not even read a number of them before having them printed.

After Chen's arrest, Zoomlion accused their competitor in Guangzhou, Sany Group Company Limited (Sany), of providing Chen with the fabricated stories. Sany, however, and perhaps unsurprisingly, denied these accusations.

After Chen's confessions, and in response to pressure from Guangdong's press regulator, the Guangdong Administration of Press and Publication, Radio, Film and Television, action was taken by *New Express*'s parent company, *Yangcheng*. Chen, of course, was effectively removed from his position as a reporter for *New Express* and had his accreditations and press card revoked. Li Yihang, president and editor-in-chief of *New Express*, and Ma Dongjin, the newspaper's vice president, were also fired. Their empty posts were filled by Liu Hongbing, Communist Party Secretary for *Yangcheng*, and Sun Xuan, a member of the Communist Party Committee at *Yangcheng*.

43.2 Judging

So, what exactly is going on in this case? One of Confucius' "Five Constant Virtues" is honesty. Was Chen acting honestly when he decided to sacrifice authenticity for fabrication? Another virtue is benevolence, the concern for the good of another person. Was Chen acing benevolently toward his readers, his industry, or even Chinese society as a whole, when he decided to submit himself to the lure of riches in exchange for his professional integrity? What about the virtue of righteousness? Would you consider Chen a righteous person, capable of rising above self-interest and understanding that his position as a reporter is a noble one, inasmuch as it is indispensable for the common good? Or wisdom? Do you think Chen was wise enough to foresee the consequences of his actions? Or propriety? Did Chen display knowledge of the importance of rules and guidelines in his industry and the legitimate reasons for following them?

When Chen decided to dedicate his career to reporting the news, he was committing himself to the service of the truth. As mentioned above, being a reporter is a noble profession. His responsibilities are to uncover meaningful stories about significant issues and inform people about them. Good reporting, therefore, can change lives, inspire constructive action, solicit support, and advance knowledge. It can hold people and institutions accountable, provide an incentive for those same people and institutions to do good, and provide warnings to communities if there is imminent danger. The role of a reporter is not a role to be taken lightly, nor is it a role to be taken advantage of. When Chen sold out his personal responsibility as a reporter for nothing more than some quick cash, he sold out the integrity of his entire industry by giving the public in China one more reason to distrust the media.

That said, what about Chen's confession? His public confession on CCTV is not the first. Many have come before him. Some may say that the confessions are coerced, that is, the perpetrators are forced to confess by the authorities, thereby submitting themselves to the role of a temporary scapegoat for an industry struggling with similar, yet currently unrevealed, scandals. It is unclear whether Chen's confession was, in fact, coerced; but, even if it was, that does not necessarily mean it was not authentic, or that Chen is not guilty.

However, if we assume that Chen is guilty and did publish the fabricated articles, using his confession as evidence, are we likewise to assume that Zoomlion is simply the innocent victim of his greed? Perhaps. "Flies don't swarm around eggs without cracks" is a metaphor used in China to explain why so few cases of media corruption are ever prosecuted. The reason is because the companies targeted by such media are oftentimes engaged in corrupt behavior themselves, and thereby submit to paying off greedy reporters who would rather line their own pockets than reveal injustice to the public. But this case differs, importantly, in the sense that Chen was the puppet of so called "middlemen", people outside of *New Express* who had a serious interest in causing harm to Zoomlion.

As mentioned in Section 43.1, Zoomlion claimed after Chen's arrest that its competitor, Sany, was the source of Chen's fabricated stories, the employer of the "middlemen" identified by Chen during his CCTV confession. Sany, in turn, adamantly denied this allegation, and due to the fact that Chen did not reveal the identity of the "middlemen" who fed him the illegitimate stories, they may very well be telling the truth. But, given the competitiveness between the two companies, and their apparent history of trying to undermine each other through corporate spying and destructive media revelations, it might not be so far-fetched a conclusion to draw. In any case, it brightens the spotlight on the core ethical concern of this case, namely, that the media can be co-opted as a weapon for wealthy individuals or corporations to slander their enemies or competitors.

Ask yourself, are your ethics for sale? Is it merely a matter of price? Are you, like Chen, able to be bought and sold to the highest bidder?

43.3 Acting

In Section 43.2, we explored the "Five Constant Virtues" of Confucius: honesty, benevolence, righteousness, wisdom, and propriety. If you concluded that Chen was lacking them when he decided to take bribes for publishing fabricated and defamatory articles about Zoomlion, then what would it take to cultivate them? Moreover, if he did embody them, how might Chen have reasoned through his decision-making process when he was initially confronted by the "middlemen" and their devious proposition?

First, he would have identified the proposition as illegal. But, he would have seen it as illegal precisely because it would harm society in the long term, and not as a means to benefitting him in the short term. Contrary to the old saying that "rules exist to be broken", just because one can benefit from breaking the law, does not mean one should do so. This is the perspective of the *Xiaoren*, Confucius' term for the kind of person who cannot rise above self-interest and sees all things only in their relation to his or her own perceived benefit, regardless of consequences. It is the *Xiaoren* that would see the law as breakable if it meant personal gain.

Second, he would have seen the scenario as immoral. The first principle of business ethics is "Do No Harm". This principle is the basis for interpreting our behavior in terms of good and bad, right and wrong, outcomes. If Chen was seeing through the eyes of a *Junzi*, Confucius' term for a person who is able to rise above their own self-interest and respond affectively to the needs of others, he would have seen that harm was the inevitable consequence of going along with the bribery scheme. This is, of course, evident in the fallout of the scandal, namely, that he lost his career in reporting, severely damaged the reputation of his firm, *New Express*, and enabled the "middlemen" to defame Zoomlion through subversive methods, however truthful or untruthful their claims actually were.

Third, he would have understood the inherent worthiness of his trade. He would have seen his role as a reporter as a call to leadership, responsible leadership, the kind of leadership that attracts and encourages, inspires, and creates. Had he embodied Confucius' "Five Constant Virtues", he would have seen his career as an opportunity to serve, not as an opportunity to exploit.

Corrupt behavior flows from an inability to see suspicious opportunities as potentially harmful, judge them as irresponsible to pursue, and act with the courage necessary to avoid them. Chen, unfortunately, might have had to learn this lesson the hard way.

43.4 Discussion Questions

1. What is the responsibility of journalists? Do they have an obligation to tell the truth in their reporting? Why or why not?
2. Do you think Chen acted immorally? If so, on what basis would you say so? If not, why not?

3. Do you think notions of good and bad, right and wrong, are purely subjective, an arbitrary imposition from rich and powerful people who stand to gain by them? If so, what would you say to defend your view? If not, what counts against such a view?

4. If you were Chen, would you sell your ethics for USD 100? What about USD 1,000? USD 1,000,000? Does the amount of money ever change your decision to remain committed to your ethical commitments?

Bibliography

China Business Network (2013). 中联重科身陷 "记者门" 矛头直指三一重工 (Zoomlion is trapped in the "reporter's door" and targets Sany Heavy Industry). *Sina.com*. Retrieved August 30, 2016 from http://finance.sina.com.cn/stock/s/20131025/105317114247.shtml.

Moore, M. (2013). Chinese newspaper apologises for reporter's conduct. *The Telegraph*. Retrieved August 30, 2016 from https://www.telegraph.co.uk/news/worldnews/asia/china/10407433/Chinese-newspaper-apologises-for-reporters-conduct.html.

Xinghua News Agency (2014). 原新快报记者陈永洲因虚假新闻被判刑1年10个月 (Former New Express reporter Chen Yongzhou sentenced to 1 year and 10 months for fake news). *Xinhua News Agency*. Retrieved August 30, 2016 from http://www.xinhuanet.com/zgjx/2014-10/17/c_133723925.htm.

Chapter 44

The Case of Xiamen University: Sexual Harassment and Higher Education in China

Helen Xu, Dennis P. McCann, and Mark Pufpaff

Abstract

In 2014, Xiamen University faced a scandal about one of their history professors sexually harassing female students. The professor was suspended, but the case became very prominent in the Chinese blogo-sphere. The case looks at the scandal from the students' and university's perspective and asks how harassment can be avoided at universities.

Keywords: Sexual Harassment, zero tolerance policy, accountability, advocacy, Goal Five — United Nations Sustainable Development Goals.

44.1 Seeing

On July 10, 2014, a blogger named "Youth Caravan" posted an article online expressing support for Ting Yang, a female student at Xiamen University, and accusing Wu Chunming, a Professor of History at the university, of seducing and molesting Ms. Ting and many other female students. The blog post also disclosed various forms of evidence, including reports of secretive trysts, hotel vouchers and receipts, and nude photos. An excerpt from the post is as follows:

> "Although most of the female students are angered, they can do nothing but remain silent. More than one victim was hurt both physically and mentally because of Wu Chunming, and some of them were in trance [after the assault] and even cut [their] wrists trying to commit suicide."

This was not the first cry for help or call for justice concerning sexual harassment at Xiamen University. Ms. Ting herself published an article online titled, *A Must-Read for Female Students of the Department of Archaeology that Defends against Bestial Behaviors*, one month before the blog post by "Youth Caravan", detailing every tactic Prof. Wu used to force female students into having sex with him. However, her plea failed to draw public attention and Ms. Ting was labeled as "insane" by the school, prompting the follow up by "Youth Caravan".

In response to the vicious online debate that erupted after these posts were published, the Professors Committee of the Department of History at Xiamen University issued a letter two days after the July 10 blog post to all faculty members stating that they would be suspending all committee activity until a conclusion was reached by higher-level leadership. At the same time, a special university investigation team was set up to consider the truth of the charges against Prof. Wu. Due to Xiamen University's zero tolerance policy concerning sexual harassment, Prof. Wu's postgraduate credentials were immediately suspended, and he was prohibited from teaching or recruiting during the period of the investigation.

In light of this, on October 9, 2014, the Ministry of Education issued *Comments on Establishing and Improving the Long-Term Effective Mechanism on Ethics and Virtues of Professors and Teachers in Colleges and Universities*, which explicitly dictated, for the first time, the government's position that all teachers and professors are prohibited, among other things, from "sexually harassing students or coercing them into having sex."

Shortly thereafter, Xiamen University itself published the *Notification of Dealing with Major Matters of Wu Chunming*, which reported that the claims against Prof. Wu were verified as accurate by the investigation team. After making public this notification, the university had Prof. Wu expelled from the Communist Party and revoked his teaching credentials. Although the action taken by the university was relatively quick and decisive, many in the blogosphere felt that Prof. Wu's punishment was far too light, given the severity of his actions. On the other extreme, some attempted to excuse his behavior, stating that there exists a "big gap" in the regulatory environment concerning matters of sexual harassment, and that Prof. Wu should not be held responsible for something he may not have known was illegal. Others, including 100 of her classmates at Xiamen University, went so far as to accuse Ms. Ting of fabricating the story against Prof. Wu, her advisor, due to her not having passed her doctoral defense.

Ms. Ting's case is only one among many, and cases of sexual misconduct are not exclusive to Xiamen University. For example, just after the conclusion of Ms. Ting's case in October 2014, another female doctoral student, this time from the School of International Relations at Peking University, sent a whistleblowing email to the university's Disciplinary Inspection Department accusing Associate Professor Yu Wanli of having sex with students and getting them pregnant. After investigations, Prof. Yu, like Prof. Wu, was expelled from the Communist Party and had his teaching qualifications revoked.

A non-governmental organization (NGO) named, A Group on Women's Rights, an organization that fights against sexual harassment among other causes in China, stated that "at least 72 on-campus sexual assault cases were reported in the media between January 2013 and May 2014." The China Women's News released a set of data on November 4th, 2014, from a survey carried out on 15 college and university campuses showing that 75% of the participants reported they had suffered from sexual harassment of various forms, verbal and physical. Another investigation, carried out by the Women's Federation of Guangzhou Province in June 2014, revealed that almost 90% of those interviewed — female students from colleges and universities in Guangzhou Province — said they had undergone sexual harassment; the investigation also stated that the areas where sexual harassment occurred most often involved public transportation, bathrooms, and offices.

44.2 Judging

What is sexual harassment?

In Amendment (IX) of China's Criminal Law and the Law on the Protection of Rights and Interests of Women, it states that "sexual harassment" is a term that contains a wide range of "unwelcome" actions or words that make someone — male or female — feel uncomfortable. "Unwelcome" here means that the person harassed has made it clear that he or she has a negative feeling in response to the action or words indicated. However, exact descriptions of the kinds of actions or words to be regarded as "unwelcome" are lacking, giving perhaps too much room for interpretation and not enough specificity for enforcement.

In the context of this case, where sexual harassment is being carried out on college and university campuses and is a condition for obtaining high academic performance scores or being granted advanced degrees such as PhDs, the victims are the targets of exploitation by predatory professors. This point, that professors are using their power to force the submission of students to their sexual desires, is outlined in the definition of sexual harassment promulgated by the Sexual Assault Prevention and Awareness Center at the University of Michigan in the United States:

"Submission is either explicitly or implicitly a condition affecting academic or employment decisions";

"The behavior is sufficiently severe or pervasive as to create an intimidating, hostile or repugnant environment"; or

"The behavior persists despite objection by the person to whom the conduct is directed."

That sexual servitude can be a prerequisite to receiving a fair grade or obtaining an employment recommendation is a serious problem in China, let alone globally, and has brought into focus the responsibilities of a professor to his or her students. In China, the existence of sexual harassment on higher education campuses and the fact that it rarely receives attention or has consequences, is due primarily to three interrelated factors:

(a) Most sexual harassment victims on university campuses remain silent rather than speak out about their abuses. A driving reason for this behavior is that there is no well-known definition of sexual harassment in China, and therefore victims and their families face inherent difficulties in understanding what is and is not sexual harassment, reporting abuses to proper authorities, prompting investigations, collecting sufficient evidence, offering testimony, and ultimately prosecuting offenders.

(b) The perpetrators typically have well-connected networks and high-profile teaching and researching backgrounds. These qualities give them protection, whether from their friends in higher-level positions in the government or Communist Party or from the universities they work for, many of whom have a strong incentive to keep them on staff to maintain a prestigious reputation.

(c) The public at large in China cannot be relied upon to consistently act as an accountability mechanism for professors to avoid engaging in sexual harassment, or as a united voice for victims seeking justice. One reason for this is, again, the ambiguity of the concept of sexual harassment. If people do not know what it means or how to identify it, it becomes difficult for them to respond effectively when it is happening to others. Another reason is public apathy, suspicion, and disparagement toward victims, in other words a general indifference or reluctance to trust the testimony of those having undergone sexual harassment. These kinds of public responses, whether intended or not, end up deepening the scars of the victim.

Given this environment, what can we say about the responsibilities of a professor? For example, former professor Wu had plenty of opportunity to be a real, lasting resource for his students, imparting to them invaluable experience and guiding them as they progressed through university and discerned their careers. Instead, he used his position to fulfill his sexual fantasies, reducing his victims to nothing more than objects, without dignity and unworthy of respect.

The philosopher Tsang said that "I daily examine myself on three points: (1) whether, in transacting business for others, I may have been not faithful; (2) whether, in intercourse with friends, I may not have been sincere; (3) whether I may have not mastered and practiced the instructions of my teacher." Given this, the professor is one who is not only concerned about accomplishing his or her own career goals but also about being a positive and imitable example to others. Wu's behavior not only violated the law but was contrary to traditional Chinese moral principles.

44.3 Acting

Given the issue of sexual harassment on Chinese college and university campuses, and the threefold reasons for its prevalence, what can be done?

If you were a student of Xiamen University...

If you were a student of Xiamen University and heard about the case of Ms. Ting, how might you get involved? A good starting point is advocacy. Spreading knowledge and increasing public awareness of what sexual harassment is helps give voice to victims who may be too ashamed to speak up for themselves. Advocacy work attempting to raise awareness about this issue could target student unions, university administration, or even external NGOs or organizations such as the All-China Women's Federation.

One option for promoting awareness would be to leverage technology. An example of this is the case of Kang Chenwei, a graduate student of Beijing Normal University, who, along with seven of his classmates, created a digital university map highlighting the frequency of sexual harassment on campus and indicating the geographic areas where such encounters happen most often. Although the effectiveness of this mapping project is not clear, it is but an example of the many creative outlets for raising awareness about the perils of sexual harassment for university students.

Another example of student activism occurred after the scandal involving Prof. Wu and Ms. Tang. More than 250 of Ms. Tang's peers, along with other graduate students across China and internationally, signed a letter proposing to supervise Xiamen University to prevent sexual harassment from occurring in the future. The student activists viewed it as nothing short of a moral imperative.

A major stumbling block for cases of sexual harassment gaining publicity on university campuses is the reporting infrastructure. For example, imagine your best friend told you one day that she had been harassed by a professor, a professor of so-called noble character and with high prestige in the eyes of the school's administration. What would you do? Although many universities in China do have a reporting mechanism for sexual harassment and related offenses, students often hesitate to use them for fear of their identities being exposed. Given this, would you advise her to report to the relevant university authorities, even though it may result in public humiliation, gossip among students, or recrimination? Or would you advise she keep silent, and just stay away from the professor, internalize the event, and try to move on? Or is there an alternative? Should student activists be demanding a pledge of confidentiality to protect those who come forward with such testimony? It is true that running from a problem is the worst way to solve it, but ineffective reporting mechanisms can end up creating more harm than good. What is a friend to do?

If you were the President of Xiamen University...
Although the announcement promulgated by the Ministry of Education provides a definition for what constitutes sexual harassment in a university, many commentators still question its clarity and potential effectiveness in holding perpetrators legally accountable. For instance, what does "improper relationship between students and teachers" exactly mean? Without a clear, detailed definition from the central government, what are universities to do, given that sexual harassment is happening on their campuses? One option would be to acknowledge the scandal honestly, disclose the details of it truthfully, and pursue the appropriate remediation regardless of the risk of backlash. Any lack of transparency can create a serious problem in bringing perpetrators to justice.

Another, related option would be to develop university-specific rules for dealing with sexual harassment. One way to establish such rules is to respond to the recent promulgation of the United Nation's Sustainable Development Goals, goal five being specifically directed toward women's empowerment and protection, and China's commitment to them through its most recent (13th) Five-Year Plan. The government's apparent focus on gender equality could be a signal for universities to develop rules and guidelines for dealing with situations of sexual harassment. Standardizing behavioral expectations for professors and providing confidential reporting outlets for students constitute one step toward China's vision of a harmonious society, one in which universities and higher-level management are able to address crises effectively and justly, and one in which both males and females are treated fairly, provided equal access to opportunity, and are respected as persons and not reduced to objects of sexual desire.

44.4 Discussion Questions

1. If you were a victim of sexual harassment, how would you respond? Would you speak up or keep silent? Why or why not?
2. If you were told by your friend that she had been harassed by a professor at her university, what would be your response? How would you advise her?

3. Do you think the punishment of former professor Wu was justified? Was it too harsh? Too light? Why or why not?
4. If you were the President of a university and a case of sexual harassment was being revealed through social media, outside of your control, how would you respond? What would be your first reaction?
5. If you had to write a sexual harassment policy for Xiamen University, what would it say?

Bibliography

China Radio Network (2014). 厦大博导被举报曾诱奸多名女生, 学生称早有耳闻. *Sina.com*. Retrieved October 17, 2016 from http://news.sina.com.cn/c/2014-07-12/222930510381.shtml.

Ecns.cn (2016). University student creates map to warn of sexual harassment on campus. *China Daily*. Retrieved September 2, 2016 from http://www.chinadaily.com.cn/china/2016-09/01/content_26670705.htm.

Tencent Education (2014). 大学生远离"性骚扰",看上去很难 (For College students avoiding "sexual harassment" seems difficult). *Tencent*. Retrieved October 17, 2016 from http://edu.qq.com/a/20141103/018456.htm.

The University of Michigan (2016). The Sexual Assault Prevention and Awareness Centre. Retrieved March 28, 2021 from https://sapac.umich.edu/.

Zhao, X. (2014). Schools rarely disclose sexual assaults. *China Daily*. Retrieved October 17, 2016 from http://www.chinadaily.com.cn/china/2014-08/12/content_18291097.htm.

Chapter 45

Charity or Not? The Case of Sun Village

Dennis P. McCann and Mark Pufpaff

Abstract

Sun Village is the name of the organization caring for the children of inmates. It was founded in 1995 by Zhang Shuqin, who became aware of the children's plight when she worked as an officer and newspaper editor for the Shaanxi Province Prison Administrative Bureau. She acquired some land, built dormitories and a school, and recruited children either from the prison or from relatives forced to take custody of them, or even from the streets. Sponsored by The China Charities Aid Foundation for Children, media coverage was very positive at the beginning. Sun Village however was turned into a business and children who lived there also had to work. This led to a lot of criticism and questions regarding what a charitable or social organization does and which rules are applied there. The case investigates these questions in the Chinese context.

Keywords: Charity, society, abuse

45.1 Seeing

The story is irresistible. A former prison matron takes pity on the children of inmates, who may be lacking in every possible form of personal care while their parents are serving their sentences, and tries to organize a shelter for them. Beginning with charitable donations, her own included, she acquires some land, builds dormitories and a school, and recruits children either from the prison or from relatives forced to take custody of them, or even from the streets; then, she feeds them, clothes them, houses them, and puts them to work, creating for them a productive routine of school lessons and farm chores, helping them to grow in accepting responsibility for their own lives in a world that has dealt them a very difficult hand. Flash forward a few years, and what was begun in an act of compassion mixed with tough love now surfaces as a successful social business, a sustainable enterprise that showcases all that is most promising in a new philanthropic culture in China, where local NGOs lead the way in addressing the real problems of a society in transition toward the ideals of a socialism with Chinese characteristics.

Sun Village is the name of the organization caring for the children of inmates. It was founded in 1995 by Zhang Shuqin, who became aware of the children's plight when she worked as an officer and newspaper editor for the Shaanxi Province Prison Administrative Bureau. Like all Chinese prisons at the time, the one in Shaanxi made no specific provisions for the foster care of the inmates' children, whose numbers are estimated currently as high as 600,000 nationally. After making the rounds of various government agencies, and finding that none of them could or would take responsibility for these children, she quit her job at the prison and used her own savings to start the first Sun Village with the mission of "providing free care and education to the children of the incarcerated". Initially set up as a philanthropic NGO, in the early years, Sun Village struggled to survive since the donations received were hardly adequate for the mission, particularly as Ms. Zhang sought to expand the number of Sun Villages — today, there are nine in operation — with the hope of eventually establishing one for every province in China. Though still far from her vision for the organization, Sun Village's expansion to date has been impressive, and was supported over the years by various government agencies and businesses, both local and international, with the list of sponsors in the 2016 China Development Brief including "China Charities Aid Foundation for Children (中华少年儿童慈善救助基金), Novartis, CYTS, Danish Chamber of Commerce, Shaanxi Chamber of Commerce, Grundfos, German Women's Organization, Rotary Club, Western Academy of Beijing, Nirvana, Daimler, Gaoli International, Lipotec, Knorr-Bremse, Doksa Foundation (香港辉煌基金会), [and] Thomson Reuters."

A breakthrough came in 2004, however, when Ms. Zhang decided to reorganize her collection of Sun Village locations as a social business, that is, as a charitable enterprise seeking to generate sufficient revenues to guarantee its own sustainability. Since that time, visitors to Beijing Sun Village in Shunyi, for example, have reported on the ecological farm in which the children work, cultivating vegetables and fruit trees, whose production is offered for sale. Other enterprises involve having the children produce artwork that is sold as souvenirs, as well as a very large mall where visitors can purchase many of the items contributed by donors at discounted prices. The resale shop seems like a reasonable innovation, given that most of the donations brought by visitors are items for which the children living at Sun Village have no immediate use. Selling these at least provides cash that supplements the revenue yielded by the other enterprises, as well as the sale of tickets to the theatrical performances given by the children on weekends, when they are not in school. The Sun Village social business has become so popular that it has been featured as a tourist attraction and listed on websites like Trip Advisor. The website, Beijing Kids, which advertises itself as "Beijing's essential international family resource", in 2014, recommended Sun Village as a place where expatriate families can bring their children for an outing. Whatever else may be said about Ms. Zhang and her enterprise, it is clear that she is a marketing genius, who has used her own previous experience in journalism to create a compelling story that everyone — government regulators, donors, volunteers, the news media, and even casual visitors — wants to see succeed.

At this point, you may be asking yourself, what could possibly go wrong with this. In May 2009, *China Weekly* published a series of inter-related articles exploring irregularities in Sun Village's registration as well as its financial disclosures. The reports indicated that Sun Village at that time was not yet properly registered either as a charitable NGO or as a social business. As anyone who has ever tried to register organizations of either type must know, the requirements for these have been quite complex and daunting. The fact that Sun Village has had such problems — *China Weekly* quoted government officials who described the situation as "a ticking bomb" and even more ominously as a "financial black hole" — has not prevented it from being sponsored by the China Charities Aid Foundation for Children. While Ms. Zhang's relationship with the Foundation apparently has been rocky over the years, she contends that in the past year, Sun Village "received over RMB

4 million from donors," all of which went directly to the Foundation, which collects, reports, and distributes the cash donations. On the contrary, Ms. Zhang has refused to disclose the revenues and expenditures of the social business, saying that "As a social enterprise, we pay our taxes and every year end we are audited and the audit is published. I think it's enough to prove that we are an honest social enterprise." Apparently, since she regards the business as a private enterprise, she owes nothing further to anyone regarding the transparency and accountability of its operations. Meanwhile, she has skillfully played upon Sun Village's ambiguous status, managing to appeal to donors eager to help extend the organization's "love" for the children of the incarcerated, while also developing a lucrative "social enterprise" ostensibly organized to make up for the fact that "the government does not subsidize [Sun Village] as an NGO."

Some of the concerns expressed over Sun Village's operations as a social business question the tough "love" bestowed on the children institutionalized there. In addition to comments questioning the theatrical performances that the children must do each weekend for visitors, there is at least one report from a New York-based Chinese NGO, "Women's Rights in China" (WRIC) that goes beyond the alleged irregularities in Sun Village's registration and finances. In August 2009, WRIC published "A Report on Beijing Sun Village's Scams, Rapes, and Child Abuse", that accuses Sun Village's management of violating "many laws, including the fund management law, Chinese women and child protection law, teenage protection law, adoption law, and much more." The report also included a number of alleged rape cases perpetrated by an employee identified as Zhang Shuqin's "boyfriend". The report is based on visits to Sun Village both before and after *China Weekly* published its series of articles — none of which so much as mention allegations of sexual abuse. Though Ms. Zhang has given several interviews since 2009, in none of these has she been asked to respond to WRIC's allegations.

45.2 Judging

What is really going on at Sun Village? *China Weekly* described the challenge of finding out as trying to follow the "Black and White Charity Road." In other words, both the good that is being done with and for the prisoners' children as well as the bad that may lurk in their exploitation to enrich an ingenious entrepreneur are real. It may be impossible to separate the two, or at least the regulatory authorities and other concerned stakeholders have been unable to so far.

If true, the most serious charges are those brought by WRIC against Ms. Zhang and Sun Village. If anyone has human rights deserving protection, surely children do, even if, or especially if, they are the children of prisoners. It simply will not do to appeal to traditional Chinese folk beliefs that would condemn such children as "bad" merely because their parents are convicted criminals. The children may be very challenging to deal with, with a range of psychological problems not usually found among their peers; they may have seen things and done things in order to survive on the streets or in the custody of unloving relatives that will require special attention, even discipline. But, their need for tough "love" in no way can excuse the atrocities alleged in the WRIC report. Ms. Zhang's idea of enlisting the children to do farm work and other chores at Sun Village, in and of itself, is perfectly reasonable. Giving an opportunity to do something constructive, starting with the cultivation of fruits and vegetables, may help the children to recover a proper sense of self-esteem that will enable them to go on to become productive adults. Ms. Zhang is right to showcase examples of her success, as graduates from Sun Village have gone on to gain admission to good colleges or join the armed forces. Nevertheless, the WRIC report describes how the worst violations have been covered up, as the children who were rape victims were paid off to keep quiet. Though an investigation through the Shunyi Public Defender's office was begun, nothing ever came of it. It is strange that, as eager as the Chinese blogosphere has been to expose other scandals plaguing philanthropic NGOs, the WRIC report apparently has not generated any significant response.

Given the deafening silence, we have to set aside the most serious of these charges and assume that they are either false or impossible to verify. To be sure, the shadows cast by them are especially dark and troubling; however, there is hope. There are other cases of charitable institutions, for example, mission schools for First Nation children in Canada, or convent schools for pregnant young women in Ireland, where similar abuses occurred, but eventually these saw the light of day. If Ms. Zhang is the "Evil Traitor" that the WRIC report makes her out to be, we can only hope that one day the full extent of her crimes will also be revealed and she will be punished.

In the meantime, this evaluation should focus on what can be known through the multiple sources available as well as Ms. Zhang's own responses regarding the illegalities involved in Sun Village's registration and her refusal to make a full disclosure of its finances. The registration problem can only partially be explained by the complexities of Chinese laws governing NGOs. Ms. Zhang has been vocal in her criticism of various government agencies, but has also blithely ignored Sun Village's spotty record on annual inspections and financial audits. All too often, those who do not wish to comply with them blame government regulations for their difficulties. Even an open-minded reconstruction of Sun Village's compliance problems will indicate that it has failed to meet the requirements for either NGO or social business registration. Ms. Zhang should know that Sun Village's problems of transparency and accountability cannot be made to disappear simply by pointing out that it pays its taxes just like any other business.

The fact is that Sun Village is not just like any other private business. As a social business, dedicated to sustaining its philanthropic activities by generating revenues sufficient to cover its costs beyond whatever it receives in donations, it must meet a higher standard of accountability. Social businesses, true enough, can be either for-profit or not-for-profit. In either case, there must be full disclosure of both revenues and expenditures, subject to an independent and professional audit. Ms. Zhang has only created problems for herself and Sun Village by refusing to comply with these expectations. Failing to provide adequate documentation on how her social business is performing, and for whose benefit, she has laid it open to charges that it is nothing but a "scam" or, if you will, a "financial black hole". The "black hole" metaphor is particularly apt, for it suggests that resources are going in, but nothing will ever come out. If that were true, then Sun Village would truly be an instrument of exploitation, in which the children it is dedicated to helping are actually being used to enrich their custodian, Ms. Zhang and her family. Since these allegations were never fully addressed, the burden of proof remains for Ms. Zhang to explain fully the nature of her social business and her personal stake in it.

45.3 Acting

If you were to advise Ms. Zhang on how to eliminate the shadows that continue to cloud Sun Village's prospects for development, what would you recommend?

In March 2016, the National People's Congress passed the "Charity Law of the People's Republic of China", which provides the legal framework for registering charitable organizations and regulating their activities. In one of her recent interviews, Ms. Zhang acknowledged that the new law simplifies the registration process and no longer requires that such NGOs be affiliated with a government department; nevertheless, she does not think it will help Sun Village: "So, we tried again but it still did not work." One recommendation might be that Ms. Zhang and her legal advisors should try again. The Charity Law is their best opportunity for overcoming the "illegalities" involved in Sun Village's currently ambiguous situation. But, if Sun Village is to be registered under this law, it must be a non-profit NGO, with adequate evidence supporting this identification. It must also rethink its fund-raising strategies so that they will be in strict compliance with what the new law stipulates about donations and how they are to be handled.

It may well be that, once the Charity Law is studied carefully, Sun Village is better advised to abandon its claim as a charitable organization and, instead, to register as a social business. There is a legal framework for doing this, and social enterprises can be registered as either non-profit or for-profit. But, in either case, Sun Village would have to submit to the appropriate regulations and make a full disclosure of its financial situation. The main point of a social enterprise is that it must serve a social purpose, as Sun Village clearly does, and that its revenue-generating activities — that is, its business activities — are structured to sustain that social purpose. If Ms. Zhang and Sun Village were to register as a social business, they could no longer claim to be a charitable organization; nevertheless, their social purpose would be recognized and they would be regulated on that basis.

Assuming, contrary to its most strident critics, that Sun Village is not a scam, the most useful recommendation might be simply for Ms. Zhang and her associates to make a clear choice of which form of registration to undergo, and to stick with it, that is, make a good faith effort to comply with all regulations stipulated by that form. Such an approach, it seems, would help dispel the shadows from Sun Village, and enable the good work that was originally intended in it to realize its full potential.

45.4 Discussion Questions

1. If you were to do a SWOT (Strengths, Weaknesses, Opportunities, Threats) analysis for Sun Village, what points would you regard as

most important for enabling Sun Village to continue fulfilling its mission?

2. Do you think that, at bottom, Ms. Zhang has a conflict of interest in the way she has organized Sun Village, as both a charity and a social enterprise? If so, how so; if not, why not?

3. When entrepreneurs fail to realize their goals, or encounter frustrations in going further, do you think that government regulations are always to blame, never to blame, or sometimes to blame? Do you think Ms. Zhang is right to blame government regulations for Sun Village's difficulties? Why or why not?

4. What do you think of Ms. Zhang's argument that she need not make any further financial disclosures about Sun Village, considered as a social enterprise, because she has paid up all the taxes it owes? If she has paid her taxes, why should she make any further disclosures?

5. What is your reaction to the allegations made in the WRIC report on Sun Village? Do you think such allegations should be ignored, when they cannot be confirmed by citing independent sources of evidence for them? Why or why not?

Bibliography

Lan, Y. China Weekly. (2009). 太阳村存在的慈善监管黑洞 (The black hole of charity supervision in Sun Village). *Ifeng.com* Retrieved September 16, 2016 from http://news.ifeng.com/society/5/200906/0608_2579_1193624.shtml.

WRIC (2009). A report on Beijing Sun village's scams, rapes and child abuse. *Women's Rights in China*. Retrieved September 16, 2016 from https://www.crchina.org/a-report-on-beijing-sun-villages-scams-rapes-and-child-abuse/.

Zhang, Y. (2013). 太阳村创始人张淑琴:孩子需资助 更需融入社会 (Zhang Shuqin, founder of Sun Village: Children need funding and need to integrate into society). *Infeng.com*. Retrieved September 16, 2016 from http://fashion.ifeng.com/baby/news/detail_2013_ 01/26/21635788_0.shtml.

Chapter 46

Fast Food and Childhood Obesity in China

Helen Xu, Dennis P. McCann, and Mark Pufpaff

Abstract

This case provides an overview on the topic of childhood obesity in China. It explains the issue and looks at different perspectives of this social problem.

Keywords: Childhood obesity, fast foods, economic growth, advertising directed at children, food nutrition labels, family diet education

46.1 Seeing

The term "fast food" has long evaded a generally accepted definition. However, for purposes of this case, we will define it broadly as food that is prepackaged, standardized in production, heavily processed, and which contains high volumes of salt, sugar, fat, and carbohydrates. A good example of such fast food in China is instant noodles; there are many others, both within China and internationally. Such food, and the companies that produce it, has become increasingly popular in China since the late 1990s.

Against this backdrop, the relatively recent growth of childhood obesity in China is being criticized as incidental to, if not consequential of, the proliferation of fast food. However, while there may be a theoretical correlation — eating a diet of fast food will increase one's likelihood of becoming obese — it is not so simple to establish concrete causation. Before we dive into that discussion, let us outline some research indicating that childhood obesity is a growing problem in China and around the world.

According to a study by the *New England Journal of Medicine*, which covered 195 countries and regions from 1980–2015, there were 107.7 million obese[1] children worldwide. Of these 107.7 million, China had the highest percentage with 15.3 million.[2] The researchers described these figures as a "growing and disturbing global health crisis". Their findings are not unique. According to the World Health Organization (WHO), "the number of overweight Chinese under the age of five is estimated to be over 41 million in 2016," with almost half of these children located in Asia. In the first Issue of the *Childhood Obesity in China Report*, co-published in May 2017 by the School of Public Health, Peking University, and the United Nations International Children's Emergency Fund (UNICEF), it was reported that the proportion of obese children seven years old or younger was 4.3%, while the proportion of obese children 7–18 years of age was 7.3%. The report also projected that if no action is taken to remedy or reverse this trend, China's proportion of obese children may rise to 56 million by 2030. In 2015, a survey from the Institute of Social Science at Peking University showed that the percentage of obese children in three areas — the rural areas, China's townships, and urban regions — was 24.62%, 15.04%, and 13.58%, respectively. This indicates that childhood obesity is more prevalent in the countryside than in cities. It also suggests that childhood obesity is no longer an affluenza, a "luxury" of the wealthy, but a widespread social problem.

Researchers in China attribute the widespread rise in childhood obesity to economic growth, a phenomenon in China which has lifted hundreds of millions of Chinese people — including children — out of

---

[1] The body mass index (BMI = the weight in kilograms divided by the square of the height in meters) measures overweightness and obesity. For adults, one is overweight if their BMI is between 25 and 29, and is obese if the BMI is equal to or greater than 30. For children, one is overweight if their BMI is at or above the 85th and below the 95th percentile, and is obese if their BMI is at or above the 95th percentile (holding constant both age and gender).

[2] Although China had the highest number of obese children compared to other countries studied, 15.3 million is only 1.1% of the entire Chinese population.

poverty, increased per capita income, increased household purchasing power, and increased the range of food and dining options available. Thus, more people, especially two-worker households, have begun eating out and consuming convenient food options — such as "fast food" — as opposed to cooking at home. This is supported by a study published by the journal *Preventive Medicine*,[3] which analyzed the relationship between a rise in disposable income and changes in eating behavior and childhood obesity rates in primary and secondary schools in Beijing, Shanghai, Nanjing, and Xian; it found that a child who regularly had more than RMB 10 per week in spending money was 45–90% more obese than those with less.

It is important to note that China is not alone in struggling with this phenomenon. For example, Brazil, another BRICS[4] country, is facing an obesity epidemic. According to *The New York Times*, "the [childhood] obesity rate in Brazil has nearly doubled to 20% over the last decade, and the portion of [children] who are overweight has nearly tripled to 58%." Anthony Winson, author of *The Industrial Diet* and professor at the University of Guelph, stated in an interview that our "diet is killing us... [even though] the prevailing story is that this is the best of all possible worlds-cheap food, widely available." This sentiment is supported by a study by Euromonitor, a marketing research firm, that concluded that sales of prepackaged food — a subset of "fast food" — and fast food proper increased by 25% and 30%, respectively, from 2011–2016. Childhood obesity in Australia, according to the George Institute, is on the rise due to 1/3 of the average Australian child's diet being fast food.

46.2 Judging

If childhood obesity is a growing problem, and garnering an increasing amount of attention in China, is fast food to blame? Perhaps. For example, as mentioned in Section 46.1, the regular consumption of fast food can increase the likelihood of obesity, which subsequently exposes such persons to a higher risk of conditions such as diabetes. This suggests that

---

[3] The study focused on the relationship between a rise in disposable income and changes in eating behavior and childhood obesity rates in primary and secondary schools in Beijing, Shanghai, Nanjing, and Xian.

[4] BRICS = (B)razil, (R)ussia, (I)ndia, (C)hina, (S)outh Africa.

diet is indeed important. Other important variables include a lack of exercise, wealth gained through familial inheritance, and one's social environment. Concerning exercise particularly, a study at California Polytechnic State University in San Luis Obispo found that exercise can actually increase your desire for a healthier diet, thus suggesting a positive and mutually reinforcing correlation between diet and exercise.[5] Given that young children are incapable of making these decisions on their own, the responsibility falls to their parents to guide them to adopt good dietary and fitness-related habits.

If parents have a responsibility to guide their children to eat a healthy diet, what does that mean for the fast food industry? Are they doomed to be ever antagonistic to healthy living, or always to be seen as undermining the efforts of responsible parents to ensure their children do not become obese? It is unfortunately not a forgone conclusion that in order to achieve profitability in the fast food industry, social responsibilities — like ensuring children are not exposing themselves to negative health outcomes by eating fast food — must be abandoned. Such thinking has historically and traditionally been anathema to Chinese wisdom. In Confucian thought, the *Xiaoren* archetype describes the kind of person who is hopelessly self-interested and cannot help but act accordingly. The *Junzi*, by contrast, is a person who is able to rise above self-interest and act with a reasonable consideration for others, in view of a common good that, to be sure, includes themselves. The *Analects* sums it up well:

"A gentleman [*Junzi*] takes as much trouble to discover what is right as the lesser men [*Xiaoren*] takes to discover what will pay." (Book IV)

In other words, the *Junzi* usually has a clear understanding of what he intends to do, and the goal he or she is able to achieve, while the *Xiaoren* stubbornly goes after fame and fortune without self-reflection or self-discipline. An important point in this passage from the *Analects* is

---

[5] The study consisted of observing two groups. One group exercised. The other group did not. Both groups' brain activity was measured by the presentation of pictures of high-caloric or health foods. For the group that did not exercise, the reward area of the brain lit up more regularly when they were shown the high-caloric food pictures. This did not happen to the group who had exercised, suggesting exercise influences how one perceives particular kinds of food.

that what is "right" does not necessarily preclude being profitable. What it means is that all things, including profitability, must be tempered by what is right in any given circumstance. Genuine business leadership does not subordinate moral decision-making to profit maximization, but guides the pursuit of profits according to what is ethically possible given the circumstances at any point in a business's lifecycle. Moreover, a company with a sense of social responsibility should be willing to work together with local governments or other authorities to address social problems, rather than trying to skirt their obligations or turning a blind eye to them.

Does the fast food industry, then, reflect more of the archetype of the *Xiaoren* or the *Junzi*? Let us look at their advertising practices toward children, as one example. Given the size and profitability of the fast food industry in China and around the world, many such companies have massive financial resources allocated to marketing and advertising campaigns directed at children. Their ability to make their food products look appealing and delicious in television advertisements, among other multimedia channels, is an important factor explaining why consumption of such products is so high; while the taste of the products in the advertisements is not necessarily deceiving — they are generally considered delicious — there is a lack of information about the health effects of eating them regularly, or in too large amounts.

Another questionable advertising technique involves leveraging celebrity endorsements. Fast food corporations are known to pay substantial sums of money to celebrities willing to endorse their products, regardless of whether the celebrities themselves even patronize the restaurants they are promoting. Many celebrities — Chinese examples include Ke Zhendong, Chen Xiao, Zhang Liang, and Chen Kun — have come under heavy criticism for promoting fast food products, their critics claiming that they are shamelessly contributing to childhood obesity while hypocritically abstaining from such food in their personal lives. Even if such accusations are true, are the celebrities really the ones at fault here? Corporations may think it is smart to use celebrity appeal to push their products, but there is an educational component about the nutritional makeup of the products that is often missing. Such an omission can hardly be considered benign if the indiscriminate consumption of fast food products actually produces harm. Corporations that willfully omit a kind of nutritional profile or cautionary announcement in advertising exhibit *Xiaoren*-type behavior, as it suggests that increasing sales takes priority over the health of consumers. A *Junzi* approach would recognize that there are ways to be profitable and socially responsible, and that the achievement of one does not have to come at the expense of the other.

China is not alone in this issue of advertising. In the United Kingdom, the Committee on Advertising Practice (CPA) has prohibited online and print advertisements for fast food products particularly aimed at children.[6] Commenting on this decision, James Best, President of the CPA, stated that "childhood obesity is a very serious and complex problem which we are committed to solving [...] these restrictions will greatly reduce the junk food ads aimed at children, while the new rule stipulates that the advertising industry shall fulfill their social responsibility and regard the reduction of childhood obesity as a central task."

Another dimension to the problem of childhood obesity is the fact that fast food processes have enabled market expansion into areas of China once passed over as cost-prohibitive. That such products can be produced at a low cost and made accessible to the public *en masse* quickly and inexpensively has opened new dietary options, particularly for those in the more rural areas of China. However, without accompanying educational information, they are consumed without much concern for their health effects. This, along with other factors, has led to an increase in childhood obesity in China's rural areas and among the country's poor. In an effort to ensure a reasonable caloric intake for their children or grandchildren, parents and grandparents are turning to fast food products. The turning away from healthier options — such as those traditionally cooked at home — could be due to the costs of more nutritious foods, the inaccessibility of nutritious options, or a lack of education about nutrition in general.

However, the problem is not exclusive to rural areas. Urban children are also consuming fast food products in larger quantities, which paired with a lack of exercise and the influence of television and Internet — as opposed to parents and teachers — upon their food consumption decisions

---

[6] There are exceptions to these prohibitions, which are primarily determined by the projected level of exposure each advertisement will have to the public. If the perceived level of exposure is below a certain threshold, the advertisement will be allowed. If such exposure is high, it will be banned.

is resulting in a rise of childhood obesity rates. Again, Confucian wisdom may point to an alternative:

> "A gentleman who never goes on eating till he is sated, who does not demand comfort in his home, who is diligent in business and cautious in speech, who associates with those that possess the Way and thereby corrects his own faults — such a one may indeed be said to have a taste for learning." (Book I)

However, strengthening individual self-discipline, while an essential first step toward personal and interpersonal harmony, is sometimes insufficient to affect the change necessary to reduce harmful trends, especially those involving children unable to help themselves. This then brings into view the critical role of parents, teachers, business leaders, and ultimately the State in guiding and educating children toward cultivating positive food consumption habits. An example of how the Chinese government took action in this regard was the issuance of its *Management Provision of Food Nutrition Label*s in May 2008, requiring all food products to include a nutritional profile. Such a profile includes listing all relevant ingredients — salt, sugar, fat, protein, carbohydrates, etc. — and their amounts, thus providing parents of young children, and consumers in general, with a guide to how such products may or may not affect health.

46.3 Acting

Going forward, how can fast food companies fulfill their social responsibilities by helping combat childhood obesity?

One way is for such companies to pursue transparency in reporting the nutritional content of their meals, paired with initiatives aimed at providing customers with more nutritionally balanced meal options. McDonald's in China is a good example of this. They began to reform their menus as early as 2005, to include "vegetables, fruits, and cereals that used less salt and better oil." They also began publicizing nutrition facts and dietary references to the public as part of their strategy to educate consumers about what is and is not healthy. The impact has been positive. In 2010, McDonald's launched a new menu with a more balanced diet; the menu reduced salt content in its hamburgers, ketchup, and chips by the total amount of 450 tons. In an effort to introduce more customization to the consumer experience, McDonald's plans to introduce what they are calling "Create Your Taste" stores in China, imitating a successful model implemented in the corporation's Australian stores. This model allows consumers to build food products based on the ingredients they value most.

Another way "fast food" companies can combat childhood obesity is by working with government bodies and relevant non-profits to help advocate balanced and healthy diets in society. For example, the Chinese Society of Nutrition was founded in 1945, with the aim to improve nutrition for all and to promote the health of the Chinese people. In collaboration with Nestlé, they implemented Dietary Recommended Intakes (DRIs) in 2011, a nutrition intake guide for preventing malnutrition and decreasing the onset of chronic diseases. For example, in addition to the Food Nutrition Label, Nestlé also included practical nutrition information, health-related tips, and the benefits associated with particular nutritional ingredients on their product package. Starting in 2007, they collaborated with the All-China Women's Federation to initiate a family diet education program, which has since become an important tool for Chinese housewives. Similar to educational programs (and academic degrees) in home economics, the family diet education program focused on educating women about nutrition, how to cultivate good dietary habits for themselves and their families, and taught them relevant home and money management skills using classroom presentations, community counseling, expert lectures, and cooking demonstrations.

Yum China Holdings, Inc., a well-known fast food company, is another example worth mentioning. In 2008, in cooperation with the China Foundation for Poverty Alleviation, they began a fundraising program called "Donate One Yuan, Give Benevolence, Offer Nutrition". The aim of this project was to raise money to provide "Love Kitchen" locations throughout rural China, and to provide residents therein with nutritious meals on a daily basis. The project raised around RMB 150 million and benefited over 500,000 residents across nine provinces. Yum China Holdings, Inc. also collaborated with the Chinese Society of Nutrition to establish Health Funds, designed to provide resources in support of balanced diets for urban residents. An example of what the resources went to were community classes on how to develop a healthy diet.

As household and per capita incomes in China rise, people have enjoyed a wider variety of food options. Many of these options, whether international or domestic, fall within what we describe as "fast food".

This creates an important decision for parents with young children. Although fast food is relatively cheap and easily accessible, parents must act as responsible decision makers for their children. Likewise, fast food business leaders, with a responsibility to the common good of society, must rise to the character of the *Junzi*, and ensure that they balance taste with health and make transparent the nutritional content of their products. Confucius spoke of the *Datong* (The Great Commonwealth) as his vision of a harmonious society. In his perspective, the *Datong* is not a destination, but an ideal situation such that everyone who lives in a country complies with social values and, in return, enjoys social security; all members of a society — no matter their occupations — can and should share a strong sense of responsibility and be willing to make a contribution toward a better society. As producers and consumers, we may be wise to adopt and share in Confucius' vision when it comes to our moral decision-making.

46.4 Discussion Questions

1. Do you think the phenomenon of "childhood obesity" is a moral issue? Why or why not?
2. As a parent, what dietary priorities would you set for your children?
3. Do "fast food" companies have a responsibility to society to offer healthy food options? Why or why not?
4. How might government regulators work with the "fast food" industry to reduce childhood obesity?
5. Imagine you were the CEO of a "fast food" restaurant chain. You discover that a growing number of children in your community are being diagnosed with diabetes due to poor diets, deriving mostly from "fast food". How would this affect your decision-making? Would you feel a responsibility to improve the health of your food offerings? Why or why not?

Bibliography

China Economic Net (2017). 我国首部《中国儿童肥胖报告》： 五项建议防控儿童肥胖 (China's first "Report on Childhood Obesity in China": Five recommendations to prevent and control childhood obesity). *Finance Sina.com*. Retrieved December 13, 2017 from http://finance.sina.com.cn/roll/2017-05-11/doc-ifyfecvz0939710.shtml.

Ordway, D-M. (2017). Obesity and weight-related deaths in 195 countries over 25 years: A new study. *Journalist Resource*. Retrieved December 13, 2017 from https://journalistsresource.org/studies/society/public-health/obesity/worldwide-children-death-trend-research/.

United Nations Health Organization (2021). Noncommunicable diseases: Childhood overweight and obesity. *United Nation Health Organization*. Retrieved March 28, 2021 from http://www.who.int/dietphysicalactivity/childhood/en/.

Wei bao (2016). 对抗儿童肥胖症 英国封杀了针对儿童的在线垃圾食品广告 (Fighting childhood obesity — UK bans online junk food ads targeting children). *Sina.com*. Retrieved December 13, 2017 from http://finance.sina.com.cn/roll/2016-12-09/doc-ifxypizk0077057.shtml.

https://doi.org/10.1142/9789811233654_0047

Chapter 47

Going Back for China's Left-Behind Children

Helen Xu, Dennis P. McCann, and Mark Pufpaff

Abstract

In 2013, Liu Xinyu, a prominent Chinese journalist, founded On the Road to School (ORS), a non-profit dedicated to supporting China's growing number of so-called "left-behind children", a term coined in 1999. The inspiration for the founding of ORS was the hardships of rural Chinese families driven apart by the need for financial sustenance. Parents would leave their children in the countryside to find work in urban factories, becoming migrant workers. Children would be left to their grandparents, neighbors, or in some cases on their own, becoming literally "left-behind".

Keywords: Society, children, family, labor relations

47.1 Seeing

There are a multitude of interrelated reasons why the phenomenon of "left-behind children" exists, but all of them are symptomatic of the choice of the parents to become migrant workers, a driving reason being that there are better paid opportunities in cities, mostly in the manufacturing and construction industries. Although it may seem counterintuitive that such migrant parents would not bring their children, their circumstances are more complicated. Most migrants live on premises at the factories or sites they work at, and in dorms with a number of other laborers, making it difficult, if not impossible, for their children to join them. Furthermore, due to their pay being relatively low in comparison with the cost of living in industrialized cities, they have trouble supporting the relocation of their families to an apartment in or even around the cities they are working in. Finally, China's *hukou* system, a registration system set up to monitor and oversee the movement of people, is structured to allocate social benefits, such as health care, insurance, and educational opportunities, only to those who are registered in the city in which they are located. Since migrant workers are not registered in the cities where they work — if they were, they would not be labeled as such — they struggle to obtain access to the same social benefits that would be necessary if their families were to relocate with them. Faced with these challenges, but still with a need to provide a better living for their families, they decide leave their children behind, without any promise of regular visits or even communication.

The result of this parent–child separation is disruptive on many levels. From a lack of love and compassion to a void of moral discipline and authority to an absence of opportunity and direction, many "left-behind children" are faced with dire circumstances. Some resort to crime, some drop out of school, some even commit suicide or die prematurely due to health complications arising from living on the streets from hand to mouth. Two examples of the latter that brought the issue of "left-behind children" to the foreground of concern in recent years both happened in Bijie City, Guizhou Province. The first, in November, 2012, involved five children who were found dead in garbage cans. They had been reported missing for a week before they were found. The cause of death was determined to be carbon monoxide poisoning, due to the inhalation of toxic fumes from the burning of trash to keep warm as the temperatures dropped. The second, in June, 2015, involved the deaths of four siblings, ranging in age from 5 to 13. After investigations, the cause of death was determined to be pesticide poisoning, the end result of an apparent attempt by the children to commit suicide. Local police reported that the children were not without access to food or water, due to their father having set up a bank fund for them which had over RMB 3,500 in it at the time of their deaths. Rather, their suicides were linked to a lack of care from and meaningful interaction with their parents, both of whom were migrants, the mother having left behind her children not three months prior to their deaths.

ORS was founded as a response to the needs of these children, and to help them lead healthy, productive, and fulfilling lives and avoid the temptations toward crime, despair, and indifference. They publish annual whitepapers on the spiritual and psychological condition of "left behind children" in China and develop and implement projects aimed at healing the wounds inflicted by the separation of migrant parents from their sons and daughters.

One such project is called "The Raindrops Radio", originally piloted in Beijing in 2015 at the Shunyi Qinghonglan School. It is a collaboration between ORS and the Voice of Literature and Art, a branch of China National Radio. The project solicits inspiring and empowering stories from experts in the areas of spiritual and psychological studies and then has celebrities, professors, or professional announcers record them into audio files. Once recorded, the files would be sent to schools for use in helping left-behind children understand love, courage, personal integrity, loyalty, and other virtues, as well as their importance for living a fulfilling life. Schoolteachers would use the recordings as a supplement for the lack of intimacy and interaction from the parents of "left-behind children", due to their being migrant workers.

Another project, titled "Story Box", espouses a similar model, where stories aimed at mentoring "left-behind children" and providing them with a sense of belonging are gathered from paedologists, writers, psychologists, and publishers of children's books, and recorded into audio files. However, instead of distributing the files to schools for use by teachers, they are distributed directly to the "left-behind children" in need, where they can be listened to on the way to and from school, and at home. "Story Box" is a collaboration between ORS and the Association of Broadcasting and Hosting in Fujian Province.

These two projects, which are not meant to replace the need for "left-behind children" to interact with their parents but provide parent-like stories for sons and daughters to listen to when actual communication with their parents is sparse, are based on ORS's ongoing research into the spiritual and psychological needs of these children. The ORS 2016 whitepaper, which compiled a total of 7060 completed questionnaires across 14 provinces, concluded that general help from society — provisions such as food, shelter, money, and clothing — while important, was not sufficient for alleviating the source of the problem, identified in the paper as primarily a lack of parental connection. The connection-centered insights derived from their research have given strategic direction to the way ORS carries out its projects. And, the results have been encouraging. As of May, 2016, "The Raindrops Radio" and "Story Box" projects have been carried out in 165 schools, covering 21 provinces, and have reached a total of 72,629 students. Their work is ongoing.

47.2 Judging

The issue of "left-behind children" is bigger than ORS, and it is deeper than simply providing emotional, moral, psychological, or spiritual support for them. However, the approach of ORS in developing solutions to the issue of "left-behind children" is cause for hope, for a number of reasons.

First, their projects are backed by research. It is not a coincidence that the core takeaway of the ORS 2016 whitepaper is the heart of their project strategy, namely, to provide a means for children to hear through audio recordings what they long to hear from their parents, to receive from a kind of mentor what they would otherwise need to receive from their parents. The ability to identify where their project efforts are most needed is likely the reason why their work has gained the traction it has. Having a strong foundation in research is also important for ORS to avoid redundancy and support other organizations already working to alleviate the issue of "left-behind children". That ORS was able to confirm that financial and material support was not the most important need of the children in question was a crucial insight, not because such support is not needed (it is!), but because they could now direct their work to where they thought it would have the most impact.

Second, they have developed strategic partnerships. Both "The Raindrops Radio" and "Story Box" projects have partners that are inherently relevant to the desired outcomes of each project. These partnerships have given ORS the reach, tools, and reputation for making their projects sustainable. That "The Raindrops Radio" went from a pilot project in Beijing to a near nationwide initiative, involving 165 schools across 21 of China's 23 provinces to date, is significant. It is reasonable to assume that at least part of this expansion had to do with the reach of their partners and collaborators.

Third, ORS has aligned their project efforts with the concerns of China's central government. For example, in October, 2016, the Supreme People's Court of China was quoted as saying the following:

"The crimes committed by left-behind children accounted for 70% of the country's juvenile delinquency cases by the end of 2013, and the percentage [has been] gradually rising."

Moreover, China's Ministry of Civil Affairs has stated that the number of "left-behind children" in China is currently — as of 2016 — estimated at 9.02 million nationwide. Other estimates range much higher, reaching upwards of 61 million. The largest distribution of these children, totaling 90% or more, is spread across China's central and western provinces, including Jiangxi, Sichuan, Guizhou, Anhui, Henan, Hunan, and Hubei. Providing meaningful outreach to such a large, growing, and widely distributed number of "left-behind children" is a major challenge, but one that ORS has viewed as an opportunity, and rightly so. Mr. Tang Jun, a researcher at the Chinese Academy of Social Sciences, stated the following in an interview with the *China Daily* newspaper concerning the suicides of the children in Bijie City in 2015:

"[The incident] showed that the government intervention measures have failed. The role of parents cannot be replaced, and the best way is to ensure that children go with their parents as they migrate to other cities to work... For decades, we have merely required a workforce from the migrant workers. If we do not provide them with more social benefit, similar cases will take place again and again."

Li Yifei, Deputy Director of the Scientific Communication and Education Research Center at Beijing Normal University, was quoted in the same *China Daily* article as saying the following:

"Intervention would also be difficult because normally the [left-behind] children would not display abnormal behavior, even if you try to ask questions. However, they generally evade or react strongly to questions about their parents... Teachers should receive psychological training to monitor the mental state of [left-behind] children. The key is to identify the [left-behind] children who might have mental problems and ensure that there will be intervention in time. However, there are few teachers or psychological workers in regions where the left-behind children are concentrated."

Given the above concerns, does not the work of ORS seem promising as a strategy for approaching them?

47.3 Acting

Let us role play to explore the responsibilities of two of the major players involved in the issue of "left-behind children" in China.

If you were the principal of a school with a large number of left-behind children...

Imagine you were approached by ORS and asked whether you would adopt "The Raindrops Radio" project as part of your outreach to your "left-behind" students. You know that your "left-behind" student population is at higher risk of dropping out than students with their parents living and working locally. You also know that these students can be ridiculed by their classmates and humiliated by the fact that their parents are migrant workers. Given the amount of time children in China spend at school, you feel that administrators have a responsibility to look after the welfare of their students to ensure they grow morally and intellectually, and all the more so if some students' parents are working in faraway cities without any means to care for them. Is there any reason not to adopt "The Raindrops Radio" project?

If you were the manager of a factory that employed a large number of migrant parents...

Imagine you overheard discussion among your migrant employees about ORS's "Story Box" project, and how it was being used by their children to supplement the time spent in between interactions with their parents. You know that your migrant employees struggle with being separated from their children. You have oftentimes wondered whether such a separation has a negative effect on their morale and productivity. You also realize that your role as a manager is to get the most out of your employees, and that their balance between work and life is important for staying energized and committed to standards of excellence in their work. You decide to discuss "Story Box" with one of your trusted employees, only to find out that while she values the role of "Story Box" in providing stories for the self-development of her children, she longs more than anything to be able to provide what "Story Box" is providing herself. You are surprised at how torn she is at the circumstances she is in, being a migrant worker away from her children. What could you do for her, and for the rest of your migrant population?

47.4 Discussion Questions

1. Do you think the phenomenon of "left-behind children" is a moral issue? Why or why not?
2. If you were a migrant parent, would you want your child to listen to the audio recordings distributed through ORS's projects? Why or why not?
3. What do you think is the responsibility of school principals and teachers in addressing the issue of "left-behind children" in their classrooms?
4. What do you think is the responsibility of factory owners and managers to their migrant workers with children back in their hometowns?
5. If you were asked to advise ORS going forward, what would be your strategic recommendations?

Bibliography

Beijing Times (2016). Keeping kids out of trouble. *China Daily*. Retrieved December 7, 2016 from http://www.chinadaily.com.cn/opinion/2016-10/21/content_27126580.htm.

Feng, W. (2015). 《留守儿童心灵白皮书》: 1000万儿童终年见不到父母 (White Paper on the Soul of Left-behind Children: 10 million children never see their parents). *China Youth*. Retrieved December 7, 2016 from http://news.youth.cn/wztt/201506/t20150618_6767481.htm.

Wan, X. and Xu, W. (2015). Deaths 'expose plight of left-behind children'. *China Daily*. Retrieved December 7, 2016 from http://www.chinadaily.com.cn/china/2015-06/12/content_20981227.htm.

Chapter 48

A Light to Shine in the Darkness: Solidarity and the 2008 Sichuan Earthquake

Mark Pufpaff, Helen Xu, and Dennis P. McCann

Abstract

The 2008 Sichuan Earthquake, also called the Great Sichuan Earthquake or Great Wenchuan Earthquake, was the strongest quake in terms of magnitude to hit China since the 1950s. It killed 90,000 people, injured 375,000 more, and left over 4.8 million people homeless. But, it also created a strong bond within the Chinese nation and led to a wave of solidarity. The case discusses what solidarity is and what solidarity means in different types of communities (families, schools, local businesses, or nations).

Keywords: Solidarity, charity, support

48.1 Seeing

May 12, 2008 marked the beginning of one of the most catastrophic earthquakes in the history of China and the world. The epicenter of the quake was in Wenchuan County in Sichuan Province and it had a magnitude of 8.0 on the Richter scale. At around 3:00pm in the afternoon, 19 kilometers below the surface of the earth, the quake began. It lasted for approximately two full minutes. The resulting devastation killed upwards of 90,000 people, injured 375,000 more, and left over 4.8 million people homeless. 1.5 million houses were destroyed and over 6 million houses were damaged. Over 7,000 schoolhouses collapsed due to the shaking, killing over 5,300 children. Landslides were ubiquitous and contributed heavily to the wreckage. Tremors were felt throughout mainland China and the surrounding countries and between 60–100 major aftershocks ensued within 72 hours of the primary quake, further adding to the ruin. In short, it was a complete disaster.

The 2008 Sichuan Earthquake, also called the Great Sichuan Earthquake or Great Wenchuan Earthquake, was the strongest quake in terms of magnitude to hit China since the 1950 Assam-Tibet Earthquake, the most devastating in terms of casualties since the Tangshan Earthquake in 1976, and the second costliest quake in world history, behind the Tohoku Earthquake in 2011 off the cost of Japan.

48.2 Judging

After the quake ended, the affected people were in serious peril. What now?

There is a certain out-of-sight out-of-mind mentality that can numb us to tragedy. Rightly or wrongly, it is not uncommon for us to nonchalantly brush over countless atrocities every day while sipping coffee and reading the newspaper. Why is our response, in general, so passive, our reaction so minimal? Perhaps because we think of news as mere information, or worse entertainment. Perhaps we think it does not involve us. Regardless of the reason, what if the news not only presented the reality of different aspects of our lives but was one big opportunity to *get involved*? What if the news made you feel like your reaction to a given event mattered? What would happen? The 2008 Sichuan Earthquake is a good example of what did happen.

Unprecedented in Chinese history, the Central Government communicated to the international community that they would be grateful for any help provided to cope with the disaster. This outward expression of need initiated a global response that mobilized immense amounts of financial and material resources. In other words, it created solidarity around the issue.

People from all walks of life cared deeply. It is important to note that aid came from many people who did not personally know the victims,

victims who otherwise might have been passing names in a daily newspaper. They helped for the simple reason that people needed help. Perhaps the Chinese government's expression of need drove people to action. Perhaps it made them feel like their reaction mattered, and would be impactful. Perhaps it initiated a compassion and sympathy that extended beyond borders, cultures, history, and languages. There seems to be something peculiar about solidarity, in that it is always directed toward the essentials, toward those things that really matter for each and every person. What do you think?

48.3 Acting

What did this solidarity look like in action?

The response to the 2008 Sichuan Earthquake was impressive. China itself mobilized very quickly; people began organizing and allocating vast financial and material resources, along with manpower, to the impact zone within only a few hours. Support came from both the public and private sectors and the general public. The international community followed suit, with the inflow of aid to China beginning after just two days. Support came from Taiwan, Japan, Singapore, South Korea, Russia, United States, Canada, Mexico, Australia, New Zealand, India, Malaysia, Vietnam, Bangladesh, Saudi Arabia, France, Britain, Netherlands, Denmark, Greece, Romania, and more. China and its international supporters worked alongside each other in the search for survivors, the building of temporary housing infrastructure, and the distribution of food, water, and medical supplies.

In total, according to a report published by the Ministry of Civil Affairs detailing donations as of November 2008, RMB 76.2 billion in cash and goods had been raised domestically and internationally.

As a current or future business leader, how would you respond? Vanke, a real estate development company in China, was the cause of severe criticism from Chinese netizens for only donating RMB 2 million and encouraging its employees not to donate more than RMB 10 each. Wang Shi, the president of Vanke who was responsible for these actions, later apologized to the public and committed RMB 100 million to relief efforts, to be invested over a five-year period. Do you find his actions sincere? Was his apology and donation an example of false solidarity, a commitment made only to smooth over outrage instead of to participate in the greater cause of rebuilding the lives of those affected by the earthquake?

In contrast, Tencent, a leading Internet and telecommunications services provider in China, was at the very forefront of the relief effort. Directly after the earthquake ended, Tencent suspended its commercial services and marketing and advertising initiatives until May 22 to focus on relief work. Over the course of six days, from May 12 to May 18, the company itself donated a total of RMB 20 million over four installments, while Gongyi.net, Tencent's public charity website, in cooperation with Tenpay.com, implemented and carried out the largest online fundraising campaign in history, raising RMB 16 million from over 200,000 netizens. In total, after only six days, Tencent was responsible for the raising of over RMB 36 million in relief aid for the victims and survivors of the earthquake. Do you see this as an example of solidarity? Do you think the practice of solidarity is also smart business and good for the bottom line?

From outside of mainland China, Formosa Plastics Group, a Taiwanese corporation founded by the now deceased Wang Yung-ching, donated RMB 100 million. Wang's response to the needs of those affected by the earthquake was compassionate and unconditional. He received praise from Chinese citizens nationwide and inspired other Taiwanese and mainland Chinese corporations to do the same.

These examples are large in both scale and scope. How do you envision solidarity on a smaller scale, perhaps in a startup environment or even in a classroom? Why do you think solidarity might be profitable as part of a business's strategy, using the contrasting examples of Vanke and Tencent for reference? How would you approach the creation of solidarity in business or otherwise?

48.4 Conclusion

Solidarity, in the case of the 2008 Sichuan Earthquake, was achieved through the Chinese government's willingness to receive aid and the international community's willingness to give it. Without this kind of reciprocity, solidarity to the extent described above might not have been possible. The cooperation between governments and compassion between people enabled a worldwide effort to honor the lives of those lost and rebuild the lives of those who survived. Imagine what the world would be like if every disaster, injustice, or act of violence garnered a similar response.

48.5 Discussion Questions

1. What is solidarity? Why do you think it is important?
2. What other examples of solidarity can you think of? How do they relate to the response seen in the aftermath of the 2008 Sichuan Earthquake?
3. Is solidarity only considered in global contexts? In what ways might solidarity exist in smaller communities (families, schools, or local businesses, for example)?

Bibliography

Balkhi, A. (2015). 25 worst earthquakes in history. *List 25*. Retrieved on February 16, 2016 from http://list25.com/25-worst-earthquakes-in-history/.

Daniell, J. (2013). Sichuan 2008: A disaster on an immense scale. *BBC News*. Retrieved on February 16, 2016 from http://www.bbc.com/news/science-environment-22398684.

Elegant, S. (2008). China's quake damage control. *TIME*. Retrieved on February 16, 2016, from http://content.time.com/time/world/article/0,8599,1739622,00.html?xid=feed-cnn-topics.

List of earthquakes in China. (n.d.). *LiquiSearch*. Retrieved on February 16, 2016 from http://www.liquisearch.com/list_of_earthquakes_in_china.

People in China give thanks to Taiwan for their donations. (2008). *The China Post*. Retrieved on February 16, 2016, from http://www.chinapost.com.tw/taiwan/china-taiwan%20relations/2008/05/17/156794/People-in.htm.

Search for China quake survivors. (2008). *BBC News*. Retrieved on February 16, 2016, from http://news.bbc.co.uk/2/hi/asia-pacific/7397489.stm.

Tencent to suspend online games and entertainment services for three days to mourn victims of Sichuan earthquake. (2008). *Tencent*. Retrieved on February 16, 2016, from https://static.www.tencent.com/storage/uploads/2019/11/09/ed3c677e9ffa9023ba0ff110fb53a11d.pdf.

Tencent donates another CYN 10 million to make total donation of CYN 20 million. (2008). *Tencent*. https://www.tencent.com/en-us/articles/80140.html.

Vervaeck, A. and Daniell, J. (2011). The May 12, 2008 deadly Sichuan Earthquake-A recap-3 years later. *Earthquake Report*. Retrieved on February 16, 2016 from http://earthquake-report.com/2011/05/10/the-may-12-2008-deadly-sichuan-earthquake-a-recap-3-years-later/.

Ying, D. (2008). Vanke says sorry with 100m yuan. *China Daily*. Retrieved on February 16, 2016, from http://www.chinadaily.com.cn/bizchina/2008-06-06/content_6742263.htm.

Chapter 49

PRC and Tax Evasion: Paying Taxes for the Common Good?

Dennis P. McCann and Mark Pufpaff

Abstract

This case discusses tax avoidance in China, which has a long history. The Chinese generally believe taxes are too high, and people do not believe that they are getting much by way of benefits in exchange for their payments. Even famous entrepreneurs share this opinion. The case discusses the relevance of tax paying in China, Confucian values, and the overall business atmosphere in China.

Keywords: Tax avoidance, tax evasion, common good, patriotic duty, Jack Ma

49.1 Seeing

Despite China's long history of tax avoidance during Imperial times,[1] the Revolution of 1949 proclaimed an entirely new attitude toward taxes, as

---

[1] Evidence of concern over the problem of taxation, how to achieve fairness in sharing the burdens of supporting the government and public works, and the difficulties of addressing the problem of tax evasion are as old as the Confucian classics. The *Book of Mencius*, for example, is filled with observations and recommendations about equitable tax policies and how to achieve compliance with them. See, for example, the passages listed in Chapter Five, "The State", in Miles Menander Jackson's compendium, *The Ethics of Confucius*

witnessed by this 1950 declaration by the State Council: "To pay tax is a glorious duty of the people and the patriotic concept of paying tax according to law should be established among the people. Tax workers should promote a closer relationship between the government and the people, raise the revolutionary standard, and hold fast to the splendid tradition of frugality and hard work." In the aftermath of the Revolution, the discrepancy between the ideal and what really goes on — in this area as in so many other areas of life — has widened. Nevertheless, in today's era of economic reform, China is now confronting renewed attempts by the government to achieve both compliance with tax laws and an end to corruption in all forms of administration, both public and private.

The ways and means of tax evasion in China are as pervasive as they are ingenious. The schemes often involve the systematic subversion of accounting procedures, ranging from the receipts meant to record various business transactions liable to VAT taxes, to the improper recognition of revenues and expenses, at both the individual and corporate levels. Some restaurants, for example, routinely provide a discount to Chinese customers who pay in cash, thus preventing the creation of the kind of paper trail left by credit card transactions that can be monitored by the taxing authorities. The cash payment remains anonymous and off the books, at least in those provided to the tax auditors. Such schemes, of course, ultimately undermine the reliability of China's economic statistics, thus making it nearly impossible for either the government or other stakeholders to determine whether and how the economy is either growing or failing to grow.

Opinion polling done in China reveals a consistent pattern in ordinary people's attitudes toward taxation. Not only are taxes — rightly or wrongly — regarded as too high but they are so considered because people do not believe that they are getting much by way of benefits in exchange for their payments. As one person recently complained, "It's like paying money as a sacrifice to an angry God." Some people, then, do what they have always done to escape the clutches of such a God. They may try to hide their property — their wives and children, their farm animals, their gold ingots, and anything else of value — in the hope that

---

(New York: G.P. Putnam's Sons, 1915), retrieved online from http://www.sacred-texts.com/ cfu/eoc/eoc00.htm. See also William Guanglin Liu's study on "The making of a fiscal state in Song China, 960–1279" (*The Economic History Review*, 68(1), February 2015, 48–78), , retrieved online from https://doi.org/10.1111/ehr.12057, for an analysis of the problems of taxation and its evasion and the Song Dynasty's attempts at policy reform.

it will not be discovered and confiscated. Like the priests serving that angry God, the tax collector, in their view, is an adversary. As far as such people can tell, the God's servants grow fat and rich, while their own needs are left unmet. The "patriotic concept of paying tax" proclaimed in the Revolution of 1949, of course, promises implicitly that such attitudes will be rendered obsolete as the people unite to achieve "socialism with Chinese characteristics".

49.2 Judging

If you were an entrepreneur trying to start up a new business in China, or if you had inherited responsibility for a family business and were now struggling to keep it going, what would you think of your "patriotic duty" to pay taxes? If you tried to check what your competitors were doing and discovered that many of them were hiding substantial portions of their business income, would you simply go along with what "everyone else is doing"? If you did not go along, if your balance sheet looked very different from that of your competitors, you might risk inviting the authorities' unwanted attention, not only on your business but also on that of your peers. If they found out you were presenting a clean balance sheet that accurately reported your income and expenses, what do you think they might do to you?

Faced with such pressures, is it any wonder that there is so much tax evasion in China? Whatever level of compliance with tax laws is currently achieved, the likelihood is that compliance is based more on the fear of getting caught than the hope of exercising moral leadership. But, is that the best we can do? Perhaps you had hoped to "hold fast to the splendid tradition of frugality and hard work." But now, as you see others getting ahead by going along with business as usual, you fear losing out. Where would you find the courage to set aside such fears, in order to do your "patriotic duty"? In the end, each of us must answer for ourselves. But, the argument for doing one's duty cannot be reduced to calculations of costs and benefits. The moral leader is one who tries to set a good example, because it is good — the right thing to do — and not simply because he may gain rewards and escape punishments for doing so.

But, what is this patriotic duty to pay one's fair share of taxes? Where does it come from? All legitimate governments, in today's world, are committed to preserving and enhancing the common good. The common good, of course, is the sum total of social conditions that enable people to live well, in accordance with their basic human dignity. It refers especially to those conditions that people, acting as individuals or in families, cannot provide for themselves, for example, police and fire protection, civil defense against natural disasters like earthquakes and floods, quality health care services, and access to adequate educational opportunities. Generally, the government stakes its claim to legitimacy on its ability to provide such services, which must be paid for through taxes that enable the government to distribute such benefits. But, of course, the taxes actually paid must be used for their intended purposes. This is why corruption is such a serious matter, for in undermining the legitimacy of the government, it undercuts everyone's sense that they have a patriotic duty to pay their taxes. The appeal to the common good, as the basis of legitimate government in China, is as old as Confucian tradition. The ideal commonwealth described in the *Liji* (*Book of Rites*) clearly indicates that the pursuit of personal virtue cannot be sustained unless respecting the common good is the first principle of our social life.

49.3 Acting

But, where to begin? Are there any examples of Chinese moral leadership that would encourage a budding entrepreneur to risk going beyond business as usual to find a better way? Maybe there is. Last year, Jack Ma's enterprise, Alibaba Group Holdings, was reported to have paid RMB 10.9 billion in taxes, thus becoming China's top tax-paying Internet firm. Granted, nobody, and no firm, is perfect. But, in a form of commerce where the incentives for tax evasion may be particularly strong, Alibaba's spectacular success shows that entrepreneurs who mean to respect the common good can fulfill their patriotic duty, while also achieving their business goals. Paying Alibaba's fair share of taxes is but one indication of Jack Ma's serious claim to be a Confucian entrepreneur. We invite everyone to take a closer look at the challenges he has faced and the results he has achieved. Perhaps, in his success, we have a role model worth imitating.

49.4 Conclusion

If Jack Ma can do it, why can't I? If you are a budding entrepreneur, you probably have heard enough of his story to know that there was a time, not too long ago, when he was more or less in the same position as you are today. He did not wait to become a billionaire before he began trying to demonstrate moral leadership. He built his ideals into the very fabric of his innovative ecommerce businesses. He believed that the Chinese people could overcome their distrust of merchants whom they did not know personally, if he could design a system that gave them good reasons to trust. We might try to learn from him. Even if we are skeptical of everyone else's sincerity in pursuing the common good, might we not risk taking the first step by acting as if we all were committed to it? Might we not decide to comply with existing tax laws, for the sake of the common good, in the hope that in setting a good example, others might be led to do the same?

49.5 Discussion Questions

1. Why did the State Council in 1950 have to declare that paying taxes is "a glorious duty of the people and the patriotic concept of paying tax according to law should be established among the people"? Why is it not enough simply to point out everyone's duty to obey the law? Why must paying one's taxes be understood as a "patriotic concept"?

2. Confucian ethics holds to a higher standard of morality than the fear of getting caught and being punished. In the matter of compliance with the law, why is the fear of getting caught not likely to be sufficient to persuade people to do their civic duty?

3. We often hear "everyone else is doing it" as an excuse for wrong-doing. We see it first, starting at school. If we assume, rightly or wrongly, that everyone is cheating on exams, are we more or less likely to cheat on exams? Similarly, with cheating on our taxes. But, is it true that "everyone else is doing it"? Is that not just a self-fulfilling prophecy?

4. Nowadays, there are frequent reports of government officials accused of some form of corruption. There are investigations, and even some-times punishment. But, even if some government officials are involved in corrupt activities, does that make it right for the rest of us to cheat on our taxes? Why? Why not?

5. What is the common good, and what is its relationship to tax policy and compliance?

Bibliography

Confucius Publishing Co., (n.d.). "The Record of Rites, Book IX: The Commonwealth State." Retrieved online from http://www.confucius.org/lunyu/edcommon.htm.

The Ethics of Confucius. Retrieved on March 30, 2016 from http://www.sacred-texts.com/cfu/eoc/eoc00.htm.

Ting, J.C. (1980). Preliminary notes on taxation in the People's Republic of China. *Boston College Third World Law Journal,* 1(1), 71–88, Retrieved on March 30, 2016 from http://lawdigitalcommons.bc.edu/cgi/viewcontent.cgi?article=1423&context=twlj.

Salvacion, M. Y. (2015). Alibaba hailed as China's top tax paying internet firm. Retrieved on March 30, 2016 from http://en.yibada.com/articles/28590/20150422/alibaba-chinas-top-tax-paying-internet-firm.htm.

Zhou, X. (2016). 'Like sacrifices to an angry god': How China's taxes are bringing down businesses. *South China Morning Post*. Retrieved on March 30, 2016 from http://www.scmp.com/news/china/economy/article/1898449/sacrifices-angry-god-how-chinas-taxes-are-bringing-down.

Index